To the memory of
JH 'Jimmy' Thomas
A former Swindon railwayman, Thomas became a prominent politician
in the 1920s and 1930s, serving as Secretary of State for the Colonies,
Lord Privy Seal and Minister of Employment.
Remembered as a champion of the underdog, he died in 1949,
and his ashes were interred at Radnor Street Cemetery.

A SWINDON RADICAL

George Ewart Hobbs
Between the Wars

Noel Ponting & Graham Carter

Published on behalf of Swindon Heritage by
The Hobnob Press,
8 Lock Warehouse, Severn Road, Gloucester GL1 2GA

The Authors hereby assert their moral rights to be
identified as the authors of the work.

All rights reserved. No part of this publication may be reproduced, stored in a retrieval system, or transmitted in any form or by any means, electronic, mechanical, photocopying, recording or otherwise, without the prior permission of the publisher and copyright holder.

British Library cataloguing in publication data:
a catalogue record for this book is available from
the British Library.

Design and typesetting by Graham Carter.

The text is set in Adobe Garamond Pro in 11pt/14pt.

© Noel Ponting and Graham Carter,
and the Estate of George Ewart Hobbs 2021

ISBN 978-1-914407-21-5 (paperback edition)
ISBN 978-1-914407-23-9 (hardback edition)

This book is a not-for-profit project; any proceeds from its sale will be reinvested into other local history projects.

Acknowledgements

We would like to extend a big thank-you to the following people and organisations for their help and support in relation to this book:

Newsquest Media Group Ltd
Peter Field, Tim Field, Molly White, Lydia Ponting, Emma Ponting,
Dr Julie Miller, Paul Plowman, Kevin Leakey,
Roger Smith (Royal Wootton Bassett Town Hall Museum),
Darryl Moody and Katherine Cole at Local Studies,
Swindon Central Library

Foreword

To us, as his oldest living descendants, George Hobbs was initially a great-grandfather on a family tree who had left posterity a few poems and a few other articles. In the family he had been remembered as a kind, intelligent and open-minded man.

He had told my mother, Dorothy, when she was still in her teens, to go and learn about as many different religions as possible – which, for a Methodist lay preacher, is open-minded indeed!

Like many families, ancestors are snippets and a few memorable anecdotes. Meeting Noel changed all that. Immensely tenacious, he was convinced there was 'more out there', and the fact we are meeting George in a second volume simply proves how right he was and that the old cliché 'tip of the iceberg' still has currency!

Noel and Graham, insatiable and painstaking local researchers, have given George a voice – a voice for Swindon and his insights into numerous religious, social and political issues of the last century from a working-class perspective, a perspective so often hidden. This voice can be deeply personal and culturally wide-ranging, conventional and unconventional, a fascinating and eclectic mix of clearly traditional views and surprisingly progressive views.

Here are science fiction and comical caricatures and from 1936, prescient warnings about nationalism and a passionate advocacy of internationalism, examination of what it means to be British and what freedom and liberty might be; reflections on topics as important to debate now as then.

Like their first offering, *A Swindon Wordsmith*, this is a detailed labour of love that shows the value of searching for 'unknown voices' to give us different perspectives.

If you are a Swindonian interested in our town's past and its voices, a lover of bringing local histories to life, or interested in the wider cultural landscape of the last century, but not from a dominant viewpoint, there will be much for the reader to enjoy here.

Pete Field & Tim Field
Swindon and Sale, April 2021

Liberty and freedom are not complete in any community unless they are the common right of every section of that community. To condition one section where another section of the same social order is not conditioned is tantamount to tyranny. True freedom is indiscriminate freedom. The freedom enjoyed by one section must be the freedom enjoyed by all.

George Ewart Hobbs

Contents

A Note to Readers • 13

A George Hobbs/Swindon Timeline • 15

Introduction • Why 'radical'? • 21

1 • Gleanings from Gleanings • 31

2 • The Inside Track • 53

3 • High Days & Holidays • 63

4 • Mrs Crabthorn: The Sequel • 87

5 • Look to the Skies: The Sun, Moon and Heavenly Bodies • 131

6 • Methodism, Faith and Fellowship • 153

7 • The Life of Reuben George • 199

8 • Freedom, Liberty and Aspects of Britishness • 223

9 • A Call for Peace, Brotherhood and Internationalism • 247

10 • The Long March to War • 291

11 • Beyond the Veil: Adventures into Spiritualism and the Afterlife • 325

12 • Immortality, the Meaning of Death and Other Theological Ideas • 351

13 • The Final Acts • 387

Illustrations • 393

Appendix A: List of Works 1924-1940 • 409

Appendix B: Glossary • 420

Appendix C: Bibliography • 421

A Note to Readers

In the course of transcribing broadsheet newspaper columns dating from the 1920s and 1930s into a contemporary, digital page layout, we had to overcome a considerable number of typesetter, compositor or general typographical errors. The task also produced a variety of grammatical challenges, most notably in the under-provision of paragraphs and commas.

More often than not, it was just the occasional word or words which needed to be corrected or, in extremis (with unquestionably missing words): re-imagined. We have deliberately chosen not to highlight these – as much for page aesthetics as simple pragmatism.

In a few cases we also encountered highly tortuous phraseology (probably occasioned in error by the author and not picked up in any subsequent proofing) where it became necessary to make low-key modifications to a sentence to make it more readable – more akin to a 'tidying up' exercise than anything else. We have decided not to identify these either, for the same reasons.

However, in a few instances, whole lines of type were found to be so disordered as to no longer convey anything intelligible. In such circumstances, great care has been taken to reinterpret the impacted sentences using as many of the key words as possible, while continuing to maintain the sentiment of the preceding text. These lines have been placed within square brackets for easy recognition.

In the stories involving the fictional character Mrs Crabthorn, the reader will also come across attitudes which are suggestive of casual sexism or sizeism, and where one of the comedic threads is the lady's palpable speech impediment (sitting along side her cherished Wiltshire accent) all reproduced in phonetic English.

Furthermore, a word readily acknowledged these days as a racial slur (and used out of context in the banter) does appear in her dialogue on a couple of occasions, and, to avoid any offence (because the last thing George Hobbs would want to do is unnecessarily offend) we have taken the opportunity to replace it with 'ninny'. Please note that where this has occurred, the replacement word has also been placed within square brackets.

As is often found in writing pre-dating the Second World War, the word 'savage' (to denote non-Christian, indigenous peoples) and the word 'imbecile' (to denote someone with learning difficulties) also make an appearance – once in each case.

In Chapter 8, the reader will occasionally find pejorative terms and negative attitudes to race and indigenous peoples, but they are included here as we seek to examine the historical record and contrast with our contemporary view.

Noel Ponting
September 2021

A George Ewart Hobbs/ Swindon Timeline

1841 ■ Construction of GWR Swindon Works authorised (February 25)
1843 ■ GWR Swindon Works becomes operational (January 2)
1854 ■ (February 6) *Swindon Advertiser* founded by William Morris
1855 ■ Mechanics Institute building completed
1864 ■ New Swindon Local Board and Old Swindon Local Board created under the Public Health Act
1869 ■ The Barracks in Faringdon Road (originally built by the GWR as a lodging house) converted for use as a Methodist chapel
1871 ■ GWR Medical Fund cottage hospital opens
1877 ■ Birth of poet and author Alfred Williams
    ■ William Dean becomes GWR Locomotive, Carriage & Wagon Supt
1880 ■ Even Swindon School opens under headmaster Henry Day
1881 ■ Radnor Street Cemetery opens
    ■ Swindon Town Football Club formed by Rev William Pitt
1883 ■ George Ewart Hobbs (GEH) born at 23 Henry Street, Even Swindon (subsequently renamed Hawkins Street), the third of four children to GWR Fitter & Metal Turner, Henry Hobbs and his wife Mary (née Dummer) (January 16)
1887 ■ Death of naturalist and author Richard Jefferies
1888 ■ Victoria Hospital opens (September 29)
1889 ■ Henry Hobbs living at 1 Jersey Terrace in Jennings Street, Even Swindon (Electoral Register)

1889 ■ GEH entered Even Swindon Infants School (October 21) and living at 1 Jersey Terrace, Jennings Street (name of parent/guardian given as Thos. Hobbs)
1890 ■ Swindon New Town boundaries extended to include Even Swindon (nowadays referred to as Rodbourne)
■ Henry Hobbs living at 71 Jennings Street (Electoral Register)
1891 ■ GEH living with his parents and three siblings at 71 Jennings Street, and listed as 'scholar' (Census return)
■ New Swindon UDC open their new town hall at Regent Circus
■ Ownership of the *Swindon Advertiser* passes to the three sons of the original founder, namely William, Samuel & Frank Morris
■ Population of New and Old Swindon: 32,838
1892 ■ Henry Hobbs living at 71 Jennings Street (Electoral Register)
■ Milton Road Baths opened by the GWR Medical Fund Society
1894 ■ Swindon Town Football Club turn professional
■ New Swindon Local Board becomes New Swindon UDC and Old Swindon Local Board becomes Old Swindon UDC
1895 ■ GEH left Even Swindon Mixed School (December 20, aged 12) (minimum age then 11 years) having entered the 5th Standard and stated to then be going on to a Higher Grade School
1896 ■ GEH entered service with GWR in the Foundry at Swindon Works (November 2), aged 13. Grade listed as 'boy', on a weekly wage of 10d (4p)
1897 ■ GEH commenced $6\frac{1}{2}$-year apprenticeship as a turner (July 16)
1898 ■ GEH's weekly wage: 1s 2d (6p)
■ Percy Street Wesleyan Methodist Chapel built, adjacent to the site of the original iron chapel (dating from 1877)
1899 ■ GEH aged 16, a member of the Percy Street Wesleyan Chapel Band of Hope, a temperance organisation for working class children from the age of six. Members met once a week to listen to lectures, and participate in activities and outings. British Methodism was an enthusiastic advocate of total abstinence during this period.
■ GEH's weekly wage: 1s 6d ($7\frac{1}{2}$p)
1900 ■ Municipal Borough of Swindon (known locally as the Corporation) created by the merger of New Swindon UDC and Old Swindon UDC
■ GEH's weekly wage: 1s 10d (9p)
1901 ■ GEH living with his parents and three siblings at 71 Jennings Street, and listed as 'locomotive engine fitter' (Census return)

1901
- GEH's weekly wage: 2s 2d (11p)
- GEH married Agnes Ann Thomas (August 23) at Swindon Registry Office
- Daughter Dorothy Agnes Emily Hobbs born (September 9)

1902
- George Jackson Churchward becomes GWR Locomotive, Carriage & Wagon Superintendent
- GEH's weekly wage: 2s 6d (12$^{1}/_{2}$p)

1904
- GEH completed apprenticeship (January 16), aged 21
- GEH formally appointed a fitter and turner (February 10), joining G Shop (Millwrights)
- GEH's weekly wage: 4s 6d (22$^{1}/_{2}$p)
- Swindon-built No 3440 City of Truro becomes the first locomotive to reach a speed of 100 mph (May 9), actually achieving a top speed of 102.3 mph

1905
- GEH's weekly wage: 4s 10d (24p)
- GEH living at 5 Jennings Street. Henry Hobbs living at 79 Jennings Street (Electoral Register)
- GEH's weekly wage: 5s (25p)

1906
- Birth of son, Reginald Henry Hobbs (May)
- Swindon tram disaster (June 1)
- Reginald Henry Hobbs baptised (June 14)
- GEH's weekly wage: 5s 3d (26p)

1907
- Death of son, Reginald Henry Hobbs, of 79 Jennings Street (April 20), aged 11 months. Causes of death given as measles, bronchopneumonia and convulsions. Buried April 25, 1907 in Plot B 1967 of Radnor Street Cemetery
- GEH's weekly wage: 5s 6d (27$^{1}/_{2}$p)

1909
- GEH appointed secretary of the Percy Street Wesleyan Chapel Band of Hope
- Swindon town footballer Harold Fleming plays his first game for England (April 3)

1910
- GEH appointed as a local preacher

1911
- GEH living with Agnes and daughter Dorothy at 79 Jennings Street. Two children born alive, one deceased (Census return)

1912
- GEH living at 79 Jennings Street (Electoral Register)
- Henri Salmet becomes the first person to land an aeroplane in Swindon (July 27)

1913
- GEH promoted to chargeman (May 10)

1914
- GEH's weekly wage: 6s (30p)
  - GEH living at 4 Jennings Street (by November 13)
  - Great Britain declares war on Imperial Germany (August 4)

1915
- GEH's booklet of poems, The British Soldier, published by Morris Bros
  - GEH's weekly wage: 7s 2d (36p)

1916
- British Government introduces conscription (January 24)
  - George Jackson Churchward becomes Chief Mechanical Engineer of the GWR
  - GEH living at 4 Jennings Street (February 21)
  - GEH's weekly wage: 7s 4d (36^1/$_2$p)
  - Birth of son, Ivor Hedley Sidney Hobbs (late May/June)
  - *My Sleeping Boy* first published (October 20)

1917
- GEH's weekly wage: 10s 8d (53^1/$_2$p)

1918
- GEH revealed himself to be a member of The Amalgamated Society of Engineers (January 31)
  - Armistice Day in the war between the allies and Imperial Germany (November 11)
  - GEH's weekly wage: 12s 3d (61p)

1919
- Death of son, Ivor Hedley Sidney Hobbs, of 4 Jennings Street (May 27), aged 2. Causes of death given as infantile convulsions and rickets. Buried on May 31 in Plot C 3617 at Radnor Street Cemetery

1920
- Swindon Town Football Club elected to the Football League
  - *Swindon Advertiser* acquired by Sir Charles Starmer via Swindon Press Ltd
  - GWR Magazine reveals that GEH was given a gratuity by the company suggestions committee, for a useful suggestion ('GE Hobbs fitter, G Shop, Swindon, 17/11/1919, £2 2s 0d [£2.10]')
  - GEH's weekly wage: 14s 11d (74^1/$_2$p)

1921
- Charles Benjamin Collett becomes Chief Mechanical Engineer of the GWR
  - GEH living in rented accommodation at 4 Jennings Street (February 4)
  - GEH appointed Secretary of Coate Amateur Rowing Club at the first General Meeting (June 29)
  - GEH's weekly wage: 13s 11d (69^1/$_2$p)

1921
- GEH living at 4 Jennings Street (October 12)

- 1922
  - Football Pink first published by Swindon Press Ltd
  - GEH living at 4 Jennings Street. Joseph Shailes living at 5 Jennings Street (Electoral Register)
  - GEH's weekly wage: 16s 6d (82½p)
- 1923
  - GWR becomes one of the 'Big Four' railway companies following the mergers resulting from the Railways Act 1921 (January 1) and the only railway company to retain its original, pre-grouping name
  - GEH appointed assistant foreman in X Shop (October 1923), becoming salaried staff
- 1924
  - GEH living at 4 Jennings Street (Electoral Register)
- 1925
  - GEH living at 15 Jennings Street (Joseph Shailes living at 4 Jennings Street) (Electoral Register)
- 1926
  - GEH appointed Foreman-in-Charge of X Shop (December 6)
- 1927
  - GWR train Cornish Riviera Express makes the longest non-stop railway run in the world, travelling 225.75 miles
  - Swindon-built GWR No 6000 King George V becomes the most powerful British 4-6-0 express passenger locomotive
  - GEH went to Southport to witness the total eclipse of the sun (June 29, commencing at 06.24 and lasting 23 seconds). Southport was chosen because it was on the central line of the path of totality.
  - Death of Major Fitzroy Pleydell Goddard, the last Lord of the Manor of Swindon (August 12)
- 1929
  - GEH's salary £350pa
  - GWR train Cheltenham Flier proclaimed the fastest steam train in the world on a regular route, covering the 77.25-mile journey from Swindon to Paddington in 70 minutes, at an average of 66.2mph
  - GEH made an honorary member of the *Evening Advertiser* editorial staff (June 29). Letter addressed to 15 Jennings Street
- 1930
  - GEH living at 15 Jennings Street (Electoral Register)
  - Death of poet and author Alfred Williams
  - GEH's salary: £380pa
- 1931
  - GEH living at 15 Jennings Street. Rostered to preach at various Methodist places of worship at Purton, Lechlade, Percy Street, Clarence Street, Shrivenham, Upper Stratton, Cricklade, Highworth and Telford Road Mission(Bath Road Methodist Circuit directory (family confirm he also travelled to Wantage)
- 1932
  - GEH living at 15 Jennings Street (Electoral Register)
- 1933
  - GEH and Agnes Ann living at 15 Jennings Street (Electoral

	Register)
	■ GEH's salary: £400pa
1934	■ GEH living at 13 Jennings Street in 1934 (Methodist Local Preachers' Who's Who)
1938	■ David Murray John becomes Chief Clerk of the Municipal Borough of Swindon
1939	■ GEH becomes Air Raid Precautions (ARP) Warden (September 1)
	■ Great Britain declares war on Nazi Germany (September 3)
	■ GEH living at 13 Jennings Street (September 29, 1939 Register)
1941	■ Frederick William Hawksworth becomes the last Chief Mechanical Engineer of the GWR
	■ Henry Day (GEH's former headmaster) passes away (November 24)
1945	■ GEH living at 13 Jennings Street (Electoral Register)
	■ VE Day (May 8)
	■ Population of Swindon: 65,520 (estimated)
	■ GEH's salary: £450pa
1946	■ GEH died intestate on (December 22), aged just 63. Resident at 13 Jennings Street. Causes of death given as uraemia and chronic nephritis. Buried at Radnor Street Cemetery (December 27) in plot C 3617, sharing the unmarked grave with Ivor Hedley Sidney Hobbs and his mother-in-law, Eliza Ann Thomas. Agnes Ann Hobbs was later buried in the same plot (July 1964)

Introduction

Why 'radical'?

> *Radical (n.) a person who favours extreme or fundamental change in existing institutions or in political, social, or economic conditions.*

This book was never intended. When, in 2019, we published *A Swindon Wordsmith*, we were satisfied that it achieved our two main aims: firstly to finally showcase some of the work of a writer who had largely been forgotten, thus paying him the tribute he deserved, and secondly to use the book to open a window on a Swindon in past times, thus giving those interested in local history a fresh vista.

George was prolific, so *A Swindon Wordsmith* could only be a selection of the kind of writing George Ewart Hobbs produced, and there was still much material that did not make the cut. But we nevertheless ended up with a weighty book that we were happy was representative of the many subjects he covered in his writing, the types of writing he produced, and the topics that particularly interested him.

Besides, the evidence was that the well had run dry, thanks to an absence of examples of his work after the mid-1920s, and this led us to the conclusion that perhaps George's preaching had begun to eat up so much of his spare time that the typewriter was put away. The microfilmed copies of the *Swindon Advertiser* at the town's Central Library certainly seemed to confirm this tailing off of George's work.

But then we made a chance but major discovery: between the wars there was not one *Advertiser* in Swindon, but two!

Any reader going into one of the town's newsagents on a Friday in the 1920s and 1930s was faced with the choice of buying the daily *Advertiser* on the one hand, or a weekly version on the other, and although one might assume that the weekly paper was largely a rehash of old news previously seen in the daily paper during the previous week, in fact it contained a number of exclusive elements, including regular columnists.

This causes a problem for modern day researchers consulting the archives at the Central Library in Swindon – because although they have a comprehensive microfilm record of the *Advertisers* that were published daily, it does not contain the weeklies. Indeed, it is easy to come to the conclusion that no such papers were ever published.

However, the *Advertiser*'s current owners, Newsquest, have a private library containing copies of the actual papers published, which were bound into huge books at regular intervals, and these are currently in safe keeping at the offices of a sister paper, the *Oxford Mail*. It is quite possible that the only surviving copy of many of those weekly editions are the single paper copies held in this Oxford archive.

So when we were kindly granted access to it, it quickly became clear that George didn't put away his typewriter in the 1920s after all, but merely transferred to writing for the weekly paper, and continued to contribute articles every week, almost right through the 1930s.

Rather than his writing tailing off, he actually became even more productive during this period than before, and rather than the well drying up, it was like a water main bursting, providing us with an additional 450 pieces of work, including 22 items of newspaper correspondence – all of which, for completeness, we felt obliged to catalogue.

Naturally this soon changed to thoughts of producing what we called a 'sequel' to *A Swindon Wordsmith*, which, if nothing else, would provide further insight into the hearts and minds of local folk in a momentous period of our history, namely the build-up to the Second World War. Indeed, we would have been happy for the new book to be – in terms of *A Swindon Wordsmith* – more of the same.

In the event, however, the *A Swindon Radical* is more than that.

Yes, we still think that the new book has much to offer the student of local history, who can still benefit from George's unique insight and his gift for pen pictures of many kinds, particularly when dealing with the build-up to the Second World War. But it also became increasingly apparent that his writing during the period covered here was something more.

Here was something quite radical.

These days, 'radical' is often used to describe someone's political views, and usually left-wing ones. And although it is true that George was, in many ways conservative (with a lower-case C), he did, indeed, have some radical thoughts about how life and society should be ordered during the ferment of the world between the wars, particularly a belief in internationalism instead of nationalism, and other ideas that sometimes evoke a sense of early socialism, even if he never called it such.

The philosophical (and often theological) thought that was already apparent in the writing showcased in *A Swindon Wordsmith*, is, we realised, writ even larger in *A Swindon Radical*.

Here is a man clearly demonstrating that everything changed after the First World War, and his surprisingly modern approach – despite his conservative instincts and a religious standpoint that appears to us, old-fashioned – is, rather, evidence of a new way of thinking.

In short: what seems like just another local history record on the surface, is, if you want to delve deeper into the mind of George Hobbs, a much more profound study of the philosophies and ethics of the intellectuals of the period, with a not inconsiderable theological body of work for us to unpick his religious thoughts, too, if we like.

This approach to life's problems and issues surfaces in much of the work covered in this book (and even in some of the fiction he wrote), but he occasionally gets straight to the heart of the matter, as demonstrated in this passage:

> "Believe or be damned, in this life and the next" was not merely the ghastly slogan of medieval ages. The spirit has survived the centuries, and still exists.
>
> For many years I have felt that the proper way to quest for truth is to question suggested truth. To say that a thing is accepted truth, and therefore there is no argument, is merely taking the line of least resistance. That is not an intelligent way of dealing with problems of which the mind must give consent or non-consent.
>
> To dogmatise, then, upon origins, especially if they have their roots planted in antiquity, is to open oneself to the charge of being presumptuous. One may theorise upon the evidence available and, eventually, may formulate a working proposition which may seem to square with that evidence. Even then, reservations must be allowed until the whole is known and understood. I claim that this must be conceded in all things if we are to face up to the great problem confronting us to-day. It is none other than the

recapturing of the young mind and redirecting it into paths of right thinking.

The youth of to-day has discovered the illogic of our teaching, which… has been entirely due to the fact that we have never got down to the problems involved. We have given a blind acquiescence to the things which are problems to our young folk. And we have made the fatal mistake of thinking they, too, should give an equally blind consent. This they have refused to give; hence their revolt.

What we are left with was recently summed up by David Olusoga, Professor of Public History at Manchester University, and a historian, social commentator and broadcaster, whom both authors of this book greatly admire. In a Radio 4 documentary, he said: "We can't talk to the dead, but you can listen to them, and we can try to feel something of what they felt."

So, in this, our second volume of the George Ewart Hobbs anthology, we continue to listen to a remarkable Swindonian, but we are trying even harder to understand what he felt, and the thought processes that led to him committing his ideas to paper every week.

And as we continue to draw attention to how prolific George the writer was, it is worth repeating that it wasn't even his day job. He was actually a time-served fitter and turner in Swindon's Great Western Railway Works, eventually rising, in 1926, to the position of foreman of X Shop, which produced points and crossings, a post he held until his premature death at the age of 63 in 1946.

Indeed, one of the discoveries we made while searching for George's writing in the *Advertiser* archives was an article, published in 1928, about X Shop, which mentions George by name. We had already demonstrated that George was a supremely gifted engineer through the inclusion, in *A Swindon Wordsmith*, of an award-winning paper he wrote about points and crossings. However, the article about the shop (which is reproduced here in Chapter 2) gives us a proper measure of the responsibility of his post when it reveals that he was in charge of no fewer than 130 men. And this responsibility would grow during the Second World War, when maintaining and servicing the railway network became a matter of national importance.

In the end, George's necessary increased commitment to work during the war is almost certainly the reason why the writing stopped abruptly in 1939; there must have been a huge demand on his time at the Works, and we should pay tribute to the huge sacrifices he must have made in what would turn out to be the last few years of his life.

His obituary refers to him having had to 'reduce his outside activities in order to keep pace with the extra work that arose' during the war years, and he was doubtless also impacted by the deaths of both his mother and his mother-in-law in 1939.

But George's life wasn't even just restricted to work and writing. Besides being a family man and a keen amateur astronomer, who kept himself well-informed on a wide range of other matters, he was also a local preacher for the Wesleyan Methodist Church: something which took him to pulpits throughout north Wiltshire and even beyond.

Although we refer to George as a family man, which of course he was, the phrase suggests (at least these days, anyway) a significant level of participation in holidays, excursions and social events together, as one family. But he certainly didn't go on Trip, the annual holiday for railwaymen in Swindon, preferring to spend the time with work colleagues, watching them playing cricket. And as for day trips: they appear to have been with workmates, too. Even those extended breaks – the few that he does reference in his articles – don't mention his wife, Agnes, or his daughter, Dorothy, by name or otherwise.

Of course, it may be that he just preferred to keep family holidays private. It is certainly the case that he was sensitive to criticism, and we can speculate that he would have wished to avoid anything considered frivolous or not in keeping with his perceived status as both a leading railwayman and a preacher.

Agnes, whom he married way back in 1901, when he was just 18, bore him three children. By the time that his articles started to appear in the local press, his daughter was approaching adulthood and, within two years, his only surviving son was to die before reaching his third birthday. Perhaps the prospect of family pursuits was just too painful a reminder.

However, by 1937 we hear: 'After all, what is more pleasant than to sit on the sands, either in a deck chair – so profusely provided at little cost – or upon the sands itself, and drink into the lungs the unpolluted ozone from the sea.'

After much searching we did eventually find one reference to Agnes and George together in a social setting, penned by a staff writer. But it was still work-related: a Swindon Press Ltd Social Club evening, held in 1931 to welcome chairman Sir Charles Starmer. Other than that, one has to go back to *A Swindon Wordsmith*, in which he referred to his 'daughter' once in Tiny and I (1917) and his 'wife' on a number of occasions in the four-part, culinary *battle of the sexes*, A Day's Effort and its Results (1921).

Then, of course, you must consider that George was a restless character or, more aptly, a workaholic. In 1938, he wrote the following, which is highly suggestive of the Protestant work ethic:

> Personally, I lead a fairly active life, and in many of those activities I find

> the rest I need. I work with fairly regular constancy because I know that my salvation lies in work. There is a lazy streak in my nature, and the antidote is continuous employment. But there comes a time – even now it is upon me – when I feel the need of the rest which a sane holiday will give.

As one might expect because of a faith to which he kept a lifelong commitment, he continued to write extensively about the Christian church and about Methodism in particular. However, the serialised articles dealing with fairly profound Old Testament matters, such as The Book of Job and The Book of Genesis (which were chiefly written as instructional material for Sunday School students), fall outside of the ambit of this book, and we have chosen not to include them here.

Having said that, we have dedicated three chapters to subjects of great religious significance to George, and which give an insight into such matters when they manifested in the minds of radical thinkers of the time; there is a relatively simple and sometimes quite charming look at faith in general and Methodism in particular and, later, a look at George's ongoing interest in spiritualism and the possibility of life *beyond the veil*, followed by a more theological look at immortality as he perceived it. All three chapters emphasise that George was never afraid to put his faith to the test by applying exactly the same radical thought processes to his religious and theological considerations that he demanded of his other thinking.

Indeed, George explains about a religious struggle of conscience that was only resolved when he realised the importance of the pursuit of truth in his own personal faith, and he admits that he had had to reject the old-fashioned blind faith that called for the word of the Bible to be interpreted literally. It is, once again, evidence of the radical thinker.

His mission to young people in particular helped to define his lifelong service to the Church and is something for which he would have been best remembered.

Another factor that had a not insignificant effect on his life was the United States of America, even though he never actually went there himself. The America of the time, with its written constitution and Bill of Rights, chimed well with his libertarian and classless world view, further helped by the fact it was the seat of so much innovation in the areas of electronics and telecommunications, as well as the emerging science of psychology, not to mention the rise of popular culture, in particular the genre of science fiction.

It is also possible that Methodist thinking from across the Atlantic was beginning to filter back to the UK, perhaps associated with the Third Great

Awakening of religious activism and the Social Gospel Movement that sought to apply Christian ethics to social problems, particularly issues related to inequality and social justice. And then, of course, there was Hydesville, New York, the home of modern spiritualism, a major area of interest for him.

We can identify a possible source for some of this. In 1909, his brother, William Hedley Hobbs, left Swindon with his wife and two young children, and headed west, arriving in New York on August 12. Like George, he was a time-served GWR fitter and turner, and having initially taken work over there as a typewriter repair man and as a machinist in a car factory, he eventually settled in Schenectady – not employed at the headquarters of the American Locomotive Company (ALCO) as you might expect, but at General Electric (GE) where he enjoyed a meteoric rise to become a mechanical designer and Chief Engineer (Master Craftsman). He also became a choirmaster and organist in a local Methodist church.

William's two surviving sons both ended up working for General Electric as well. Ernest Hedley Hobbs is said to have helped install the first radar on the aircraft carrier USS Enterprise (CV-6). Launched in 1936, it was one of 14 ships to receive an early RCA CXAM-1 Radar in 1941. The other son, George William Hobbs, is said to have helped develop the use of the binary system in modern computing.

If one takes into account the evidence that George was an avid reader of *Reader's Digest* even before the UK edition was first distributed in 1938, then all the news and current affairs from the USA – particularly that relating to emerging technologies – must have seemed like science fiction to someone still working in the post-Victorian steam era. What is certain is he would have found it all intellectually irresistible.

It is important to put George's radicalism into the context of a town that was, on the surface, both spiritually and socially conservative, and returned both Labour and Conservative Members of Parliament during the inter-war years, at a time when its profile was 'redbrick industrial' and its demographic was broadly working class (which was all particularly tough on George, as he always voted Liberal!). At heart, however, Swindon had other ideas.

Whereas, in other towns, the old order of self-interested politicians and the Anglican clergy might still have held sway, even as attitudes changed after the First World War, in Swindon the railway company was still all-powerful.

Meanwhile, the strong local tradition of non-conformist worship still provided an attractive alternative to the conservatism of the Church of England for many, and – most important of all – it satisfied the town's instinct for self-improvement and innovation, which still found fertile ground among the generally intelligent, often gifted and always highly skilled workforce behind the walls of the Railway Works.

This was evident in the groundbreaking organisations they created, such as the Mechanics' Institute and the GWR Medical Fund. Furthermore, Swindon continued to expand rapidly by attracting workers from outside the town, outside the county and, in time, outside the country. So it was always in a state of flux, always more likely to have an open mind rather than trust to convention, and evolved, naturally and practically painlessly, into the modern, multi-cultural and largely tolerant town that it has now been for many years.

George Ewart Hobbs is nothing if not one of the products of this enlightened community, and if he had not been born a Swindonian, perhaps his drive and abilities might have landed on too-fallow ground for them to blossom.

Never afraid to look for new truths and speak his mind from the pulpit or via his weekly column in the *Swindon Advertiser*, or correct what he saw as fallacies or errors in its letters pages, the list of causes for which George advocated is a lengthy one – ranging from calling for the overthrow of the Christian church establishment, to a firm belief that psychic phenomena really do happen, through his long-term flirtation with spiritualism. And he champions an opposition to capital punishment at a time when national public opinion was not yet ready for it. He also shows support for pacifism and disarmament, a hatred of convention and the pomp and ceremony of nationhood, and even gives support for the Church of England vicar who 'dared' to marry the former King Edward VIII to Wallis Simpson.

To this we can add a number of issues which, at the time, were by no means of mainstream concern, notably climate change, wildlife conservation, the pros and cons of boxing, bad parenting and child neglect. And there are a few other matters that got local people a bit 'hot under the collar', notably an infamous BBC broadcast by John Betjeman that was less than favourable about Swindon, and he also has something to say about the gazumping of cinemagoers, chain letters, hoarders and profiteers.

Later in the book you'll find a chapter dealing with his cherished liberties arising from having the good fortune to be born 'a Britisher', a chapter covering his desperate calls for peace and disarmament, and a further one dealing with the various key staging-posts as the planet descended into the Second World War.

There are also radical literary experiments seen in the continuing situation comedies of the redoubtable Mrs Crabthorn, and – even more ahead-of-its-time – science fiction, although we have chosen to publish a serialised short story about a Franco-British space mission, called *A Visit to Venus*, separately, as a companion to this book. This is partly because we thought it deserved to live as a standalone book, but probably mainly because we thought how chuffed George would have been to see it presented as such!

Elsewhere we get to learn something of the camaraderie George experienced inside and outside of the Railway Works, and we also devote a chapter to his great friend (and fellow *Advertiser* columnist), Reuben George, another radical thinker from Swindon's history who has so far also been largely overlooked.

And, of course, we would be failing in our duty if we didn't also include a chapter on George's favourite hobby, astronomy.

Although the COVID-19 pandemic impacted on our efforts to promote *A Swindon Wordsmith*, we did manage to give three presentations prior to lockdown, one of which was to the Swindon Society – where we had the good fortune to meet a lady, Jean Allen, for whom George had once provided a personal reference, when she was a young girl. She remains the only person that we've met who actually met George and, given that he passed away 75 years ago, it will always remain a highlight of our mini book tour.

We remain content that after so many years of relative obscurity, an extraordinary man has been given his voice again, and by reading this book, you have the chance to 'listen' to him at length, and witness a radical thinker at work. And just in case you haven't realised how radical his thinking was, in the last chapter, The Final Acts, we have included one of the very few examples of his work published during the war.

It is a letter to the *Advertiser* in May 1940, entitled Dandelions as Food – and you can't get much more radical in your thinking than that!

Chapter 1

Gleanings from Gleanings

Although George Hobbs had a virtually blank canvas on which to paint his pen pictures of life between the wars, in May 1937 a general heading was adopted for his *Advertiser* column to explain what he saw his remit as: 'Gleanings'. Each week he would, he said, 'endeavour to extract some item of topical news and comment upon it'.

In fact he returned, again and again, to favourite and familiar topics that had always captivated him, so – as this book will demonstrate – it is possible to gather a body of work on a number of those subjects that is large enough to justify building into a whole chapter. But that's not to say there isn't also much value in many other aspects of life that captured his imagination and were the target for his philosophical pen.

So we will begin our survey of George's work in the period covered by this book (the late 1920s and 1930s) by looking at some of the other items that interested him from time to time, with the idea of seeing what can be gleaned from his Gleanings!

What do they tell us about the times he lived in? Or the town he lived in? Or the man himself? Or the way George and other radicals thought? What they certainly afford us is a look into the past through the eyes of a natural wordsmith, vividly reflecting the changing patterns of life as they happened.

When George wrote his first article under the heading of Gleanings, the 'item of topical news' he chose to focus on was, of all things, marriage. It was indeed, a topical question, thanks to a Bill that was going through Parliament at the time, which eventually became The Matrimonial Causes Act 1937. It was also the year in which the ongoing scandal of the former King Edward VIII (by then Duke of Windsor) and his marriage to American divorcee Wallis Simpson divided opinion.

Not surprisingly, his writings reveal attitudes to marriage were quite different to those prevailing today, but we might be surprised that some aspects don't necessarily match our assumptions.

The omission of the word 'obey' from the marriage ceremony, for instance, might seem a comparatively recent development, but George informs us that it was an issue as early as 1937. He reported how Anglican Bishops were 'concerned at the repeated omission of "obey", and they intimated that disciplinary action would be taken against those of the clergy who offend'. So the Church hierarchy was actively trying to retain the word, seeing it as a point of principle or policy, and not something that should be left to personal choice.

Unfortunately, George gives us no hint about his position on this particular controversy, so we are left guessing, but otherwise he is a priceless barometer of attitudes, revealing increasingly enlightened and liberal views. This is despite the fact that, as a lay preacher and a deeply religious man, for whom faith was always a key part of his life, we might expect him to be conservative in his views on topics such as marriage. In fact, he is likely to be far more pragmatic than one might anticipate.

In an age when most couples still opted for a church wedding, for instance, George writes: 'The mere fact of passing through a religious ritual does not constitute marriage in its real sense. No one is more married by going through a church ceremony, and no one is less married by going through a civil ceremony.'

The Matrimonial Causes Act 1937, when it was passed, changed the grounds for divorce; until then it only included adultery, but now extended to cruelty, desertion for three years, 'incurable insanity', incest and even sodomy; times were certainly a-changing, but not necessarily quickly, because divorce clearly remained a blame game, and 'marital breakdown' was not grounds for divorce until 1969, by which time George had been in his grave for nearly a quarter of a century.

Likewise, attitudes to capital punishment – a subject that George would repeatedly return to in his writing – were beginning to change, but only as part of a longer evolution.

He always argued the case for the abolition of capital punishment, decades before this view gathered enough pace to succeed, and whenever he returned to the subject, it was invariably provoked by incidents that had brought it back into public consciousness.

In January 1923, for example, the *Advertiser* published a letter in which George referred to 'the tragedy of the week', which readers would have understood to mean the execution, just three days earlier, of Edith Thompson.

Along with her lover, Thompson was hanged for the murder of her husband, and the case attracted much controversy. For a start, female murderers were generally spared the death penalty, and when they weren't, it invariably led to a re-evaluation of the arguments for and against capital punishment; much later, it was the controversial hanging of another murderess, Ruth Ellis, in 1955 – the last woman to be hanged in Britain – that did as much as any single event to finally turn the tide in favour of abolition.

In the case of Edith Thompson there were two additional circumstances to add fuel to the fire: doubt about the evidence presented at her trial, and – some weeks after she was executed – the emergence of rumours that her hanging had been botched. It is now on record that Thompson collapsed and was carried, virtually unconscious, to the gallows. George firstly argued against capital punishment on the practical grounds that it did not act as a deterrent, but most of his letter took the moral ground. Hanging was 'barbaric in the extreme', and he said accounts of Thompson's last hours, in particular, 'simply nauseate'.

Incidentally, he might be surprised, if he were alive today, to find the controversy over the execution of Edith Thompson continues, a century later. There is even a website (edithjessiethompson.co.uk) seeking 'the truth about Edith Thompson'.

In his 1923 letter, George made no direct reference to his faith as a factor in his argument, but he did say that 'the real design of punishment' should be 'reformation', and he expanded upon this idea when he returned to the subject in 1930, the year that a Parliamentary Select Committee recommended – in vain, as it happened – that capital punishment should be suspended for a five-year trial period.

George entered the reignited debate by stating: 'Capital punishment, with all its attendant horrors, is not only vindictive and barbaric, but is devoid of logic in principle and in effect. There is not one single redeeming feature in the whole process.'

And it brought him back to an important aspect of the debate: the question of redemption. As he pointed out, executing someone removed the opportunity for them to redeem themselves, and as a religious man, he thought it important that even a murderer should have the chance to redeem himself before his god.

Because we live in more secular times than George, we might put less store by the need for religious redemption than he did, but providing opportunities for social redemption is an argument that has largely been forgotten in the debate, and is now seldom heard.

It should also be noted that George saw the public appetite for capital punishment as a symptom of a wider immorality. 'The public conscience,' he wrote, 'is smug, fat and self-centred.'

Another six years later, in 1936, capital punishment was, yet again, the subject of one of George's articles, but even if public opinion was shifting, he would not live nearly long enough to see it reach its tipping point. It is interesting to reflect that he was born only 15 years after the last public execution in Britain, and it would be 19 years after his death (1965) before capital punishment for murder was suspended, finally being made permanent in 1969. However, execution was still a theoretical punishment for treason or piracy with violence as late as 1998, when it was finally completely outlawed, more than half a century after George's death.

His arguments may not have had much effect on the long debate of capital punishment, but his early commitment to the right side tells us much about the man. It has never been a question of *if* he was man ahead of his time, but rather *how far*, and in this case the answer can be counted in decades.

George's thoughts on *corporal* punishment are as revealing as they were on *capital* punishment, but for different reasons.

When, in 1937, he wrote about parental discipline, we might have expected him to paint a picture of attitudes that were very different to today's more enlightened attitudes. But if we thought that corporal punishment was still the default in schools and homes in the years just before the Second World War, George puts us straight. In fact, he informs us that such an era was by then three decades in the past, explaining:

> No-one would wish to return to the days of the "heavy father". And one feels the absence of a cane in the home – a rod of correction which almost every home possessed 30 years ago – is all to the good. "Spare the rod and spoil the child" is not necessarily true. A child can be spoiled by the application of the rod. Often, when the rod had been administered, it was not used by a cool, judicious hand, but by a tempestuous, angry head. And where temper rules, correction is impossible.

Yet, even in remarking on this shift in attitudes during his own lifetime, George leaves behind a suggestion that the decline of corporal punishment hadn't necessarily come about for the right reasons. Most of us, today, have come to the conclusion that corporal punishment is unjustifiable under any circumstances, and that is a good enough reason for outlawing it, but it is possible to read between George's lines and conclude that he believed corporal punishment could still be acceptable if it was meted out in a sober, reflective frame of mind.

Perhaps the most radical thing about attitudes to these moral issues was not how much they shifted during George's lifetime, but rather that they had begun to move at all. Often the most radical change is not found in the end result, but when people dare to tackle long-held and apparently sacred beliefs that are considered beyond question. In this respect, George was clearly not afraid to challenge these beliefs, and was consequently always prepared to stick his neck out in pursuit of the truth and new ways of finding resolutions.

Perhaps the best example of this is an article written by George in 1936. As a deeply religious person and also a man of his time, there are certain delicate subjects that we might not expect him to bring up in polite society, including the columns of the *Swindon Advertiser*. Probably top of the list is sex – or, at least, sex education.

But we would be wrong. George reveals a major shifting of attitudes during the 20th century, even if previous generations' inability to overcome the delicacy of the matter was seen as the reason for former attitudes. For him, the question had changed from whether it was too difficult or inappropriate to give sex education to children, to whether it was right to pass on the responsibility to the education system:

> During the last 40 years we seem to have passed from one impossible condition in our social evolution to another. Forty years ago a false standard of modesty stood in the way of preparing young folk for the facts of life. Parents paled before such a dreadful suggestion. Then came the world war, with its Cinderella-like transition from reticence to brutally open candour. There was but little attempt at restraint. Gradually there emerged from the chaos a new order of things. Open candour was replaced, not by a return to pre-war modesty – which, after all, was sincere though misguided – but to a post-war, pseudo modesty. Parents consider it indelicate to deal with this phase themselves, but agree to the responsibility being shouldered by the educational authorities… This, however, in all conscience, can be but a poor substitute for the real solution. It lacks that very essence which is essential to success – sympathy and a gentle understanding. Real success and achievement are attained only when the father and son are true pals, and when the girl and her mother confide in each other… And there I will leave it.

In other Gleanings, George deals with the question of newly married couples considering the question of starting a family – when is the time right? – and what he has to say on the subject once again demonstrates how attitudes in his lifetime, compare with today's; or rather: how they differ.

What appears to be the primary consideration is not – as we could be excused for guessing – whether a couple could afford children yet – but rather 'the curtailment of social pleasures'. It is a subject referenced in various other articles in the late 1930s, telling us something we may not have considered before: how leisure opportunities were shaping people's outlook, and what they wanted from life. Previously, the pub or club might have lured the man of the house to spend time outside the family home, but now there were other distractions to tempt young couples out to enjoy leisure pursuits together.

George notes the practice of young children being left unattended at home while their parents 'go out to amuse themselves at the cinema, etc'. He implies that this is common practice, even among more respectable members of society.

He returned to the subject several times over the years, complaining: 'The parents who will leave a young child locked alone in a house while they attend some function or another are committing a grave wrong against their child,' adding: 'I have been told of parents who have excused such conduct on the ground that they have attended a religious meeting. I claim that no possible excuse can condone such conduct.'

George's main reason for being so appalled by children being left *home alone* (as we might say today), however, is curious. While we might be concerned about physical harm that the child might suffer or bring on itself because of neglect, George had concerns about the mental impact: 'No one can possibly dream of the harm which shocks a child's nerves when it awakens to find itself alone in a deserted house.'

In another article, dated 1937, George demonstrates his particular disappointment in young parents, whom, he suggests, are more self-centred than those of his own generation, accusing them of being too 'gay' (obviously meaning fun-loving, rather than the modern meaning). 'Modern parents are gay,' he says, 'while their family of one or two are growing up, and gayer still when they are "off their hands"'.

The reference to a 'family of one or two' reminds us that we had now entered an era when families were much smaller than they had been, say, when George was a child, when it would have not been unusual to have seven, eight or more siblings.

George also noted a change in the way children perceived age, so that parents now might be considered 'old at 50'. He follows up his observation with an odd one about a supposed new vanity in men: 'Old they never will be, what with modern dentistry and cosmetics, in which latter men as well as the fair sex indulge.'

George is, yet again, astute in seeing radical social changes not just when they are happening, but also when they are approaching, and this time he feels it is a change for the worse. The new-found freedom and opportunities that young people and young couples enjoyed would, he feared, mean that 'they would not become the companions, the chums, the pals of their children'.

More profoundly, however, he reminds us of the cloud of mortality that still hung over parenthood – and we should not forget that George was the voice of experience, having suffered the death in infancy of two of his three children. And childbirth was still a very real danger for women.

'The fear of child-birth,' he wrote, 'is, with some, a very real cause for childlessness.' He does not say what 'the fear' is, exactly, but we can surmise that he is referring both to the pain and the stress of the process in the 1930s, but also the real possibility that the mother and children were both at risk of death during childbirth. What it informs us, as we try to understand what ordinary life was like in George's time, is every couple had profound decisions to make before deciding to start a family.

George also comes up with another surprising consideration that he thought every potential mother in the 1930s had to make before committing to have a child (or deciding not to): the possibility that if the baby was male, she might lose her son in a war. It would be safe to assume that very few would-be mothers in Britain today would even give a moment's thought to this, and students of history might be excused for overlooking this as a real concern for young parents, even though it was a time when the First World War was still a dark memory, and the threat of the Second World War was looming.

But George underlined the reality when he wrote:

> The brutal vocabulary of the day expresses that fear. "Will my boy become cannon-fodder? Have I – a potential mother, fit, healthy and strong – to agonise for my son, sacrifice for him, train him to be good, upright and manly, and then hand him over to be the victim of senseless national jealousies?… and, by that argument… refuse the state of motherhood.

As one might expect, the subject of war was very much in George's and everyone else's mind from the middle of the 1930s onwards, and in subsequent chapters we will see George's vivid assessment of the situation as it ebbed and flowed between seemingly inevitable war and false hopes of peace.

Among huge questions about armament and appeasement, however, he gives us insights into human nature that is closer to home. In October 1938, for example, when war seemed to have been averted, he wrote: 'Thank God, it is not to be, and our minds are released from the strain of the past few weeks.' But this showed up the panic-buyers, who had stocked up on food in expectation of war, and George left no-one in any doubt about his feelings on the matter:

> All over Britain, they have been hurrying again from shop to shop, trying to return the food they had bought. Those who have made extensive and unreasonable purchases of perishable provisions deserve no sympathy. They may atone for their unpatriotic action by giving the goods to hospitals and charitable institutions.

If, however, the international situation and the way it brought out the worst in some people were reasons for pessimism, however, George tempered it with an optimism about the younger generation, and how they might one day become the world's salvation; throughout his life, he never lost sight of the fact that young people were the key to the future, and was always keen to do his best for them.

And, yet again, he recognised the radical changes that were happening, and the need to adapt his own thoughts accordingly. In an article in 1939 he was considering the question of shyness among young people and concluded:

> I am not sure, however, that modern youth is afflicted over-much with this malady. I imagine there is a tendency towards its opposite – in modern parlance "cockiness". Modern youth is very sure of itself, and of its place in the general scheme of things.

If this sounds like a kind of rebuke, however, at least George tempers it by adding:

> We must give youth its chance. At least, in the world of affairs, it cannot make a bigger mess of things than we have. And, if I mistake not, I seem to glimpse that youth is approaching the major problems of our national and international life with a clearer perception, and with a stronger resolution, than we who are older... Good fortune goes with its endeavours.

And this brings us rather neatly to a 21st century question that the younger generation of today seems to be taking rather more seriously than the rest: climate change.

Although climate change would seem to be an entirely modern phenomenon, George at least provides some evidence that it was a consideration as early as the first half of the 20th century.

In a Gleanings article published in 1938, he remarked on changes in climate that had been noticeable during his lifetime, and even considered the possibility that it might be the result of a more significant trend... before ultimately coming to conclusions that we now know – with the benefit of better data and better understanding – to be wrong. At the same time he provides us with a little insight into leisure time in Swindon during this era, in terms of ice skating; it is well recorded that a frozen Coate Water reservoir was an annual favourite among skaters, but George informs us that trips along the frozen canal to neighbouring towns and villages was common too.

> ...time was when every ironmonger in Swindon had a brave display of skates in front of his shop – "Skeletons", "Acmes", "Wooden-bottoms". If I remember rightly, the skeleton skate required straps, even as did the wooden-bottom. The "Acme" required no strap; a clip arrangement gripped the heel and the tread of the foot.
>
> The old canal usually froze over, just before Christmas, and the ice sometimes held to the end of February. Hundreds of folk gathered, the learners keeping to one of the "Pounds" – the stretch of water between locks – and the experts taking journeys to Purton, Shrivenham or Wootton Bassett... A skating Christmas is rare to-day, but it was not so rare, 40 years ago.
>
> I imagine that climatic changes occupy many thousands of years, probably millions. That changes have occurred is proved by evidence which is accepted as true and reliable... It is therefore probable that early man of our temperate zone experienced a climate very much different from what we experience to-day. But I imagine that every change came gradually – so gradually that it was imperceptible to any one age. A too-sudden change would probably mean the extermination of life in the affected regions. So that, even though we are experiencing some sort of change in weather conditions during the past 40 years, there is little probability of it being the beginning of climate change. Hence, as the man said when informed that the world would probably last another hundred million years, "We may rest content that no great change is imminent."

In another article he says: 'That some tremendous change is taking place in the earth's climatic conditions cannot, I think, be denied,' and, looking for an answer, he wrote a whole article that considered whether the cause of climate change could be found in the phases of the moon and sun.

A radical thinker he undoubtedly was, but it never occured to him that climate change might be man-made.

Another apparently modern idea that interested George, a century ago, is what we would now call 'green industry'. In 1922, he wrote an article for the *GWR Magazine* called The Erection of a Stirling Water Tube Boiler at Swindon Works.

The first thing to note about it is George's skill in making a highly technical subject easily digestible for non-skilled readers; not all articles in the magazine (by other authors) pass this test! It reveals how the GWR had a principle of maximising efficiency at a time when not all industries were so advanced. Or, as George put it: 'Cheeseparing [penny-pinching] is foolishness, but the elimination of waste is scientific in its process and has an affinity to the law of progress and development.'

This was an era, indeed, when the GWR was at the cutting edge of power production and recycling, since not only was Swindon Works home to the world's largest private gas works, but other locations in the Works used processes designed to generate what we would now call 'green energy', such as powering sawmills and other parts of the Carriage & Wagon Works through the complex process of burning sawdust and other waste.

The article also reveals that groundworks for the installation of boilers led to palaentology discoveries, which George admitted had his fertile mind boggling:

> Cutting into virgin soil upon this particular site has often affected the writer somewhat strangely. On four occasions distinct evidences of prehistoric marine life have been revealed, causing the imagination to run riot, and the thoughts to dwell upon the mystic fascination of early life upon this planet.

Another subject that George touches on is boxing, and this tells us something about the man himself, specifically the willingness of the truly radical thinker to not just delve deeply into a subject, but to keep an open mind and, where necessary, be prepared to think again.

He had written about boxing before, and admitted he had been 'vehement in my condemnation', but in October 1923 he explained how he had accepted an invitation from a local boxing coach to experience the sport, at first hand, in the New Drill Hall, in the GWR Park. He doesn't reveal whether he actually donned gloves and climbed into the ring, but he certainly benefited from watching the sport at close quarters, apparently for the first time.

The article is headed 'Does boxing brutalise?' and George's conclusion is:

> My experience of Friday last convinced me that boxing as a sport is much maligned. It is a sport that no rake [a habitually immoral man] could possibly indulge in – it therefore tends to clean living. It is a sport, too, in which tempers are chastened and not indulged. And as it tends to make

men clean and develops the better that is in them, I dare to affirm that boxing has a high moral tone.

The boxing club encounter also reveals something about how information and knowledge spread in those times. Today we can all make judgements about boxing because even if we have not attended an actual match, at least we have all seen one on television. George did not have that luxury, but needed to actively seek out or accept an invitation to a match, and perhaps he based his earlier conclusions on what he had seen of boxing before – possibly at the cinema or even in boxing booths at the fair, both of which tend to suggest brutality rather than its true sporting and highly regulated context.

More than anything, perhaps, George's boxing articles are a lesson in not making assumptions based on inadequate information, and surely has a message for us in modern times, where apparent 'truths' propagated on social media often turn out to be incorrect, ill-informed or deliberately misleading.

One can almost feel George kicking himself for coming to his earlier wrong conclusion about boxing, based on insufficient data. His writing on the subject probably also relates to another problem of modern life: the divisions caused when people underestimate the complexity of an issue, and feel they have to pick sides, without really understanding what the arguments are, for and against; George knows full well that 'Does boxing brutalise?' is too basic a question, and impossible to answer with 'yes' or 'no'. There is a strong sense of him anticipating how this was already becoming a problem for him and his contemporaries as communications developed, and perhaps he saw, in boxing, a microcosm of much graver issues and the darker clouds that were brewing internationally in the 1930s (as seen in Chapters 9 and 10).

Anyway, he evidently became a boxing fan in the end, because, in 1938, in another Gleanings, he explained how he had risen at 2.20am in order to listen to a radio commentary of a re-match between Welshman Tommy Farr and American Max Baer at Madison Square Garden. Part of his enjoyment, he said, was the thrill of listening to a live commentary from the United States, although the thrill of the contest was clearly a factor too.

Another sport, speedway, also had George scratching his head for answers to not just a localised debate, but wider and deeper questions, not least the decline of Christianity. As a churchman and a man of unshakable faith, George was perhaps better placed than anyone to chart the decline of the Church between the wars. But while we might again assume him to be a conservative member of the older generation in remaining faithful to his beliefs, another Gleanings, written in 1937, shows him to be much more of a pragmatist and realist.

His views are brought to the fore because of an argument that was evidently raging in Swindon at the time, which George called 'the controversial problem of the Wroughton Sunday speedway racing'. It seemed that some public opinion was objecting to the running of races on the Sabbath, and one might expect that George would be among them. In the event, he did not offer us his own opinion on the issue specifically, pointing out that the argument, actually, was rather missing the point.

He began by praising sport in general for its effects on mind and body, and pointed out that speedway was 'on a par with golf, tennis and cricket, all of which are played on Sunday'. But the meat of the matter is elsewhere, and he adds:

> However unpalatable it sounds, let us who are in the Church admit an undeniable fact. The church has long since not only lost its grip upon Mr and Mrs Everyman, but has utterly lost its grip upon their children. The latter fact is more tragic than the former. And in this lamentable admission, scarcely a minister, lay preacher or Church member is free from blame.

He went on to say that 'the causes of the Church's lost grip are manifold,' but traced it firmly to the First World War:

> Into a world of intellectual doubt and of political upheaval the Great War came. That war not merely changed the geographical markings of the world; it changed the outlook upon life – mental, moral and spiritual. Thinking, action, feeling underwent a revolutionary change.

This is something that modern historians often recognise, but reading George's interpretation, less than 20 years after the end of the conflict, we can see how the 'revolutionary change' was recognised even by those living through it; people like George could feel the ground shifting.

In his view, however, the decline of religion was also caused by other forces, and as he deconstructs it, he provides us with probably the strongest evidence of his own progressive and liberal attitudes. Indeed, it is irrefutable proof, if it were needed, that George – somebody whom we might assume to be conservative in his approach to religion, because of his faith and his many articles on the subject, as well as his age and the era in which he was brought up – was actually the polar opposite of conservative in his approach to religion.

He cites an improvement in education as another reason for the decline of religion, and says it is society's – and especially the Church's – reaction to this that he thinks is to blame, explaining:

> The new education gave to youth analytical minds. They began to sift,

explore, experiment. But along each new line of thought they found the doors barred and marked "Forbidden". The older minds, standing aghast at youth's onslaught upon what had been the teaching of years, whipped and lashed them back again into their own dark and dusty modes of thought. There could be only one ending to such a condition. It was long since broken upon the Church.

This 'huge revolt' he said, was 'misguided – or, better still, unguided – and tragic', and he continued:

> They demanded that a line be drawn between folk and tribal lore, symbol and figure – and that of actual history. Almost entirely their requests were met with indifference – in some instances with hostility and threats of expulsion... Youth has revolted! The profound indifference of the Church to the changing needs of the times has cost the Church its virile youth.'

He then describes the current (1937) state of worship in Swindon, which he calls 'spiritual anaemia':

> Go to almost any church in Swindon on a Sunday morning, and the best congregation but half-fills the building. Many of the churches, with seating accommodation for between four and six hundred, have between 20 and 40 in the congregations. Some congregations average about 12. In many of the churches the same tale can be told on Sunday evenings – churches sparsely filled. Especially is this true during the summer months.

And then back to the topical issue of the day:

> I have come to this conclusion – a conclusion from which I cannot escape. If Sunday speedway racing is menacing the spiritual life of the people, the apathetic response to spiritual stability in the Church itself is more menacing. And the Church will never stop the former until she has purified and cleansed herself from the worst sin of all – sleep. When she becomes awakened, alive, virile, strong, she will be able to answer youth's great need – a reinterpretation of the great truths of Christianity.

As for the speedway controversy: there is an ironic twist because although the version of the sport practised at Wroughton in the 1930s was called 'speedway', it was more akin to what we would now call moto-cross or scrambling, taking place on an undulating random-shaped track. When the professional and international sport that we now call 'speedway' came along, on an oval track, whatever concerns there might have been about sport taking place on the Sabbath were soon overtaken by another issue: its close association with dog racing, which shared the track, and which was built on gambling; the two sports have gone arm-in-arm, ever since. So George, who was known to be a great opponent of gambling, may not have been so approving of 'speedway' after all.

His writings also share his thoughts about another two-wheeled pursuit: cycling, revealing how life was quickly being transformed in the 1930s as bicycles began vying for diminishing space on Swindon's roads.

We should point out that George was a keen cyclist and it was his default method of transport. Ironically, his senior position in the Railway Works probably meant that he was one of that elite band of pre-war citizens who could have afforded a car if he had wanted one, but never owned one. He seems to have made up his mind as early as 1923, when he explained that he 'knew as much about a motor car as a motor car knew about me', and added: 'Carburettors, radiators, friction clutches, sparking-plugs, and all the other technical terms of the motoring fraternity was to me a foreign language.'

His obituary offers more insight into his transport solutions ('In days gone by, he often travelled to the outlying areas in a horse-drawn trap, in order to keep his engagements'), and we know that he sometimes took the train; the former Wantage Road railway station, for example, was conveniently situated in the village of Grove, as was the Wesleyan chapel where he preached.

Some views on cycling are aired in an article in 1936 that was written in response to a new law that banned children under seven from cycling on the road without adult supervision. It informs or reminds us that in the 1930s road safety suddenly became a greater concern because there was both a marked increase in traffic and a rise in the number of young cyclists. This was due to a new affordability, but probably also because whereas, until then, the bicycle had primarily been a means for adults to get from A to B more quickly than walking, suddenly cycling became a leisure pursuit, which children often did just for fun. As George put it: there was always a risk 'of limb', but 'now it is not so much the risk of limb as risk of life'.

What is perhaps most interesting is the apparent perception, shared by George, that the main problem was not so much the increase in traffic as the poor skills or recklessness of young cyclists. This was such a problem that George felt that – in complete opposition to modern attitudes about the many benefits of getting people, and especially *young* people on bikes – 'cycling to school is to be discouraged'! He also advocated the introduction of a test, which all cyclists should pass before being allowed on the roads. Evidently, the problems caused when cyclists and impatient motorists have to share the same space has always been an issue!

However, George had a particular bee in his bonnet, which was the danger and foolishness of cyclists who rode without holding the handlebars, and he argued there should be a law against it. One correspondent, who simply called himself 'Cyclist', wrote to the *Advertiser* to say that, effectively, there already was a law. And he went on to suggest that 'what power Mr Hobbs' pen may possess should be directed towards getting the police to use the powers they already have', before making the valid point (which still holds true) that: 'nearly always a cyclist who acts in this foolish way is the victim of his own folly, whereas the reverse is the case when a motorist acts in a foolhardy manner.'

Several of George's other articles in the late 1930s are preoccupied with the issue of road safety in general and cycling in particular. In a decade that started with worldwide recession and ended in world war, such concern over the nuts and bolts of road safety might seem to be comparatively trivial, but it does underline how rapidly town life was changing, and how the 1930s was the decade in which the previously safe and quiet streets of Swindon were transformed by increased traffic, perhaps never to revert.

Indeed, we should not lose sight of the fact that even the bicycle was not long past being considered 'new-fangled'. The 'safety bicycle' was only developed and perfected during George's lifetime, and in his childhood he would have seen cyclists riding around town on 'ordinaries': what we would call penny-farthings.

They is also evidence of how language was changing in that, in a 1936 article, George refers to a 'push-bike'. It's a term we are still familiar with today, even if its use is perhaps in decline. Obviously, 'push-bike' was always necessary to differentiate the humble pedal cycle from motorcycles, but the irony is that when George used it, it was to emphasise that he was referring to the significant increase in cyclists on main roads, compared with the perhaps more-familiar motorcyclists; in other words: motorcycling, not new-fangled cycling, was the norm.

While we are on the subject, we should dwell a little longer on of the joys of George Hobbs's writing: his vocabulary and the language he uses. His skill as a wordsmith is clear enough, but another attraction is that – like all good journalists – he is informed about the latest vernacular, and is not afraid to use it.

A good example of this is the word 'wangle', a verb and noun which is roughly a 20th century equivalent of 'scam'. In a (1939) letter to the *Advertiser* he noted how Swindon cinemagoers were up in arms because when the sixpenny seats were sold out, they were offered shilling (5p) alternatives, only to find themselves sitting in seats that had previously cost sixpence ($2^1/_2$p). George notes that such 'wangling' had been outlawed in London. At the time, the word was relatively new, or at least it had a new meaning. Used by printers by the end of the 19th century to describe arranging matters to one's own convenience, it began to be used in terms of 'swindle' or 'swindling' only during the First World War.

George even invents some words that you wouldn't actually have found in the dictionary, including "pussyfootite", and through his writing we can also watch words evolving.

The award for the most charming use of language probably goes to 'jumptiddy-wagtail', a game that George refers to in an article dated 1922. These days it is one of those rare words that returns only one result if you enter it into Google, turning up in part of a memoir about schooldays by a child who attended King William Street School, Swindon, from 1916. That refers to 'leapfrog jumptiddly-wagtail', so is clearly a fiercely local phenomenon – but still one that George can use with confidence that his readers will understand.

In *A Visit to Venus*, a science fiction tale published as a companion to this book, George uses the word 'tabloid' to describe something in tablet form; the modern meaning, based on the size and shape (and later the immorality) of certain newspapers came later. The same story also has evidence of words evolving and changing: 'optical *delusion*' instead of illusion, and 'phantasy', not fantasy.

While much of the language George uses is familiar to us, some of his cultural references demonstrate how certain aspects of life have changed over the last century. In a letter to the *Advertiser*, for instance, he says someone might think him 'an Ananias', with the clear expectation that readers will understand what he meant. Actually, it isn't difficult to guess Ananias was some kind of fool, but how many readers, today, would know that he was a disciple who lied to the Holy Spirit?

There are other examples, in George's writing, of words that are now obsolete, but whose meaning can still be guessed. When he uses the phrase 'sheer funk', for instance, he is clearly describing panic, and he even manages to deliver a surprise word during a comic article about a cricket match, informing us that he was positioned at 'long stop', a fielding position (on the boundary, directly behind the wicketkeeper) that is all but obsolete in the modern game.

There are plenty more of these little gems to be discovered, but our last example, for now, can be found when George says something allegedly 'sets up a positive radio', meaning it generated a general feeling of postivity.

What he was specifically referring to were the claims of those who indulged in the sending of chain letters, or 'the "prosperity chain" menace' as he called it. Each generation has its annoying crosses to bear – think of it as the early 20th century equivalent of today's cold-callers on the telephone, or internet spam – and in 1933 he wrote to the *Advertiser* to warn of the nuisance, and how it might harbour deeper problems. Chain letters were posted or delivered by hand, and implored the receiver to send a similar letter to, say, six friends, usually with a warning that breaking the chain would lead to misfortune. On the other hand, it was also suggested that expanding the chain would somehow bring prosperity to the sender or the recipients.

While also alerting us to the prevalence of what he calls "poison pen" letters, he also pleads that 'much could be written of the harm perpetrated by the "chain letter" fiend', concluding 'the rank stupidity of the passers-on of these letters is a puzzle to any sane person'. George was also upset that the chain letter he received in his letterbox included a reference to God, which he considered blasphemous, although he was more concerned by the worry that breaking the chain might cause 'a person in indifferent health'.

Chain letters might seem petty concerns to us today, but we might find a parallel in the spreading of malicious, unchecked or deliberately dishonest or misleading information on social media, and in that context it should not be surprising for us to find a sensitive and sensible man like George frustrated to see the gullible taken advantage of.

On a lighter note – although it may still a real problem for some – George tells us something about social awkwardness in the 1920s when he describes the annual dinner of one of the workshops in the Railway Works, which he attended:

> Usually menu cards are embarrassing to the ordinary individual. You study the queer jumble of words, believe you have solved the puzzle, and then to show the rest of the company your mastery of languages, ask in a lordly manner for what you want…
>
> The menu in this case was mercifully printed in the mother tongue, and its contents suggested satisfaction to the palate of the most fastidious: soup, turbot with lobster sauce, roast chicken, beef and mutton, ham, vegetables, sweets, cheese and salad. A dinner which everyone enjoyed.

Incidentally, apart from two apparently professional or semi-professional musicians, the rest of the evening's entertainment – 'vocal and instrumental melody' – was provided by fellow members of the shop, underlining the extent to which people, in those days, were able to generate their own amusement.

Another beauty of George Hobbs's body of work is the ability to throw light upon an aspect of Swindon's heritage that is not recorded elsewhere. In one of his early Gleanings articles, written in 1937, he returns to a favourite subject – cycling safety and a possible need for a change in the law – and makes a reference to magistrates that reveals something profound about what we might now call 'public service' in the 1930s. George remarks that he would have liked to have been a magistrate: 'But, alas! it cannot be… I am "out of the running".'

It is surprising to find that an able, upstanding and respected figure in the community, and a manager in the Railway Works – easily the town's largest employer – should find himself automatically disqualified from the Bench, and perhaps other public service. The reason, as George explains, is that he is 'not actively engaged in party or TUC work. My only jobs, apart from factory life, are an intense love of writing and an equally intense love of preaching. Neither, however, comes under the category of "public" work.'

It is a telling insight into how society was organised. Although he doesn't openly condemn this state of affairs, we can detect a frustration in George's words, and an annoyance that trade unionists and people with strong party affiliations had been allowed to monopolise key offices. This had not previously been the case in Swindon, where very senior railwaymen and prominent local figures – all of whom were backed up with a record of success in their fields – seemed to rise, naturally, to public offices; the town's first mayor was George Jackson Churchward, the Chief Mechanical Engineer of the Great Western Railway. In excluding people like George, the system was now apparently shifting towards putting control of local affairs in the hands of less able petty politicians, with rather less of a social conscience and vision than previously, who were surely less able than people like George Hobbs.

Swindon has long endured a self-consciousness about its external image that almost borders on paranoia at times, and whenever there are criticisms of the town from outsiders, they are either quickly being repudiated by loyal Swindonians, or else others from the town line up to agree with criticisms, taking the opportunity to further rubbish their home town. George shows us that this is nothing new, in a debate he opened up in 1937.

Swindon had been criticised in a radio broadcast by John Betjeman, and George, via the letters page of the *Advertiser*, leapt to its defence, also defying those who suggested that Betjeman had a point. The continued expansion of the town – which is still an issue today – seems to have been the real catalyst for the debate, as George quotes the broadcast as saying Swindon was 'floundering about like a helpless octopus, spreading its horrid tentacles out into quiet village places'. He joked that he had struck Betjeman 'off my visiting list', although it should be said the poet (who was Poet Laureate from 1972 to 1984) did have a soft spot for Swindon, despite its faults.

Housing has always provided fodder for Swindon's critics, although the mushrooming of streets of small terraced houses in the second half of the 19th century, which might have been considered a weakness, is probably now considered a strength. George Hobbs lived in several such houses throughout his life, but interestingly always chose to rent, rather than buy.

This was despite clearly having the means to purchase his own house, if he had wished to, and it is something of a puzzle why he chose not to.

However, we get a clue in another Gleanings, from 1937, when he is talking about a debate concerning the supposed shoddiness of newly built houses, compared with older ones, but notes:

> There are thousands of folk who would prefer to pay a reasonable rent rather than own a house. Many, however, are faced with the fear of being turned out by a capricious owner, and in consequence they are forced by that fear to purchase. Newly married couples are forced to one of two alternatives – either to occupy rooms or to purchase a house. In buying they have no choice. They must purchase according to their means.

From this we could conclude that, in the 1930s, whether or not one bought a house, rather than renting, was governed more by the insecurity of being at the mercy of a potentially disreputable landlords than other considerations, such as cost or the desirability of owning property. And it does give the impression that buying a house – albeit a potentially inferior one – was more affordable than we might, in hindsight, expect.

George also informs us that the buying of a house takes 20 years: significantly less than the 25- or 30-year mortgage we might expect today. And there is an irony in that there was evidently concern over the quality of houses built in Swindon in the 1930s, and yet perhaps the most sought-after houses in the town are those built either during that decade or the 1950s.

George gives us an insight into public reaction to George VI taking the throne when his Gleanings considers the views of those writing letters to the *Advertiser* following the coronation of 1937. We might assume that support for the monarchy was pretty water-tight in the 1930s, but it appears otherwise, with George noting how one correspondent complained of the coronation: 'this exhibition of vain-glorious wealth and medieval absurdities was deserving of tears'. It was, after all, the decade of the Great Depression and immense social hardship, played out against the backdrop of a discredited king, Edward VIII, who not only divided the country by abdicating so he could marry his American divorcee lover, but turned out to be a friend and ally of the Nazis in Germany.

These pre-war doubts over the royal family emphasise just how successful George VI and Queen Elizabeth the Queen Mother were in winning back support, largely through their stoicism during the war.

The debate about the coronation and hence the monarchy was apparently inspired by the release of a full-length feature film of the ceremony. It was the first coronation to be filmed in such a way, and the first to be broadcast live on the radio. George tells us that cinema audiences weren't sure whether they were expected to stand whenever they heard the National Anthem in the film. More surprising was that the film was received, by some cinemagoers, with mirth, which outraged some and puzzled others, including George, who wrote: 'I honestly cannot see where "laughter, guffaws and giggles" should be met with in a film of such character as the Coronation… there are times when we just have to bear with what we feel to be wrong and unseemly.' Although he does not reveal his own thoughts about the monarchy, he does question whether those standing for the National Anthem during the film are loyal, or were just 'bowing to convention' – but it does provide us with perfect trailer for Chapter 8, in which George considers Freedom, Liberty & Aspects of Britishness more deeply.

The above is only a selection of things that might be gleaned from George's Gleanings; there is much more in *A Swindon Wordsmith* and the rest of this book, and we believe few people can have given a better insight into life between the wars, the radical changes that were happening, than our George.

And we finish this chapter – and start our transcriptions of George's articles with one that paints a mostly charming picture of Swindon in 1937. He refers to the opening of the underpass in Rodbourne Road and the building of the Railway Works' massive A Shop, at the time the largest covered workshop in Europe.

Gleanings [28, extract] By George E Hobbs
(First published: November 19, 1937)

Times have changed very materially since I was a lad. In some instances the changes are for the better, in some very much for the worst. This applies to the aspect of paternal control and also that of the child's attitude towards its parents. The latter naturally is largely the effect of the former.

In my boyhood days my father was the authority upon the hours I kept, and woe betide me if I was out beyond the hour he stipulated I should be in. Usually the hour fixed was 8 o'clock in the winter and 9 o'clock in the summer months. When I was a little older, and the evening classes were inaugurated, the time was extended to 9.45 – the time allowed for the journey on foot from the Technical School – now the College – to Jennings-street. If I remember rightly, the evening classes were from 7 o'clock to 9.15, three nights each week, and this after working in the factory from 6am to 5.30pm...

I well remember one incident of my younger days. Owing to paternal strictures I missed an experience which I would have given much to have enjoyed.

In my earlier boyhood days a level crossing stood where now are the Rodbourne-road bridges. When the bridges were constructed we knew them by the name of "tunnels", and still call them by that name. The proper name naturally would be "bridges". But we who saw and remember the excavations and general construction also remember that "the line had to be tunnelled". Hence the name "tunnel" is still upon the lips of those who saw the work executed.

On more than one occasion I have enjoyed a ride upon the gates of the level crossing as they swung to prevent traffic from crossing the railroad, or back to permit free entry across the "lines", the signalman, of course, threatening me with sundry penalties if he could but catch me.

And, by the way, I well remember a man, who lived in Jennings-street, being killed by a broad-gauge engine, just east of the crossing. I remember it, though only a lad of tender years, because I saw his wife going towards the fatal spot, and observed her return. The pathos of that scene is in my memory yet.

And then came the conception of the "tunnel", and the work began. A temporary road was constructed where the lofty "pattern tank" now stands, and rejoined Rodbourne-road somewhere between the GWR west entrance and the Rodbourne-road Workmen's Club. The great "New Erecting Shop", one of the marvels of modern building construction, was possibly then not even a dream.

At long last the "tunnel" was completed, and the excitement was intense when the date was fixed for the road to be opened. Ropes stretched across the road at both ends, and when these were removed the new road would be officially in use.

How we youngsters waited and waited! Whatever the cost to us, we were going to be the first through that road. Seven o'clock in the evening wore on to eight, and still no sign of the withdrawal of the ropes. Half-past-eight, quarter-to-nine – and I began to feel very worried. My elder brother, by virtue of his two years' seniority, ordered me home. No, not for a thousand whackings!

I was going to be one of the first through that tunnel. But as the minutes slipped by, my determination to achieve began to diminish in power. For a few seconds it wavered between "the first through the tunnel" or "the first to find it awkward – and hot?"

At five minutes to nine my courage entirely petered out, and I bolted for home, and safety. If my memory does not play me tricks, my brother arrived home about ten minutes past nine, he having been one of the first to run through the tunnel.

Chapter 2

The Inside Track

"For a quarter of a century past, not a single railway accident involving loss of life has occurred in Great Britain as a result of defective equipment or maintenance of track." The Points and Crossings shop rejoice in this fact and I take some little pride that it has contributed to the safety of the travelling public.

(George Hobbs, February 1929)

Millions of words and hundreds of books have been written about Swindon and its railway history, but few, if any, sources come close to informing us about what is was really like, nor the reality of day-to-day life than the writings of George Ewart Hobbs.

Many examples of the window that George opens up to us were highlighted in *A Swindon Wordsmith*, and the following provides further insight into his and other Swindonian railwaymen's lives, both inside the factory walls and outside.

Our first example deals with the way in which Remembrance was marked in the years soon after the war, when the wounds of losing workmates would still have been raw for many Swindon railwaymen, George included. *A Swindon Wordsmith* contained an illustration of his own personal grief.

However, our example from 1922 conveys how the initial grief turned to something just as significant, which was 'keeping their memory green'. Because Remembrance and its annual events have become so familiar to us, and because it continues to be an important part of the national consciousness, all these years later, it is easy for us to assume that this was inevitable, and that Remembrance would prevail. Can one detect, in his words, a tangible fear that, actually, their fallen friends would be forgotten?

An unanswered question is why he and his colleagues were so intent on marking the 1922 anniversary on November 11 itself, whereas we have become accustomed to shifting ceremonies and services, if necessary, to Remembrance Sunday. It seems to be important for Swindon railwaymen to mark the day collectively, as comrades, and in the workplace.

However – lest we forget their debt to their employer – notice how George feels obliged to point out that the honouring of the war dead was 'by permission of the management'. Because even when it came to something as important as Remembrance, nobody should be in any doubt that the company needed to be acknowledged as somehow generous in allowing so many men a short break from work so they could honour their lost colleagues and other war dead.

The second piece demonstrates how railwaymen's social lives also often ran parallel with their workmates'. George's account of the annual dinner for him and his colleagues in G Shop reveal that while there was some professional or semi-professional entertainment, it was mostly supplemented with much 'vocal and instrumental melody' by talented members of the shop; clearly, in those days, people were ready, willing and able to provide their own entertainment.

There is also much of the formality that we might expect of such an occasion in that era, and perhaps George's light-hearted treatment of the menu cards is a thin disguise for the social awkwardness that he and others felt.

But while the article otherwise provides us with a charming and quite vivid view of the social life of Swindon railwaymen in the 1920s, he forgets – or perhaps found it unnecessary – to inform us of whether any women were invited! Apparently not; not even *Mrs* Hobbs.

Our final selection is an article that wasn't written *by* George, but was partly *about* him. It was by an uncredited writer and appeared in the *Swindon Advertiser* as part of a series giving readers a behind-the-scenes view of various parts of Swindon Works, in this case X Shop, where George worked from 1923, taking over as foreman in 1926.

It is included here partly because it gives a rare (albeit too brief) insight into his place of work, a sometimes forgotten corner of the Works, but also because it includes a profile of George himself. Thirdly – just in case we forget that George made his living as an engineer, and his great writing was never his day job – it underlines the immense knowledge, experience and skills he must have possessed to be put in charge of 130 men who were, themselves, also highly skilled; don't be fooled by his modesty, elsewhere, when talking about his technical brain!

Perhaps most importantly, however, it leaves us in no doubt about George's status in the Works, even among the 'old originals': those long-serving engineers who had been around for decades, but still looked up to George, a younger man, as their boss.

This respect would also have translated to reverence and trust in life outside. So the readers of the local publications George wrote for – almost all of whom would have had some connection to the Works – would have understood that here was a man of great standing in the community, whose words were worth reading, and his radical ideas worth considering, regardless of how light-hearted they were sometimes inclined.

The article also reminds us that while the GWR might have won international recognition and left a glamorous legacy because of its locomotives, in fact Swindon Works also provided most of everything else that was required to run a huge railway network, including the rails that its famous engines ran on.

Swindon GWR Shopmen at Dinner
Talent Revealed at Annual Gathering of "G" Shop
A Fine Spread

(First published: January 28, 1921)

An evening of excellent fare and of artistic surprises was enjoyed when the "G" Shop of the Great Western Works held their annual dinner and social at the King's Arms Hotel, Swindon. A company of 55 sat down to dinner, of whom among the visitors present was Mr Beer, late foreman of the shop, and several old friends who had spent the greater part of their working lives therein.

The tables, of which there were three, were tastefully and invitingly decorated, and the company sat down to a dinner which reflected the greatest credit upon Host Godwin, his good wife and the capable culinary and waiting staff under their joint supervision.

Usually menu cards are embarrassing to the ordinary individual. You study the queer jumble of words, believe you have solved the puzzle, and then to show the rest of the company your mastery of languages, ask in a lordly manner for what you want.

You really want a nice piece of chicken – preferably that portion ambiguously termed the "Parson's Nose" – and to your utter surprise and dismay – seeing you are a "Pussyfootite" – along comes the smiling waiter with a bottle of whiskey with the cork drawn, and you find yourself let in for seventeen and sixpence extra. Or else the waiter, being a decent sort of fellow, bends over you and says *sotto voce*: "We do not serve up buckets of coal, sir!" – and you collapse.

The menu in this case was mercifully printed in the mother tongue, and its contents suggested satisfaction to the palate of the most fastidious: soup, turbot with lobster sauce, roast chicken, beef and mutton, ham vegetables, sweets, cheese and salad. A dinner which everyone enjoyed.

Talent from the Shop

Following the dinner, the company settled down to enjoy an evening of vocal and instrumental melody. And the general expression was one of surprised gratification. Except for Mr W Richardson, an artist of wide renown and excellent entertaining abilities, and Mr P Hyde, an accomplished pianist, the programme was entirely local – applying the term to the shop.

It was indeed a pleasurable surprise to find such high talent among those whom one rubbed shoulders with day by day.

The greatest praise is due to the following gentlemen who contributed to the success of the evening: Mr F Hyde, pianoforte solo; Messrs HD Harris, WC Chapman, EE Knighton, R Patton, H Cook, W Woodruff, H Rudman and PS Smith, who contributed songs; two quartets were finely rendered by Messrs Chapman, Woodruff, Patton and Walker; a duet in fine style by Messrs Chapman and Patton. A very amusing impersonation was given by Mr AH Manning at the piano. Mr W Richardson, the well-known "mirth raiser" of the Wags, was greatly appreciated by his entertaining songs and patter.

During an interval in the programme, toasts were proposed and responded to. "Our Noble Selves" was proposed by the Chairman, Mr AH Chapman, and responded to by Mr G Marshman and Mr JD Smith, foremen of the "G" Shop.

To the chairman was also entrusted "The Visitors" and was reminiscently responded to by Mr A Beer, late foreman of the shop and Mr James of the Neath Division. The last toast was "Our Host and Hostess" suitably responded to by Mr C Godwin.

As members of the "G" Shop social club, our best thanks are due to the committee, and to Mr T Walker, our indefatigable secretary, for providing such an evening's real enjoyment.

Remembrance Day in the GWR Works Mr GE Hobbs' Impressions of a Memorable Occasion – Hymns on Sheet Iron

(First published: November 17, 1922)

By permission of the management, short services of remembrance were conducted in several of the shops in the GWR Works. In the "A" Erecting Shop the service was most impressive.

At about 12 minutes to 11.00am, work suddenly ceased, and immediately several hundred men made their way to the south-east corner of the shop in which is placed the handsome memorial erected to the memory of those who had participated in the Great War. On a small raised platform, Messrs Plaister, Jarvis, Holbrow and Hood, foremen of the various sections of the shop took their places with Mr E Morse, a chargeman who was to take the prayer of the service. Over the door upon two long pieces of sheet-iron, two hymns had been written. This dispensed with the need of books, and even from the back of the large concourse of men, the hymns could be plainly seen.

Keeping their Memory Green

At 10.50 am, Mr Plaister the senior foreman stepped to the front of the platform and told in brief, feeling sentences the reason of the service. It was to keep green the memory of those of their shopmates who had paid the supreme sacrifice in the great world struggle.

Mr Plaister then announced the first hymn, "Through the Night of Doubt and Sorrow." The singing, which was accompanied by a band of instrumental music, was sympathetically taken up by all who were present.

Mr E Morse offered up the prayer and upon its conclusion came the sibilant sound which called the whole of the town to the two minutes of impressive silence. A longer blast terminated the silence, and the concluding hymn, " O God, Our Help in Ages Past," was announced and heartily sung by all present.

Mr Plaister was then handed a beautiful wreath of flowers which he placed at the base of the memorial. "This wreath," he said, "is placed here to the fragrant memory of those who gave their lives in defence of their country."

The singing of the National Anthem concluded the service.

A United Service

In the "X" Shop the men of the "X" and "C" (carpenters) shop joined together in a common service. Messrs J Hayward and Gooding, foremen of the "C" shop, Mr Kirby of the "X" shop, and Mr Sims of the Steam Hammer shop, attended, and Mr A Christopher conducted the service. Mr B Selwood accompanied the singing upon an organ which had been requisitioned for the occasion. Following the singing of the hymn, "Lead, Kindly Light," Mr Christopher read a short lesson, and then engaged in prayer. Following the two minutes' silence a brief address was given, and the service concluded by the singing of the hymn, "All People That On Earth Do Dwell."

Round The Memorial

In the "K" (coppersmith) shop, the men gathered around their war memorial for their service. Mr S Hale attended, and, and Mr T Reeves conducted the service. In the vast emptiness of the old "W" shop gathered the men of the "T," "P1," "P2" and "V2" shops, and to this service came a large number of men from the "V1" shop as well. Messrs Fricker, Peskett, D Williams and Fox attended, and Mr A Zebedee conducted. The "W" shop war memorial was taken from its case and placed upon the bench which formed the platform.

Mr Fricker conducted the band which accompanied the singing. At the conclusion of the service the hymn "Onward Christian Soldiers" was sung. The hymns, as at AE shop, were written upon long pieces of sheet-iron.

Swindon at Work
A Series of Illustrated Articles on the GWR Works: "X Shop"

(First published: January 13, 1928)

In railway work it is the locomotive which commands the principal attention of the ordinary observer. This is, perhaps, only natural because of the spectacular nature of the appeal which engines like "King George V" or the "Caerphilly Castle" make to the public eye.

"Oh what a lovely engine," is the comment one frequently hears passed on these triumphs of modern engineering, and this is not surprising considering the combination of grace and power that these latest GWR locomotives represent. No apology need be offered, therefore, for dealing primarily in this series of articles with the work of locomotive construction, and my purpose has been to describe in as popular a manner as possible the process of engine building from the raw material to the finished article.

There are, however, certain shops in the Swindon works which have little or nothing to do with the actual work of locomotive construction but which are every bit as important in railway organisation as "A" shop and other "show" departments of the factory. How many people who go into ecstasies over the intensely interesting operations of engine erecting stop to think of the vital part played by the shops which turn out the permanent way material for the whole of the Great Western system.

It is only necessary to stand outside a great railway terminus like Paddington station and observe the vast network of rails which branch out in all directions to realise how important it is that the track should be as near perfection as it is possible to be. Yet most people, I suppose, see the engine and forget the rails, on which the safety of travelling, to a great extent, depends.

With a faulty track the finest engine in the world would very soon come to grief, but fortunately for the safety of the public, the Great Western Railway pays just as much care and attention to accuracy in the production of permanent way material as in the construction of locomotives and carriages.

Smooth and Safe Running

There is a shop at the Swindon works – called the "X" shop – which is specially set apart for the manufacture of permanent way material such as crossings, switches, single and double compounds, etc, and I can bear testimony to the excellence and thoroughness of the work carried on in this shop, which contributes materially to the smooth and safe running of GWR trains.

Two foreigners who had come over to study British railway methods were heard to say that of all the railways the GWR was foremost for its smooth and comfortable travelling. This is a tribute not only to the men who make the engines and carriages but to the men who are responsible for constructing the rails, points and crossings, because the absence of jolting and oscillation which is such a conspicuous feature of travelling on the GWR is as much due to the excellent track as anything else.

There is nothing shoddy about the work turned out in "X" shop. From foreman down to apprentice lad, all the employees realise the importance of their allotted task and how vital it is that there shall not be the slightest flaw in the rails over which the mighty GWR expresses rush about the country at speeds of over a mile a minute. It was put to me in this way – that the workmen realise that the lives of their own wives and families may depend on the soundness of the track and that, therefore, they put the best into their work. It is the human element which governs the remarkable degree of accuracy and efficiency of the work of "X" shop.

Incidentally, and in view of the use today of the $97^{1}/_{2}$lb [44kg] sleepered and ballasted track, it is interesting to observe that the permanent way of the Stockton and Darlington Railway – the centenary of which was celebrated about two years ago – was originally laid with 28lb [13kg] fish-bellied rails, supported on some sections on oak blocks taken from old English and French men-of-war, and in other sections on stone sleepers of an average size 2ft [61cm] long, 1ft 6ins [46cm] high, and 1ft [30cm] deep.

It will also be profitable to note the development in the various types of rails. Going back over half a century ago the first rail of any importance was what was called the hollow crowned bridge rail, which was laid on longitudinal timbers and braced across with transoms. Then there came the double head rail and it was thought that after the head was worn it could be reversed and run on the foot, but the idea was found impracticable.

Next there was the true bull head rail, called the 68D type, but this had two great faults. In the first place the head was so much larger than the foot that in the cooling process correct straightening was impossible, and the second fault was the tapered head. The radius of the head was so nearly coincident with that of the tyre that serious frictional resistance was set up.

Then came the 92 type rail and the same fault was evident, in that the radius of the head was so nearly coincident with the radius of the tyre. The rail mostly in use today is the 00 type, but with the introduction of the British standard 95, the rail of the future will, probably be the 95 BS for main line work and the 85 BS for branch lines.

30 Years' History

"X" shop was opened in 1897, when the work was transferred from Reading. Previously all the permanent way materials were turned out in Reading, but with greatly increased demand it was found impossible to cope with it adequately there, so the whole department was removed to Swindon. During its 30 years' history an enormous amount of intricate and highly skilled work has been carried out in "X" shop, and I was particularly interested in a chart which showed the variations in the output of the shop during those years. This indicated a decided slump after any great national crisis, such as, for instance the Boer war (1899-1902) and the European war (1914-1918).

Again a slump was revealed after the general strike of 1926, but since then there has been an upward tendency. The average output of the shop today is about 50 crossings and 30 switches per week, and as the maintenance work for the whole of the GWR system and absorbed lines is done here, it will be readily understood that the staff of 130 men are kept busily employed.

Mr W Kirby was the first foreman of the shop and held the position with credit to himself and satisfaction to the Company until last year, when he entered on a well-earned retirement. He was succeeded by Mr George E Hobbs, the present foreman, who had acted as Mr Kirby's assistant from 1923 to 1926.

Mr Hobbs entered the service of the Company in 1896, and spent 29 years in "G" shop before being promoted to the staff. He is well known in Wesleyan Methodist circles as a very acceptable local preacher, and he has also a very facile pen, as his frequent contributions to the columns of the *Swindon Advertiser* show.

To Mr Hobbs, work is not a drudgery but a pleasure and that he has imparted some of this spirit to the men under him is evident from the good feeling which exists throughout all ranks in the shop.

"A happier 12 months I don't think I have ever spent," said Mr Hobbs regarding the past year's work, and he went on to pay a glowing tribute to his men. "A finer body of men no foreman could possibly wish and it is a real pleasure to be in charge of them. Every man is out for the honour of the shop and getting the work done in an efficient manner. I have got the utmost confidence in every single man in the shop," he said.

Before leaving the personal side, reference must be made to one or two of the "old originals" as they are called – men who have been connected with the shop ever since it was opened. There is Mr R Pockett, who rose from the ranks to his present important position of shop inspector and piecework checker. It is his duty to inspect and pass the work before it leaves the shop, and the task could not be in better hands.

What struck one about these "X" shop officials was the pride they take in their work. "What a lovely piece of work," said the foreman as we were looking at a job which had just been completed. I confess I did not see anything beautiful about it but the foreman was looking at it with the trained eye and when the well-shaped lines and curves were pointed out to me I was able to see that there is something artistic even in such a commonplace object as a section of rails.

Another interesting personality I had the pleasure of meeting was Mr Bert Rose who was a squadron sergeant-major in the 6th Dragoon Guards in the Boer war. He retains his soldierly bearing to this day and is a fine specimen of manhood. He too is one of the "old originals," and others who come under the same category are Mr J Parin, Mr W Godsell and Mr J Godsell.

Chapter 3

High Days and Holidays

My only jobs, apart from factory life, are an intense love of writing and an equally intense love of preaching
(from Gleanings [12], first published July 23, 1937)

You would be quite excused for wondering why on earth we would lead (on a chapter about holidays of all things) with a quote from George regarding work. Of course, the two are opposite sides of the same coin. And if you have in your mind's eye a picture of him on the platform at Swindon Station at the start of Trip Week, wearing a 'kiss me quick' hat and armed with all the paraphernalia for a day on the beach at Paignton or any other archetypal old-fashioned holiday, then you'd be wrong. Very wrong indeed.

It's not the case that he opposed the taking of holidays. On the contrary, he positively extolled the virtues of taking an extended break from the toils of work. It's just that his 'take' on what constituted true rest didn't fit the Trip Week narrative.

He certainly wrote about Trip in the context of the fictional exploits of Mrs Crabthorn; there must have been more than enough material gleaned from conversations with workmates to inform his writing. But, as for taking part himself? There's certainly no evidence that he did, and no personal anecdotes have been found in any of the hundreds of newspaper articles that appeared in the *Swindon Advertiser*.

There may well be a number of reasons for this. Firstly, excursions to the beach in the company of hordes of other Swindonians (with all the ancillary frivolous expenditure, as he might well see it) really wasn't his thing. He seems to have found it deeply uncomfortable to be in the company of people who were spending significant sums on personal gratification rather than using their time and effort contributing to the public good. Secondly, could he justify the cost to himself, particularly as he was known to be generous to those less fortunate than himself? And did he really have much spare time to devote to such an enterprise given all his other interests?

Tim Field, one of George's two great grandsons, has recently let me have this interesting observation following a visit he made to Swindon's railway museum, STEAM, with his family, some years ago. "I had been looking at all the photos as I'd gone round," said Tim, "seeing if I could spot family members. When I got to the final section, 'The Great Western on Holiday', there, in front of me was a huge picture of people waiting to board one of the Trip trains, and in the centre of the picture was my Nan with my Uncle and Mum. No sign of George, or Agnes, come to that. And yet there was a tradition during my childhood of all generations going on holiday together. I suppose he might have been the photographer, but I doubt it, somehow. However, he certainly would have arranged their passage."

We do know that George sometimes visited Derby (another railway town) and we can but speculate that this was with a former Swindon railwayman or a friend from Methodist circles, given that he stayed there at a private address. In Gleanings [74] we learn that he stayed a few days in Walton-on-Thames and visited the parish church there.

In the following articles, we find out that, instead of going away during Trip Week, he thoroughly enjoyed socialising with his G Shop workmates over a game of cricket, even playing in one of the matches himself.

You get the feeling that George was never more contented than when relaxing with his work colleagues. The *esprit de corps* that he experienced was simply an extension of the feelings of pride and brotherhood that bound them all together during the working day: happy summer days he recalled in 1922 when he wrote:

> The men who work in the "G" shop of the G.W.R. Works are quiet, inoffensive men until the approach of the holidays and then they are apt to get out of hand. Not that they fall foul of the police, but their exuberant spirits are evidenced in challenge and counter-challenge being hurled about with disdainful indiscrimination. Cricket, football, swimming, boating; anything but marbles, buttons, or "jumptiddy-wagtail," the challenges fly, until order is obtained out of chaos, and it is decided to hold a cricket match.

Also included here are two travelogues: one documenting a day trip with G Shop to the Isle of Wight, and the other recording an outing to the Wye Valley with X Shop. They are a timely reminder that there used to be an age when group outings were popular, especially works outings. Notice how George makes no reference to himself or his workmates taking guests; presumably the men who worked long hours together also took trips together, leaving the ladies at home.

Finally, we have three articles in which George examines whether a good holiday can also be achieved on a budget.

He also looks at what comprises a successful holiday, and the relationship between holidays and improved mental wellbeing, particularly against the background of global unrest immediately prior to the Second World War – something that resonated in the time that this book is being written, when the upheaval of the Covid-19 pandemic of 2020/21 was causing many to reassess how they utilise leisure time, and its effect on mental health.

A Cricket Match Record Tale of Two "G" Shop Teams
By George E Hobbs
(First published: July 15, 1921)

Swindon is a sad place during Trip week, and the saddest day of all is Trip day. Early in the morning, while it is yet dark, the juvenile portion of the town's inhabitants inflame the ire of somnolent parents by demanding to be dressed in full holiday regalia and catch a train that has no desire to transport them for at least another three hours. Presently the door bangs behind them and they troop towards the station amid all the excitement and joy inseparable from Trip morning.

Halfway to the station, Father discovers he has left his pass behind. Mother expostulates in terms of biting sarcasm, and with the terrified cries of the children in his ears, Father dashes back to rectify the omission. A frantic search ends abortively and then he discovers it is in his pocket all the time.

Father criticises unsparingly humanity in general, and certain members of his family in particular. But he does not criticise himself; for father is above reproach.

They are in the train at last – it may be the wrong one, but it doesn't matter. The whistle blows and Swindon, the once gay town, is left deserted, desolate and sad.

But no! Swindon was not quite deserted. There were a few left behind. And some of the few decided, previous to the Trip, to relieve the monotony by playing a cricket match. The match duly came off on Friday last upon the Rodbourne recreation ground, wickets being pitched at 7.00pm.

Now, although one of the opposing teams had the honour of my assistance, I trust that my account of the match will be fair and unbiased.

To write of all the difficulties that were encountered and how they were overcome, would fill the Advertiser many times over. So, ignoring all the troubles of the selecting committee – who to leave out and who to include – I come to the time when the gladiators began to assemble upon the field of battle.

Missing Stumps

When the weapons came upon the field, carried in a bag by two stalwart gladiators, it was found that three important members of the equipment were missing. Three stumps, called in sporting parlance 'wickets', had wandered off somewhere in the wilderness, and got lost.

After the match was over, I no longer wondered why the stumps were missing. To see them fly out of the ground, with the bails journeying up towards the moon, would render any respectable wicket busy with an excuse for non-attendance.

We got over our difficulty, however, by applying to a genial attendant, who supplied us with three potential trees and a hand-saw.

I do not know who won the toss. All that I know is that our side – The Players – had to bat first. The other side – The Gentlemen – of course, fielding.

When we saw our first two men, fully accoutred and ready to withstand the onslaught of the enemy, I could scarcely forbear a cheer. The scene was dramatic in the extreme. If the contestants had but taken some portion of the equipment in his hand, and marched in a circle crying , "Ave Cæsar! Morituri te salutant," it would not have been unseemly, for each was out to slay the honour of the other.

There was the demon bowler, looking at the ball as though imparting secret instructions as to its journey. At the other end of the pitch, the wicketkeeper, stern of visage and restless upon his feet, waited for the first attack. The field was well placed, the umpires – autocratic and unbending – are in position, the scorer in a place of safety, and the battle commenced.

It was only about two minutes after the battle commenced that the first casualty occurred. Philosophers philosophise about opportunity being caught by the forelock or else it is gone forever. But in this case, opportunity had used pomade upon its forelock and it slipped through our first champion's fingers. One run only was recorded, and he – our first hope – was ignominiously run out.

But there were still nine good men and true waiting to take up the challenge, and number three went in with grit enough to hit the ball to – well, to anywhere. Unfortunately no geographical position can be assigned to where he did hit the ball, for he hit it nowhere. The ball had evidently been well tutored by the bowler; for, escaping the vicious swipe of the ball, it hit the middle stump clean out of the ground.

I felt sorry for the enemy's wicketkeeper. No sooner had he taken the trouble to stand the wickets up and fix the bails than they were down again with the bails flying over his head. I think he feared the bails much more than he feared the ball. And so wicket after wicket went down until it came to the turn of number seven to go in.

Number seven, I need scarcely say, was myself.

Not in Practice

I must admit that it was quite twenty years since I last played cricket. On that occasion no runs were recorded against my name upon the score sheet, but two black eyes were recorded against my will upon my face. The bowler mistook my two eyes and nose for the stumps. Remembering this, it was scarcely any wonder that I shook with physical ague.

Nevertheless, I donned the pad, seized the bat and walked with head erect to the duelling pitch. I could see murder in the eyes of the bowler, but much as I am partial to poultry, I was determined I would not leave the pitch with a duck.

But, alas for good resolutions! This one went the same way as those I make on New Year Eve.

The first ball I missed, accidentally. The second ball I hit, accidentally. The third ball hit my middle wicket deliberately – and I left the pitch with a duck, a sadder but wiser man.

The match must have been very interesting from the spectator's point of view, for at this juncture the game had to be stopped for a few minutes to clear the crowd from the field. One of the fielders had to take the crowd by the hand and lead the enthusiastic little toddler to a place of safety.

And then the Gentlemen went in to bat, and the Players went out to field. My position was "long stop", but right through the Gentlemen's innings I was continually belying my position, for I did not "stop long" in one place. It was all very well for those on my side to yell "run!" I can only run about the speed of a steam roller, and I must be going down hill at that. But, to run almost as far as Stratton two or three times in succession was beyond a joke. I was very thankful when their crack batsmen 'gave in' without being 'out', and then I had a little respite.

When stumps were drawn (without gas*), the score stood: Players 25, Gentlemen 97. My side would have done better if the scorer had only been a gentleman. Previous to the match I called him on one side and offered him half-a-crown to credit our side with 20 runs to start with, but he refused – the base villain. If he had only given us that 20 runs we could have held up our heads. As it is, cricket is a subject the Players do not care to discuss.

Both teams were made up from the "G" Shop of the GWR Works, and one is happy to record that the real good fellowship exhibited during the match made the evening worthwhile. May that good fellowship last long.

*drawing flames

Cricket Through Expert Eyes
By George E Hobbs
(First published: July 13, 1923)

When writing upon a subject about which I have but hazy ideas, I am careful to maintain a reserve commensurate with that lack of knowledge. But when I write of things upon which I have expert knowledge, reservation is thrown to the winds. I become bold in my statements and definite in my opinions. Hence, in writing of the summer game known as cricket, no criticism can possibly be levelled at the statements I make. One other beside myself has expert knowledge of this most fascinating game, and he has the inextinguishable honour of bearing the same noble surname as myself – J.B. Hobbs of Surrey*.

What he and I do not know about cricket need not be translated into the German language or the Billingsgate dialect. It would not be worth knowing. I write therefore of cricket in general, and of a match I witnessed in particular. The match – in particular – was played on "Trip" Friday, between two "G" Shop elevens, upon the "Duke" at Gorse Hill.

Cricket then is a game played between two opposing sides, each consisting of eleven men. It is essential that the game be staged in a field of wide dimensions on account of the ferocious propensities of certain players under stress of excitement. If a large field cannot be requisitioned, it is permissible (and even advisable) for spectators to dig themselves in and view the match through periscopes.

Equipment Before Players

Cricket can only be played with becoming dignity by the use of certain equipment which is brought upon the field of play in a long, coffin-shaped bag, and reverently placed upon the short, sweet grass of the aforesaid field. The equipment according to cricket law is of far greater importance than the players. If one of the players fails to arrive upon the battleground, the play may proceed. But, if only one portion of the equipment fails to arrive, then there is consternation in the camp – unless some genius is able to produce an approximation of the article missing.

When, after minute inspection, the equipment is found to be intact, certain members of the equipment inelegantly termed "stumps" are removed from the bag and driven into the ground. Two sets of "stumps" are pitched three in line and 22 yards apart. These are pitched under the microscopic vision of the umpires, and must be perfectly upright and each level with the other.

With modern appliances, fixing the stumps in proper alignment is a simple matter. No umpire attends a match without taking with him a "plumb-bob," a "straightedge" and a "spirit-level" – at least, that is the "G" Shop method, and "G" Shop always adopts the best methods.

The Curtain Up

When the "stumps" are plumbed, squared and levelled to the fastidious satisfaction of the umpires, the arena is cleared of non-combatants and the duel to the death commences.

The captain who has "won the toss," either by bribery or fluking (which is a distinction without a difference), callously orders two of his men to march forward in order to face eleven men who are thirsting for their blood. After the laborious efforts of the umpires in fixing the stumps, they are to see that no bowler deranges their symmetrical beauty.

"Play!" cries someone and the bowler, leaping high into the air, hurls the balls with lightning velocity at the poor fellow defending those beautifully arranged stumps. If the defender is successful and strikes the ball hard – with his eyes shut – then the eleven fielders run about and throw the ball at each other; while the two defenders run past each other just to express their joy.

If the ball be driven "outstation," it is termed a "boundary," and the defender who has secured the boundary, if he be a true sportsman, is then supposed to poke out his tongue at the bowler. This is done in order to intrigue the bowler to reckless action.

Sometimes a defending batsman walks out to the playing pitch and back again, just for exercise. At such times it is considered ill-bred to ask the defender how many runs he has made.

Advice to Umpires

Another thing often forgotten by umpires: if a defending batsman should happen to hit the ball with his eye instead of the bat, it is decidedly wrong to give that man "Out, Leg Before Wicket". The right term to use should be: "Out, Eye Before Wicket". Two fielders should then carry the defender from the pitch, give an internal application of brandy and an external application of raw beef – two pounds of prime cut should always be kept with the equipment.

In the event of a bowler failing to dislodge a batsman after exasperating attempts, it is permissible for the bowler to wink at the wicketkeeper. Upon receipt of the wink, the wicketkeeper will wait for the next ball up, which upon its receipt, he will tap the wicket with his foot and dislodge the bails. The batsman is then considered "out". Great skill is needed for this movement: the art lying in the movement being unobserved.

Having proved to the reader that my knowledge of cricket is of a wonderful order, it can occasion no surprise that I went to see and record my shop-mates' match. It was a real pleasure to be upon the field with them, for they all are as jolly and as happy a company of men as one could wish to meet. One only I had occasion to find fault with, and that was my friend Norman. He appointed himself director of applause, but really he was quite inefficient – for he insisted upon applauding the "duckers" and sympathising with those who made runs.

Good to Watch

Play commenced at 7.00pm and concluded at 9.00pm. No great score was recorded but, even so, the game was good to watch. Mr F Wheeler captained one eleven and Mr S Taylor the other. Messrs J Tanner and E Pinchon very efficiently performed the duty of umpires.

The score was as follows:

Mr Wheeler's XI			Mr Taylor's XI		
W Brown	c McGill b Westwood	2	H McGill	b Harris	5
F Wheeler	b Westwood	10	W Knighton	b Wheeler	0
A Higgins	b Westwood	2	R Manning	run out	1
A Woodfield	c Westwood b Westwood	0	F Herbert	lbw	5
G Merritt	b Manning	9	F Westwood	b Harris	5
H Harris	b Manning	0	S Taylor	b Wheeler	5
R Patton	b Westwood	0	W Groves	c Wheeler b Harris	1
I Rees	not out	3	F Waldron	b Harris	1
F Handel	b Westwood	0	C Ovens	b Wheeler	4
Extras		5	A Albinson	not out	4
Total		31	Extras		9
			Total		40

Several ladies graced the playing field with their presence, and all spent a most enjoyable evening. Mr HA Wilkins was also present to watch the varying fortunes of "G" Shop versus "G" Shop.

*Jack Hobbs, the England cricketer, still considered one of the greatest batsman ever to play the game, and the first professional to be knighted (in 1953). There is no evidence that George Hobbs and Sir Jack Hobbs were related!

Beauties of the Isle of Wight
Swindon Party's Happy Outing
By George E Hobbs
(First published: June 15, 1923)

The "G" Shop Social Club journeyed to the Isle of Wight, via Southampton, for their annual outing. The party, 47 in number, assembled at the MSWR station, proceeding to Southampton in two saloons attached to the 7.30am train from Swindon. Some of the party detrained at Southampton West in order to enjoy a walk through this part of the town and also to view the magnificent Cenotaph, erected to the memory of the men from Southampton who fell in the war.

Arriving at Southampton Dock station, an hour's stay enabled one to view the monument erected to the memory of the Pilgrim Fathers, who rather than submit to the intolerant ecclesiastical rule of James I, dared the terrors of the sea in a diminutive sailing ship; seeking freedom for the expression of their religious beliefs in America.

As one thought of the tiny "Mayflower," and then glanced across the narrow stretch of water to where two mammoth liners were docked – the "Mauretania" and the "Majestic" – one realised a little of the indomitable courage and zeal which sustained them through the vigours of the venture.

The voyage to the Island by the steamship "Princess Beatrice" was most enjoyable. Southampton Water evidently realised the dignity of the distinguished company on board the vessel. It was respectful, subdued, and even deferential.

But the Solent, more autocratic because of its distant relationship to the Atlantic ocean, was not quite so respectful or subdued. It was but a short sharp growl, but the menace in the growl said: "G Shop party? Faugh! Who are you, I should like to know? I could swallow the lot of you in a brace of shakes!" – and it had the audacity to spit right in my face.

At Carisbrooke Castle

Brakes* conveyed the party through Cowes – the first impression of which is rather disappointing – out into the beautiful open stretch of the Island, on to Carisbrooke. One thing only marred the enjoyment of the drive, and that was the hat of the gentleman who guided our horse powered limousine to victory – and Carisbrooke. It was an ancient, beavered topper, and really it should either have been mercifully strangled, or else superannuated long before the Romans thought of visiting Albion.

One looked out upon the landscape and thanked God one was alive to view the beauties of nature – and then one looked at that antiquated topper, and – ugh! – cold shivers chased each other down one's spine. One compensation alone was ours – the horse-motor attendant apologised for his hat before the journey commenced.

Following lunch – mark that, please, lunch! – at the "Eight Bells Hotel", the party visited Carisbrooke Castle. Even in ruins and decay, certain portions bespeak its former magnificence and impregnability. The age of the Castle seems to be lost in the mists of antiquity. Conjecture, however, is ripe, and portions of the older structure suggest a latter ninth or early tenth century origin. Some experts have fixed its origin much earlier, even suggesting a time before the Roman invasion.

If the origin of the castle lies in obscurity, there are indications that progressive renovations have been executed. There is a fine old 13th century window to be seen, while the inside gate of the "Great Gateway" is of 14th century origin. The window of the room in which Charles the First was imprisoned is still intact, while his daughter's – Princess Elizabeth – room, and her bedroom, in which she died in the year 1650, is also in a fair state of preservation.

No one visiting the castle should miss the sight of the donkey drawing water from the great well. This well, constructed in 1588 – the year in which the Spanish Armada challenged the might of England – is 200 feet deep. From the top of the well to the surface of the water is a sheer drop of 161 feet.

A wooden bucket is attached to a rope which is closely wound around an oak windlass. Upon the shaft of the windlass, a huge lattice framed wheel is attached, 15 feet 6 inches in diameter. When the bucket has been lowered into the water the little donkey steps out from his hidden recess and steps into the floor of the wheel. Immediately he begins to walk, the wheel commences to revolve, and slowly the bucket ascends to the top of the well. Although the donkey gets no "forrader" in his position, he actually walks a distance of 300 yards – which is a little short of a quarter of a mile.

A Beautiful Tableau

Having concluded their survey of the castle, the party moved on to Whippingham, where a visit to its famous church was greatly enjoyed. One saw the royal pew, and the magnificent tomb of Prince Henry of Battenberg. But that which held one's attention most, and which profoundly stirred the deepest emotions of one's being, was the sight of a tableau in pure alabaster over the altar.

The tableau depicts the "last supper", and as one stood and watched, each figure in bold, clean relief told again that story of tragedy, of pathos and of supreme heroism. If other parties should be visiting Whippingham, a sight of this wonderful and exquisitely wrought tableau should not be missed.

Tea time found the party back in Cowes, and, after tea, the return journey to Southampton was commenced.

Upon crossing the Solent the party had a most inspiring view of a huge leviathan of the deep going out to sea. The liner was the "Arcadia" and she was bound upon a three month's cruise among the Norwegian fiords.

Returning to Southampton, a visit was paid to the fine old walls, still magnificent in their defiance of time, then on to Dock station and home. It was a day of perfect enjoyment, splendidly organised, and certainly reflects great credit upon those who had the management of the outing in hand.

Beauties of Wye Valley
A GWR Shop Outing,
Described by GE Hobbs

(First published: September 5, 1924)

Those folks who have been privileged to journey in foreign lands have invariably waxed enthusiastic over vistas of wondrous scenic beauty met by them in their travels. From India, Africa, America and Australasia come claims of unrivalled natural beauty. Unanimity of opinion is impossible because degrees of scenic virtue depend largely upon the temperament of the individual mind.

To one mind there is no appeal like the rugged sublimity of a mountain group, with its precipitous cliffs and yawning chasms. To another, the open spaces and rolling prairies. To one the near aspect, to another the distant view.

Be the claim from foreign lands what it may there are scenes in old England that ravish the very soul of a beauty lover. A journey through the Wye Valley is a journey of exquisite sweetness. The beauty of the Vale is one of the highest order – that of the serial beauty of continuity. The prologue is encountered early upon the journey, but never is the epilogue reached. Each turn of the road reveals a new chapter of the charm, stirring the emotions to their deepest depths.

Such were my thoughts, when, on Saturday last, I enjoyed a journey through this exquisite spot.

It was the occasion of the "X" Shop annual outing, and a large company from the shop, including the chief foreman, Mr W Kirby, journeyed from Swindon to Gloucester in order to enjoy a sight of the Valley of the Wye.

From Gloucester the journey was taken through Newnham, Blakeney, Lydney, on to Chepstow, whereupon the first stop was made. The view along the route is very beautiful, and constantly the ever widening estuary of the Severn could be seen.

At Chepstow advantage was taken of the hour's stay, in viewing the ruins of the eleventh century castle upon the banks of the River Wye. Much of this magnificent structure is still standing. The existing structure comprises four courts, a court house, guard house, and five outflanking towers.

At Chepstow

As one stood within the defences of this relic of bygone strength, one had but to allow the imagination scope in order to hear the clash and din of arms and the shouts of mail-clad warriors. One of the most interesting features to be seen in the castle is the spiral stone staircase built in "Henry Martin's Tower". The walls here are 12ft thick, and the stairway leads to a dungeon below, and upwards to three floors, which were minor state rooms. Each step is made with a large "boss" at what may be termed its pivotal centre. In the centre of the boss a 2-inch or 2½-inch square hole is cut (this was seen at the top step) through which some tying medium is passed. Whether it was bar iron passed through or a lead core run down was impossible of solution. The other end of each step was, of course, built into the 12ft thick walls.

The next halt was made at Tintern, where lunch was partaken at the Anchor Hotel. Afterwards the ruins of the 10th century Abbey were inspected. This noble edifice is beautiful even in ruins, and from the standing walls one can easily visualise something of its former glory. That glory, however, consisted in strength of walls and in the vastness of interior spaces. There are no decorative carvings. One record reads: "Superfluities, and notable curiosities in carvings, paintings, pavements, and other like things, which may corrupt the early purity of the Order and are not consistent with our poverty, we forbid to be made... nor any painting except the image of our Saviour." All the altar appointments had to be painted in one colour. It was rather a shock to one, when standing in front of the great East window, visualising as one did the beautiful effect of stained glass, to find that the order ran:- "Let glass windows be white only."

Tintern to Monmouth

The journey from Tintern to Monmouth is picturesque in the extreme. Such a journey must be personally undertaken to fully appreciate its glorious beauty.

At Monmouth a short stay was indulged in order to view the monument erected to the memory of the Hon CS Rolls, one of the pioneers in aviation, who lost his life whilst flying at Bournemouth. The monument is a carved, life-sized figure of the Hon CS Rolls in full flying regalia, holding in his hands a small aeroplane of the older type. It is a beautiful monument and worthily perpetuates the memory of this gallant gentleman.

From Monmouth the journey was continued to Ross, where tea was provided at the Swan Hotel. Previously a visit has been paid to Ross Church. As we entered the portals of the church, one of the party reminded us of a melancholy event. He informed us that the last time but one he had entered the church it was in the company of Patrick Mahon, the Crumbles murderer. Mahon's signature is in the visitors' register of Ross Church.

Two trees are growing within the church. Each trunk is about 4in in diameter, and the height of the trees is about 10 feet. An interesting legend is attached to this remarkable growth. An infidel dying said that if there was a God, two trees would grow out of his tomb. The trees are growing out of a tomb – hence the legend. Rational folk need no proofs of this character. If proof is needed of a supreme being, of a divine and intelligent architect, a sight of the Wye Valley is all-sufficient.

In an after-tea speech, Mr. Kirkby thanked the officers and committee for the splendid outing enjoyed by the whole party. It was an outing of this character that helped to adjust the little differences which may occur in the daily round of workshop life. The names of Messrs J Robins, H Godsell and T Reed were mentioned as having given of their best in order that the outing should be a success. And certainly the committee are to be congratulated upon the huge success of the outing. In a very able speech, Mr Hands replied for the shopmen, and Mr J Robins replied for the committee.

Holidays
By George E Hobbs
(First published: July 9,1936)

I think we cannot do better this week than write of holidays, because this is Swindon's holiday week.

To-night and early to-morrow morning thousands will be speeding away from Swindon to various parts of the British Isles – perhaps some even to the nearer seaside resorts of the Continent. All are on holiday bent, and, even now, are happy in the thought that for a time the hooter will not be heard and the clang of industry will be silent. The holiday-makers will be able to relax and enjoy rest and a complete change of scenery.

Like every other community, Swindon folk are as complex in their ideas of an ideal holiday as they are in their daily hours of rest and relaxation. Some will find their ideal in the gaiety and fun of Blackpool and similar places. Others will find their ideal in the quietude of some seaside nook, or in the healthful charm of the countryside. It is strange, but true, that some seek rest in restlessness. Others are content with the peace of a serene relaxation. Wherever the destination, whatever the ideals, if the essence of holidays is realised – that of regeneration of recuperation – then the holiday will have been well spent.

To many people there is one particular bugbear which is apt to spoil a holiday almost before it begins. A holiday can be enjoyed on a minimum of expenditure, and one can be spoiled on a maximum. Some will leave for their holidays disgruntled because there is not too much in the family exchequer. Such a holiday is already doomed to failure, because it has begun with discontent.

That a holiday needs money is very true. The question is: how much is needed so that the maximum of pleasure can be attained?

* * *

To begin with, it must be taken into account that the folk who let rooms depend on the "season" for their means of subsistence throughout the year. It may be thought that the terms in some instances are high, as indeed they are. But as this is a necessary item in the expenditure this is first allowed for.

To offset this expenditure, which, among other items, is the man's responsibility (all slander actions to be fought after the holidays), the wife and mother is relieved of the distraction of cooking, preparing meals and the subsequent washing-up. For one week in the year, at least, mother, who so sadly needs it, gets a rest from these things.

Personally I am glad the fates decreed my entry into this world as a male. The man in the work-shops obtains a variety of changes in his daily calling, even if he has a cantankerous boss. But the woman, day after day, sees four walls, dishes to be cleaned, children to be watched and washed, a line of apparel which occasionally has the unhappy knack of breaking on a squally day, and a multiplicity of other jobs which daily grow more and more monotonous. Therefore, viewed in the light of mother's rest and change, the expenditure upon the rooms is not excessive.

Then comes the vexed question of what constitutes a real "slap-up" time. I am thinking now more particularly of the family groups. A has one child and is in a fair job. B has four children, and not such a fair job. Quite the natural instinct is for B to wish for his children the same chances of enjoyment as A. To do this, however, B must spend four times as much as A, and B cannot do this, much as he would like to do so. The money saved simply won't run to it. B, moreover, is conscious that his children cannot appreciate the "why" of the difference between their three-half-pence each and A's child's six-pence. But in these circumstances B has the chance of a lifetime.

He has the power of logically reasoning that real joy and happiness are not measured upon a money basis. What he lacks in finance he can more than make up in service. For a week he can become a boy again and share in the inexpensive joys of his children. He won't look foolish even if he does paddle in the sea with the youngsters instead of longing for that seven-and-sixpenny charabanc tour, or that five-shilling boat trip.

He should balance against his desire of the more expensive things the fact that charabanc tours are apt to be dusty and hot, and sea trips may make one of the party sick. On the sands are no expensive seats, and sea-paddling will bring discomfort to none.

* * *

Looking back over my past experience, I honestly think that much money may be spent during holidays which does not bring one particle of compensation.

In this I am not thinking of our young folk who reckon to have a good time and "blow the cost." These dear young folk are all lovable. About Wednesday of Trip Week mother and dad in some other part of England receive a message, brief but expressive: "Dear Mum and Dad, – Stumped. Could you please send on a £1. Love, Jack (or Jill)."

No, I am not thinking of these. I am thinking of those to whom the saving for holidays has been difficult. A good deal of joy is lost in grieving for the unattainable. And when the unattainable has been attempted it is followed by ragged tempers and further loss of joy. And that is bad for a holiday.

I think the best type of holiday, and one which will be the most successful, is the one that has been systematically planned. I do not mean that the itinerary has been mapped out, but that from the funds available a daily allocation has been apportioned. If this is done then those with the all too limited exchequer will know how they stand daily. Such a method will avoid a too-free expenditure at the beginning of the holiday and a lack at the end.

Above all, I would stress again that, while money must have its place in the holiday scheme, real recuperation cannot be purchased. Some sort of gratification can be purchased, but contentment of spirit – which is the essential to recuperation – cannot be bought.

* * *

To every family man, to every mother, I wish for you with your children a real joyous holiday.

Some of the young folk will be journeying to resorts different to that of their parents. This is as it should be, for there must come a time when independence must be attempted. But for youth, amid gaiety, it becomes a time of forgetfulness. I do not mean that moral codes of honour will be forgotten, but that filial bonds may be temporarily lost sight of. Father and mother will be thinking of these young folk, and a letter to them will be greatly appreciated. To write a letter will occupy not more than a quarter of an hour, and the cost but three-half-pence. This will be but a small expenditure of time and money compared to the joy of mother and dad that they have not been forgotten.

Gleanings [10]
By George E Hobbs
(First published: July 8, 1937)

This week will witness a great exodus from Swindon. Folk, according to fancy or necessity, will journey to quiet little rural villages or inland towns, to sea coast villages or towns of a restful character, or to the more garish resorts of noise and bustle. Wherever it may be, each destination will represent a personal interpretation of what constitutes a holiday. And this leads me to my topic for this week. What constitutes a successful holiday?

Everyone, whatever his or her job, needs, at some time or another, a holiday, or change from the usual occupation. Every effort is a tax upon energy, and, while an evening's recreation or a night's sleep may yield back some degree of stimulation, there comes a time when a complete rest and change is necessary.

"Fatigue" is the price paid for overtaxing capacities. Even engineers are acquainted with "fatigue" in their use of steels and the like. Doctors are more acquainted with it, however, because they have to deal with human obstinacies. There comes a time when the problem which was easy of solution becomes one in which even the formula eludes the mind. The difficulty which has been met with a smile is now met with irritation, almost with despair. The little pinpricks which had been passed over as the inevitable routine of factory and business life, are now sword-jabs which reach the vital parts of our constitution. These are the sure signs that "fatigue" has set in, and that a rest, a holiday, a means of recuperation is necessary.

* * *

Knowing that the Swindon "Trip" is arranged upon a previously-advertised date, preparations are made so that all shall be ready for that date. The first thing of importance is the destination where the hoped-for recuperation will be found. As I have already said, fancy or necessity will lead the way.

That recuperation cannot be found in a mad, exhaustive itinerary is unquestionably true. To rush from one scene of excitement to another is a further tax upon energy, and one eventually finds the need of a second holiday to get over the first. True rest and recuperation can come only by supplying the needs to repair the lowered energies and capacities. In many cases the need is for a restful tonic to mind and spirit.

Some will find this in the peace and charm of the countryside. Here there will be no late nights and hectic days. Body, mind and soul will be recuperated by the perfect rest and change – in the birds singing their morning hymn of joy, in the soft rustle of the leaves as the wind breathes upon the pine, the oak and the beech, in the sweet scent of the hay and in the perfume of flowers. All these act upon the jaded nerves like a tonic wine of rich vintage. They take away the shadows which had gathered – the sure sign of the need for rest and change. They fill the soul with new courage for the daily battle which shortly must be renewed. They give new meaning to life and a new solution to life's problems. They create a new purpose, a reinvigorated love, a revitalised service. And then the calm of a summer's evening when "Heaven is touching earth with rest," never more appreciated than in that solemnity which comes to the countryside in the evening.

There is a wonder in the dawn, but there is something indescribably "searching" in the evening twilight. There is something which draws one out to reach for the highest that is in one. And in that "drawing out" there follows an infilling of joyous strength and power.

* * *

But certainly not all will find rest and recuperation in the countryside. Many will journey to the seaside resorts of our land and there seek the rest and change they so much need. After all, what is more pleasant than to sit on the sands, either in a deck chair – so profusely provided at little cost – or upon the sands itself, and drink into the lungs the unpolluted ozone from the sea.

Nature – or, if you will, a benign Creator – has decreed that the oceans of the earth shall safeguard the continuance of His creatures. A fresh water ocean would long since have exterminated the race. The saline properties of the ocean not only counteract the effect of poisonous gases which would arise from the millions of decomposing bodies, but also cleanse the shores. Only a saline "motioned" ocean could preserve life, and one of the properties of the "ordered" ocean is its life-giving ozone. There is, therefore, at the seaside the inexpensive means of providing rest and the necessary recuperation which the factory worker needs.

To the reflective mind there is much to stimulate down by the sea. One can forget – for one week at least – that "wars and rumours of wars" are still a part of our life's problems. In fact, it is partly in the forgetting that "rest" will do its beneficent work.

There is a source of inspiration in the sea itself – its power, its extent, its tempests and its tranquillity; the outline of the bay and the rugged rocks out at sea. One can day-dream of the immensity of years in which the devouring sea ate away the softer ground, and thus formed the bay in all the wonder of its conformation, but could not erode those sentinel rocks. In all their rugged grandeur they stand as a defiance of the sea's power and might. Those rocks were once part of the mainland, but now they are the eternal evidence of what once was.

And, if we come down to matters less elevated, there are other joys at the seaside. Good food is as essential to a successful holiday as are the other multifarious sides. I am not sure that I know of anything nicer than to come down to breakfast faced with a freshly-caught fish, nicely browned. Bacon and egg savour too much of Wiltshire and of Swindon. A freshly-caught mackerel, browned to a turn, can rarely be surpassed. Personally I should not worry if it was any other kind of fish as long as it was freshly-caught and properly served up. A good breakfast – at least, a satisfying breakfast – augurs the beginning of a good day.

* * *

I think, however that the first essential to a successful holiday is contentment with the circumstances under which the holiday is to be taken. A limited amount of money only can be saved for the holiday, the amount lessening according to family responsibilities. It is hurtful, perhaps, to see others "cutting a dash," and feel that you cannot hope to attain to anything like that degree of expenditure.

Even so, it still remains true that a mind in which dwells discontent is certainly not in a fit state to receive that necessary rest and to achieve recuperation. No song of birds, no whisper of the wind, no starlit sky, nothing in sea, land or sky, can yield to a discontented mind, peace and rest. They can yield peace and rest to a wearied mind – to a mind fatigued by months of hard thinking and hard work in the battles and problems of life, but not to a mind diseased with discontent; for discontent is a disease of great potency.

But if the holiday is begun with contentment and maintained throughout the whole period then it must be one of success.

My only wish to all readers of the "The Swindon Advertiser" who will be going away on holiday is that it will be a happy time, and I wish them a safe return.

Gleanings [69]
By George E Hobbs
(First published: September 9, 1938)

One of the disturbing features of our modern life is its extreme restlessness. It is not that we are busy, but just restless. We rush from one thing to another, and in these extremely rapid transitions we are chasing something which we do not name, yet in our inmost thoughts we desire more than all else – rest, peace and tranquillity of soul. The pity of it is that, while the object in view is of a concrete nature, the pursuit merely ends in chasing a shadow. We try to find these desirable and necessary things just where they are not, and in a way which defeats the end in view.

In whichever way we turn we find the evidence of this purposed quest. The world at large is perplexed with its apparently insoluble problems. And everywhere to-day there is universal heartache, distress of mind and weariness of soul. The request – to use a biblical simile – is for bread; instead, stones are found. The desire is for fish; the realisation is serpent. The plea is for a medicinal tonic, yet we take to ourselves harmful drugs. It is little wonder, then, that our search, prosecuted as it is upon wrong lines, ends in disappointment and distress of mind.

*　*　*

Let us take a homely and everyday illustration before we enlarge upon the greater issues involved.

We come to a point when we feel jaded and worn. The solution is a holiday right away from the scene of our daily activities. The place is selected, and preparations are pushed forward for the week or ten-days' holiday. But the holiday is foredoomed to cancel out what is so necessary to achieve – rest and peace – because the start is made with an incorrect outlook. That which is proverbial is not always true. "A change is as good as a rest" is true only when it is conditioned by the virtue of the change. Contentment must be the centre and soul of every changed circumstance; otherwise a change will not and cannot be as good as a rest.

The day of the holiday arrives, and the curative rest begins by relaxing during the train journey. But, with the destination reached, the cure which has begun abruptly terminates. "Of course we cannot sit about and mope," we say, with a mistaken view of what rest demands. And so animation begets animation. Fun-fairs, swimming, dancing, boating, walking, etc., with hours growing later and later as the holiday progresses, all with a desire to extract every ounce of "pleasurable" excitement from every conceivable minute. And so the holiday ends. The return journey is made with the consciousness, not realised until this moment, that what has been sought for has not been found. What is found is dissatisfaction, resentment, a conscious "fed-up" feeling – all because energies which had been already sorely taxed and, in consequence, needed rest, had been made to function over and above their capacity. And the result must ever be chaos and distress. Whenever we overtax our capacities we have to pay the penalty, for Nature will never permit herself to be abused. Therefore, in order to be the best we can be it is vitally necessary that we have rest.

* * *

There is a strange link between the physical and the psychical – between "mind and matter," as we say. The new science of psychology is discovering this truth in a thousand ways. And it is not too much to assert that in the years to come many of the problems which we now treat upon a physical basis will be found to yield more readily to a psychical formula. Certainly those who have to administer our penal code are discovering this truth, and the work of reclamation is beginning to be based upon saner lines than those of punishment. It seeks to discover the fundamental causes of misdemeanour rather than to flog or punish the misdemeanant.

It is somewhat along these lines we discover the vicious causes of irritable tempers, frayed nerves, discontented outlook and that "fed up" feeling. These are definitely mental diseases and are primarily due to a state of existence in which the healthful balm of rest is absent. It is indeed true that, while a bad temper can be traced to physical suffering, it can also be traced to an over-taxed or overworked body. The remedy is rest and a sane relaxation. But it must be sought and obtained in the proper way.

* * *

I think it is true to say that hard work has never killed a single individual.

Hard work is often a man's salvation, and often – not always – one finds rest in work.

Personally, I lead a fairly active life, and in may of those activities I find the rest I need. I work with fairly regular constancy because I know that my salvation lies in work. There is a lazy streak in my nature, and the antidote is continuous employment. But there comes a time – even now it is upon me – when I feel the need of the rest which a sane holiday will give. I am beginning a ten-days' holiday in which I hope to laze, sleep, wander by the side of Old Father Thames, visit old churches and find sanctuary within walls of ancient grandeur.

* * *

I had reached this far in my article when I remembered I had once gleaned from the D'Alroy Daily Diary. I got out my notes and found it suited my present mood. The gleaning is from that diary of 5 September, 1935. Here is something of what is written:–

"Where shall I find peace in these hurrying, scurrying days? Where shall I find a moment's respite in these swiftly passing years?

"There is a quietude to be found in little country churches – a calm that enters into you, if you will but seek it and relax. There is a peace, too, in the country itself, amid the fields and hills and hedges, in the gentle flow of streams and in the stillness of quiet lakes.

"There is peace in cathedrals, in places that have a history, a future and a past; for such buildings have nobility and a deep sense of permanence and fortitude. From them we may borrow much, as one borrows from a bank. For before we can borrow from them we must deposit something in exchange. So leave your cares and troubles behind you, and come to these quiet places alone.

"Then stay alone and rest. Rest there with bigger things and bigger people than your own little world allows. Such peace, passing understanding, comes only to those who are ready in training, so to speak – to receive so great a gift."

And then the diary goes on – "Everyone can find peace who is willing to pay the price of peace. Nothing worth having can be obtained otherwise than in exchange for something else."

* * *

And the price of peace, that which we give in exchange, is the disinterested service we give to our fellows.

Here, then, is that rest so vitally needed by us all. Not the glare of footlight and the noise of fun-fair, but the calm inspiration of the countryside – the tranquil peace which is shared both by the little country churches and the great cathedrals.

Some time ago I visited Bristol Cathedral. I trod softly, for I had caught sounds of other days and of other lives. Music, soft and soothing, seemed to breathe from the great organ. It floated upward and outward, and then, as though it merged with other music, flawless and perfect, it floated downward again. I seemed to see the serenity of peace upon the faces of those mystic forms as they passed before me, and I prayed that this peace should be my peace.

The vision passed, and I came out again into a world of distraction and unrest – a world torn by bitterness and strife – a world seeking with hellish purpose to destroy itself. And I prayed again that the peace and calm I had just visioned should come to the world. The world is astray, and everything astray must be restless until it again finds true anchorage within the haven of that which is noble and true and Godlike. Until then storm and stress must be ours.

Chapter 4

Mrs Crabthorn: The Sequel

Me and John 'ave decided long ago who was the 'ead of our 'ouse.
An' I can tell yer – it ain't John
Mrs Crabthorn (June 17, 1921)

The character of Mrs Crabthorn (sometimes Crabthorne) first appeared in print on July 1, 1920, in *Trip Eve and Trip Day: A Comedy of the Train and of the Washtub*, and then a further 11 pieces, ending with the adorable rhyming poem, Mrs Crabthorne at the Seaside, three years later. We thought that her adventures (and her rôle as George's protagonist-general) had simply run its course at this point.

She did, in fact, enjoy a brief revival in the latter part of 1926, with a further, two escapades, and then, only then, does she seem to go into happy retirement. Of course, you would then have to spare a thought for the physical and emotional wellbeing of her long-suffering husband, John.

But then, in January 1930, like all literary franchises for which there is insatiable public demand, the character of Mrs Sal Crabthorn made a dramatic reappearance in *The Return of Mrs Crabthorn*, with George (somewhat predictably) coming off second best. Indeed, George went out of his way to state that he had been 'inundated with special requests to resurrect that old nuisance' – and what's more, it honestly seems that that was the case.

Interestingly, George also felt compelled at this time to issue a disclaimer, making it abundantly clear that he knows of 'no one of that name'. Could it have been that lawyers acting for the literary estate of Mary Botham Howitt were starting to take an interest? As explained in *A Swindon Wordsmith*, a Mrs Crabthorn appeared in a work by that author, providing the possibility that George's not dissimilar character was inspired by her.

However, it was probably more likely that someone in Swindon with a similar name or character traits felt that they were being defamed.

George's 'old dame' went on to enjoy an extended run up to the May of 1930, finally bowing out with a valedictory episode, just over two years later.

In this chapter, you will find **Mrs Crabthorne at a Football Match** (October 29, 1926). She provides an account of the match against Bristol City – played at the County Ground on the previous Saturday – and lets us have her thoughts on the psychology of the crowd.

The game ended as a 2-2 draw, despite the Town being two up at half-time, in front of a crowd of 20,057. For the record: Bristol City ended up becoming Champions of Third Division South for the 1926/27 season, and Swindon Town finished a creditable fifth. Harry Morris was Swindon's top scorer for that season, finding the back of the net on an amazing 47 occasions.

Swindon Town historian Paul Plowman reports that "Morris was voted greatest ever player (in a poll to celebrate the club's 125th anniversary) by the club's supporters in 2013, and still holds the record for goals scored in a league match, season and career (216). He was top scorer in each of his seven seasons at the club [1926-33] as well as the first Swindon Town player to score five goals in a single game."

Not long after the death of his daughter, in 1937 he emigrated to Sweden, where he managed IFK Göteborg (1938-41) to great success. He also worked there for the British Consulate throughout the Second World War, helping many escaped prisoners of war to return to Britain. He died in California in 1985.

Listening-in to Mars (November 5, 1926) contains one of the greatest, comedy one-liners of all time, and features a trick played on Mrs Crabthorn by Eby & 'Ria's boyfriend.

It was announced in January 1901 that Nikola Tesla had picked up a wireless transmission, reportedly to be of planetary origin (and possibly from the inhabitants of Mars) while conducting electrical experiments on Pikes Peak, Colorado, in 1899. This is the obvious inspiration for the story, but there may have been another explanation.

George's brother, William Hedley Hobbs, had emigrated to the United States in 1909, eventually settling in Schenectady, New York, where he later became Chief Engineer for General Electric – which was not only headquartered there, but became the testing ground for many advanced radio technologies. Union College in Schenectady became a premier place for the study of electrical engineering in the early part of the 20th century, and Swedish engineer Ernst Alexanderson of GE made the first demonstrations of his television broadcasts in the city in 1927.

One can only imagine what George must have made of his brother's letters from America.

The Return of Mrs Crabthorn (January 24, 1930) is the one where George states that he was inundated with special requests to resurrect 'that old nuisance', and also includes the previously mentioned disclaimer, under 'Author's note'.

Also included here is a comical travelogue in five parts: **Mrs Crabthorn Has A Day Out – The First Stage of a Visit to Clifton Zoo [1]** (January 31, 1930); **Mrs Crabthorn's Visit to Clifton Zoo [2]** (February 14, 1930); **Mrs Crabthorn's Visit to Clifton Zoo [3]** (February 21, 1930); **Mrs Crabthorn at the Zoo [4]** (February 28, 1930); and **Mrs Crabthorn Demands an Explanation [5]** (March 7, 1930)

George accompanies Mrs C on a trip to Bristol Zoo and documents various calamities at Swindon Junction Station; while en route to Bristol; upon arrival at Temple Meads; and finally, in the monkey house. And then, in a piece bookending the whole saga, George relates the consequent fall-out from the excursion after his lady friend unexpectedly turns up at his home demanding an explanation for the way she was portrayed.

Then there is a two-part story: **The Crabthorns and the Dunmow Flitch [1]** (March 14, 1930) and **The Crabthorns and the Dunmow Flitch [2]** (March 21, 1930). It doesn't take long to realise the heavy irony of a storyline predicated on happy marriages. Just imagine for a moment a mock-judicial version of a gameshow like *Mr and Mrs* – one in which you could win a side of bacon – and you'll get the idea.

The very suggestion that John and Sal would stand any chance of persuading anyone (even during a comedy trial) that their relationship was the epitome of matrimonial bliss would be, well, frankly ridiculous. But here they both are, attempting a dress rehearsal ahead of travelling to Essex to convince a jury that they had never 'wished themselves unmarried'.

Here's hoping that they hadn't already paid over the entry fee...

Next in line is an attempt to chronicle an exercise in spring cleaning chez-Crabthorn – although here it is used in its broadest sense to encompass the full (if only aspirational!) redecoration of three rooms, related in three installments: **Spring Cleaning – Mrs Crabthorn Makes a Start [1]** (March 28, 1930); **Spring Cleaning at Crabthorns' [2]** (April 4, 1930); **Spring Cleaning at Crabthorns' [3]** (April 11, 1930). In scenarios brimful of classic, though clichéd slapstick, it's hard not to think that George drew inspiration from Charlie Chaplin and Laurel and Hardy, as well as other Vaudeville-turned-movie stars of the time. Or for more recent comparisons, think of the antics of Charlie Cairoli or The Chuckle Brothers.

As an aside: the Brimscombe Brewery of Smith & Sons at Far Thrupp near Stroud ceased production around 1914, and the premises were acquired by the Stroud Brewery Co in 1919.

In **Mrs Crabthorn's "Gost"** (May 2, 1930), the Crabthorn children play a trick on their mum by making tapping sounds on the window – and John gets bashed (again). George (of course, playing himself in the sketch) says he has 'No patience with such foolish tales' as ghosts, and it's quite possible that wrapped up in this piece of banter is a jibe at the séance mediums who had been revealed in the press as frauds, particularly those who claimed to receive messages from the spirits of the dead in the form of 'rapping' noises.

Last but not least, **Mrs Crabthorne Prepares for Trip** (July 7, 1932) is the final instalment, and much is left to the imagination. But you get the distinct impression that there is a sizing mismatch between Mrs C and her intended beachwear.

You might argue that Mrs Crabthorn made more comebacks than Lazarus, but it seems that, this time, she really did go into retirement.

Mrs Crabthorne at a Football Match
Her 'Impressions' of the Leadership Fight
Told by Geo E Hobbs

(First published: October 29, 1926)

Sir, – The following has been sent me by my old friend, Mrs Crabthorne, for insertion in the columns of the Swindon Advertiser. I would that I could have refused her request, but I am ever weak-willed where this lady is concerned. She wished me to "Hedit" the stuff before sending it on. I assure you, sir, I have tried to do as she wished. I sat up two nights with three English dictionaries, two French, one Latin, one Greek, one giving American slang terms, and one written exclusively for Sergeant Majors, in order to decipher her hieroglyphics, and find out what exactly she was writing about. But all to very little purpose. All that I could deduce with any degree of clarity was that my esteemed friend had written down her personal views upon last Saturday's football match at the County Ground. As you will observe, she has taken as her text, "The Watchers Watched," or "The Sicology (Psychology is what Mrs Crabthorne intends) of a Football Crowd."

If you can see your way clear to accept her "Himpressions", then I thank you on my own behalf. At the same time, should you observe the least sign of distress among the compositors while fixing this stuff, please stop it at once. I've already had one nightmare over it, and I wish to save them a similar experience.

Again: if after reading her MSS you decide not to proceed with it, then may the good saints preserve me! Her closing admonition to me was significant. Said she: "Hif that don't show hup in the Hadvertiser, I'll pulp yew thro' the heye of a niddle."

Yours in Fear, and Trembling,
George E Hobbs

Mrs Crabthorne's Story

I went to see last Saturday's match at the County Ground. The match was between our brave Swindon boys an' a team sent hup from Bristle – called Bristle Sity. I don't usually go, cos, as John ses, "If a woman 'as got seven nippers to baff, she ain't got no time to see the things that hinspires." By this, John means that football hinspires – an' I find as it does.

Last Saturday I told John he'd 'ave to baff the nippers as I intended goin' to see the match. An' I may say, in parentisis, that wen I speaks like this it's final.

So off I goes.

When I harrived at the field, I ses to a 'andsome looking bloke, "Wich way do I get hin?" Course I knows I'm built on generous lines, but that's no hexcuse for hinsolence.

"In, Mam? In?" asks 'im, laffin'. "Better get over the top. You'll never get through the turnstile."

If that feller sees this in print, let 'im remember it was only me delicate upbringin' that stopped me from tiffin 'im one on 'is conk.

I got in thro' the big doors wen the bobby wasn't looking, an' took my place in the hinclosure side stand. I 'adn't bin there a minit wen somebody shouted, "Take the shutters down from the front of the stand. I can't see the field!"

The fool! I cuddent see any shutters. But a nice young man led me to the hend of the stand ware I 'ad a nice view – of the crowd.

Some Who Were There

It was very hinteresting to watch the folk as they came in. First one I noticed was a feller with a robin in 'is coat; 'e 'ad a gleam in 'is heye which sed: "Let me stand among the Bristle supporters, so that I can yell 'Ooray!' wen the're feelin' blue. An' show 'em wot sports we are wen things are goin' bad with us." A reglar Daniel 'e looked, 'eroic an' staunch. Only 'e forgot 'isself, 'e cussed as much as 'e yelled 'Ooray!'

Then there was the toffs bringin' their little ladies wiv' 'em. 'Appy the gents looked wen they came in, but their gobs fell wen they found there wos six deep in front of 'em. If John served 'is little Sal like that I'd keep 'im off beer an' baccy fer a month. Course they ought to 'ave come wen the dicky bird goes after worm – early.

Then there was them what come in with a "I'm going to git a place, [damn] you!/'Ose toes yer walkin' on?/Move hup, I'm come-to-stop" attitude.

But there wos many and many with 'appy patience on their dials. They wos willin' to take their chance of a view without pushin' an' shovin' folk into the middle of nex' week.

An' then a shout went hup. I looked to see wot 'twas about, an' my gracious didn't I blush. Me dial went quite scarlit. Why, them fellers 'ad next to nothin' on 'em. An' then I laffed. I remembered seein' John, me 'usband, once like them chaps; 'e wos going to play fer some team. I mistook 'im fer Sammy, me youngest bye, an' as it was time fer Sammy's afternoon nap, I picked 'im hup an' put 'im in the cot. It was only when a voice sed "Wot you doin', Sal?" that I seed it was me 'usband.

As everybody seemed content wiv the costoom of the fellers in the field I concluded 'twas all right, so I settled down to watch all I could see.

A little feller, wiv short blue 'nicks on an wiv a wistle in 'is mouth, waited to see that all the blues wos one hend an' the reds at t'other hend of the field. He blowed 'is whistle an' away they went. But o' lor! football is funny. But the crowd is a jolly sight more funny. For instance: the little feller with the wistle didn't kick the ball at all; 'e keep runnin' hup and down the feeld tryin' to get out of the way. Course, I was told that wos 'is dooty, so I hexcused 'im. That, an' to keep the players in horder. But this is wot amused me. Hif 'e blowed 'is wistle agen the Reds, then the Red supporters yelled advice wich can't be found in the Bible, while the Blew supporters yelled "Good," an' told the Reds to go to the Gasworks, or some other place of perfume an' 'eat. But if it 'appened vicy versy, then the yelling wos vicy versy. So the pore little feller 'ad a warm time. I thought at one time one of the chaps in red wos goin' to 'it 'im a biff on 'is nob. But I suppose 'e saw the little feller wos not hup to 'is weight so 'e let un go.

I don't think the red supporters ought to have called the Bristle Sity teem "Dirty devils," just cause they got mud on their nicks. It might 'ave bin true, but 'taint a nice term to use in front of a lady like me.

The Excitement of the Moment

One chap behind me made me jumpin' mad. Wen the ball was goin' hup to the Bristle hend 'e got 'is harms round me an' squeezed me in a most disgraceful way. An' then wen the ball shot into goal 'e kicked me ware no lady ought to be kicked. I told 'im I'd 'it 'im in the lug for two pins, an' 'e sed: "Madam, my haction wos over haccentuated thro' the hexcitement of the titanic struggle in the arena below, also thro' the excitability of me temperament. So, charmin' leddy, pray hexcuse me."

In the face of such a 'ansome appologetty I could do nothin' but hexcuse 'im. But lor! 'twasn't long 'fore 'e kicked me in the same place, so I took it out of a little feller in front of me – an' kicked 'im.

'Twas a beno to see the dials of the folk durin' the diff'rent fortunes of the game. "Fry's" pitcher of an-tic-i-pasion an' real-i-zasion, hetcetera, was no where in hit. As the ball was goin' hup the field, you'd see fust, a look of wonder. Then 'ope – with heyes beginnin' to hopen wide. Then joy – with lips prest tight an' heyes opened wider. Then as the ball was cleared a great long "oooooh!" – an' dials an' heyes resoom'd their normal hattitude agen. Like waves on the beech at Portland the crowd swayed, until I got near seasick a watchin' 'em.

One last comment, then I'm done

I'm not a vin-dic-tive sort of woman, as me 'usband'll tell yew. But if I could 'ave that Bristle chap, wot kicked the Robin feller on the ground for five minutes with a fryin' pan in me 'and, I'd make un a necklet with the rim of the pan. I'd see 'is 'ead went thro' the bottom of the pan. Allowing for all the hexcitement wich wos bound to be present, 'twas the worst bit of a great strenuous game. Course there was doubtful things on tother side as well. But 'tis a pity wen tempers get the better of a bloke cos 'e's beet fer a minit.

Yours, hetcetera,

Mrs Sal Crabthorne

Listening-in to Mars
A Comedy of the Crabthorne Household
By George E Hobbs

(First published: November 5, 1926)

The close proximity of Mars to the Earth, and the suggestiveness of the consequent discoveries, has given abundant scope to those who have the happy art of weaving probable truth out of the discovered truth. The novelists who grip the public mind are those who, while soaring high in flights of fancy, yet keep within the bounds of ultimate possibility. Hence there are those who write of "the inhabitants of Mars", and even of the inter-communication between that planet and our Earth. Not only have novelists indulged their fancy upon this point, but practical sane men have asserted such as truth. No one would associate "flight of fancy" with the nature of Nikola Tesla, the…

* * *

I had just completed the above (which, really, was the commencement of an article for the Swindon Advertiser) when I was very rudely interrupted by that old busybody, Mrs Crabthorne. I am sorry to write of the lady in this way, but candour compels me. I would not mind so much if she was only like the ladies according to the poets – "Angels, treading lightly, light as air." But Mrs Crabthorne is temperamentally tempestuous. She came into the room with the stealth of a whirlwind, and with the stately grace of a steam roller uncontrolled.

"Sonny-me-lad," she wheezed, "we've 'ad a message from Mars on me wireless set. An'…"

"Message from you grandmother?" I interrupted irritably.

"Can't, you chump, she's dead," replied Mrs Crabthorne. "An' I ain't no spiritu'list. I tell yew we've 'ad a message from Mars."

"Don't be absurd, Mrs Crabthorne," said I, wishing she would cease her cackle and get out. "If a 14-valve set gave a negative result, how on earth can you obtain a positive result from a one-valve set? It is preposterous!"

Trusting that would be final, I turned to resume my writing. Mrs Crabthorne, however, has the grace of a consistent tenacity of purpose. She is so hide-bound that it disturbed her not a whit when I turned my back upon her.

Said she sweetly: "I don't 'no wot yew mean by them funny words, sonny, an' I don't s'pose yew do. Just swank, nothin' else! I tell yew again we've 'ad a message from Mars, an' yew've got to come an' year it."

"Do you think I'm a fool?!" I answered hotly. "If you're…"

"If I'm one you ain't, I s'pose yew wos goin' to hinsinuate?" queried the good lady, with studied sarcasm. "Well, yew can take it from me I ain't one, so put yer own construction on me answer. Yew've got to come an' listen in."

When Mrs Crabthorne speaks thus, mine, as so often in the past, is "but to do or die." But often I wished I had a Gatling gun so that I could blow the dear soul a million miles the other side of the moon. I need scarcely say I went to her abode.

John, her husband, a cute little fellow, gave me a wink when I went it. I must confess that for the moment I could not judge the significance of that wink.

"Mister 'Obbs, come to year that Mars feller talk," said Mrs Crabthorne to her husband. "Chune in John, an' don't stan' there lookin' like a kid that's lost 'is dummy."

John "chuned" in, or at least he attempted to do so. A series of weird sounds proceeded from the loud speaker which, for the moment, I thought to be gentlemen cats arguing over a feline triangle.

"Hatmosferets!" explained Mrs Crabthorne, sententiously. "We always gets them things 'till we chune hout of the hearth's hatmosferet belt."

"Perhaps you are out of the belt Mrs Crabthorne?" I ventured. "It may be one or two comets knocking up against your wavelength."

Before my lady friend could give me the retort courteous, John did a curious thing. He switched off the set. Then he raised the sitting room window blind and lowered it again.

"Wot yew playin' about with the blind for, yew Ninny?" asked Mrs Crabthorne, her temper rising to boiling point. "W'y don't yew chune in prop'ly 'fore the clouds stop yew reachin' Mars?"

I did not catch John's answer, but nevertheless he complied with his wife's loving request. In a moment I heard a voice. It was like that of a man whose voice was deep bass in calibre, but venturing now into high soprano.

"Hello! Hello! Mars calling! Professor Doem, of…"

"There yew are, yew hold Ananias! Now will yew believe?" yelled Mrs Crabthorne in her excitement, shaking me until my teeth rattled.

"Just a moment, Mrs Crabthorne," I cried, dodging another demonstration. "First let me correct your Bible history. It was not Ananias who disbelieved, but Thomas. Ananias was the one who told untruths. And I'm thinking very seriously there are one or two here. What can a Martian know of the English language?"

"Call me a liar, will yew!" Yew wobblin' jelly!" said Mrs Crabthorne, belligerently. "Of course they'd 'no Henglish! Ain't Henglish the greatest an' purest langwige in the yewniverse? An'..."

"But English is not a pure language," I ventured, merely to put the good lady right. "It is..."

"Dry hup, an' year wot the Mars feller's talkin' about," applied she rudely.

"Mars calling!" reiterated that funny voice. "Professor Doem wishes to know who got in on the Swindon Town Council. Did Reu..."

"Wonnerful! Wonnerful!" cried Mrs Crabthrone in an ecstasy of feeling, dancing round the room like an elephant. "Yes. Oh! yes. Course Reu..."

I am sorry to say before Mrs Crabthorne could finish her sentence, pandaemonium reigned supreme. In her excitement she unfortunately trod upon the cat. Now no self-respecting cat will tolerate for one moment twenty-nine and a half stone upon its steering apparatus. The cat immediately protested against the insult by puncturing Mrs Crabthorne's leg with four sharp claws.

With a yell a [Native American] might have envied, the poor tortured lady capsized. I naturally ran to save her from falling. John also was bent upon the same mission of mercy. We both met with a violent impact, and even before Mrs Crabthorne reached the floor I had cannoned John underneath his faithful spouse, while I landed in the coal scuttle.

And still that horrible voice went on: "Mars calling!" and something about Professor Doem. But for the time being I should not have become excited even if Neptune had called. I was too firmly fixed in the scuttle. Presently I was able to extricate myself, and then I turned to sort over the casualties.

I dare not enlarge upon the scene that ensued. How I levered Mrs Crabthorne from off John, and the physical wreck I found him. Nor dare I tabulate the good lady's vocabulary. It was weird, monstrous, yet withal convincing. Without bidding them "Adieu," I journeyed home.

It was a puzzle to me how the whole thing had been faked and who was responsible for it. The sequel was not long in coming.

A day or so later I met John looking somewhat worse for wear.

"We had a [devil] of a time after you went," he said sadly. "'Course 'twas a trick we put on the missis. Eby, that's our third youngest, got 'Ria's chap to fix a long speaking tube from the shed at the bottom of the garden to the loud speaker. We disconnected the aerial, and what Sal thought was the atmospherics was Eby howling up the tube.

"Sal found it out," he concluded pathetically. "Eby's got to stand now to have his meals – he can't sit down. And as for 'Ria's chap, well, the doctor said he may be able to leave his bed in a fortnight. And as for me – no beer for a month."

It's a cruel world.

The Return of Mrs Crabthorn
George E Hobbs Revives an old Character
(First published: January 24, 1930) F

No creature on this earth is more deserving of sympathy at the moment than the writer of this article. To disclose the reason is to reveal a painful episode.

Not only have I been inundated with special requests to resurrect that old nuisance Mrs S Crabthorn, but have had a visit from the old dame in person. I am reluctantly compelled to connect the two – the innumerable requests and her ladyship's visit – and feel that no request would have been forthcoming but for her.

I have recorded the exploits of this elephantine fairy, her husband John and the Crabthorn chicks, until I have wearied of them. I recorded their historic journey to "Weymuff", Mrs Crabthorn's "Moonlit flit from Rodbern to Souf Swindon", "Her adventures with a Robot", "Teaching her to drive a car", "Guy Fawkes' Night", and a host of other adventures. I went out of my way to put my study at Mrs Crabthorn's convenience. I constantly paid her compliments, only to be met just as constantly with abuse and scorn. Now by the decree of a cruel fate, I have to go through it all again.

Mrs Crabthorn's visit to me proved anything but a happy one. As veracity was ever my strong point, I must record exactly what occurred.

I was in my study preparing a recondite treatise upon "Mechanics" when I was startled nearly out of my wits by a strange sound. It was a kind of rumble, gradually growing in intensity. An icy hand seemed to grip my heart. Was this the end of the world? My alarm turned to anger when I heard the rumble accompanied by an all-too-well-remembered voice:

"Ware are yu, sonny-me-lad? I'm a-comin' in. Ah! 'ere yu be. Now wot about it?"

"For the love of Mike, go away," I gasped, as soon as I could get breath. "I thought you were dead, or hoped you were."

"You'll get a thick ear in a minnit," said she of the fairy form. "Now wot about me in the Adver agen?"

"For heaven's sake, no! I am far too busy for any such nonsense. You go to…"

"I aint goin' then. An' yu ought to be 'shamed of yourself talkin' to a lady like that. Yu…"

"I was merely going to say," I interrupted, "You go to the editor and ask him to write up your adventures. I am far too busy."

"Wot doin'?" asked she, with her usual grace and charm.

"I am engaged upon a treatise dealing with the laws of 'Mechanics'," I answered shortly, wishing she would depart without wasting more time.

"About th' insititoot wot gives th' Trip, or the rendevios where John gets 'is beer?"

"My dear lady, NO!"

"Aw right, sonny-boy, don't git yer braces twisted. Now wot do yu mean by 'Meecanics'?"

"Mechanics," I answered with what patience I could command, "deals with the laws relating to force; and force is any cause which moves, or tends to move, any portion of matter. Now, Mrs, Crabthorn, please go!"

"Arf-a-mo, sonny-me-lad. Arf-a-mo. Yu got it wrong. Th' perlice is a force but they ain't meecanics. They comes under th' 'eading of th' uniformed staff. I've 'nowed meecanics cuss 'em. Me 'usband John 'as. Course, I can see some 'nalogy. Yu said, force moves or pertends to move portions of matter. I've sin 'em move portions of matter in a 'and cart – them as 'ave 'ad one over th' hate. It works out there, don't it, mister 'nowall?"

There is a finality to the patience of the most tolerant. My patience had reached its limits. Personally I am a man of peace. But for Mrs Crabthorn to invade my study and interrupt me with the nonsense of her walnut of a brain was more than I could stand.

"You are an ignorant and obnoxious female!" I shouted heatedly. "The more I see of you, the more convinced I am that Darwin was correct in his deductions. Now please go before I have to remove you."

"Move me!" said she, pugnaciously. "Yu silly hass, yu cuddent move a wops off a norange 'nless a bobby wos stood by yu."

I must admit that had I been cooler I should have acted with more discretion. It must be remembered that Mrs Crabthorn weighed 22 stone; with a measurement around her wasp-like waist of six feet, two-and-a-quarter inches.

But my blood was up. I rose from my chair to set the battle in array.

"Aw right, sonny-me-lad," said Mrs Crabthorn, mistaking my action, "Yu needn't begin to be chiverous now. I don't want year seat. I kin stand."

"Stand!" I roared. "You're going to see what applied mechanics means."

And with that I charged.

* * *

A man told me the other day he once had a "tap" on the head with a "quarter" hammer. He said he had been given to understand there were one million stars visible to the naked eye. He thought on that occasion the "tap" must have given him a telescopic eye, for he solemnly avowed he saw more than a million.

I have no idea how many I saw when I met Mrs Crabthorn's elf-like form. All that I remember before losing consciousness was trying to solve the well-known problem of what happens when an irresistible force meets an immovable object.

The honours this time were with my lady friend.

Author's note: It must be distinctly understood that in reviving Mrs Crabthorn – an old character of mine through the Advertiser – I know no one of that name. If such a name exists, my selection of it is purely accidental.

Mrs Crabthorn Has a Day Out
The First Stage of a Visit to Clifton Zoo
By George E Hobbs
(First published: January 31, 1930)

I quite agree that a sense of humour is an asset. Especially when it is the other fellow who steps on the banana skin. Personally, I am very sensitive to ridicule. I hate having my leg pulled.

I really had no idea of what would be involved when Mrs Crabthorn requested me to escort her to the Clifton Zoo. Of course I knew her to be an abnormal woman in size, weight and thirst. Still I thought I could manage a day at the zoo without looking too foolish.

I arranged an early start in the morning, before folk were astir. Being tactful, I assigned no reason for this decision. Unfortunately, I quite overlooked the fact that a popular excursion was booked for that day. When I arrived at the station I found to my chagrin quite a host of folk had gathered. How fervently I hoped nothing untoward would occur.

Alas! for my hopes. We met it instantly.

Until that day I was unaware Mrs Crabthorn had "nerves". It appears that when she ascends stairs, the height of which is above normal house stairs, she is apt to feel giddy. Not in the "flighty" sense, but in the unstable equilibrium sense. She sways from the vertical posture.

We had almost reached the top of the Down platform steps when, with a sound like a whale in distress, she collapsed. Down the stairs she rolled with the grace of a 50-gallon cask.

Apparently, she was well corseted, for she reached the bottom without falling asunder. How fervent was my prayer of thankfulness that I had not been immediately behind her when she began her graceful glide. I should have been rolled like a pancake, but corrugated in contour. Mrs Crabthorn told me later it was a "wee drappie" that had brought her round. I may add that the "wee drappie" was from a full pint bottle at starting, to half an inch below the label at finishing.

On the Lift

The difficulty now was how to get her on to the platform. A sympathetic porter suggested the "lift" which had recently been installed. It was a kindly thought, and between us we piloted Mrs Crabthorn on to the lift. But the lift would not lift. It seemed to start, but sank back again with a groan. The porter suggested taking her up a piece at a time. He recognised the futility of this, however, when I pointed out that as far I knew she was made in one piece. But it is said that necessity is the mother of invention. Necessity was present, so we invented. Mrs Crabthorn was induced to mount the stairs again with two porters astern, acting as collision mats; I, at the top of the stairs, pulling gently on a rope. My reward was picturesque and to the point.

"There yu are, yu daft [ninny]. Why didn't yu think of that at the beginnin'?"

I swallowed the insult with becoming meekness and felt thankful that all trouble was at an end.

But it was not at an end. Not by a very long way, as the sequel will show. We met it again when trying to enter the compartment.

The width of the carriage door was one foot, nine inches. The width of my friend on the minor axis was two foot, four inches, and on the major axis two foot, six-and-a-quarter inches. I stayed my friend on the platform so that I could work out the problem of entry by mathematics. The formula I used was a simple one.

Let CDW = carriage door width.

And CMAW = Crabthorn's minor axial width.

Then CDW/CMAW = result.

If the result proved less than unity, it would be awkward. If over unity, it would be well.

I found to my infinite sorrow that no mathematician, however skilled in figures, could squeeze CMAW into CDW with comfort; my figures revealed there would be an appreciable, abdominal and posterioric overlap. The position was further aggravated by the fact that entry had to be made upon the corridor side. This involved what accountants term "a double entry".

Squeezing Her In

Seeing that theory would not solve the problem, I reverted again to practice. I requested my lady friend to stand close to the doorway so that her minor axial width would be on the same plane as the carriage door width. To my intense annoyance, all the passengers had vacated their seats in order to witness the attempt.

"Now, Mrs Crabthorn," said I, "when these kindly porters push, please contract across your minor axial width. You'll soon be on your seat."

She was – but not in the way I meant.

It appears she is not of the contracting sort, with the result that at the first push Mrs Crabthorn was wedged tight in the doorway. Thinking she was in peril, all the passengers made a rush in order to render assistance. It was a kindly thought, but the action was too impetuous. The combined force pushed her out of the first doorway and wedged her in the second. Again there was a heave, and with a cheer she was dislodged from the second doorway. But such was the force of the second push that my lady friend was propelled across the compartment, and the opposite door being open, she went through the doorway, on to the line.

In my excitement I unfortunately became involved in the final push.

I followed my lady friend through the door, not by choice, but by compulsion. She had found her seat all right, but before she could regain her composure I cannoned into her, amidships. With a sound like a wail of a Scot's bagpipe, she sank back to rest.

A sympathetic doctor, viewing the ruins, gave his opinion that Mrs Crabthorn was stunned. But I pointed out that could not be, unless she carried the few brains she possessed near to where I butted her. I differentially suggested she was simply winded.

When She Came Round

At that moment Mrs Crabthorn came round. If she had been winded, she was certainly not in that condition now. In the narrow space of five short minutes I learned more about railways, railway porters, and my own ancestry than I had ever known before. If her vocabulary was lurid, at least it was understandable. One had no doubt as to her meaning. It was not so much in her forcible language I objected as to her ideas upon evolution. She inferred there were some with whom she was acquainted – and here she was very pointed – that were a first cross between "a hass an' a hape". I dare not record her reply to my objection.

Eventually we found accommodation in the guard's van, to the secret annoyance of the guard. If I had only known what awaited me on the journey I should have "gone on the club"* – never to Clifton.

(To be continued)

*Taken sick leave

Mrs Crabthorn's Visit to Clifton Zoo
Her Experiences on the Journey
from Swindon to Bristol
Related by George E Hobbs
(First published: February 14, 1930)

Although I do not worry over much of what folk think of me, I feel it incumbent to correct an error when one is made. Mrs Crabthorn has spread the rumour that I am snobbish and unchivalrous, basing these ideas upon our journey to Bristol. I categorically deny these foolish statements of hers, and will place on record the happenings of that unhappy journey. Unhesitatingly I must confess she was a source of anxiety from start to finish. She was altogether unreasonable, blaming me for everything that went wrong.

After the guard had recovered from his grouch, he became quite friendly with my lady friend and found her a seat upon a packing case.

Now I have been informed that before an elephant attempts to cross a bridge it always tests the stability of the bridge by pressing one foot upon it. My wisp of a fairy did not take this precaution, with the result she went straight through the case. With scarcely any effort she made a beautiful omelet of two gross eggs.

I am fairly quick to appreciate the pointed barb of satire, but I failed utterly to see any point in the guard's comment upon the unfortunate occurrence. He said, "She was like an old broody hen a-hatching out chicks."

I suggest that no respectable hen would make an omelet of eggs placed under her maternal charge. I thought Mrs Crabthorn's comment was much more logical, and entirely free from all suggestions of satire. Said she: "If the blamed box 'ad bin made as it ought to bin made, it woodn't 'ave busted."

We got rid of the unholy mess at "Bassett". I wished we could have unshipped Mrs Crabthorn as well: but the fates decreed otherwise.

Upon the resumption of the journey the guard found my lady friend a somewhat precarious seat upon a sack of potatoes.

Now the most simple-minded of individuals know perfectly well that no railway track can be built straight throughout its entire length. At some part of the track, curves are inevitable. Of course, this makes little difference to passengers seated comfortably in the first and third class coaches. But a little difference is expected when one is seated upon a sack of potatoes.

Another thing the most simple-minded knows is that when curves are met with, one should bend to the curve and not from it. Mrs Crabthorn was evidently unacquainted with these principles. At the first appreciable curve we met she followed the line of least resistance. From her exalted position upon the sack of potatoes my lady friend executed two beautiful geometrical figures. She constructed a tangent to the curve and a parabola from the "spuds".

I did not have time to prove Bode's law of equal areas in equal times in her parabolic flight. I was too concerned over the posture of my friend. She had descended into a conglomeration of luggage, but which way up I could not determine. The position was further aggravated from the fact that the train continued to swing to contrary curves. Presently I heard a muffled voice: "'Elp me out, yu Didmarten 'ens!" – and I knew then she was head downwards amid the luggage.

"Guard," I said anxiously, "how are we going to face her?"

"I'm blest if I know," he replied sourly. "Why not let her stay where she is? At least she's out of mischief."

"But we cannot do that," I remonstrated. "Why, man, don't you see she's wrong way up?"

At that moment there came a terrible shriek from Mrs Crabthorn.

"Great Scot!" ejaculated the guard.

"I bet she's got her head down by that cage of white mice. I'm taking them for my nephew."

In haste we attacked the pile of luggage, while the shriek turned into a roar. Just as we extricated Mrs Crabthorn from her unenviable position the train dashed into Box Tunnel. Through some inexplicable cause the light became extinguished. With the fear of the white mice upon her, my lady friend raged about the van. Box after box I heard crash.

"For the love of Mike, stand..."

I got no farther, for at that moment the elf-like form of Mrs Crabthorn cannoned into me, and in trying to save myself I caught the guard on the starboard quarter.

Before now I have found infinite joy in disentangling an awkward ball of twine. Not for one single second did I enjoy the disentanglement of that mix-up in the guard's van. I attempted to locate my leg, but an impolite remark from the guard revealed it was his. I tried again, but an indignant protest revealed a second error. Only as we emerged from the tunnel into the light could we appreciate who was who.

I must admit my temper was short, but in common fairness to the other two, must also admit that my vocabulary was placed third on the list. Mrs Crabthorn's oration, while it lacked the dignity of Mark Antony's, was far more expressive and was explosive to a degree. The guard merely consigned my lady friend to a place, the geographical position of which is unknown.

A sigh of relief escaped my lips when we ran into Temple Meads station.

(To be continued)

Mrs Crabthorn's Visit to Clifton Zoo George E Hobbs Continues the Story of Her Adventures

(First published: February 21, 1930)

It seems to be a generally accepted tenet of belief, based, I presume, upon the story of Eve and that of Pandora, that women only suffer from curiosity. My experience at Temple Meads proves the contrary. Masculine as well as feminine passengers de-trained in order to ascertain how we had stood the journey down. Seeing the interest she had engendered, Mrs Crabthorn strutted about the platform as though the Lord Mayor had come to do her homage.

I felt very sorry for the guard. No one was more conscious than I to what trouble he had been put. At the same time, having deposited Mrs Crabthorn safely at Bristol, I think he should have been content. Unfortunately, he was not content. He felt it incumbent upon him to blazon out a parting message for the convenience of the passengers.

"The coupling on the brake van's busted, and we's got to shunt her off," said he maliciously. "And the driver's been cussing the fireman for burning a ton more coal than usual on the journey down."

My lady friend, however, is equal to all occasions. One may say with truth that though her repartee at times lacked dignity, both in diction and deportment, it was always effective. It was so upon the present occasion.

"Take yer old train," said she pugnaciously, "an' tie it round yer neck. An'… an'… winkles an' welks to you, my young upstart!"

I thought the guard very wise at this juncture in sounding the retreat and calling off his forces.

It will be but a waste of time to detail the awful difficulties encountered in transporting Mrs Crabthorn from the down arrival platform to the street. If a cruel fate decrees that I take this lady again to Bristol, I trust a subway will have been constructed. I could then roll her down the stairs.

Of course, it [just had to] be that this day of all days was a gala day at Bristol. Strings of bunting and flags of majestic size floated in the breeze. It was but natural that my lady friend should take it into her fool head that the decorations were for her.

"They 'no'ed I was a'comin'," said she; the words being accompanied by a peculiar sound. I looked at her in alarm. Her face confirmed my fear. She was about to faint.

"Are you ill?" I asked anxiously, fearing a scene.

"Hill?– yu daft [ninny]. I was laffin'."

"And does your face always look like a half-deflated football when you laugh?" I asked thoughtlessly.

"Like a wot?!" she yelled belligerently. "I'll bust yer…"

I have always realised the futility of giving way to anger. It invariably leads to instability in more ways than one. It led my little fairy to the state known as "hors de combat".

Some thoughtless person had evidently been enjoying the delights of a banana and had forgotten to deposit the residue in one of the public receptacles provided for such things. The aforesaid residue had been indiscriminately thrown upon the pavement. In the midst of Mrs Crabthorn's inelegant censure, her right foot found that unfortunate skin. When she placed her dainty "fourteens" upon it, she was in a vertical posture. In less than two seconds she was in a horizontal posture. Two seconds of time is of very short duration; yet in that brief period my friend performed some exquisite acrobatic feats. I closed my eyes in dismay, not because I feared her husband, John, would be a widower, but because the riot of colours displayed offended my aesthetic taste. Rainbow ringed stockings stood at defiance with yellow and blue petticoat and multi-coloured patchwork nether garment.

I was glad to close my eyes, for it made my head reel. But the closing of my eyes could not prevent me from envisioning again those graceful geometric figures. One foot and ponderous leg performed a circle as through it disclaimed relationship with the other portions of her anatomy. The other foot and leg seemed to follow an independent course. One could not decide for the moment whether they intended leaving her for good, or remaining attached to her person. That they decided upon the latter course was evident from the mighty thump with which her heel struck the pavement.

"What is this?" asked an authoritative voice, breaking through the assembled crowd.

"Thank heaven you have come, Constable," said I, "for really I am at a loss what to do."

"Humph!" muttered the constable, thoughtfully. "What was it, 'Johnnie Walker' or 'Old Tom'?"

I hastened to assure the arm of the law that nothing internally had caused the wreck, the cause being external.

"Didn't ought to be hurt much," he ventured. "She seems well padded."

I disagreed with the constable's deductions, emphasising the fact that all bulging parts were essential parts of the lady herself.

The constable's comment upon this revelation I must leave unrecorded.

"Whistle an ambulance," said he shortly to the crowd. In a few moments a motor ambulance was on the spot. Six men attempted to raise Mrs Crabthorn – and then the unexpected happened.

It was impossible for all six to be at the head of the fallen queen. To raise her equally all round some had to be at the other end. No sooner had the two men at the south end each taken a leg than Mrs Crabthorn awoke from her stupor.

Oral rockets, squibs and wheels followed each other in discordant succession, the natural consequence being that the men, astonished at the strength and extent of her vocabulary, dropped her again.

Luckily the part upon which she fell contained no brains and was well cushioned with flesh. The added shock took her from every dictionary extant. She invented one of her own. With infinite patience and care she analysed the pedigree of each of those six men. She told the constable his origin and his ultimate destination. Then fixing her baleful eyes upon my unoffending self she delivered her soul thus:

"As fer yu, my young cock sparrow, I'll speak my thoughts when we get to the monkey 'ouse."

(Final episode next week)

Mrs Crabthorn at the Zoo
The Final Episode
By Geo E Hobbs

(First published: February 28, 1930)

After Mrs Crabthorn had recovered somewhat from her contact with the pavement, she intimated that the fall had "mammered" her brains. Discretely I refrained from enquiring the meaning of the verb "to mammer". Her meaning may have been "muddled", which, to me, would have been plain. Had she used such a word it would have been awkward for me. With my usual love of truth I should then have been under the painful necessity of informing her she could not muddle what she never possessed. This would have led to a further painful necessity – the necessity of replying to such a statement. I did not feel equal to a war of words with this champion in repartee, hence my discretion.

Mrs Crabthorn attempted a dispersal of the crowd in characteristic vein.

"Wot you waitin' for, you daft ninnys? Think this is a 'nagery?"

One little lady was equal to the occasion. In a very cultured voice and with a sweet dispositional attitude, she answered my lady friend's query.

"Yes, fatty," said she. "We thought the orang-outang had busted out from the zoo, and the feller by you was the keeper."

A deep silence followed this challenge to Mrs Crabthorn's supremacy in rhetoric. Her waistline heaved until I thought that no self-respecting tape or safety pin could possibly stand the abnormal strain.

"Calm yourself, my dear Mrs Crabthorn," I began. "I do not think this lady intended to be rude. I…"

But by this time Mrs Crabthorn had recovered sufficiently to take a further part in the argument. With womanly solicitude she first told me to "mind yer hown hinterference." Then she detailed her wishes respecting the little lady, finally telling her to go upon a very long journey, where she would find warmth if not comfort.

It was all very regrettable. Unfortunately the little lady was as pugnacious as Mrs Crabthorn was cantankerous. Before I could interfere the little lady had removed her halo. Bending her sunny little bobbed head she charged my lady friend in a part known in vulgar parlance as the "bread basket".

Fortunately for Mrs Crabthorn she is built somewhat upon the lines of our globe – she bulges along the equatorial zone – the result being that while the barest of grunts escaped Mrs Crabthorn, the little lady was conveyed backwards by the recoil, finally coming to a rest upon her natural sitting-place.

I dread to think of what further might have happened had not the "arm of the law" returned at that moment. The crowd dispersed like magic, and Mrs Crabthorn and I were left to our own sweet selves.

By the time we reached the zoo I had heard quite a few comments upon my "manly" conduct in protecting a "weak woman agenst hinsult". Also a few upon the dire consequences resulting in a second meeting with "that short-skirted little minx". I was devoutly thankful when we passed through the gates, for I hoped that now all trouble was over.

Alas, for such hopes!

"Oo! Gosh!" said she, as we entered the garden. "There's a woppin' dawg."

"Lion," mildly corrected a bystander, before I could speak.

"Oo's a liar?!" she yelled, bristling like a cat with its tail in a gin.

It was with difficulty I appeased that feminine volcano, pointing out to her that the gentleman had merely corrected her zoology.

It was a weary, dispiriting job showing her round; all the time aggravated by a huge crowd that insisted upon accompanying us. Mrs Crabthorn's comments upon zoology were to them as entertaining as they were inaccurate.

A very regrettable accident occurred while we were in the monkey house. There is nothing vindictive in my nature. Yet I felt that the accident had a semblance of poetic justice.

Mrs Crabthorn had been very pointed in her comments when she stood in front of the "little old men" – the apes. Her comparisons were odious and offensive to a degree. Not that she intended to hurt my dignity. It was just her idea of pleasantry.

Concluding her caustic comparisons, she went to look at the droll little monkeys performing upon their rotary trapeze – and she went a trifle too near. A little hairy paw shot out, presumably, to grasp Mrs Crabthorn's hat. He missed the hat but found her nose. On the human principle that "finders keepings", the monkey endeavoured to take into the cage what he had found. A deadlock occurred when he found the face would not follow the nose. Owing to the pressure upon her nasal organ, Mrs Crabthorn could pronounce no word with the consonants "n" and "m" contained therein. All that one could hear clearly was: "Oh be dose! Oh be dose! Dab 'ib! ad dab 'ib agaid!"

Luckily for my fairy queen, something gave way. It was the skin off her nose. The monkey sat back suddenly – and squeaked. Mrs Crabthorn sat back suddenly – and cursed. Every branch of the monkey tribe came under review, and such was her spleen that my poor humble self got mixed up with the anthropoids.

I am really sorry to show how human I am. I am afraid I gloried in my triumph. Mrs Crabthorn was obsessed with what the little lady had said to her about the orang-outang. The little lady said she resembled it. Could I show her one?

I took her back to the monkey house, in the centre of which was the orang-outang. When she saw his great flat face and ungainly shape, I trust with all my heart I shall not be present when she sees the little lady again.

Our return journey was a nightmare. I hope no reader will wish me to write of it. I want to forget it.

Mrs Crabthorn Demands an Explanation By George E Hobbs
(First published: March 7, 1930)

A few days ago Mrs Crabthorn paid me a surprise visit. She came to demand an explanation of my article upon our day at the zoo. The visit was not one I should have sought. It was both undignified and disastrous. I record that interview with reluctance and sorrow.

Hearing the front gate behave as though old Thor had struck it with his hammer, I looked through the window to identify my visitor. It was Mrs Crabthorn. Grim determination was stamped upon her face.

Instinctively I knew I was "for it". I could read her mission at a glance. She had evidently misunderstood my account of the visit to the zoo and had called for an explanation. I do not mind confessing that I profoundly dislike an argument with that woman when she is riled. In the circumstances I felt my best policy would be for her to imagine I was "not at home".

Now it appears that when Mrs Crabthorn suffers from mental storms, either her vision becomes impaired or she becomes forgetful. I am not clear even now which of the two caused her to fall over the doorstep. Fall she did, and great was the fall thereof!

I think it must have been her head that reached the door first. My opinion was based upon the law relating to similarity of sounds. It was the same sound one hears at the cokernut shies when a successful thrower records a hit. This deduction was strengthened by an additional fact. The comments following the impact were similar to those uttered by the attendant whose head had been mistaken for the nut. It was futile for me to hope that such a reverse would cause my lady friend to depart. Mrs Crabthorn is nothing if not tenacious.

Rat-a-tat went the knocker. It was ferocious, menacing. No response came from my side of the door. A dull sound, accompanied by an awful yell, puzzled me considerably until I heard text and context explained by Mrs Crabthorn. It was a garbled account, mixed with choice epithets.

From what I gathered it seemed that her eagerness to gain admission was accentuated by disappointment at my non-appearance. The knocker had come down upon the nail of her middle finger. A mighty bang followed the termination of her monologue.

There was a clatter of falling pieces in the porch. It was significant. I knew then that the knocker had knocked out its swan song. It would never function again. Still, I was able to view things in their right perspective. I felt I would far rather obtain the services of a good mechanic to fit a new door-knocker than I would the services of a good surgeon to fit me out with a new face.

Finding the knocker would never function again, the shy little fairy assailed the door with fist and foot. I fear that at that moment I forgot my usual serenity of temper and became hopping mad. How fervently I longed for a machine gun. I verily believe I would have blown Mrs Crabthorn far beyond that bourne from whence there is no return. Hastily I went to the door to remonstrate with her.

"What do you mean by this unseemly conduct?" I began heatedly.

"What do hi mean?" echoed she, advancing with menacing steps. "I Ii'm come to wallop the 'ide off you – you lim of a scribbler. 'Ere, John, come an' 'elp me."

It was the first I knew that John was with her. He is such a tiny little fellow that one day Mrs Crabthorn bathed him in mistake for Ely, their third son. So now I supposed he was behind his elephantine spouse with his heart in his boots.

I naturally retreated from Mrs Crabthorn, not because I was afraid of the onslaught, but merely to give the dear lady breathing room. Three folks in a narrow passage, especially with the prospect of a mix-up, is not hygienic.

Mrs Crabthorn mistook my action, and advanced. This left me no other alternative but to ascend the stairs. From a respiration point of view it was becoming more unhealthy at every step. To my surprise and disgust Mrs Crabthorn followed me up the stairs. John, however, knew how indelicate the action was and recorded his disapproval.

"Come back, darling," said he mildly. "You must not go up those stairs with Mr Hobbs."

"Hi'll come back in a minnit, you little worm," she called back fiercely. "When hi've settled with this hape hi'll sit on you."

Of course, Mrs Crabthorn meant this merely as a figure of speech. A literal application was far from her mind.

When I reached the head of the stairs I thought it high time to rebuke the ascending and panting lady. I can honestly affirm, whatever version Mrs Crabthorn may suggest, that my rebuke contained no malice aforethought. It was kindly intended and kindly administered. To show that I was not angry I addressed her as "Dear Mrs Crabthorn," and placed my hand upon her shoulder in a friendly way. All that I know was that she went backwards down the stairs. As she fell she clutched my hand – and I went with her. We went down more or less in unison. We parted company at the bottom.

I do not think I ever saw a sweeter expression on Mrs Crabthorn's face as when friendly help laid her out in the sitting room. It was like that of an angel, calm and placid. As she was coming round I heard her mutter – "John."

I had forgotten the poor little chap. We found him sadly flattened. It took quite a time to knead him back into the shape of a man. Poor old John. His wife had sat on him all right.

The Crabthorns and the Dunmow Flitch
The First Rehearsal:
Described by George E Hobbs

(First published: March 14, 1930)

The saying about the face being the mirror of the soul is unsound both in theory and practice. A tempestuous face will reflect a tempestuous soul; but a beatific countenance may not be the reflection of a benignant soul. One learns by experience.

When I saw the angelic smile upon the face of Mrs Crabthorn I was not deceived. It sat oddly upon her, reminding one of a picture painted by a futurist. It was all angles and no curves.

The smile made me nervous. I could not fathom its meaning. To make matters worse, Mrs Crabthorn insisted – positively insisted – upon buying a new knocker for the front door and having it affixed.

"That's all right, my young cock sparrow," said she in answer to my protest. "Hi 'nocked the blamed 'nocker off, so hi'll 'nock it on agen."

I was not left long in doubt as to what this seeming kindliness portended.

"Me an' John's goin' to try for the flitch thing – side of a grunter or summit like it. We wants you to come hup termorrer night as we're 'avin' a full dress re'ersal."

"My dear Mrs Crabthorn, I am afraid you are mistaken," I replied gently, but firmly. "The 'Dunmow Flitch' is a peace trophy, not one given for war."

The smile slipped its moorings in an instant.

"Wot you mean, you, you, bobtailed looney! John an' me never scraps. 'E noes better. John signed the harmistyce the day after we got spliced. Hi made 'im."

"Did domestic disharmony commence so soon after the nuptials were celebrated?" I asked, surprised.

"'Ere stow it, Mister Dickshunry," said she rudely. "Talk Henglish so's hi understan's. Wot 'appened was this. Next day after he was spliced John ups an' ses that as man was made fust 'e was to be 'sidered 'ead of the 'ouse."

"Quite right," I interjected. "That, of course, is as it should be."

"Ho, his it?!" replied she, with disdain. "Then get this into yer thick 'ead. Hi ups in a minute an' shook John 'til 'is chin 'it 'is forrid. 'You little worm,' ses hi, 'hi'll 'ave you know that in this 'ouse hi'm goin' to be 'ead, tail an' middle piece – get me?'"

I nodded in silent sympathy for poor old John. What an awful experience it must have been for him when his 'chin 'it 'is forrid.'

I felt that such an attitude as this did not augur well for the 'Dunmow Flitch', but thought it wiser not to say so. Mrs Crabthorn is such a positive woman that I no longer wondered [about] John taking the line of least resistance. I appeased my lady friend by saying that from what I knew of the Crabthorns' domestic life, I thought they had a good chance. I did not enlarge upon the point that the good chance I meant was a good chance of losing.

Diplomacy only comes by wisdom, and wisdom only by experience. Very reluctantly I consented to attend the "full dress re'ersal".

I am sorry to say the first attempt proved a dismal failure. I do not blame Mrs Crabthorn for its non-success. It was altogether due to unforeseen circumstances. Fate can be very cruel at times.

John is too much of a gentleman to tell crude untruths. Like me, he has learned wisdom. The only untruths of which he is guilty are "diplomatic" ones. Unfortunately for John, Mrs Crabthorn is a difficult woman to convince.

When I arrived I naturally expected to find the stage set for the peace and love display. Instead of this I saw a very irate woman.

"What is the matter?" I asked, much concerned at her wrath.

"Matter?! You daft ninny! Use yer heyes if you can't yer brains. John ain't come 'ome from work."

"Perhaps he is detained at…"

The words died a violent death. The front door opened and a happy little squeak floated through the air:

"There ain't no sense, a-sitting on a fence

All by yourself in the moonlight."*

I thought it wonderful that a man could display such care-free joy after a hard day's work – and with such a wife. Evidently John had entered into the real spirit of the evening. It was to be of joy and peace.

Then the sitting-room door opened, and with a playful flick in came John's bowler hat. Just pure, innocent fun, on the principle that if the hat remained where it was thrown the owner was welcome. If, however, it was returned with a dent in it, then it was a delicate hint that the owner was not welcome. In the present case the hat remained where it was thrown. It could do no other, seeing that Mrs Crabthorn jumped and stamped upon it. The hat received dents without being returned.

John came in, a happy smile upon his face, but a trifle unsteady at the knees.

"Pleased to meet you again, John," said I, rising and holding out my hand. John tried to grasp my hand, missed it and fell under the table.

"Ware you bin, you little toad?" shouted Mrs Crabthorn, still stamping upon John's hat.

"Bosh made me… me… overtime darling – all by shelf in moonlight"– and John prepared to sing himself to sleep.

Mrs Crabthorn ceased to stamp upon the hat. There was an ominous calm. Sensing a storm, I perched high upon the sofa's head. I could see by the expression upon her face that Mrs Crabthorn was about to show me what it involved to be the ''ead, tail and middle piece' of a household.

Luckily for the little man, he was too far gone to take any interest in the proceedings. It mattered not to him whether his head pointed north, south, east or west. He just smiled and snored alternately.

Alas for the first attempt!

(Next week: The second attempt)

All By Yourself in the Moonlight (1928), by Whispering Jack Smith, Tommy Handley, et al

---

The Crabthorns and the Dunmow Flitch [2] The Second Rehearsal: By George E Hobbs
(First published: March 21, 1930)

Many, many years ago, when time was young, a lady came to live upon this old world of ours. Before her advent, if aught went awry, man took the blame unselfishly upon his own shoulders. After her advent man very naturally placed the blame where it should be placed – upon his lady mate. In process of years there came a time when the balance of power became equal. So that when man blamed woman, she took half and slipped the other half back upon the shoulders of man. Man did not relish this equalisation of power. He fought hard to regain the lost half of his kingdom. He miserably failed.

In further process of years the balance of power again became unequal. Not that man had regained his lost half, but that woman had driven him from the other half. Woman now reigned supreme. Hence, to-day, we live in an age when woman is the overlord – or overlady – of man.

Wheresoever trouble is found in the present day world, woman is NEVER to blame. The saying, "A woman in the case," has long ceased to have any meaning. Such [a] saying is as dead as the dodo. It is man and man alone who must be blamed, even when there is nothing more upon the table than tea and scones.

In the event of a reader suggesting that the foregoing is a misrepresentation of the facts, it must be distinctly understood the fault is not mine. John Crabthorn must bear the brunt, for the critical analysis is his. He had studied this fascinating question previous to marriage, he informed me. Marriage not only supplied him with added data, but gave to him absolute and incontrovertible convictions. As John pathetically said to me the morning following the breakdown: "There's no trouble in our house but what I'm the cause, even though I ain't there. Who the missis'll blame when I hands in me check I'm blowed if I knows."

After a short pause, he added: "P'r'aps she'll marry another bloke. Lor! What a time he'd get, to be sure."

I took the opportunity of warning John that when the second rehearsal was due, not to deviate from the path home. "Keep straight ahead," I implored him, "and do not stop until you get right into the kitchen."

Of course, I meant John to use sense in carrying out these simple instructions. He obeyed me literally. It was a vile evening, wet and muddy. John went blundering past the front door and into the kitchen.

"Here I am, darling," said he with a happy smile upon his face. "Now we are ready for our evening of bliss."

"An' yu'll be ready for the hundertaker 'nless yu go an' shut thet front door yu galoot," replied she with menace in her tones. "An' wipe yer dirty boots on th' mat. Ain't yu got heyes to see I've scrubbed th' passage for the occasion?"

John hurriedly retraced his steps to comply with the gentle request of his wife.

"Now come hon an' show wot a good, kind 'usband yew can be to yer pore little wife. Kiss me first, yu fool! Ain't yew just come in from work?!"

If the truth must be told, John had not kissed his wife for years, one reason being that he was at a physical disadvantage. John was very little taller than his dear wife's waist – or what is the waist on ordinary women. In order to kiss her, John either had to stand upon a stool or his wife had to bend down. For the osculatory contact upon this occasion Mrs Crabthorn did the latter. Being anxious to demonstrate to me that her affection for John was genuine, she bent down quickly and with determination. Her enthusiasm proved her ruin. As she stooped quickly her aft quarters caught against the head of the sofa. Poor little John's face was upturned for the kiss. As his wife shot forward like a blizzard that had lost its way, her dear little head caught John upon the point of his chin. Before I could assist in the salvage, John went quickly to sleep.

In my excitement I quite forgot the significance of the evening.

"Stand back!" I called to Mrs Crabthorn as she struggled to her feet. "Stand back! You must not hit a man when he's down. Go to your neutral corner. One-two-three-four."

"Five! You block'ead!" – and I was just in time to dodge something that flashed like a meteor past my head. I dread to think where I should have been at "six" if "five" had reached its destination.

I protested hotly against this unprovoked assault. To my surprise and secret joy, Mrs Crabthorn was penitent. Together we collected John and found to our mutual satisfaction he was still in one piece. A small glass of "JW" which has been appropriately interpreted to mean "Joy Worker" brought John round, and soon we sat at table, a happy and joyous family. A spotless cloth covered the table, the best "tea-set" brought into service, and what with "fancies", two kinds of jam, etc, it seemed destined to be a glorious repast. (Seemed! Seemed!)

As a special favour, John was permitted to have his particular delicacy for tea (pickled onions), and then the tragedy happened.

Everyone knows that unless extreme care is exercised, this delectable vegetable is apt to assume the characteristics of tiddlywinks. They shoot upward and outward as the knife attempts to sever, or the fork impale them. When once in flight, gravitation plays strange tricks with them. One never knows their destination until too late. With a sigh of satisfaction John made an attempt to impale an onion with his fork so that he could sever it. The onion resisted capture and shot into Mrs Crabthorn's steaming tea-cup. John retrieved it with his fingers, scalded them, and with a yell, shot the onion into the jam.

Unfortunately the jam had not been made to the correct consistency. It was fluid in nature and red in colour. The tablecloth rapidly assumed the colour of the jam. John salvaged the onion at the same time that Mrs Crabthorn found her temper. She did not "lose" it. She found it good and proper.

As I peered cautiously through a chink in the door I sadly realised that the "Flitch" was off. The "fancies", the jam, the onions, the tablecloth and John were all mixed up together.

I have finished with all rehearsals, Sals.

Spring Cleaning
Mrs Crabthorn Makes a Start
By George E Hobbs
(First published: March 28, 1930)

It is said that every season has its compensations as well as its difficulties. Each season, however, is not equally balanced. Some have more compensations than difficulties! Others have few compensations, but many difficulties. Spring comes under the latter category. There are few compensations because spring is spoilt by two characteristics which are diametrically opposed to the happiness of man. They are love and spring cleaning.

At the moment I am unable to determine which is the more disturbing factor. Love robs man of peace before marriage, and spring cleaning after marriage. These two factors make man "look at heaven and long to enter in".

Oh my dear, fair readers. If you were honest in your marriage vows, when you said "Love, honour and cherish thee," then never, never spring clean!

"The Boss" and Her Assistants

There came a sinking feeling to my heart when Mrs Crabthorn asked me to go up and help in her spring cleaning. I was only to assist, she informed me, as she herself would be the "boss", John the chargeman, and I the leading hand. From this I gathered I was to be considered as the "gang".

As Mrs Crabthorn intended having three rooms completely renovated (papered, painted, etc), she thought it best that John and I should have a day off. We could then manage things comfortably. John, being allowed beer, was to work on the system known as "day" work. I, having free access to and the use of the Corporation tap, was to work "time and thirds".

I took my note-book with me, thinking I should gather some interesting data. With John on beer and I on water it would really resolve itself into a "wet" and "dry bob" contest. My mistake was that I did not reckon on the umpire – the boss.

I had no knowledge from what source the combination overalls – provided for John and I – came. I only know I had hysterics when I saw John in his. To where the legs had vanished I had no idea, for the "seat" was round his ankles. When I could compose myself I suggested putting half-a-dozen tucks in the body part so as to bring the legs into view.

"Sh! – Sh!" cautioned John with a warning finger upraised, and that is all I could get from him. I quickly saw, however, there would be trouble when John went to mount the step-ladder.

As I attempted to don the pair provided for me I recognised the source and quickly discarded them. The sense of the fitness of things has ever been my strong point. Dignity is an essential part of my make-up.

The Cat's Noble End

The parlour being the first to attack, we made our way thitherward. Moving the furniture was a job quickly accomplished. I was not permitted to touch the piano, the reason I was to discover later. To my surprise the piano was moved by John and his dear wife with the greatest of ease. Unfortunately the cat become an irreparable casualty during the removal of the furniture. I felt really sorry for the cat. It ought never to have had its nine lives extinguished at one fell swoop by the missile that struck it.

Mrs Crabthorn had a "family" Bible resting upon the parlour table, with brass clasps and profusely illustrated. It was her "treasured hornament, with hall the fambly names hon the front page". The Bible with all the names of the Crabthorn tribe fell upon the cat and flattened it out like a pancake. Like Tennyson's vision of systems, it had its day, and ceased to be. Mrs Crabthorn took the loss of the cat very bravely. Thus did she sum up the tragedy:

"The pore critter cuddent 'ave died a nobler death. 'E died with a good book on 'is chest."

I did not like to contradict my lady friend. As a matter of fact the cat died with the book on his back. Still I do not suppose the position of the book would affect the destination of the cat either way. Nor do I suppose that the Bible suffered any more loss of dignity by killing the cat than by being used as a "hornament".

Mrs C's "Medicine Chest"

Under the able direction of Mrs Crabthorn, John and I commenced stripping the walls. Seeing the job progressing favourably, my lady friend withdrew in order to prepare for lunch. No sooner had she vanished than John produced a piece of wire and skilfully unlocked the piano. The piano was devoid of all parts that would produce harmony, but it did contain that which was capable of producing melody.

"Here y'are, mate," said John, after he had wiped his mouth, but forgot to wipe the neck of the bottle. "Have a swig of this. I've got one on the missis this time."

"No, John," I replied sorrowfully, "Such an act is altogether unbecoming of a gentleman. If the piano is Mrs Crabthorn's own medicine chest then I think it should be taboo to you."

I am glad to record that my gentle reprimand made John ashamed of his action. He put the bottle back – after he had had another long pull at the neck. When John went back to the paper stripping I was pained to note that one eye was looking east and the other looking west.

So that John should come to no harm I suggested that he remained upon the floor and I would do the ladder work. But John had now reached the argumentative stage. He was the chargeman, while I was merely the leading hand. It was the chargeman's duty to give orders; the leading hand's duty was one of obedience. With this admonition he ascended the steps, poised for a moment on the top step but one, lost his balance and fell.

I have seen the "swallow" dive performed on four occasions, but never with such grace and never with such an ending as that attending John's dive. With arms outflung he descended and dived head foremost into the bucket of paste prepared for paper-hanging.

Just as I pulled the poor little fellow's head out of the bucket the door opened, and in came Mrs Crabthorn.

(This distressful narrative is continued next week)

Spring Cleaning at the Crabthorns' [2] George E Hobbs Continues the Story of His Adventures
(First published: April 4, 1930)

Falling head foremost into a bucket of paste is amusing to the unsympathetic onlooker only. The victim invariably is the least amused of all. At the same time such an experience is attended by compensatory blessings. One shudders to think of what discomforts would attend a header into a bucket of lime-wash. Lime-wash has no thirst-quenching values. On the other hand, "paste" is fairly high in vitamins.

When I retrieved the head of John from the paste bucket his face was as barren of features as is the disc of the planet Venus. One could but guess the location of eyes, ears, nose and mouth. Mrs Crabthorn had mixed that paste with her usual "know all" attitude. It had the consistency of oatmeal porridge. Hence, John's head resembled a football minus the lace holes and lace.

The difficulty of knowing just where to commence removing the sticky substance was solved by John himself. He coughed, and then, through some inexplicable cause, sneezed.

Having his eyes filled with paste, he simply could not see if anyone stood in the direct line of cough and sneeze. The result was that his dear wife received a generous portion of the paste with the vitamins thrown in, *gratis*.

A Warm Few Minutes

It was "clear decks for action" in a moment. In less time than it takes me to write this line, John's ears and eyes were freed of the paste.

I think at that moment Mrs Crabthorn surpassed anything I had ever seen of her or heard from her. She pranced about like a [Native American] performing the "death dance" at the torture of a captive. One massive arm and hand shook John up and down in perfect rhythm, accompanied all the time by a breathless, running commentary. A very wide field was covered during her oration. It embraced husbands in general, husbands in particular; even including chargemen and leading hands. The address was picturesquely illustrated throughout, and, like all up-to-date orations, concluded with a grand climax. It consisted in doubling John up in the form of the letter "V" and sitting the poor little fellow back in the bucket of paste.

The Crabthornian Bouncer

"There, yu little toad!" said she with malice aforethought. "That'll teach you to look where you're a-sneezin' another time." Having delivered herself thus, she bounced from the room.

It is a truly marvellous sight to see Mrs Crabthorn bounce. If the reader can visualise one of the "King" Class engines going down a hop, skip and jump upon the permanent way, then the reader can easily visualise the Crabthornian bounce.

It was a sad job making John presentable again. I stripped him of his combination overalls and put them aside for washing. I wished I could have done the same with his head. The paste and the hair of his head typified the screen version of love. There was a close and clinging embrace between the two.

By lunch time John was almost himself again. I was profoundly thankful to observe that Mrs Crabthorn's face had resumed its usual lamb-like expression.

My lady friend had prepared an excellent five-course lunch, the menu consisting of three helpings of bread and two of cheese. For drink I was again beholden to the usual Corporation supply. John was indebted to a Mr Stroud, who lives near the Thrupp, some little distance from Brimscombe.

The "Medicine Chest"

After lunch Mrs Crabthorn thoughtfully suggested half-an-hour's rest for the workmen, while she herself would look in the parlour to see what progress had been made.

"Gosh!" exclaimed John upon the disappearance of his darling. "Now I'm for it agin. The missis is gone to the piano – what you called the 'medicine chest'."

In a few moments Mrs Crabthorn returned. I have been told that the face of the sphinx is inscrutable, mysterious, baffling. The face of Mrs Crabthorn was decidedly in contradistinction to that of the sphinx. It was like an open book, distinct and readable.

"'Ow did you come to stick your 'ead in the paste?" asked she, looking at John.

John looked sickly. I felt I must help him out or he would give himself away.

"John slipped from the…"

"You mind your own hinterferences, my young cock sparrow," said she, with an ugly glitter in her eyes. "Hi hast John, not you."

"I slipped, darling. I…"

"What made you slip?"

Now, the most astute sometimes make mistakes. It is not due to thoughtlessness, but rather to being over zealous. Seeing that John would incriminate himself through sheer nervousness, I calmly stepped into the breach.

"Mrs Crabthorn," I began impressively, "It was the combination overalls you supplied to John that made him slip – not what you think. He…"

"An' what do hi think?"

"You think John touched the brandy in the piano"

"Ho! – an' 'ow do you know what was in the piano?"

"Well… you see," I began. Then too late, I realised that instead of helping the little man I had given him away.

I went back to my work in the parlour in a very sad state of mind. It was an hour before John put in an appearance. I expected to see a battered wreck. Instead, John's face was smiling.

"It's all right," said he, the smile broadening into a grin. "The swig the missis had took effect before she could clout me. She wanted to kiss me, but I dodged her. She's asleep now, sleeping like a babe."

I rather liked the simile, "sleeping like a babe".

Spring Cleaning at the Crabthorns' [3] The Final Episode: Related by George E Hobbs

(First published: April 11, 1930)

When I write of "The Final Episode," I intend conveying to the reader that it was final so far as I personally was concerned. John saw the job through to its completion. I take off my hat to John, for he is now one of my heroes. I have had a glimpse of the job since its completion, and, although I had a severe attack of internal spasms, I still take off my hat to him. He at least achieved something, whilst I failed – miserably failed.

I have to confess I cravenly deserted the Crabthorns in the midst of their spring clean. The confession takes me farther. I registered a solemn vow that should the fates decree my life upon this planet to be double that of Methuselah, never again will I undertake the awful duties of paperhanging. Such duties should be undertaken by a genius only. I, alas, am not a genius!

I weathered through the process of washing off and whitening the parlour ceiling fairly well. I fell from the plank twice only. The first time I was lucky enough to fall upon Mrs Crabthorn, with very little hurt to myself. The second time, John was fortunately my collision mat. Of the two I preferred Mrs Crabthorn, although I must confess John's language was the more refined. It is strange how easily some folk lose their tempers over trifles. As it was I who fell, it should have been mine whose temper was tried. Instead, it was Mrs Crabthorn who raised all the storm. She is most unreasonable at times.

Hanging Wallpaper

It was the paperhanging that got me good and proper. I have often wondered what thoughts passed through the great Napoleon's mind when he withdrew from the field of Waterloo in a hurry. I know now! It is not a plain or garden type of defeat that hurts. It is when defeat is aggravated into an ignominious rout that the hurt is of a painful nature. The paperhanging not only defeated me, but mercilessly drove me from the field with dishonour.

When all was ready we took the kitchen table into the parlour in order to cut the paper upon it and apply the paste. The transfer of the table was a rather difficult undertaking. It necessitated perseverance, patience and push. John supplied the perseverance, I the patience, and Mrs Crabthorn the push.

Perseverance and patience carried the table to the parlour door and push took it through. Unfortunately the parlour door accompanied the table upon the final stages of its journey, followed by choice and fervent remarks from Push. John and I re-hung the door before we commenced to "hang" the paper.

Now I feel sure that had Mrs Crabthorn been a little more generous in the price paid for the wallpaper, many of our troubles would never have occurred. Instead of giving fourpence-halfpenny a roll she gave threepence-three-farthings only. I think it must have been the "three farthings" that decided her course of action. Mrs Crabthorn could never resist the lure of a packet of pins in lieu of the farthing change. As she bought a roll at a time, she became the proud possessor of six packets of pins.

What It Looked Like

The paper was artistic to a degree. Its design was elusive. As fast as one caught the idea it escaped. At one time it resembled a medley of intertwining flowers, flowers that no mortal eye have ever yet seen. At another time it resembled Dante's "Inferno", while again it resembled a cross between a wandering comet and a ground plan of London pushed out of shape.

I tremble to think what thoughts a man would have could he but see that paper with one over the eight inside him. I feel sure he would imagine he had got them again. The fascination of that design was such that if John had not reversed the paper for pasting, I verily believe I should have commenced to put straw in my hair and to imagine I was a [Native American]. Thank goodness that a pair of solar goggles averted the disaster.

Then we commenced the job that finally routed me. John cut the first piece of paper and cut it a foot short of the length. I chided him upon his inaccurate measuring and said I would cut the second piece. I did – and cut it a foot too long.

John began to banter me, but I froze his banter with a glance of displeasure. I very naturally reminded him that his was carelessness; mine, an unfortunate accident. We got over the difficulty in the old-fashioned way. We took a bit off the swings and put it on the roundabouts. It mattered not a jot about the symmetry of the design. The design would have connected up even if one piece had been at right angles to the first.

John applied the paste to the first piece cut, I hung it to the wall. I was rather bucked by the way the top part of the paper adhered. In brushing down, however, I found the lower part exceedingly mountainous. I applied the brush with vigour in order to take out the lumps – and John's pale face came through the paper. It was very regrettable, but how was I to know that John was behind the paper? It was rather annoying too, for, of course, it spoilt my first effort and the first piece of paper.

The second piece fell to the floor as I was about to jab it on the wall. It took John and I a good ten minutes to straighten it out again. Even then it had several rents and one or two parts were missing. We decided to fix it as it was and fill in the missing parts afterwards.

The Crowning Disaster

The paper, however, was intractable. It had a will of its own. It positively refused to be hung in a decent manner. First it went one way, then the other; finally, when at rest, it had a perfect adhesion at an angle of forty-five degrees. This meant we had to cut two triangular pieces in order to bring things square again.

By the time I had hung four pieces, the design was wandering in every direction. Not only so, but the details of the design began to wander also. Colours merged and then separated again, only to re-emerge and separate once more.

And then came the crowning disaster. The first three pieces, with its rents and holes and triangles, fell from the wall – a ruined, inglorious heap upon the floor.

Sadly, I hauled down the flag, kissed John, shook hands with Mrs Crabthorn and went home. Not for a King's ransom would I attempt paperhanging again.

Mrs Crabthorn's "Gost"
By Geo E Hobbs
(First published: May 2, 1930)

I have undertaken some strange duties in my brief existence upon this earth, but never one so strange as that which befell me a day or so ago. (The morbid and the timid should not read this narrative.)

Mrs Crabthorn came to me in a state of extreme agitation.

"We've got a gost at our 'ouse," said she. "An' yu've got to come an' clear 'im out."

"Got what?" I queried, surprised into ungrammatical phrasing.

"A gost!" she answered solemnly.

I turned away in scornful disgust. I have no patience with such foolish tales.

"The best thing you can do," I advised her, "is to take more water with it. If you do not you will be seeing snakes as well as ghosts."

"D'yu mean hi gets boozed?" asked she, threateningly.

"I would not be so crude, my dear lady. Pray calm yourself, and, at least, try to be logical."

"Wot yu mean?"

"I do not doubt you have seen spirits," I answered. "But they are of the liquid variety and fiery to the taste. Give it a rest or..."

"Hi means wot I ses, Mister 'Obbs. I ain't a-leg pullin' – struth an' honour."

An air of sincerity about Mrs Crabthorn impressed me even against my better judgement. Finally Mrs Crabthorn brought matters to a head with a definite request to see for myself. I politely refused, and this revealed that she was the keener logician.

"'Tain't cos yu don't believe, but cos yu're afraid!" was her challenge.

What could I do in the face of such a challenge? I went to her house.

When I arrived at the abode of love – and "gosts" – I was surprised at two things. First, that the "kids were a-bed", and, secondly, "the kids 'noes all about the gost." I thought what brave little children they were to go to bed in the dark and yet know of these peculiar happenings.

"Are they not nervous?" I asked.

"Not so finnickey as yu is," she replied pointedly. "Yu".

She paused. I held my breath. Upon the kitchen window there came a tap, tap, tap.

"There 'tis," cried Mrs Crabthorn wildly. "'E's started 'is hantics. Go an' see if it's 'im!"

"B-b-better w-wait a m-moment," I answered calmly. "D-d-don't d-distress yourself. B-be like me, se-serene…"

"Oh! Luv-a-mussey!"

Dived Under the Table

The kitchen door began to open mysteriously and noiselessly. Mrs Crabthorn dived under the table. It was very foolish of her to be so scared. It made her lose her sense of values. She berated me soundly for being under the table first.

The situation was further aggravated by the gas light failing – Mrs Crabthorn having forgotten to replenish the meter with the requisite coins. A soft, rhythmic padding was heard. What could it be?

"Where are you, darling?" came a squeaking little voice. "I ain't got no matches. I… oh lor! The devil's got me!"

It was poor little John. His terror must have been awful, for his dear wife had clutched both his ankles.

All thoughts of mysterious happenings must have vanished from the mind of Mrs Crabthorn. She naturally believed John had been making a fool of her. Now, with her temper well alight and the darkness intensely black, chaos reigned supreme. A volcanic eruption must be a tame affair to the merry mix-up that ensued. Chairs and table chased each other in gleeful abandon. Luckily I was able to locate the combatants, for a squeak from John and a grunt from his loving spouse constantly revealed their whereabouts.

Struck a Match

No respectable ghost would dare venture into such a scene as this. I felt heartened by such a thought and hastily struck a match to re-light the gas. By this time John had ceased to take interest in anything. Mrs Crabthorn, too, was quiet, and for that mercy I was truly thankful.

I found poor little John under the wreckage of the table sleeping the sleep of the just. And what a sight the table was, to be sure! For all the world it resembled a quadruped seated upon its haunches. Two legs were still intact; two had ceased to function. Three chairs could boast of but one sound leg between them, while two of them had lost their defence – their backs.

"Th' dratted little worm," said Mrs Crabthorn as she emerged from her contemplative mood, "Hi'll teach 'im to play gosts. Ware is 'e?"

"You have killed him," said I solemnly.

"An' hi'll do th' same for yu, Mister Know-all. Wy don't you get 'im some brandy – an' some for me?" said she nastily.

"Have you any in the house?" I queried.

"No!" she snapped. "They got some next door. Go an' ask 'em."

Buttons on String

Meekly I went to do her bidding. As I was about to call over the wall to ask help of the kindly neighbour something caught my eye that drew me up with a jolt. A piece of string was suspended from the bedroom window above. Attached to the string were three buttons. I thought again of the "kids were a-bed", and the "kids 'noes all about the gost".

I know it was unforgivable upon my part. I called Mrs Crabthorn out and showed her the buttons attached to the string. As she re-entered the house I fled up the garden path. I had no desire to see the bed and the "kids" served like the table and poor little John.

I shall go to Mrs Crabthorn's no more.

Mrs Crabthorne Prepares For Trip
By George E Hobbs

(First published: July 7, 1932)

I have been asked to resurrect "for one week only," as the cinema posters have it, a character that once waddled through the columns of the Advertiser. I would much rather have been excused, for the old dame fairly got on my nerves. Still, I've always been obedient to the call, and if I must be troubled with her, well, thank heaven, it is for one week only.

Upon one thing I am fully determined. In no circumstances will I have her at my house. The last time she "honoured" me with a visit, one chair developed bow legs, and the settee, even yet, has not fully recovered from an inverted curvature of the seat. Hence my determination is to seek her rather than be sought by her.

I had written the above before my interview with Mrs Crabthorne. After the interview I wished more than ever I had been excused. Her reception of me was anything but of a dignified nature.

Mrs Crabthorne is in possession of the most wonderful tongue possible. It is far sharper than any two-edged sword. To make use of the correct simile, her tongue has the combined virtues of a broad sword and a rapier. It slashes and it pricks.

"Golly, John" said she to her wizened husband when I went in, "look wot the wind's blow'd in."

A watery smile lit up John's pale face.

"Pleased to see you again, Mr Hobbs," said he, looking to his wife for approval.

The Soft Answer

"Pleased? You little wart," said she, acidly, "well, I ain't. The sooner he's gorn the sooner I'll be 'appy agen."

"Pardon me, Mrs Crabthorne," I replied, as politely as the circumstances permitted. "It is no wish of mine to be here, I assure you. My presence is due to the fact that I have been requested to interview you upon your forthcoming exodus."

"Hexodus? Wot yu mean?"

"Well, to put it plainly, your forthcoming trip to the seaside."

"Ho! Is that wot you means. Who wants to 'no about it? Not the heditor of the Adver?"

"Good gracious, no! He doesn't care a–a–"

"Goo hon, don't mind me. I ain't delicate."

"What I was about to say," I recovered quickly, "was that the editor is not particularly anxious. It is some of the Advertiser readers who wish to know."

"Then tell 'em to go to…"

"Mrs Crabthorne!" I expostulated.

"Ah, ah Smarty. I wasn't goin' to say wot yu thought. I was goin' to say, "Tell 'em to go to Weymuff."

"Yes, yes," said I hastily, "and is Weymouth your objective this year?"

"This yer 'oliday, d'yu mean?"

"Yes," I answered, helplessly.

"Well, then, 'tis, Mr Nosey Parker. And we're goin' fer the week this time."

"That's real good," I answered, enthusiastically. "I hope it will keep fine for you."

Only Words This Time

Mrs Crabthorne unbent at my gracious wish for her happiness – so much so that she insisted upon my viewing some of her preparations for the week's stay at the seaside.

"Rose Janet, me third gel, ken..."

"Fourth, my love," interposed John, mildly.

"Ain't I 'er mother – fat 'ead?" demanded Mrs Crabthorne, belligerently. "Don't I 'no the order which the kids wos barned in?"

John quilted, relieved to find it was to be no more than words this time.

"As I wos a-sayin'," began Mrs Crabthorne again, "Rose Janet, me third gel, ken swim like a tadpole."

"I beg your pardon, Mrs Crabthorne. What did you say?" I asked.

"Me gel, Rose Janet, ken swim like a tadpole," she reiterated, with the emphasis upon tadpole. "An' I'll just git 'er swimin' costoom to show yer."

As Mrs Crabthorne returned, who should make her appearance but Rose Janet. She looked at her mother in horror.

"Mother," she cried, "what have you got? That's my..."

"So 'tis, gel. So 'tis. I must 'ave got the wrong 'uns. Wot you laffin' at, yu daft loon?"– turning to me.

An Animated Dialogue

"I was certainly not laughing, Mrs Crabthorne," I replied. "As a matter of fact, I felt embarrassed."

"Yu felt hembarrassed?" she queried, with a sneer. "John, tell 'im wot 'e is. I'm too much of a leddy."

Mrs Crabthorne disappeared, presumably to get the "right uns". Rose Janet, in high indignation, followed her. John and I were alone.

"Mr Hobbs," said John with agitation. "I'm in a terrible mess."

"Gambling, or drink, John?" I asked.

"No, worse than that. Far worse, I..."

A singular commotion was taking place overhead. Instead of John completing his complaint, he went to the door to listen. An animated dialogue between Rose Janet and her mother came floating down the stairs. John turned even more pale.

"Hark at that," he groaned. "Sal's fair lost her balance over Trip. She's made herself a beach suit to wear at the seaside. And here I have..."

"Don't worry, John," I whispered. "If it's a question of a loan to tide you over, I'll see to that."

"Worse than that," replied John, miserably. "Hark, here's Sal. For the love of heaven, don't laugh."

Poor John!

In spite of the vigorous protestations of Rose Janet, down the stairs came her elephantine parent. I have had nightmares before to-day, but never one equal to the sight now disporting itself before my view.

A glorified orange, with a pip at the apex for a head, and two pips in the southern hemisphere for legs, apparelled in a multi-coloured pyjama suit, stood before me.

"Wot yu think of this?" demanded Mrs Crabthorne, triumphantly. "I'm a wearing this on the sands at Weymuff. Fits me figger like they does on the pictures."

Mrs Crabthorne went to bend. The pyjamas refused to follow the contour... She fled!

"Mr Hobbs," said John, quilting hard, "what can I do?"

"They say that chloroform is pretty effective and safe, John," I replied, thinking of the beach suit.

"Then I'll take some," replied John, sadly.

"You?" I queried.

"Yes," said John, huskily. "Fact is, I forgot to put in for the passes."

Poor John! I wonder where he will spend Trip day!

Chapter 5

Look to the Skies! The Sun, Moon and Heavenly Bodies

...the telescope was invented, and the mind of man figuratively gasped at the wonderful and undreamt of beauty that opened before his view
(George Ewart Hobbs, November 7, 1919)

Astronomy was George's one and only true hobby (his work in the GWR was exactly that: work, while preaching was his calling, and writing was his vocation).

Yes, he was briefly involved in the setting-up of Coate Amateur Rowing Club in 1919, but that was as a committee member and not as a competitor.

His obituary referred to him as a 'keen astronomer' and from his many articles on the subject it is clear that he was in awe of the stars and the solar system throughout his adult life.

In the science fiction epic *A Visit to Venus* (published separately, as a companion to this book), the reader will find countless references to planetary science and prevailing astronomical theory – the perfect vehicle for George to share some of his not inconsiderable knowledge as a hobby star-gazer. Much of this he relates via the character of crew member, Jim who asserts in Chapter 8:

I have no wish to vaunt myself, but both Sandy and Paul will agree I was the keenest observer, astronomically. It was my supreme delight when upon watch to observe the starry heavens, especially the displacement of the planets among the stars.

Allied to this, he also wrote extensively on the origin of man and the possibility of extraterrestrial life – all the time attempting to marry his faith with emerging scientific thought.

In Other Worlds Than Ours (Part 1), published in November 1919, George refers to this theological conflict of centuries past:

> The telescope revealed that a sharp line of demarcation separated imaginative speculation from actual truth. The popular belief taught and supported by the most powerful organisation in the world – the Church – was that the sun, moon and stars made obeisance to the earth. The telescope, assisted by that recondite branch of study – mathematics – revealed the contrary to be the truth.
>
> Instead of the sun obeying the dictates of our globe, the earth was controlled by the sun. And what was even more terrible, the findings of astronomers led them to declare that this earth of ours, important and essential as it was to man, was one of the smallest known globes in the galaxy of orbs that filled the immensity of space.
>
> The bitterest opposition followed this declaration. It was the height of absurdity, and the grossest blasphemy to say that this immense world of ours, upon which the Creator had expended so much care and wisdom, was smaller than those minute points of light in the heavens. The evil one had taken possession of these foolish astronomers and had perverted their minds. Thus, in the vain attempt to make imagination truth, and truth imagination, the tortures were applied; and not only were bodies twisted out of human shape, but minds of wonderful god-like capacity were rendered imbecilic in the process of exacting recantations.
>
> Happily we live in days where individual opinions no longer render men liable to the tortures; and truth or imagination can be expressed without fear of wrack or scourge.

In this extract from Other Worlds Than Ours (Part 6A), from January 1920, George goes to great lengths to distance astronomy from astrology. And we learn more besides:

> Folk are still living who confuse astronomy with astrology, and in consequence, reject the truths of the former science with the same smile of contempt as they reject the reputed truths of the latter. I have no quarrel with those who reject the deductions of astrology, for I believe – and my opinion may be taken for what it is worth – that the planets can influence human beings, only in so far as they influence the physical condition of the

Earth. That is to say – as I have tried to show before – every planet has a disturbing influence upon every other planet in the system. This influence is such as to cause the planet thus disturbed to swerve slightly from its path.

As climatic conditions are largely influenced by the faithfulness of the Earth to its orbit, it naturally follows that when, by Solar "pull" and planetary conjunction, the disturbance is greater, there must come a corresponding effect in the climatic conditions upon the Earth. If the change be momentarily severe, and that severity, operating upon constitutions that are not strong, carries individuals to their graves, then, in this sense, it may be said that the planets have an influence upon human beings. But when I am told that I shall be quarrelsome, or at least, that I must set an extra-strong watch upon my temper, because I was born when Mars was in the ascendancy, is, to my mind – to use an inelegant term – bunkum.

I believe I was born when Venus – the goddess of Love – was in the ascendancy; in fact, was near the meridian, so that the time was most opportune for me to make my bow to the world. Yet I have been informed before now that I was in possession of "a devil of a temper" – which I sincerely trust is an over-exaggeration of that temperamental quality I exhibit when told that "unbaptised children are lost", or suchlike foolish utterance.

But to resume: the science of astronomical research stands entirely upon a different basis. It is as fundamentally sound as astrology is fundamentally unsound. Astronomy does not deal with fantastical suppositions, but with truth as demonstrated by immutable law. The discovery of Neptune by mathematical calculi – locating a planet by figures before locating it by sight – is proof positive of its stability. And the discovery, or re-discovery, of Ceres is another proof that the findings of astronomers are "faithful – and worthy of all acceptation.

And in the final part of the series, from April 1920, we get a good insight into what George actually believed – and must have surprised a not insignificant number of people into the bargain:

That is to say, I believe that life – so far as the Solar system is concerned – first dawned upon the planet Mercury. And life which flourished upon Mercury was similar to that which is found upon the Earth. Its highest creation was sentient beings – men and women, as we know men and women upon this planet. I reason so because it seems to me out of harmony with logic to believe that Earth is the only planet upon which sentient life can exist.

I imagine the Great Architect had a more utilitarian purpose in creating the host of heaven than merely as a spectacular display for the special delight of Earth dwellers. To believe otherwise is to reduce the Great Intellect to that of a common or garden type of showman.

And he rounded everything off with this astounding statement:

> Mercury then, in all probability, has had its prehistoric man, crude and undeveloped in intelligence. Then civilisation grew and developed with science, philosophy and art. And then Mercury grew old, his glories were departing. But life was not being annihilated from the system: for as life was ceasing upon Mercury, it was commencing upon Venus, and, ceasing upon Venus, commencing upon Earth. As each planet radiates its heat away and becomes a solid globe, so I believe it becomes a world with sentient beings as its highest tenants.
>
> Lastly, I believe that this progression will continue until Neptune, the outermost planet of the system, will be the only world upon which life is found. Then possibly, upon the decay of Neptune will come the great cataclysm – when the system will be born anew.

Taken in isolation, and alongside what we now know, thanks to discoveries made in the space race, it would be easy to dismiss George's speculations as preposterous nonsense, and even naive. But they are anything but, indeed reflecting what this book is essentially about: the radical thinking of a man prepared to think outside the box, and for whom even the earth is too small to contain his interest and wonder. Or, as he concluded after setting down his ideas about the progression of intelligent life from planet to planet:

> Yes, these speculations are unorthodox. But sometimes accepted orthodoxy is in error. Whether this be error or truth, one thing I know: it has provided me with hours and hours of keen enjoyment.

George's mind was no less confined by the possibilities of science fiction, in which his dabblings reached a peak with the longest and most ambitious of his tales, *A Visit to Venus*, published in installments in the *Swindon Advertiser* in 1927. Our intention was to include it as a separate chapter, but we decided that it deserved more individual treatment, so it is published as a companion to this book. We think George would have been rather pleased to see it as such.

George's flights of fancy into the fledgling world of science fiction were documented in *A Swindon Wordsmith*, where we pointed out that he was something of a pioneer and ahead of his time, but *A Visit to Venus* is testament to him being rather more. That's because it owes rather less to the modern idea of science fiction, with its reliance on violence, action and confrontation to cover up think storylines, than more cerebral efforts.

Indeed, there is more than a touch of early *Star Trek* and *Star Trek: The Next Generation* in *A Visit to Venus*, thanks to its deep consideration of moral questions. This even includes the idea at the core of *Star Trek* in the beginning: man seeking out new civilisations and resisting, according to the Prime Directive, the temptation to meddle.

When his characters boldly go where no man has gone before, they find Venus is a kind of Heaven, or at least a version of Utopia, and George's story – like all the best science fiction – is less about alien worlds and races than human ambition and frailties.

The four articles that are included in this chapter start with **The Solar Eclipse – Impressions of a Swindon Lecture** (November 2, 1927). Here, George provides an account of a lecture he attended at Euclid Street School looking back on the total solar eclipse of 1927 – something he travelled up to the North of England to witness with his own eyes, armed with a pair of binoculars (and, we trust, a pair of welder's goggles). His first-hand account, with the headline Pen Picture of the Solar Eclipse, had made it to the front page of the *Advertiser* the following day, and was reproduced in full in *A Swindon Wordsmith*, published in 2019.

Even now you can still feel his sense of excitement in his comment:

> I could not help my thoughts winging back to 29 June, 1927. On 28 June I journeyed to Southport hoping to see a sight I knew I should never see again – the next solar eclipse in England will not take place until 11 August, 1999.
>
> At 5.13 am on 29 June, I saw the beginning of the moon's passage across the sun. Every phase of that wonderful phenomenon I watched with ever-increasing interest. For 23 breathless seconds the sun remained completely eclipsed, the only light coming from the marvellous corona and the crimson prominences radiating from the sun's vast circumference.

In the 39th edition of his **Gleanings** (February 11, 1938) – and despite all the courtesy in the preamble – George repudiates astrology and in particular the views expressed by Mrs Grace Burnett of Dixon Street, in her letter of the previous week, in which she stated:

> Personally, I think the sun, the moon and the planets control everything. They are the forces of good and evil, and their collective forces make the Great Being – the complete system. The moon, next to the sun, is the glamorous planet or force, said to contain no dust and no noise. Some say it controls evil forces, because so much evil is done at night. Whether that be so or not, the moon goes on laughing and weaves his silver spells over one and all.

And the *Advertiser* of the following week contained her reply, of which the following are extracts:

> We country-born folk have strange ways of believing in God. The sun, moon, stars, wind and rain are all God to us – the complete God…
>
> Astronomy or astrology as a science does not appeal to me. I study and travel and love the sun, moon, stars and elements as a kind of Romany, but not of the "cross your hand with silver" type…
>
> Alfred Williams walked with his eyes on the sky. Richard Jefferies went into "the open spaces" to commune and think, and Mr Hobbs "spends hours feeling the Invisible Presence (which to me is the All Visible) when watching with awe the beauty of the moon."
>
> Why do they all get some kind of influence from the heavens and open spaces if there is no influence there? The biographies of great writers, poets and thinkers tell us that they all drew greatness from these sources.

There is no evidence that George continued the debate.

Again in **Gleanings** – this time number 62 (July 22, 1938) George reviews a series of radio lectures presented by the then Astronomer Royal, Dr Spencer Jones – to which he added his own musings and deductions. The subject in question was "Is there life on other planets?" and this article covers the episodes dealing with the Moon and the planet Mercury.

Science in general and astronomy in particular held him in awe. As he says, 'I hunger for knowledge as a hungry man yearns for food', and in relation to the talks he adds: 'Each… has been full of interest, and has helped one to get away, for a while at least, from "ARP" and "wars and rumours of war".

Finally, in the 65th **Gleanings** (August 12, 1938), George considers Venus, the planet featured in the final broadcast, rounding off Dr (later Sir) Harold Spencer Jones's series on the potential for life elsewhere in our solar system. George references his story *A Visit to Venus* in the course of the review, saying: 'I found this planet an excellent subject upon which to base that story. I took advantage of all that was known about her and called upon my imagination to fill in the details.'

It was, in effect, a blank canvas, especially compared with what we now know, since Venus offered almost nothing to telescope gazers and only revealed its secrets when visited by probes.

Indeed, for all the knowledge George gleaned about the cosmos, it was mostly confined to the solar system, and even then keeping oneself abreast of new discoveries brought only a fraction of the knowledge we have today. So it is easy to regret, on his behalf, that George was born too soon (but then that always applies to all seekers of knowledge). Just how little was known is demonstrated by an article written in 1938, in which he reported on a new development: 'a telescope with a lens one hundred inches wide', which had shown there were two more moons orbiting Jupiter than previously known, 'making eleven in all'. In 2021, we know of 79.

It is a great credit that he retained a fascination with astronomy throughout his life, even though the science was still quite rudimentary, and rarely offered any proper answers to the many questions in his mind, and only death could rob him of his insatiable thirst for knowledge and understanding of all things in both heaven and earth.

The Solar Eclipse
Impressions of a Swindon Lecture
By George E Hobbs
(First published: November 2, 1927)

Those who were privileged to listen to the lecture given by Professor Turner at Euclid Street Schools must have felt well repaid for the time spent. The lecture dealt with "Eclipses, with special reference to the Solar eclipse of June, 1927." It was a lecture, interesting, educative and inspirational.

The lecturer first revealed the immense difference in planetary sizes by a method that was at once novel and gripping. A narrow strip of wood, 24 inches long, had at one end a small white-headed pin which represented the moon.

At the other end was another pin with its head as large as a small playing marble. This represented the earth. One inch of the rod represented 10,000 miles; so that the rod being 24 inches long, the distance between the two was 24 x 10,000, which gave a result of 240,000 miles. This is the distance separating the earth and moon.

The audience gasped when the relative size of the sun was compared to the scale model of the earth and moon.

To demonstrate this, Professor Turner opened a large, white umbrella which was eight feet across. How diminutive looked the tiny marble against the umbrella. And too, how diminutive looked the marble against the football which the lecturer held to view and which represented the larger planets of the system, such as Jupiter, Saturn and Uranus.

Incidentally, Professor Turner dealt with that wonder planet in the constellation of Orion – Betelgeuse. Far mightier than our own sun, and so vast that its diameter would reach far beyond the orbit of the earth. Yet, so attenuated is the fabric of its constellation that our own sun would outweigh it with ease.

Path of Totality

Passing to the subject of eclipses, a slide was shown, demonstrating how a solar eclipse was produced.

From the sun to the earth, lines were drawn tangential to both, and intersecting at a point near to the moon's orbit. When the moon passed centrally across, near to the apex of the angle thus subtended, and the tangents to sun and earth became also tangents to the moon, then the light of the sun was obliterated at some position or other from the earth. This position was the path of totality.

Above or below this central position, partial eclipses of varying magnitudes would ensue. This was followed by a mechanical slide of a very fascinating nature. The earth was seen in motion around the sun, with the moon in perfect phasing around the earth. Professor Turner showed the "families" of eclipses upon the screen. Passing from south to north in certain difficult periods, and from north to south in similar intersecting periods.

The periods thus formed revealed a faithful return in 18 years, 11⅓rd days; though the position ever moved westward. The "Saros" cycle of eclipses of which the eclipse of 1927 formed part, was also shown.

A slight digression came, pleasing and instructive in its features, in a screen version of a lunar landscape, with the earth shown in space. It was "daytime" upon the moon, yet stars were seen surrounding the earth. Professor Turner said this was by no means an exaggeration, and was entirely due to the airless condition of our satellite.

The ringed craters upon the lunar landscape were seen, and this led to an interesting probable explanation of their existence. The present writer has often seen this beautiful feature and had believed them to be due to volcanic action. While Professor Turner did not disprove this possible cause, he suggested that certain astronomers believed they were caused by meteoric impact. It was certainly an interesting suggestion as to a possible cause.

A beautiful screen photograph was shown of the total eclipse of 1919. This photograph was taken at the moment of "flash spectrum" reversal and clearly revealed that beautiful phenomenon known as "Bailey's beads". It was a wonderful sight, and it evinced from the audience spontaneous applause.

Eclipse Phenomena

An ingenious slide, mechanically controlled, was then placed upon the screen. In a few moments, a solar eclipse was shown.

The moon entered upon the limb of the sun, and in stately (though somewhat rapid) progression passed over the sun's disc. Those who had never witnessed the real thing could easily obtain an excellent impression of the majesty and awe of eclipse phenomena.

Professor Turner made the interesting announcement that solar prominences could now be photographed without waiting for a total eclipse. This was performed by means of a camera known as a "spectroheliograph". The special spectrum line with which the photograph is to be taken is isolated, the main body of the sun blotted out and the prominences can then be taken.

Photographic slides were shown of solar prominences taken by this method. Fiery tongues shot out into space, some reaching many thousands of miles.

Then came the time for which personally I had been waiting. That was a photograph of the eclipse of June 1927.

I went north to Southport last June in order to witness that wonderful sight. My impressions were recorded in the Swindon Advertiser the day following the eclipse. Therefore, I waited with ever-increasing interest to see again on the screen what I had witnessed at Southport.

The Preparations

Professor Turner told the audience of the preparations made to photograph the eclipted sun at Southport; of the difficulties encountered due to inclement weather, and of their hopes and fears.

The sun's disc was "caught" by means of a huge mirror and his image held by means of a clockwork attachment. Trained upon the mirror was a twin telescope, 40 feet in length, and by this means the photograph was taken.

First, the lecturer showed a photographic slide taken by an ordinary camera. Then, a larger photographic slide taken by the Astronomer Royal at Giggleswick. It was a wonderful photograph, full of interest, and with the beautiful corona showing around the dark edge of the moon. But I frankly confess I received somewhat of a shock.

In the Advertiser I recorded what I saw at Southport. I wrote that the corona was visible as pearly white upon three quadrants of the sun's limb, but upon the top righthand quadrant, it was blood-red. From the centre of that blood-red quadrant an eruptive prominence protruded far out into space. I was somewhat perturbed at not seeing it upon the screen.

As Professor Turner was unable to remain after his lecture owing to indisposition, I sought a few minutes interview with him through the good offices of Mr R George.

Professor Turner was kindness personified, and in response to my query he confirmed my statement as to the existence of the grey prominence upon the top righthand quadrant of the sun's limb.

In conclusion, I should like to tender my thanks to the officials of the WEA for the evening's enchantment. I would not have missed it for a great deal.

Gleanings [39]
By George E Hobbs
(First published: February 11, 1938)

I already had a roughcast article on the presumed "message of the stars" when Mrs Grace Burnett's interesting letter appeared in last week's issue of "The Swindon Advertiser". In consequence, instead of making a study of astrology part of my Gleanings this week, I shall endeavour to give all my allotted space to it.

As Mrs Burnett suggested in her letter, a study of the heavenly bodies, especially that of the planets which constitute our solar system, is an absorbing and fascinating topic, and like music, is never exhausted. But the question I want to get down to is just this: have the planets any influence upon individual lives?

This article will be culled from my roughcast copy, and is in no way even the suggestion of a criticism of Mrs Burnett's interesting and thoughtful ideas.

* * *

Milton has represented Adam, when rising in Paradise in the full perfection of his senses, as being profoundly moved at the beauty and glory of the wonders he saw around him. We do not rise at a bound into this enchanted wonderland; we grow into it gradually. We see, among other things, the night sky as very young children. It develops into familiarity.

To the uninstructed it is the same scene every night. There is no change of a spectacular nature. Today, if never before, we see things only when there is swift movement before our eyes, and we hear them only when a thunderous noise smites our ears. Familiarity with sameness brings contempt and, in consequence, we lose the thrill and inspiration of that which lies close at hand.

To me it seems altogether inexplicable that one can look upon a cloudless night sky without feeling a sense of awe, or without a desire to know something of its teaching and meaning. And when, in her peerless splendour, the moon holds sway at her court, the sight is beautiful and inspiring. Many hours have I spent drinking in its delight and charm and, feeling the Presence of the Invisible, have worshipped. But it seems to me that a profound difference exists between a study of celestial physical phenomena and that of what I may term celestial psychical influence.

* * *

It has been said that the science of astronomy grew out of the science of astrology – in other words, that astrology is the older science. To me this is like putting the cart before the horse, for I imagine the opposite to be nearer the truth. I very much question whether today astrology can be termed a science in the true sense of the word, any more than mythology can be termed a sound religious system of belief. It probably was termed a science in the ages that are gone, just as what we term mythology was a standard and accepted religious cult

There is a bed-fellow affinity between astrology and mythology and I am going to suggest that both belong to the distant past. Each has a part in the long development of human culture, and each is instructive in that it forms part of the fabric which built up human knowledge.

Astronomy – the study of the laws which govern the physical constitution and behaviour of star and planet – IS a science. It is the queen of the sciences. Discoveries of motions, densities, constitutions, velocities etc, have been translated into laws – laws which have been tried and proved and which by their intrinsic fidelity to truth, have been the basis of subsequent discoveries. And while there are thousands of problems still unsolved, and even mistakes made, yet it is true to say that astronomy as a science is both logical and sound.

* * *

But I have said that, while it has been claimed that astronomy grew out of astrology, the opposite is more near the truth. And I think that reflection must prove this claim.

Five of the planets were known to the ancient people – Mercury, Venus, Mars, Jupiter and Saturn. Their discoveries are lost in antiquity. It is said that the Chaldeans, about 2000BC, mapped out the constellations, and also discovered that eclipses repeat themselves in the "Saros Period" – a cycle of 18 years. Even before this, the five planets were known. They were undoubtedly noted because of their wanderings and periodic displacements among the "fixed" stars.

Certain of the stars were ever constant to their position in the heavens; others were seen to "shift," to move, to wander. Long before "influences" were assigned to these wanderers, the scientists, the philosophers, the wise men among the ancients recorded the movement of each of the five. And the study of their motions and journeys among the stars was purely astronomical.

I have a note by me, culled from "The Splendour of the Heavens," which reads as follows: "In or about 408BC, Eudoxus, a Greek scientist, demonstrated planetary motions by the aid of geometry, thus inaugurating the era of scientific astronomy as distinct from philosophical speculation." But even the era of philosophical speculation was definitely based upon actual observation, and that observation of planetary motion was astronomical.

* * *

Now I think it is unquestionably true that among the ancient folk, religion formed an integral part of their lives. However crude their system may seem to us, to them it was very real. Naturally they could not conceive of one great, supreme God, but created for themselves many gods. Everything which baffled solution was controlled and governed by a god – a different god to suit each unsolved difficulty. The harvest and plenty, the drought and famine, the thunder and lightning, the wind, dawn, night, river, sea, earthquake, etc – all had their duties.

What more natural, then, that in process of time the wandering planets should become gods? And with the identification of god with planet, there dawned the cult of astrology, of the presumed influence by and from the planets.

The planets having been studied (which comes under the science of astronomy), the optical characteristics of each suggested a name from their galaxy of gods (which comes under the cult of what we term mythology), and from this developed "influence" by the planets (which became the cult of astrology). I think there is but little difficulty in associating names with physical characteristics.

There is the little planet nestling close to the sun. He is elusive, quick to appear, as quick to disappear. He is difficult to see or catch. What more natural than that he should become "Mercury", the swift one, the flying god or, better still, the flying messenger of the gods?

And that beautiful orb which seems to have tenderness, the queenly beauty, the radiance and sweetness of woman. How appropriate to call her "Venus", the goddess of love!

And then that sinister red one, which seems to menace by its advance among the stars, and again to retreat. No more fitting name can be given than that of "Mars", the god of strife and war. And, farther out, the slow grand circuit of the mighty one. Nothing hurried, but just an exclusive, aloof majesty of being. What more fitting than that this one should be the king of the gods – "Jupiter", the high one who ruled from Olympus?

And the fifth, on the outskirts of that which was known to the ancients. How easily it fits into the cult of mythology! Who should come next to the king but the renegade, the usurper – "Saturn," the evil one, the Satan of the bunch?

* * *

Here we have them complete as known to the ancient peoples. When other planets were discovered, mythology was called in to give them names – "Uranus", the heavens; "Neptune", god of the sea and ocean; and, more recently, the new discovery was named "Pluto", god of the dark internal Hades of the earth.

To me the teaching of planetary influence upon individual lives is based upon fallacy. The movement of the planets is purely mechanical, controlled entirely by the mechanical laws instituted by the Great Architect of the Universe, and can have no possible psychical influence upon a single individual.

* * *

For months I have studied readings as given by three leading journals. There have been times when things seemed to fit, but in the main they have been miles wide of the mark. I am convinced that the times when things seemed to fit were pure coincidences of chance, and not of purpose. When I am convinced that the planets influence my life I shall have to get down to a reconstruction of my ideas of law and justice and God.

Until I am convinced I must still believe that astrology is the relic of past ages – and fallacious in its claims.

Gleanings [62]
By George E Hobbs
(First published: July 22, 1938)

"There are two things that fill my soul with holy reverence and ever-growing wonder – the spectacle of the starry sky, that virtually annihilates us as physical beings, and the moral law, which raises us to infinite dignity as intelligent agents." So wrote the great German scientist and philosopher, Immanuel Kant.

I wonder how many react to these great facts – one visioned, and one experienced – as did Kant.

What an inspiring sight is the starry sky! How it thrills with its majesty and splendour. Golden orbs, and orbs of silver and of ruby. Giant stars, impregnable in their grand isolation and shining undimmed through countless aeons. Stars of lesser magnitude, no less beautiful because of their diminutive appearance, each contributing its quota to the stability of the Universe.

What a book from which to read! How simple yet how complex and profound! Here there are pages of written matter which an elementary intellect can comprehend. And, too, there are pages which will benumb the finest intellect the world has known. The complexity of the book but adds to its inspiration and charm.

* * *

Sometimes, when I contemplate the advances made by science, and the wonderful opportunities opened to our student youth of to-day, I feel regretful of my lost opportunities. I hunger for knowledge as a hungry man yearns for food. But my powers to assimilate and retain are regretfully small. I feel I ever want to urge our youth of to-day never to shirk the opportunity to assimilate knowledge. The masters of teaching of this present age are probably the finest any age has seen. The opportunities afforded to our students are legion. And to me there is no worse crime than a refusal to learn where capacity is in evidence.

But to return to our subject.

* * *

From a study of the heavenly bodies by the people of antiquity the science of astronomy was born. Gradually, more and more secrets were wrested from the tardy bosom of Dame Nature until, after many vicissitudes of fortune, the great edifice of present-day knowledge was built. It has been a wonderful achievement in a wonderful science. And happy must be the folk who are engaged in the research works involved. Happy, too, must be those folk who are in possession of telescopes of sufficient power to see at least the nearer wonders of the Universe.

In a study involving such tremendous possibilities it is a natural contingency of thought that speculation should occasionally be indulged. Such speculations begin when the path of that which is known forks into the path of that which may be. If the uninitiated indulges in speculation then the result will be exaggeration and misconception. But if the expert indulges, as occasionally he does, then one can listen with thoughtful attention.

For a week or two past Dr Spencer Jones, the Astronomer Royal, has broadcast a series of talks on "Is there life on other planets?" Each of the talks has been full of interest, and has helped one to get away, for a while at least, from "ARP" and "wars and rumours of war".

After dealing briefly with the general construction, or, better still, with a general description of the Universe, Dr Jones asked a question that has often agitated the minds of thinkers. "Can it be," he enquired, "that throughout the vast deeps of space nowhere but on our own little earth is life to be found? Most people, I think, would find it difficult to believe that this can be so. The mind rebels against this seeming waste of creation."

I imagine that little difficulty would present itself if the Universe merely consisted of our own Solar System of sun and nine planets. One could then suspect that life had once flourished upon each of the succeeding planets from Pluto to where we find it at present – upon our own little planet, Earth. But when we are reminded – as Dr Jones reminded us in his first talk of the series – that our own sun is but one member of a system comprising "something like one hundred thousand million stars, or suns," and that "this vast system is merely one amongst millions of more or less similar systems in the region of space we can probe with our telescopes," then a serious difficulty does occur. It would seem to constitute a breach of the law of sanity upon the part of the Creator.

* * *

But Dr Jones was not content to dwell upon reasons why life ought to be found upon other bodies in the great galaxy of systems. Rather, he placed each body known to the keen eye of the observational astronomer, and to the colleagues of allied departments, under a cold, critical analysis for the presence of life as known to the earth.

He agreed, in passing, that "one of the greatest difficulties in discussing this subject is that we know so little about life, in spite of the great progress that the science of biology has made". In other words, if the fundamentals of terrestrial life constitute difficulties, it is almost impossible to formulate what kind of life could exist outside the laws which restrict and condition it. The search, then, would have to be made for the presence of life analogous to that of the earth.

* * *

Dr Jones gave certain essential conditions which a planet must possess if life is to be found upon its surface. The first essential was that of temperature within certain narrow limits. "We must conclude," said he, "that if on a planet we find either a very high or a very low temperature, it is extremely improbable that life in any form could exist on it." The next essential for which to seek is "the presence of water, either in the liquid form or as vapour". The third essential is the presence of an atmosphere in which oxygen and carbon dioxide must be constituents. There must be an absence of poisonous gases.

It is of more than passing interest to note that the astronomer "with his delicate instruments, can measure the temperatures of the planets; he is able also to obtain some information about the composition of the atmospheres".

The first celestial body Dr Jones placed under analytical test for the presence of life was that of our own satellite, the moon. Only a quarter of a million miles from the earth, she afforded an excellent opportunity for study. Telescopically the moon is an interesting study. Before my telescope ceased to function I enjoyed a sight of the mountain ranges, the great ring craters and the wide, somewhat featureless, "mares" or supposed seas.

Interesting, but what of the presence of life? A schoolboy, answering his teacher upon this very subject, said: "There's no nothing on the moon except nothing." His mind evidently wandered near the truth, but his way of expressing it was unorthodox.

Life is not possible upon the moon – though it may have been possible in the æons long since past – because there is neither atmosphere nor water. This is how Dr Jones describes the conditions upon the moon: "So we have the strange picture of a world without any atmosphere at all; there is no breeze to rustle, no sound to break the deathly silence; no air; no water; no life, either animal life or plant life, not even of the most primitive types – for that must be the inevitable consequence of the complete absence of water or water-vapour, of oxygen and of carbon-dioxide."

* * *

There are temperatures upon the moon, but they are erratic and extreme. During the day, which is about 14 of our days in length, the "sun strikes down in pitiless fury from a cloudless sky." Dr Jones said that at noonday the temperature would be well above boiling point, while at midnight there are about 150 degrees of frost.

Another reason for the absence of life upon the moon, and one I think I had not appreciated before, lies in the fact that the moon is subjected to a continual meteoric bombardment upon its surface. We are naturally familiar with these phenomena as they apply to the earth. We call them "shooting stars". But we upon the earth are protected from these visitants by the thickness or density of the atmosphere. As they strike the outer layers of the atmosphere they are disintegrated by friction and are dissolved. But upon the moon there is no such protection, and a constant rain of meteors descends upon its surface. And so life is entirely ruled out in so far as our satellite the moon is concerned.

* * *

From the moon Dr Jones passed on to the little planet Mercury. This planet, about the same size as the moon, lies closest to the sun. At one time it was conjectured that another planet circled even nearer than Mercury to the sun. To this supposed planet the provisional name of "Vulcan" was given. It is now no longer believed that this planet exists. Life is ruled out upon Mercury for a similar reason to that of the moon. His proximity to the sun renders life impossible on account of the tremendous heat which must strike his surface. The proportion of heat his surface receives to that of the earth is nine times terrestrial tropical heat in the winter. If life is barely possible along earth's equatorial belt, what must it be like with nine times that amount? And, too, Mercury is discovered to possess no atmosphere and no water vapour. His complete year is but 88 terrestrial days, and he passes through his complete seasonal changes in that time.

We will think of the other planets in our next article.

Gleanings [65]
By George E Hobbs
(First published: August 12, 1938)

The quest for the evidence of life on other planets – as given by Dr Jones, the Astronomer Royal, in his broadcast talks – is nearing its end. One more planet is examined, that of Venus – the "Hesperus" of Milton's famous poem. How these lines come back to one:

"Silence was pleased: now glow'd the firmament
With living sapphires: Hesperus, that led
The starry host, rode brightest, till the Moon,
Rising in clouded majesty, at length
Apparent queen, unveiled her peerless light,
And o'er the dark her silver mantle threw."

One writer describes the appearance of Venus in this delightful manner. It is a comparison of contrasts without being odious. "Jupiter," he wrote "may shine with his strong pale-yellow light, and Mars, when favourably placed, may emit a brilliant fiery-red lustre, but neither of these objects can compare with the refulgent beauties of Venus. She forms a resplendent picture, either in the morning's dawn, heralding the sun's rising glory, or in the evening's twilight lingering over the glow where he has just set amid gilded clouds."

* * *

Delightful as is the appearance of the "Goddess of Love and Beauty," our search must probe deeper than mere beauty. Our quest is to see if there are indications of life upon her surface, and, if so, what kind of life.

When I wrote my fantasy, "A Visit to Venus," which appeared in the columns of "The Swindon Advertiser" as a serial, I found this planet an excellent subject upon which to base that story. I took advantage of all that was known about her and called upon my imagination to fill in the details.

When we come to Dr Jones' commentary upon Venus we shall see what prospects there are for this planet to contain life. Before dealing with that commentary, however, let us gather a few details about this interesting planet.

Venus is our inside neighbour, swinging upon her orbit 26 million miles nearer the sun. Being on the inside, she presents two remarkable features – one which can be seen at short periods by means of the telescope, and one which I can never hope to see. The first of these features is the fact that she passes through the same beautiful phases as the Moon, from crescent to full and full to crescent. The second feature involves a little complex explanation.

Venus circles the sun thirteen times to the Earth's eight times. So that every eight years (13 for Venus) the two planets should be similarly placed. If this actually was the case then, every eight years, we should experience the wonderful sight of Venus passing in front of the sun – the "Transit of Venus" as it is called.

* * *

I have seen a total solar eclipse, with the thrills which must last a lifetime. Once I witnessed a lunar rainbow, which is exceedingly rare. But, alas! I shall never see Venus transit the sun. The reason is that, while the 8–13 years cycle will continue until doomsday, Venus, true to her feminine characteristics, is erratic in her path. Her path is tilted to that of the Earth, so that at times she passes above the Sun, at other times below the Sun. At times, however, viewers from the Earth are favoured, and when a transit occurs upon the north limb of the Sun it will occur again, eight years later upon the south limb. The last transit occurred in 1874 and again in 1882, which is the eight-year cycle. It will not occur again until 2004 and 2012. By that time I shall be – well, much too old to bother about the transit of Venus. There are two irregular periods in which no transits occur. These vary between 105½ and 121½ years.

* * *

While there never has been the romance attached to Venus as there has been to Mars, certain features are supposed to have been seen upon her disc. An astronomer by name of Schröter claimed to have discovered certain markings which became known as "Schröter's Mountains". But this and other problems we will leave to the skilful analysis of Dr Jones.

The Astronomer Royal said that Venus was a disappointing sight in the telescope. The phases were beautiful, but "we hope to find some evidence of continents and oceans on a world that in some respects is so similar to our own. But," continued Dr Jones, "we are doomed to disappointment. We can see no well-defined markings at all."

Dr Jones went on to say that what markings had been seen were very illusive. Whatever they were, they certainly could not be permanent features. By this presence of permanent features it is deduced that the surface of the planet is hidden by dense and opaque clouds.

Endeavours have been made to pierce the dense pall by means of photographic plates termed "haze-cutting" plates. These plates are specially sensitised for the infra-red light rays. Quite remarkable results have been achieved by this means on the planet Mars, the photographic plates revealing what the eye is unable to perceive. On Venus, however, the results are negative, the dense materials surrounding her surface refusing to yield up the planet's secret.

* * *

Now if it is true, as Dr Jones emphatically declared, that the markings found upon Venus are "very illusive" and "certainly not permanent", it is difficult to see how the axial rotation of Venus – ie, the length of her day – can be determined. I believe it to be true that the only sure and effective method by which time measurement can be reckoned is by observing the rotation of features. And these, to have any virtue, must essentially have a permanent basis. The axial rotations of both Uranus and Neptune are unknown owing to the difficulty of observing markings of a permanent nature upon their discs. Hence I see the difficulty the pronouncing upon the daily rotation of Venus.

Dr Jones first agreed to this difficulty, but in the next sentence pronounced a definite knowledge upon the problem. Said he: "Because we are unable to see the surface of Venus, and because the cloud details are so ill-defined, it is difficult to find out how long the day of Venus is." And then: "We only know that it is considerably longer than our day, and probably equal in length to about four of our weeks." This means that as the year of Venus is just about equivalent to five-eighths the length of our year, it would give Venus about 7½ days a year.

* * *

What really intrigued my mind was the suggested implication that there are other means of detecting a planet's rotation, beside that of permanent features. The fact remains, however, that there is no decided opinion upon this matter, for the length of day ranges in supposition from 23 hours to 224 days – the length of the year of Venus. If the latter be true, then this phenomenon is analogous to that of our satellite, the Moon. It means that just as the Moon always presents the same face to the Earth, so Venus always presents the same face to the Sun. One face is eternally bright with sunlight, the other eternally dark and cold. And there we must leave this very interesting problem.

An interesting achievement of modern astronomical science was revealed in the fact that the heat from Venus can be measured. To use Dr Jones' own words: "This amount of heat may be measured with an extremely sensitive and delicate instrument called a bolometer, which is capable of detecting the heat from a candle, three miles away. It is possible to measure with this instrument the heat received not only from the bright face of Venus, but also from the dark face. We find that the temperature of the sunlit face reaches 80 or 90 degrees Fahrenheit, whilst that of the dark face falls to about 40 degrees below freezing point."

* * *

But, alas! All the improved methods of applied science but reveal greater and more conclusive evidence that life, as we know it, does not and cannot exist outside our own little planet Earth. The search for the two great essentials – water-vapour and oxygen – has proved abortive, and conditions generally upon the planet Venus, so far as can be ascertained, are against the possibility of life upon her surface.

One last picture of Venus, and then the survey of the Solar System is complete. This picture is in the nature of a prophetic conjecture.

"On Venus," said Dr Jones, "we seem to see a world with conditions somewhat similar to those that the Earth passed through, millions of years ago. The comparative absence of oxygen would appear to indicate that life on Venus can be, at the most, primitive plant life. At the surface, beneath the thick cloud later, conditions are likely to be extremely hot and humid, extensive oceans and swamps may abound, and it seems reasonable to expect that the first forms of animal life to develop will be fishes and other marine types of life. It is possible that life may be in a process of development, and that in the millions of years to come Venus will be the home of higher and higher types of life and ultimately – who can tell – of intelligent life."

* * *

I wonder! Has the System seen intelligent life long before that of the Earth?

Chapter 6

Methodism, Faith and Fellowship

No two men can claim divine inspiration for their beliefs if those two beliefs are antagonistic to each other. Obviously one must be wrong, And perhaps, both are wrong.
George Ewart Hobbs (June 15, 1928)

To me, prayer is a matter of personal need.
George Ewart Hobbs (October 4, 1935)

It's difficult to imagine any aspect of George's life that wasn't borne and consumed by faith, in particular his love of Methodism. Indeed, in *A Swindon Wordsmith* we made reference to the fact that he had a special 'calling' to bring the Christian message to as many as would listen (or read) – whether they be regular churchgoers, Sunday School pupils, members of the Band of Hope at Percy Street (where George was secretary in 1909), members of the Wesley Guild or readers of the *Swindon Advertiser*.

He was manifestly non-parochial in his preaching of the essential truths of the Christian church, and the 1930s see him reaching out to as many worshippers as possible, whether they be in chapels on the Bath Road circuit or beyond.

Occasionally he writes – evoking memories of Alfred Williams, and Richard Jefferies before him – of a connection he feels with the Wiltshire landscape, which harks back to pre-Christian times and reveals something of a deeper, neo-pagan spirituality. In this extract from a much longer piece entitled A Delve Into The Past, which appeared in 1936, he wrote:

What, then of the past? Have we never wandered in the rich, historic district surrounding Swindon and wondered of the past? It is strange but true.

Whenever I walk along the Moredon Road and look across towards Swindon Hill, Liddington Hill, Bassett Down, Broadtown etc, I always seem to have the tingling sensation of some past association. Put it down to a fanciful but vivid imagination if you will. But, there it is – and it is a true experience. Often I have suddenly stopped, as though as I had caught the meaning, only to find it had eluded me and was gone.

Such "fancies" are never satisfied with the time of Cromwell, or of Cœur de Lion, or of Alfred the Great. But ever they creep back to a greater antiquity – to the time when Boadicea, brave in her reckless determination to rid Britain of Roman invaders, led the Iceni in person, only to take her own life when defeated by Suetonius.

But never have I visioned an association with the warriors. The fleeting, illusive shadow is ever associated with the priesthood. Occasionally I glimpse again the stately oak which I know was the symbol of the Supreme One – with the mistletoe clinging to its trunk, symbolising man's dependence upon the Supreme One.

Sometimes of an evening, I almost seem to connect the gentle rustle of the breeze, as occasionally it gathers in volume, with the wild, low chant of the priests as they wind their way slowly through the oak groves to the circle of their ritual worship.

I do not believe in reincarnation, though this to some folk is a very positive belief. But I must confess to the fact that these "fancies" are very strong at times.

Records confirm that he was a regular preacher at the High Street Methodist Church in Wroughton, the Play Close Methodist Church in Purton, and the High Street Wesleyan Church in Wootton Bassett, as well as the Congregational Church in Haydon Wick and the Primitive Methodist Church in Wootton Bassett – even before Methodist union in September 1932.

It appears that 'The Prim' in Wootton Bassett (also known at the time as 'Hillside Methodist Church') developed a particular affection for George – and it seems that the feeling was mutual. His recorded appearances in the pulpit certainly exceeded those of other locations at the time. A report in the *Swindon Advertiser* on October 5, 1932 referred to 'a welcome reappearance in the pulpit' and the following year he was referred to as a 'Special Preacher'.

What is particularly wonderful is that this delightful chapel survives to this very day as a place of worship. Now known as Royal Wootton Bassett Methodist Church, the current building dates from 1838 and, from the outside (barring the new entrance porch), it is largely as George would remember it.

On the subject of secularism and Church unity, we find this extract from a piece he wrote in 1938, in which George proudly emphasises his very senior position at the Church of England Little London Mission in Old Town, Swindon:

> The popular belief for years has been that an unbridgeable gulf existed between Conformity and Nonconformity. Yet it is safe to say that such belief was one of an accepted fancy rather than of reality. True, one has often found a "we-have-no-dealings-with-the-Samaritan" spirit – a spirit hard, stupid and unbending. But such a spirit was never so prevalent as popular fancy imagined. Everybody said it existed, so everybody said it was true. Give popular imagination something upon which to bite, and every sprat in the sea becomes a whale.
>
> It is possibly true that time was when I, as a Nonconformist lay preacher, would not be tolerated as the leader of an Anglican Mission Church, which I now am. But times have changed and are changing – changing, we very much hope, for the better. The latest scheme is one which will kill the "exclusive" bogey for ever.
>
> Some time ago the various Methodist Churches pooled their powers and became known as "The Methodist Church". Such terms as "Wesleyan", "Primitive Methodist", "United Methodist", etc, are now no longer recognised. It is now one Church, united in one common bond and for one common purpose.
>
> And now he have the conception of a greater and wider unity – the possibility of the children, who saw that self-expression could only be achieved by leaving home, coming back into the great family circle again. The separation certainly has done no harm, for the parent has learned wisdom and tolerance. And the children, through years of struggle and misunderstanding, have learned many lessons which will stand them in good stead in the new commonwealth of spiritual endeavour.

In *A Swindon Wordsmith* we lamented the fact that his undated piece The Virtue of Gratitude seemed to be 'the closest we will ever have to one of his own sermons' – given that his series Pen Pictures of the Pulpit saw George reporting on the sermons of others. Well, subsequent research has revealed that an address entitled 'Gratitude' was delivered before the Wootton Bassett Brotherhood at the Memorial Institute on Sunday 5, April 1931, suggesting it was, indeed, a sermon.

Interestingly, the only other undated and unpublished sermon known to exist (to which we were kindly given access by George's descendants) was a lengthy, typewritten piece entitled The Life of Charles Bradlaugh, and we found that an address with the same title was delivered to the Hillside Methodist Fellowship on November 3, 1936, although a much shorter article about Bradlaugh appeared in the *Swindon Advertiser* on May 8, 1931.

In the circumstances, it would be unusual if there weren't numerous other examples of 'cross-over', where articles would appear in the *Advertiser* followed by a talk before an audience or congregation regarding the same subject matter – and vice versa.

One such instance involves a sermon entitled The Fall: Historic or Symbolic? which was given to the Hillside Methodist Fellowship on February 2, 1937, only for an article of the same name to appear in the *Swindon Advertiser* on October 7, 1937.

Another example, which appeared in print the previous year, relates to the poet and revolutionary, Lord Byron (hardly a non-controversial figure for a churchman raised during the Victorian-era, but further evidence of George's willingness to raise difficult subject matter and break with convention).

Further instances will be found elsewhere in this book, particularly his articles relating to world peace, power and immortality.

But faith and 'The Church' tends to be the keystone upon which much of George's work is carried. There is much from which to choose and, clearly, only a selection can appear in these pages.

His canon of religious works include lengthy series such as The Creation of the World, Bible Narratives for Young Students, Bible Stories and The Book of Job, as well as a number individual pieces, many of which are either heavily doctrinal or aimed particularly at Sunday School scholars. Consequently, a good number fall outside the scope of this anthology, but George's writing on religion cannot be ignored, especially when they reveal the radical in him; his faith might have been unshakable, but he wasn't afraid to question if it meant getting closer to the truth.

In January 1935 he wrote:

> The attitude of those who declare the Bible to be built upon myth and

> legend is no more unreasonable than the attitude of those who declare that all between its covers is literally and historically true. As a matter of fact, I am convinced that the former attitude of mind exists only because of the latter. The unreasonable dogmatising of the literalists has created the equally unreasonable thought processes of their antagonists. I seriously claim that if we are to understand the most glorious book in the whole realm of literature it must be agreed that allegory, tribal folklore, metaphor and simile form part of its content. Even so, every word and every sentence, allegory and metaphor, point definitely to some aspect of truth.

His full-throated opposition to a literal interpretation of the Old Testament and his distaste for all matters of religious dogma became central to his mission, particularly in relation to young people, who were already starting to turn their back on Sunday school and formal church services, in pursuit of outdoor recreation and other more secular types of amusement.

Children across the country were starting to think for themselves and assert their independence of thought – all gained through better education and a revolution in social attitudes in the post-First World War era.

In 1937 he wrote a piece about the controversy surrounding Sunday speedway racing in Wroughton, opposing those who felt the sport should not take place on the sabbath, and revealing how he thought the crisis faced by Christianity in Britain at the time would benefit from some home truths:

> However unpalatable it sounds, let us who are in the Church admit an undeniable fact. The Church has long since not only lost its grip upon Mr & Mrs Everyman, but has utterly lost its grip upon their children.
>
> The lamentable fact is that the average religious person of today suffers from spiritual anæmia. Go to almost any church in Swindon on a Sunday morning and the best congregation but half-fills the building.

He was certainly never afraid to court controversy, particularly given the fact that 'Victorian values' still held sway in many aspects of church and family life. Furthermore, he often found the opportunity to defy the strictures of formality and convention just too irresistible, as here:

> Most, if not all readers will know of the controversy surrounding the relationship between Edward VIII and American socialite and divorcée Wallis Simpson which led to the King's abdication from the throne in December 1936. Few however will know of the furore surrounding the couple's subsequent marriage in France on 3rd June 1937. The ceremony was performed by the vicar of Darlington, the Reverend Robert Anderson Jardine without the formal consent of the Church of England who, at the time, forbade the marriage of divorced partners.

Called by the press 'the poor man's pastor' by virtue of his working-class parish, Jardine was a member of The Protestant Truth Society, the leader of which said of him; 'Mr Jardine is quite fearless in his advocacy of any cause which he judges right and would pursue his own line regardless of the consequences to himself.'

And on June 4, 1937 he was moved to write a letter to the *Swindon Advertiser*:

> Sir – Probably the Rev Anderson Jardine does not require publicity. I want, however, to place it on record that I, for one, raise my hand to him in salute.
>
> A man of grit, and one who is not afraid to defy convention. More power to your example, Rev Sir.
>
> Yours etc,
>
> George E Hobbs

Surely this is an instance of George admiring his own steadfast convictions in the character of another churchman, but Jardine paid a heavy price for his brave actions; he was forced to resign and under considerable pressure, he ended up emigrating to California.

Only two weeks later, we read of George having broken another latter-day taboo:

> There is much need to plead for a more sane dress for summer wear, and therefore a need to defy convention. Last Summer, upon particularly hot Sundays, I took my religious services in an open-neck sports shirt. In all probability, if the day is hot, unbearably hot, I shall follow the same course this year. It is nothing short of narrowness to say that I lose dignity by so doing.
>
> It seems to me that the snag which we trip is that the criterion of our sincerity lies in outward demonstration rather than in inward response.
>
> The cry of the old Prophet was, "Rend your hearts and not your garments."
>
> Life's best is not expressed in external show and pomp, but in the quiet submission to that which leads to a higher dignity of human endeavour.

And the following year, we witness George making what amounts to a mini manifesto on what he sees as everything that was wrong with society, and suggests some remedies – all of which provides further evidence of his political 'direction of travel' as well as his overt radicalism. In an extract from Gleanings [34] which appeared in the press on January 7, 1938, he states:

> I sometimes think that there are two very profound mistakes made today by would-be world reformers. The first is that of over-concentration upon the mass, in which the individual is lost. And the second is that the wrong emphasis is placed upon the remedies to be applied.

Numbers of public men and women agree that conditions need rectifying and that society needs purging. But their vision is so wide that they seem to lose sight of the individual in the mass called "society". And when they talk of "remedies" they think in terms of institutions, order and machinery of the social world, and, not only do they again lose sight of the individual, but they place an incorrect emphasis upon the remedies to be applied.

I suppose it is another phase of the "mass" period in which we live. In the realm of commerce we have mass production. In the realm of thought we have mass thinking. In consequence, in the realm of morals we have a determination towards mass reformation. And to this end we set up mass machinery. I imagine that never in the history of the world has it seen such a medley of machinery set up with the laudable intention of making the world a better place in which to live. Institutions, orders, guilds, social service centres, councils, committees, sub-committees, sub-sub-committees, and so on, until there seems no room for more. All our powers are expended upon mass reformation, instead of upon that which matters most – individual reformation.

We forget that there are depths which can be plumbed in the individual which are lost in the mass. As a lay preacher I know the glamour that lies in facing a congregation when one has a message to deliver. Yet I am more than ever convinced that the best work lies in personal contact with the individual. It is impossible to reform the mass until the individual has been reformed.

And he continues:

There are four factors which have the power of "bettering conditions", but I doubt very much whether of themselves they can give life. They are money, education, change of systems and religion.

Money! A man and his wife are living in a hovel. They are gross, beastly and sensual. A fortune comes their way and they are able to move into a mansion. Their conditions are "bettered". From penury and want and dirt they have wealth and plenty and spotless cleanliness. But has the change given them life? Their material circumstances have changed from the grinning skeleton to the completed human form. But it is not true to say that death is as complete as formerly? There is no moral advance, but rather the "bettered" conditions have given them more scope for the indulgence of what had gone before – sensuality and bestiality. There is no indication of an advance towards life.

Education. This can, and does, better conditions. Knowledge is better than ignorance, for knowledge is undoubtedly power. But too often knowledge defeats its own ends. We learn too much, and in the learning we discover that we are naked and unclothed. Our academic culture has produced in us a cold, calculating materialism. Instead of advanced education doing its proper work and teaching us humility, we become as gods and we see no audacity in pointing out to the Creator where He has made mistakes.

Revolutions in Systems: Yes, these may better conditions. Community of interests may be better than the competitive system. Equality of opportunity may be better than opportunity controlled by rich relations. Socialism may be better than Imperialism. But these of themselves cannot give life. They are soulless systems replacing soulless systems.

Religion: How we plead for this. Yet religion can be as lifeless as the Dead Sea. Religion can stimulate and lead unto life. It can also lead unto death. I suppose that the greatest religious race of history were the Jews, and the greatest religious era was when Jesus of Nazareth walked the earth. Yet it is true to say that the Jews of that day were as dead as mutton. There was no life of sweetness, of tolerance and of love.

If true reformation is to come to the world it first must begin in the individual. And it also must produce – if it is to be of lasting value – not merely better conditions, materially, but better results morally and spiritually. It must produce Life!

And perhaps, just perhaps, we learn a little more of his personal 'take' on a particular moral issue – that of *felo de se* or suicide.

Mr John George 'Jack' Wise was a respected local businessman and a stalwart of Percy Street Methodist church, having served there as Church Treasurer and Sunday School Superintendent for many years. Tragically, he was found dead in the sea at Weston-super-Mare on January 4, 1939, having left his grocery business at 178 Rodbourne Road the previous day, commenting to a colleague "I'm going out for a little while."

He never returned to the shop and, in the absence of any suggestion that Mr Wise was preparing to take his own life, the coroner had no alternative but to record a verdict of 'Found Drowned'. At this time it was still a criminal offence to even attempt to take your own life, although secularisation and the medicalisation of suicide were helping to shift public opinion towards greater sympathy for those suffering from mental distress. Nevertheless, there would have still been many in the wider Church at the time who would have regarded it as a 'mortal sin' to commit 'self-murder'.

George, who was a great friend of the deceased, had often written of his wider concern for those suffering from mental illness – hardly an easy subject for a member of the laity to concern himself with, back in the late 1930s, particularly alongside his other pastoral duties. Accompanying the report on the funeral service, George penned a short appreciation – an extract from which appears below. Note the implied expectation that the deceased will be received into heaven by a God of compassion and redemption, rather be judged at the court of religious dogma.

> In business he was scrupulously honest, not merely to his customers, but to his own conscience. There came a time when he felt he ought not to sell tobacco or cigarettes, and although he knew it would mean loss of trade, he adhered to his principle and sold no more. This high conception of his moral dealings animated him throughout his business life.
>
> In religious outlook, Mr Wise's interpretation of the "Word" was almost literal. He kept rigidly to the old Evangel [Christian gospel] and was happy and contented in its teaching and in its expression. He was tolerant to those who thought differently from himself. One always knew just where Mr Wise stood religiously. And in that stand he was zealous to a fault.
>
> Now tragically, he has passed over. We mourn his loss. But the Great Spirit into Whose Presence he has gone will understand all the circumstances.
>
> To the family, great sympathy will go out in their hour of darkness.

In the articles chosen for this chapter, we find George deepening his mission to young and old alike. We also find humour as well as some of the radicalism that would colour much of his thinking during the 1930s. But above and beyond everything else, we find him reaching out to the forgotten, the unheard and the ill-treated with selfless compassion – both as a pastor, friend and champion of the underdog.

In **The "Fall": Historic or Symbolic?** (October 7, 1927), George argues that this Biblical story set in the Garden of Eden is one of allegory as opposed to a depiction of a literal event.

In **A New Year's Message** (January 4, 1929) we learn that the *Advertiser* was also sent out on subscription to Swindonians in all parts of the former Empire, as well as the USA and Argentina – and George takes advantage of this 'reach' to tailor a message of hope and cheer for different sections of the community.

George strays somewhat overtly into the field of socialism as he commences an analysis of power and its potential for good and evil in **Power [1]** (March 13, 1931), and in **Power [2]** (March 20, 1931), George seeks to highlight the achievements of those individuals, even those thought of as 'extremists', for whom powerful thought led to beneficial reforms to society – although, regrettably, no mention is made of the exact situation or situations to which George seems to be referring.

In **The First Christmas** (December 24, 1931), it is not the excesses of capitalism which fall within the writer's crosshairs, but members of the wider Christian church – or rather those who hold clerical office and who then accept a stipend which goes beyond providing for their basic needs alone.

The two-line quote, by the way, is taken from the third verse of It Came Upon *The Midnight Clear* by the American minister, Edmund Sears (1810-1876).

The Call to Prayer (September 6, 1935) sees George once again exhibiting his uncompromising credentials as a radical, tackling the urgent call to prayer made by Church leaders, doubtless in response to the Abyssinia crisis, but in an amazing show of defiance, he declares that he will not pray that God will prevent war, stressing: 'I am audacious enough to say there are some things that God cannot do.'

The four lines of poetry quoted in the main article are taken from *The People's Anthem* by Ebenezer Elliott (1781-1849), a onetime Chartist also referred to as 'The Corn Law Rhymer'.

In many ways, **Life's Success** (June 19, 1936), a heart-felt and particularly well-written article, could be viewed as a companion piece to the earlier articles Making a Success of Life (1922) and Spirit to Achieve (also 1922), and is concerned with how emerging technologies are used or misused – whether to be in the genuine service of mankind or whether to be employed in the field of warfare.

Mrs Crabthorn aside (see Chapter 4), humour plays a relatively minor role in George's writing in the 1930s – until we come across **The Humour of Life** (June 26, 1936), made up of light-hearted moments in the career of a travelling preacher.

Methodist Union in 1932 brought the three main denominations (the Wesleyans, The Primitive Methodists and the United Methodists) together as one church, and **The New Methodist Hymnal [1]** (July 24, 1936) and **The New Methodist Hymnal [2, extract]** (July 31, 1936) are George's own personal critique of the new hymnbook – the first such book since John Wesley's original collection in 1779.

He includes two verses from the hymn *Jesus, Friend of Little Children*, by Walter John Mathams (1853-1931), and the final verse from *He Who Would Valiant Be*, by John Bunyan (1628-1688).

Lessons of Harvest (October 9, 1936) reflect the fact that Harvest Festival was one of George's most cherished occasions (and reports in the *Advertiser* show that he conducted services at the Little London Mission in both 1937 and 1939). He also wrote about it in the following year, too, the following extract summing up his thoughts on the subject:

The idea of personality – somehow or somewhere – is revealed in the very nature of harvest thanksgiving services. That is, our gratitude is expressed to a Person. It would be utterly illogical to express thanks to something which is dumb and deaf, and utterly incapable of response.

And so, in the life principle of the seed, in the wonder of its release towards development and fruition, we see the hand of a Person whom we call God. It is to Him we express our unstinted gratitude for the fruits of the earth.

The Present Menace [extract] (February 26, 1937) could quite easily have been placed in Chapter 9, but is included here because it reiterates his willingness to take on the Christian establishment for what he believes as their collective cowardice in the face of militarism and re-armament.

In **Gleanings [4, extract]** (May 28, 1937), George advocates reform of the House of Lords, in particular for the Lords Spiritual to include the heads of the Non-Conformist Churches, as well the Salvation Army.

Originally part of a longer article on the merits of motorbike racing at Wroughton on a Sunday, **Gleanings [13, extract]** (July 30, 1937) is included here because of the way it highlights an existential crisis for George and the wider church movement, and how is he is determined to pull no punches in his open criticism of the religious establishment.

Radical or not, **Gleanings [73, extract]** (October 14, 1938) is included as further evidence of his enduring, personal commitment to the younger members of the congregation.

The chapter is concluded with **Gleanings [87, extract]** (January 27, 1939), which finds George reaching out to those suffering from anxiety and stress, as the country slips inexorably towards war with Nazi Germany.

It is also significant for its frank admission that George had, at various times, been similarly affected – most notably following the sudden death of his son, Ivor Hedley Hobbs in May 1919.

The "Fall":
Historic or Symbolic?
(First published: October 7, 1927)

Controversy has raged for many years around the origin of man. At times the contending camps have been vigorous in defence and attack. At other times the inevitable reaction set in, and for a time: peace.

Now, since the Presidential address given by Sir Arthur Keith, controversy is again revived, and lectures, debates, sermons, etc, are once more the order.

Where discussions follow lectures one persistent question reveals the general difficulty of accepting the "common stock" theory. That question relates to the "Fall" of man. And, certainly, if there be a "Fall", then the Biblical story must stand in its literal verity. On the other hand, if there be not a "Fall" then it clears the way of difficulty to an appreciation of the "common stock" theory, and the "Fall" idea becomes symbolic.

Hence the title of my subject: "Is the Biblical story of the Fall of Man symbolic or historic?"

First, we shall be upon safe ground by saying that Sin – personal wrongdoing – is a fact of universal experience. The fateful termination to the general description of Naaman is true spiritually of universal man: "But he was a leper."

No one, I think, will be foolish enough to deny the existence of Sin and its universal sway!

Secondly (and this is not a sermon), Sin is a fact of antiquity.

Just as men sin to-day, so they sinned yesterday. We may traverse back through the pages of history, even to the most ancient of records, and there we find the existence of sin. So true is this record that we are led to say that Sin is not only universal but of a great antiquity and that the history of the world is a history of wrong-doing.

The Origin of Sin

But is it a history of wrong-doing? Let us see if it is not rather a history of a continuous moral struggle – which is a vastly different thing.

We shall still be upon safe ground when we say that everything existing relative to man had an origin. Just as the world and man had an origin, so qualities – good and bad – had an origin. Whether one quality – evil – had its origin in one definite act at a definite period, or was a process through a developing conscience is the difficult problem now before the court.

The origin of Sin in the Universe is much too profound a problem for discussion here. Just as the origin of the life principle has baffled, and perhaps ever will baffle human intelligence to solve, so the origin of Sin in the Universe has ever baffled human intelligence to solve. The problem is profound in that if we believe in the personality of Satan then Sin antedates man probably by infinite time. We do not know, neither would it be of profit to pursue it.

It is the origin of Sin in man that is here under discussion, or as we shall presently see, the origin of Moral Conflict.

We have not to go to modern school-men and thinkers for a suggested cause, but must go right back to the dawn of written communication, to the time when philosopher and thinker tabulated their thoughts upon papyrus, or chiselled them upon tablet and monument. Even then we are not at the source, for the written or chiselled word was the product of oral tradition. It may be well understood by the reader, yet it will bear repetition. We must never lose sight of the fact that probably many centuries elapsed before the first crude system of written communication was established.

The Biblical Story

Now let us take the Biblical story of the "Fall", a story with which we are all familiar. We will take the story in rapid sequence.

Having made heaven and earth in six days, the Lord creates man in His own image, gives to him a helper to meet and places both in a beautiful garden. Man is given dominion over all living creatures, and has perfect freedom – save in one direction. He must refrain from the fruit of one single tree only. He has full sanction for every other fruit. But this one is taboo.

But one of the created creatures – the Serpent – tells the woman that the taboo is simply the result of a jealous guarding of Divine Knowledge. "He knows," said the serpent quietly, "that if you eat of this fruit you will not die. And what is more, your knowledge will be equal to His knowledge. Ye shall be as gods, knowing good and evil."

The results of eating the fruit thus forbidden were too good to be ignored. The woman partook, gave some to her husband, and the "Fall" was assured. [Now lost in their newly found knowledge, having been tempted by the fruit which would give them eternal life, they were expelled from the garden and became wanderers.]

Such is the story with which we are all familiar, and from which has arisen insurmountable difficulties of acceptance.

An Allegory

Now shall we look at the story from a different view-point. The view-point of an allegory.

In the dawn of written communication an inspired writer, viewing the titanic struggle between the forces of Right and Wrong, writes an allegory. His wanderings had taken him into the forests; into the haunts of the beasts of the field. He has noted the crafty, subtle, sinuous movements of the snake, and for his allegory sees there is no fitter symbol for the forces of wrong.

In his meditation he fails at first to find a fitting symbol for Right. No beast with which he is familiar have qualities or habits which can possibly represent the symbol of goodness.

Presently it begins to assume shape. In brooding over his subject he sees a Great One whom he can neither name adequately nor describe. He terms him "the seed of the woman". The Great One and the Serpent are brought into conflict.

The writer of the allegory is profoundly conscious that the struggle will be severe, and the victory will not be won without acute suffering upon the part of the victor.

The Great One's foot is upon the Serpent's head – which is the vulnerable part of the beast, and the part he intends to crush. Slowly the crushing pressure is applied. And in crushing the beast's head the Serpent's fangs penetrate the Great One's heel.

Here, then, is the story of the "Fall" reconstructed from God's curse upon the Serpent. The verse itself (Gen, 3-15) is really a condensed version of the story told in detail. It is purely allegorical – a story of moral struggle told in symbol.

The Pith of the Parable

And here, to my mind, is the pith of the whole parable. It suggests with very strong force the beginnings of recognition of opposing moral forces in the world of man. Instead of a newly created man "falling" from an "innocent" and "perfect" state, it is the account of man in the long transition of his development arriving at a point when he first fights the Beast in his nature.

We see man, not as beginning with a fall from blissful innocence, but we see him at a point where he struggles at an ascent from gross ignorance to knowledge and wisdom. Not as being cast out from a garden of delight and pleasure, but the commencement of a "pilgrimage to a city of truth and light".

It took countless ages to prepare the earth as a home for man. First there came low forms of life which endured for long ages before there was any sign of conscious existence. Then there came in proper sequence those pre-human beings, with nothing to distinguish them from other animals. Then came forms more clearly resembling man. Gradually, as development advanced, early man began to feel the stirrings of a conscious direction of Effort. The struggle was beginning between the Serpent and the "Seed of the Woman".

It was then the dawn of choice began.

It was not a matter of "disobedience", but of developing powers of choice between the higher and the lower – between the Beast and the Divine. The lower choice brought the consciousness of Sin – "I was naked and I hid myself."

Man was haunted not by the voice of an angry god, seeking him in a garden, but by the voice of an awakened conscience speaking in his own heart.

If it be still claimed that man "fell", then with more force and logic it may be claimed that he has ascended. A consciousness of shame following a wrong act reveals a live moral consciousness. Where no shame is felt then the moral sense is dead. When to early man the consciousness of a wrong choice brought distress of mind, it marked a decided ascent in human consciousness and human development.

The "Creation of Man" was not something done in a moment and finished with. It was the beginning of a process, a process which Tennyson suggests is not even yet complete.

George E Hobbs
A New Year's Message
(First published: January 4, 1929)

In writing a New Year's message two questions present themselves: What kind of message shall it be? Who are the folk to whom the message will be addressed? The second question is difficult to answer, for the Swindon Advertiser not only has a wonderful circulation locally and in the surrounding districts, but in various places throughout the world. It would be interesting to tabulate the places where the Advertiser is read. To my own knowledge, copies are sent to Canada, USA, West Indies, India, Australia, New Zealand, the Argentine and Africa.

The business man who is struggling heroically to avert disaster will have a different outlook from the man who has had a successful year. The families who live in those areas of acute suffering and want will have different needs to the families whose breadwinner is in safe employ. How futile would it be to write a message of hope and cheer to the man who can look back on the year 1928 with delight and satisfaction. The year has been one of remarkable success to him. He has been advanced in his position and his income has materially increased. If success finds him ill-adapted for her treasures a more suitable message probably would be one of caution against pride and its attendant horror, snobbery. No message of hope and cheer is suitable to the man who looks down upon his fellows because he has been fortunate enough to move a few paltry steps up the social ladder. Some ladders are very unstable and are unable to bear the weight of that extra poundage of the head that swells.

And dare I write a message of hope and cheer to the one in whose soul hope has almost died? Everything looked bright to him once. Eden opened its gates when he took his young bride to the house he had prepared for her. His joy was full to overflowing as he looked for the first time upon his own child. He has now an added responsibility – the responsibility of training a new, fresh life. Then through regrettable industrial conditions he is discharged. A hopeful search for employment becomes a despairing search. The eyes of his wife, full of patient suffering, haunts him, goads him, crushes him. The cry of the child has weakened his faith. He is not far from the pit of despair. What message can I, dare I, write to him?

And then I think of those far away, and whose link with home is the Swindon Advertiser. And I think of those who will commence the New Year with the sorrow of a great loss upon them. A life of great promise has been cut down with the swiftness of an eagle's swoop. The immediate relatives and friends are even yet staggered and dismayed with that pain which is unequalled in human experience. These too, will need a message.

With all these varying needs there must, of necessity, be a varying message for the New Year. So:

To the proud: There is a selfish elation in pride, but no joy. If you wish for the deepest joys that life offers for the New Year, then, "except ye become as a little child" you will miss it.

To the one who has almost lost hope: This is a difficult task, because I am aware not only of your gradually diminishing hope, but also of the bitter feelings that have been engendered in your breast. Yet I know of no better words than these I am about to write for you. The original is in the past tense. Let me transpose into the future tense for you:

> "I will wait patiently for the Lord, and he will incline unto me and hear my prayer. He will bring me up out of the horrible pit, and out of the miry clay, and he will set my feet upon a rock and establish my goings. He will put a new song in my mouth, even praise unto Him who is going to help me." There is hope in the future.

And to those far away whose eyes are ever turned towards the homeland: How poignant are your thoughts at this time of the year. You are lonely – but not friendless. Just as the atmosphere circles the earth, so He who is the Friend of all, circles the earth. He is the companion of the lonely heart in the crowded city, on the prairie and veld, and in desert and bush. I imagine it needs tremendous courage to face a daily home-sickness. May that courage of yours be steadfast, unflagging, until under the dispensation of Providence, you see the shores of the old country again.

And to those who face the New Year with the hand of bereavement heavy upon them: Death is inevitable, it is the lot of all, yet its presence is never felt without grief. But could we glimpse behind the veil, how much would our sorrows lessen. We cannot see – or, at least, many of us cannot – and all that we see and feel is loss – just loss.

To you, may each succeeding day take somewhat from its terror and sorrow. May each day grow brighter and brighter until not that you will have forgotten, but that the shadows will have dispersed.

To all: may the coming year be one of high endeavour. May we find our duty and do it cheerfully. May we find in service to our fellows our highest joy.

Power [1]
By George E Hobbs
(First published: March 13, 1931)

Those of my readers who have read Jack London's "Iron Heel" will remember the outcome of Ernest Everhard's address before the "Philomaths" – a society composed of the ruling classes of America. Everhard brought against them a strong indictment of mismanagement, which naturally provoked a lively debate. Of the debate itself I shall have little comment to make. I am using the incident simply as a jumping-off place for this article on "Power".

After the discussion has waged for some time, with the bitterest of recriminations, a clear-minded, hard-headed opponent of Everhard answered his indictment.

"This is our answer," said he, with brutal frankness. "We have no words to waste on you. When you reach out your vaunted strong hands for our palaces and purpled ease, we will show you what strength is. In roar of shell and shrapnel, and in whine of machine-guns, will our answer be couched. [We will grind you revolutionists down under our heel, and we shall walk upon your faces. The world is ours, we are its lords, and ours it shall remain. As for the host of labor, it has been in the dirt since history began, and I read history aright. And in the dirt it shall remain. So long as I and mine and those that come after us have the power, there is the word. It is the king of words –

POWER. Not God, not Mammon, but Power! Pour it over your tongue till it tingles with it – Power!"]

The Only Answer

"I am answered," said Everhard, quietly. "It is the only answer that could be given... Power shall be the arbiter, as it always has been the arbiter... We have coined that word over till our minds are all a-tingle with it – Power! It is a kingly word." "Power" is a kingly word, but it is a word indicative of a capacity that can be wrongly used. It is profoundly wrong as illustrated above. The world is rapidly becoming more sane in its outlook upon life. It is realising, slowly but surely, that "in roar of shell and shrapnel and in whine of machine-guns' represents an aspect of power which is foolish and immoral. Little or no good can come when power is represented in terms of force of the basest kind.

But there is an aspect in which "power" is desirable – something to be preferred above gold and silver. It is the aim of the article to indicate the right kind of power.

One of the definitions of power given by the dictionary is "ability to act". This definition, however, does not express the idea of my thoughts. I want to define power not merely as "ability to act", but, rather, as "ability to achieve" – to achieve in the highest and noblest pursuits of life, to achieve in the highest duty and noblest service – the service to one's fellows.

Power in Thinking

Now it suggests itself to one's mind that to achieve in any undertaking the initial stages of that undertaking should be upon the right lines. A faulty foundation will presage an indifferent and imperfect super-structure. It therefore seems imperative that achievement – the final act – must be preceded by power in thinking.

But do our thoughts matter? Our thoughts do matter, because, in every case, thought determines what we are. Action – upon which judgement so often rests – is, after all, but the culmination of a process. That process is thought, desire, action. It matters little if the duration between thought and action be a second or a year; the process is the same. A "thoughtless" action is a misnomer. There is no such thing. An act may be performed through insufficient thought, but no act can be a thoughtless act. Thought, conscious or sub-conscious, must precede every act of a normal person.

It has been said – and freely said – that the difficulty of the age is to get men to think. This does not seem a correct statement of the facts. Men do think.

The question is: do men think with power, or think dynamically? Or is the order of their thinking that which makes them heedlessly follow the crowd?

Popular Consent

One hears, at frequent intervals, of something which is known as "public opinion". I would suggest the more appropriate term would be "popular consent". Public opinion demands thought; popular consent is too often due to its lack. It is capricious and moody, and has much stability as the whirling sands upon the sea-shore. If popular consent is to change into its rightful place and become public opinion it can only be so transformed by vital individual thought – thought which ignores the clap-trap of sensationalism; thought which will rise above the fear of an adverse criticism; thought which is powerful, dynamic, fearless, yet, withal, which is sympathetic, compassionate and kind.

If, therefore, the foundation-thought be of power, we are already beginning to tread the path that will lead to ultimate power – the "ability to achieve".

But merely to think with power is not nearly sufficient. There must of necessity be the sequel – power in action, or actions of power.

I have said that action is the culminating effect of thought. Taking the implication of the fore-going we may say: What a man thinks, so his actions will be. Here, however, we may be met by an apparent paradox. While it must ever be true that thought must precede action, it does not always follow that actions of power will follow powerful thought. The trouble is that a very human element is apt to creep in. The source-thought may be powerful, but the expression of that thought may be weak, through fear. "To know what is right, and fear to do it, is cowardice," is a saying attributed to Confucius. And many have had to confess to their moral cowardice.

If we are to render service to our fellows, if we are to assist in the bringing of a nobler age, then thought must find expression in actions of power. This will be developed in the next article.

Power [2]
By George E Hobbs
(First published: March 20, 1931)

I concluded in my last article with the suggestion that, if we are to achieve the highest and best, then powerful thought must find expression in powerful action. Let us proceed from this point. There is a quality in extremists I am bound to admire.

They may be a nuisance – oftentimes they are a positive nuisance. But, as our American friends say, they "put over the goods". They know the joy of ultimate achievement.

History has proved over and over again, that when powerful thought has developed in proper sequence to actions of power, reforms have come. A case in point: in the middle of the 18th century the conditions in England were far from idealistic. The Enclosure Acts were despoiling the villages, and the seeds of industrial anarchy were being sown in the towns. Immorality, cruelty, ignorance and vice were rampant. Religion was formal and lifeless. Macaulay says: "The clergy made war on schism with so much vigour that they had little leisure to make war on vice."

Then a change came over England. But the change was not due to Parliament, nor was it brought about by organised churches. It was due to a small group of men neither wealthy nor influential. They were men who transmuted powerful thought into actions of power – and the Wesley brothers revolutionised England.

Slave Question

John Brown had powerful thoughts upon the slave question. He saw the sights that sickened his soul and he transformed powerful thought into action. Powerful thought, to him, meant actions of power, and actions of power led to his execution. If one could have pierced the veil and asked if he regretted his actions, he would have replied: "No – the slaves are free!" He would have appreciated that ultimate power was the "ability to achieve".

But arguments and illustrations are of little value unless they can be made of practical utility. The appeal of the article is just this: are we powerful in our thinking, or are we the wobblers? The hoary story of the political canvasser has not yet lost its point. The lady of the house told a persistent canvasser that her husband was always of the persuasion of the visiting canvasser. To the Liberal he was Liberal; to the Conservative he was Conservative; to the Socialist he was Socialist.

"A damned nuisance!" was the unexpected reply.

Crude, very crude – but true. Every wobbler is a damned nuisance, and I find no reason to modify that adjective even though it shocks Editor, Printer and Reader. One never knows where the wobbler stands – at least one does, for he stands nowhere. The wobbler is unstable, weak and vacillating.

Individual Thinking

If we are to attain to the highest reward of human service – that we leave the world a little better than we found it – then such achievement must begin with solid individual thinking. It can be attained by no other way.

But if we are satisfied that our thoughts are of power, can we apply the second test? Are we powerful in our actions?

Carlyle has said, "The end of man is an action, not a thought, even though it were the noblest." To stop short at powerful thought is a job not even half done.

To write of powerful action is an easy task. It requires no effort. To perform an action of power is not an easy task. It does require effort, and very much more beside. Powerful deeds can never be performed in a snug chair by a bright fire, singing, "Rescue the perishing." Neither can they be performed by throwing the onus of a brighter England, or a brighter world, upon the shoulders of Deity. I have ever been conscious of the false sentiment which characterise the first four lines of Elliott's hymn,

> "When wilt Thou save the people?
> O God of mercy, when?
> Not kings alone, but nations!
> Not thrones and crowns, but men!"

Higher Moral Culture

This job is not God's but man's. The people will be saved – and by "saved" I mean brought to a higher moral culture – just as soon as, and no sooner than, powerful human thought is transmuted into actions of power. Not actions of force, for force is alien to the principles of true development. The need is for actions of Power – actions in which self is eliminated, which perhaps, is the hardest task ever assigned to an individual.

It will be as well to suggest here that when powerful actions are attempted they may not be attended by hearty approval, even from one's best friends. It may be found that the reverse is more often true. No photograph will appear in the public press, or if it does will probably be underlined "The latest fanatic". If a pat on the back is looked for it will have to be – as the popular song says – self-administered. It will probably come from no other source. No, the heroic mind will not look for these things, for, like "popular consent", they have no value in the great scheme of human improvement. The heroic mind who will dare powerful deeds will not fear the blast of revilings, or of ridicule, or of misunderstandings – the cruellest of all. The heroic mind who would gain "the city of light" will set his face steadfastly towards that light, and with unswerving steps will plod on to the goal of the 'ability to achieve'.

There is today a clarion call for powerful thinking – and actions of power. In the highest and best sense I conclude this article with Holmes' wonderful lines:

> 'God gives us Men! A time like this demands
> Strong minds, great hearts, true faith and ready hands;
> Men whom the lust of lucre does not kill;
> Men whom the spoils of office cannot buy;
> Men who possess opinions and a will;
> Men who have honour; men who will not lie;
> Men who can stand before a demagogue
> And damn his treacherous flatteries without winking.
> Tall men, sun-crowned, who live above the fog
> In public duty and in private thinking;
> For while the rabble with their thumb-worn creeds,
> Their large professions and their little deeds,
> Mingle in selfish strife. Lo! Freedom weeps,
> Wrong rules the land, and waiting Justice sleeps.'

The First Christmas
By George E Hobbs
(First published: December 24, 1931)

Instinctively, this week, we turn to the Christmas festival. And just as instinctively we think of the first Christmas Day, which, in the scale of time, was but as yesterday. In the years that followed there came to the convictions of man the epochal value of that event. So profound was its importance that history received an indelible cleavage. All history is identified by that cleavage, and became known either as "BC" or "Anno Domini." The dividing line was the first Christmas Day.

It is in the progress of years that the lustre of that immortal event is seen. To the contemporary mind of that day it had no significance in any way. Except to a very few it was just an ordinary event. A babe was born who was just as sweet as, and no sweeter than, any other babe. There was no halo about his head – at least, no greater and no lesser halo than about the head of every other child. And, so that the contemporary mind be not unduly blamed for short-sightedness, no single person of that day could, by any manner of investigation, prove that the child was supernormal. There is not a Doctor of Medicine or a Bachelor of Science, not a physiologist or a psychologist, but what would have been baffled in an attempt to discover super-normal conditions or qualities in the new-born babe. He slept, he drew sustenance from his mother, he wept. In the early days of his babyhood he was just as mentally ignorant and just as morally innocent as every other normally-born child. In all things surrounding the infant stage of this babe we must not claim more than sane reasoning will permit.

A Wonderful Appeal

And yet, although superior excellence was impossible of detection, this child, Jesus, was destined to rock the foundations of empires, and change the face of history.

Without stressing any suggestion of super-normality about the event of his birth, one does not hesitate to say there is a wonderful appeal in the message of that birth. Yet truth demands the admission that to a large number the appeal falls upon deaf ears. And truth further compels the admission that even to many who call themselves Christians the message of the Babe of Bethlehem is grossly misunderstood.

The first striking appeal is the place of his birth. He who was to shake the very foundations of life itself, transforming its values, and revolutionising its customs and outlook. He who was to crush the mighty and raise into prominence the lowly and degraded – born in a stable and cradled in a manger! He who had been described by seer and prophet as "Wonderful", "The Mighty God", finding his first bed in the straw that bedded down the cattle! Yet even this is not incomprehensible. We would have the circumstances no different from what are recorded. Yet incomprehensibility is found in the interpretation of this message of humility and lowliness.

How can the "followers" of this supreme example of lowliness and poverty roll in the lap of luxury? I am not now referring to men of the commercial world. They have their own code of the fitness of things and if they follow that code that is their affair. No, I am not thinking of these. I am rather thinking of those who lead the Church He founded, the leaders of the cause he espoused; rather of the cause which was his very life and existence.

How any person can be a minister, a Bishop, a Vicar, a priest in His great work, and obtain the advantage of one single penny beyond his need, passes my comprehension. It is contradictory to every phase of His life and to every ideal of His teaching.

It serves no useful purpose to play with words or conditions. He who would serve his Master as Minister, Bishop, Vicar, or Priest, faithfully and in the full consciousness of the obligations of his office, can never, honestly, make one penny beyond his needs and the obligatory needs of his family. To advance one step beyond this is to render one's life but a farce, a travesty which makes the man in the street ridicule that which should be lofty and noble.

The Duty of the Church

Another striking appeal of the Christmas message is that contained in the angelic song, "Peace on the earth, goodwill toward men."

For 2,000 years this message has been flashed annually throughout Christendom, and yet at this Christmas time we shall repeat, as we have repeated oft and again:

"Beneath the angel strain have rolled
Two thousand years of wrong."

And the words will still be true and applicable. [Wherever there is wrong, there is also the] antithesis of peace, and whatever disturbs peace or prevents its consummation is wrong.

It has been suggested over and over again that it is the incumbent duty of the Church (I use the singular to denote all) to preach peace. But the suggestion is wrong, and those who suggest it errs through ignorance. The duty of the Church is not to preach peace but to practise it.

When all the internal bickerings, the many jealousies, the lines of social distinctions, and the cliques are entirely eliminated, then, and then only, will the Church be able to practise peace. And when she does practise peace there will be little need to preach it. The example set will commend itself.

When once the Church has purified herself, then will come the glorious chance of passing on to the world at large the belated bequest of Christmas. Being peaceful internally, she will tolerate war no more. Believe me, the Church universal, united for peace, is strong enough to prevent the greatest nation from waging war. But strife with lethal weapons is not the only kind of warfare. Having mutual goodwill internally, the Church will seek every avenue and strive every endeavour that goodwill shall be expressed universally.

Where conditions are found that prevent the expression of goodwill to men, it will then be the duty of the Church to alter those conditions. And this state of affairs will quickly come if the Church will listen to the Christmas message, "Peace on the earth, goodwill to men."

May I take this opportunity of wishing all readers of the Swindon Advertiser every good wish for Christmas.

The Call to Prayer
Is This Attitude Based on the Right Concept?
By George E Hobbs
(First published: September 6, 1935)

In writing this article I am animated by one desire only. Religious leaders are calling the Churches to prayer upon a matter of grave urgency. As a lay preacher, interested in the cause of universal peace and in the betterment of mankind, I want to contribute my share in the scheme of things. But when I give service I want, first of all, to be sure that I have the right concept for, and in, that service. I therefore want light upon this difficult problem. Have I the right concept if I respond to the request of the leaders of religion?

There is no desire to appear ultra-religious, but I have always understood that prayer in the main consisted of praise, as expressed in adoration; thanksgiving, as expressed in the joy and gladness of life; and supplication, as expressed through some special personal need.

In public prayer the same idea obtains as in the attitude of private, or personal prayer. The preacher takes the needs of his congregation and presents them as a whole. As the needs of all are more or less identically similar, the preacher uses the plural "we" in a singular sense.

In praise, thanksgiving and supplication the "we" becomes intensely singular because – as in the case of private prayer – there is affinity in thought and desire between the supplicator and the supplicated.

A quagmire of contradictions?

But when I traverse beyond this concept is there not a danger of finding myself in a quagmire of contradictions? I think we must agree, if we are true to our sense of the fitness of things, that many of our prayers lack wisdom. In many cases we revert, perhaps unconsciously, to the old pagan attitude of prayer. In times of drought or pestilence the gods were angry and earnest prayers were directed to the gods that they would turn from their anger and smile again upon the earth.

The Christian era holds many examples of prayers to God for "His Mercy" upon the people in times of devastating epidemics. In time, however, human intelligence was brought to bear upon schemes of sanitation and hygiene, and man proved the truth that he was "to work out his own salvation".

And so I come to the larger issue – the issue which now confronts the Churches and has led them to a call for prayer. I am to pray for peace. I am to pray that God will influence the League Council that war may be averted. I am to pray that God will thwart the desire of those who wish for those things which must lead to war. But am I showing a renegade spirit if I do not respond to such a wish?

There is a striking scene in the life of the Christ which will illustrate to a profound degree the point I have in view. The Christ is standing upon a prominence outside the city Jerusalem. Upon His face is a look of unutterable sadness. The tears start to His eyes – and this is his soliloquy: "How often would I have gathered thee as a hen gathereth her brood, but ye would not!"

The Christ with all His magnetism and power, stands helpless and baffled before the perverted will of the people. The Christ knew the value and power of prayer as none other did, yet He did not pray to His Father that He would turn the heart of the people to Him. He knew that God would do no other – that He could do no other – than what He had already done and was doing. Constantly He was urging His wisdom and tolerance and love upon the people. And the people themselves, having the powers of free choice, must yield to wisdom and save themselves and the world, or yield to mischief and destroy themselves and the world.

Misconceptions of Deity

I am audacious enough to say there are some things that God cannot do. If He did He would belie His own nature. Just as it is impossible for God to hate the vilest of men, so it is equally impossible for Him to force His will upon men. He exhorts, but never forces His will.

When the Great War paralysed the world, the thought processes of men's minds became paralysed also. The misconceptions of Deity were truly appalling. God, to me, is a God of love and of infinite compassion. He is also a God of wisdom and of supreme justice. If I thought in my mind that He could have prevented that war, and did not, He would be to me a devil. Just as the Christ, so God stands helpless against a perverted will. The perverted will of man was responsible for that hell, and all the lessons accruing therefrom have been wasted upon his pretended intelligence.

It seems to me an insult to Deity when we sing:

> "When wilt thou save the people?
> O, God of mercy, when?
> The people, Lord, the people–
> Not thrones and crowns, but men?"

By such sentiments we throw the onus of action upon God, whereas the onus of action should be upon men. It is man who has the awful dynamic of choice. That choice is influenced towards the best and noblest by infinite love and wisdom. If in face of this beneficent influence man determines upon the worst, God is helpless – and man must pay his dues.

We have failed in our duty

I believe the call to prayer issued by the Churches to be one of real desire for world peace. I also reluctantly believe it to be futile in its objective. Thousands of times in thousands of Churches since the world war has been prayed, "Give peace in our time, O Lord." This prayer has been prayed with far less fervour than, "Lend me sixpence until Friday, Jack." And now we are up against vicious realities again: the panic has set in, and in that panic we throw again the challenge upon God. Is this a fair and just concept? Most emphatically it is not.

Yes, I shall answer the call to prayer, but I shall not pray that God will prevent war. I shall pray that God will help me to be a man of peace, and that I, by precept and example, may show the warlike man that peace and love and tolerance are best. Let us bow our heads in humiliation and shame that we who call ourselves Christians have utterly failed in our duty.

Life's Success
By George E Hobbs
(First published: June 19, 1936)

If I were asked to give a brief definition of the phrase "Making a success of life", I think I should answer something like this: "Finding contentment in service". Perhaps a more qualified definition would be: "Finding real contentment in disinterested service".

One hears quite often of folk of whom it may be said that they have been successful in life. But my definition would scarcely apply to them. They have made some sort of success of life, but it would not be true to say they have found contentment in service. On the contrary, they have found discontent in service, and in the very success they have achieved, paradoxically, they have discovered failure.

Life is made up of paradoxes. One of the greatest is discovered in these words: "He that findeth his life shall lose it, but he that loseth his life for my sake shall find it." It seems difficult to square the logic of such a saying – to lose in the finding and to find in the losing. Yet life has proved its logic sound, and has verified its truth over and over again. The lamentable fact is that so many lose in the finding and all too few find in the losing. The trouble is that we have placed a false value upon "success" and in consequence the whole perspective is blurred and distorted.

* * *

One of the most poignant moments of any human life must be the realisation, when too late, that life has been useless and wasted. To such, even with achieved wealth and position about and upon them, the closing days must be bitter and sad. And further. To such, upon whom the conviction has come of a future existence, the future must be of a gloomy and distressing anticipation.

If, therefore, my definition be true, that, "finding contentment in service" is the solution to a successful life, how can it be applied? It seems to me that the key is the motive which prompts and inspires service.

A man designs an aeroplane or a submarine. His whole soul is wrapped up in his careful planning and ultimate achievement. He visualises, in the case of the air-craft, the possibilities of swift and safe flight, bringing distances nearer for traveller and for essential goods. In his vision he has gone farther. He sees in his machine the means of breaking down racial barriers and the possibilities of linking up the peoples of the earth in a closer bond.

With his submarine he visions the means of safe and peaceful underwater travelling; his craft no longer subjected to destructive surface elements. In beautiful weather he can skim the surface; in stormy weather he can dive beneath its tumult.

If these are his motives, and his designs become an accomplished fact, then, so far as he is concerned, he bids fair to make a success of life. He has contributed something to the world's benefit. He finds "contentment in service".

* * *

But – and there can be no equivocation upon this point – if his motive is to design a machine which will devastate a people from the air, or smash a ship to destruction from beneath the water, then he cannot, by any stretch of the imagination, make a real success of life. Such a "success" is definitely opposed to "finding contentment in service". To find contentment in such service, or to suggest that it can be found there, is to insult the God-like in human endeavour. To say that destruction must be met by destruction is not an answer to a problem, but an excuse to cover it – an excuse all the more deadly because its plausibility sounds like reasoned logic. Much of this so-called reasoning is dangerous in the extreme.

But, reverting again to our designer and his motives, it is possible, of course, for his motives to be beyond challenge, but that others have adapted his design for work contrary to his intentions. If this is so, then it frees the designer from responsibility and fastens it upon the usurper. There is, however, another case which cannot stand in the same category.

* * *

One of the most diabolical of all human inventions is that of poison gas. Here there can be no mistake as to motive. That kindly individual who is out to excuse every human endeavour which goes astray can find no excuse to offer here. He is baffled and staggered before the enormity of the crime, for it is beyond explanation or excuse.

The inventor of poison gas can have no false ideas about his invention. Neither can he entertain the thought that his motive is good and beneficial. He knows, as clear as the fact that two and two make four, that his invention is to kill, and to kill in the most horrible manner. He also knows that where his invention is partially inhaled the victim never, as long as he lives, really recovers from its effects. Oft and again conditions will be ideal for a return of its presence, and the victim finds a perpetual cause for cursing the inventor who forgot his manhood.

Can such an individual find "contentment in service"? If I, for one instant, thought this possible, I should have to assume the fact that Satan can disguise himself in human form. Only the Devil himself could find contentment in a service of agony and destruction. No human soul can find contentment in service if that service oppresses, or degrades, or hurts his fellows. Every service which leaves in its trail suffering and sorrow negatives success and contentment to the one by whom that service is rendered.

* * *

And now let me follow the bent that is in me. I wonder if I could issue an appeal to our young folk forceful enough to be heard – to you who are students old enough to understand my appeal, to you who are in the upper classes of our Primary Schools, and especially to you of our Secondary Schools and College.

You want to make a success of life? Then you can achieve this if you begin your life on right lines. You must have your sport and fun and relaxation. Sport will build and develop your muscles, quicken your eye and brain. Fun and relaxation will give you that saving grace of humour and will make you companionable. But remember you are members of a social order. You live in a community which is governed by laws. Those laws are supposed to be based upon equity and justice.

The creators and administrators of those laws are men whose ideas are fixed – many of them trained in schools of thought that are now antiquated and obsolete. They do not like breaking away from old traditions and old customs.

* * *

You must not despise your heritage, but you have the golden opportunity of taking your heritage and interpreting it in terms of the future. You will make our future laws, and will interpret our future art. You will take hold of nature's new secrets which she is so tardy of releasing, and you will bend them to your will. You will take hold of new sciences and harness them to do your bidding. You will specialise in medical and surgical research, and new methods will be yours in the combat with disease. You have a wonderful future. What will you do with it?

Will you do as many of us have done – get all you can and give nothing in return? Living selfishly, prostituting your gifts and powers to the highest bidder. Or will you dedicate your powers, your knowledge, your gifts to the benefit of your fellows? Believe me, if you do the latter you will make a success of life, and you will find that pearl of great price, "Contentment in service".

The Humour of Life
By George E Hobbs
(First published: June 26, 1936)

The title of my article is a little unfortunate – as titles sometimes are apt to be. One thinks of a subject, which one fondly imagines will be suitable for an article; and then the title bothers one much more than the writing of the article. Happy are those who can keep a title for all winds and weathers, and then write under it any topic, from a split in the Cabinet to murder on the high seas, such titles as "Gleanings", "Here and there", or "Ramblings", but when one is tied down to a given topic then the title is apt to give the writer grey hairs before his time. The idea I have before me is the humour one can get out of life – and things. I always feel sorry for anyone who can see no humour in life. It seems to me they are missing so much that helps life forward. I know there is much to depress and sadden. On the other hand, there is much to brighten the days and give an added zest to life.

Sometimes the cause borders upon the trivial, yet those who have eyes to see, and the gift to appreciate, can quickly discover its humour and enjoy it. Life in its ordinary, everyday expression supplies a fund of illustrations which one may enjoy alone or in company.

* * *

A short time since I was on may way home when I saw a little chap menaced by one much bigger than himself. By all the laws of weight and size the little fellow should have taken to his heels. To the surprise and chagrin of the bigger lad, he did not do so. He stood his ground defiantly. The sturdy stand of the little chap caused the other to lose heart and it was he who turned to run. No one could have acted quicker or with truer judgment. The seat of the big lad's trousers was the mark; the distance away, just the length of the little chap's leg. Nothing could have been truer than the foot which followed the leg. Plunk! – and the big lad started on a homeward flight, minus a little loss of prestige. The scene was most amusing – brief and effective.

A dear old brother, very enthusiastic but not given to "speechifying" once addressed an audience of which I was a member. He laboured through for a while, and then, finding time was against him, said: "Well, friends, it's no use. I must finish this on some previous occasion."

Some of the richest humour is that which tells against oneself. Personally, as long as the humour is clean, I never mind which way the wind blows. I am a Methodist lay preacher, as some know to their sorrow. And it is generally stated that "You don't do it for nothing". We are credited with bringing back from country appointments "sacks of potatoes" or anything that is in season. This is why some of us have "poacher's" pockets in our coats. Not, of course, to carry sermons, but to bring home anything which is floating round and cannot find an owner. To all and sundry who fondly imagine my leg can be pulled upon the subject I heartily agree to the commandeering of all which is at all movable.

To one in particular I was serious, because, without offence, he was serious in his questioning. I told him that never in my preaching career had I done this – and promptly forgot the subject.

A few Sundays later I was conducting services at Grove, near Wantage. Following the evening service I found that my host had packed a basket with vegetables for me, with carrots displaying their green foliage from the edge of the basket. My protest hurt my host, so manfully gripping the basket I made for the train. Fortunately, no one in the compartment knew I had fallen from grace, in consequence I could hold my head high. But alas! Nemesis was near at hand.

When I emerged from Swindon station the usual Sunday evening crowd had foregathered. And, of all the ill-fortune, the first person I saw was my friend, the critic. In his natural delight at finding me a second Ananias he capered about like a jack-in-the-box, drawing several of his friends' attention to the one who "never, O, never, did such a thing in all his life". I melted quickly into the crowd and lived to enjoy the whole episode. The sad part is that not even to this day will he believe that was the first and only time.

* * *

Sometimes humour is found in that which is intended to be serious. I recall one such experience. In my choir-singing days – days before my voice sounded like a rasp – we went one Sunday evening to give a sacred concert at another church. We contributed anthems, sacred songs, duets, etc. All went swimmingly until it came to the "vote of thanks" to the choir. The gentleman who proposed the vote was evidently in his best style of oratory. His intentions were good. What he put over alas – not so good! Said he:

> "Friends, I ses agin what I've said afore. What folks want to go to the the-a-tre to be amused for I can't think. To-night I've been amused more than I can say a-listening to these friends with their songs and things. I asks you all to give 'em a good 'earty clap!"

As I said, his intentions were good. But, ye gods, "amuse" with sacred song and music! Still he may have used the term advisedly and in strict accord with his reactions. We may have been amusing in our efforts at seriousness. Who knows?

And so life is touched day by day with its salvation of humour and fun. Life is not intended to be morbid and dull, and he who shuts from his life the saving grace of humour is missing the joy and tonic of life.

* * *

What a profound change has come to the Christian aspect of life to what obtained in my early days. Time was when the sombre dress and the pensive look was the hall-mark of Christian virtue. The ugly, inartistic dress denoted modesty and purity. Gay clothes hid the moral freebooter. The carefree laughter of someone who had seen and appreciated humour had something of the devil hidden somewhere. Life in those days was a thing of cemeteries and churchyards. All that has now changed. It is a good and beneficial change. And while Christianity can still supply solace and comfort to human souls in the darker experiences of life, it also accompanies them in the fun and frolic of life.

* * *

The Christian life which is untinged by humour is like a rose without fragrance. Its beauty is real, but it is the beauty of austerity. It lacks that which would humanise it and make it attractive. A morose outlook attracts none. A humorous one attracts many.

The New Methodist Hymnal [1]
By George E Hobbs
(First published: July 24, 1936)

The compilers of the new Methodist Hymnal are to be congratulated upon the excellent production they have presented to the people called Methodists. When Methodist Union became an accomplished fact, it was thought that a "united" hymnal should synchronise with so great a movement. This has been done, and the result is a happy one.

The Hymnal was compiled by a select committee under the presidency of the Rev Luke Wiseman, himself an acknowledged authority upon Methodist hymnology and music.

The book is not as yet universally used, one of the reasons being the cost of change-over. Although it is a tacit understanding that members should obtain their own copies, this does not always work out in practice. Hence a supply must be purchased, and these are usually marked "for the use of visitors". Then, too, where there is a good choir there are music editions to purchase, besides a special edition for the organ and one for pulpit use. A church, therefore, must consider its financial stability before undertaking the burden of a change-over in its Hymnal.

Many of the Methodist churches, however, have changed from old to new. This in its train has produced its little problems. And the problems, really, are not connected with the hymns, but with the tunes.

Many of the tunes are new to the congregations, and the most liberal-minded congregation in the world of Methodism is apt to be very conservative-minded where tunes are concerned. If the new tune should be of the "Cwm Rhondda", or "Rimington" type – one that grips instantly by its sheer tunefulness – then all is well. But if the tune has a "choir" rather than a "congregational" setting, then all is not well. It seems to me that when new Hymnals, in particular, are introduced, there should be not only "choir practice" evenings, but "congregation practice" evenings as well. Every church-goer knows that a bad sermon is bad, but it is not half so bad when the singing "goes with a swing". On more than one occasion I have been greeted, when leaving the pulpit, with "At least, the singing has been good, Mr Hobbs." "At least" was the compensation of the service.

The idea of a congregation practice evening is my contribution to the "Suggestions Committee" of the Methodist Church.

In the first preface of the new book there is a short history of the development of Methodist hymn-books into the present one. Towards the end this sentence occurs:

> "This hymn-book is issued for the use of British Methodists, and for not a few Methodists beyond the seas as well. It is the first such book since Wesley's first collection of a hundred and fifty years ago. Its publication therefore might be called an historic event in Methodism."

The second preface is historic in that it is John Wesley's original preface to his first compilation of hymns, and is dated "Friday, October 20th, 1779".

If we compare the new book with that of the late "Wesleyan" book, it approximates to it in its sectional divisions. There are, however, one or two new features. There is a delightful collection of hymns under the title, "for little children". To most preachers no service is complete without a hymn for, and a talk to, the young folk. Personally, I do this at the evening as well as the morning service, if there are young folk present. And such a hymn as "In our dear Lord's garden", sung as children can sing, is a sacrament in itself.

What appeals to me most strongly in the children's section is the entire elimination of that which is morbid and sad. Young life, buoyant with the joy of living, revolts against the cemetery aspect of life. And so, in this section the compilers have been mercifully wise. The hymns selected are attractive by the simplicity of their theology and the beauty of their poetic expressions. Take this one for perfection of rhythm and poetic beauty:

"Jesus Friend of little children,
Be a friend to me;
Take my hand and ever keep me
Close to Thee.
Teach me how to grow in goodness
Daily as I grow;
Thou hast been a child, and surely
Thou dost know."

The tune set to this hymn is as delightful as the hymn itself.

In the section, "Pilgrimage, Guidance and Perseverance", there is a hymn included by John Bunyan. It is, of course, in the true Bunyan style, and makes odd reading. It evidently recalls the days when the belief was that Christians could be assailed by apparitions. The last verse reads:

"Hobgoblins nor foul fiend
Can daunt his spirit;
He knows he at the end
Shall life inherit.
Then fancies fly away
He'll fear not what men say;
He'll labour night and day
To be a pilgrim."

It is recorded that St Augustine described a hymn as "a song with praise to God". If this is so – and I think we shall agree with this definition – then any hymn which would distort this idea should never find place within the covers of a hymn-book.

* * *

In the old "Wesleyan" hymn-book there was one hymn which I am glad has found no place in the new Methodist book. It contained faulty theology and thereby distorted the truth. In no way could it be called "a song with praise of God". One verse of the hymn read:

"Thou hatest all that evil do,
Or speak iniquity;
The Heart unkind, the heart untrue
Are both abhorred by Thee."

This verse was evidently inspired by one of the Psalms, in which the human but vindictive psalmist thunders out, "Thou hatest the workers of iniquity." But both happen to be a distortion of the truth. If such were true then it would relegate to the fable stage such incomparable stories as "The Prodigal Son" and "The Lost Sheep". Both the psalmist and the poet got mixed between "worker" and "work". It is the work that is hated, not the worker.

* * *

The hymn-book is compiled in such manner as to suit all tastes in vocal religious exercises. I am giving my personal opinion now when I say there is nothing lost in introducing a little ritual into the Methodist Church services. The chanting of the Lord's Prayer was frowned upon for a considerable time. It is now a regular feature in most of the churches.

At the end of the book, "Ancient Hymns and Canticles" are included. In this connection Trinity Methodist Church, Gorse Hill, chants the "Te Deum" in place of the second hymn on the first Sunday morning service of each month. Those of us who have been privileged to take this service must agree that it is a good innovation.

There are also Psalms and passages of Scripture set to music. These of course, are only possible where there is a choir capable of leading the singing.

For those churches that still retain the "after service" – that is, an informal meeting following the evening service – there is a delightful collection of "Verses", fifty in number. These will assist very greatly in the spontaneous singing, which is a feature of these meetings.

I imagine that no hymn-book has ever embraced so wide a scope as that of the new Methodist hymn-book.

The New Methodist Hymnal [2, extract]
By George E Hobbs

(First published: July 31, 1936)

[The hymn O Worship the King, All Glorious] consists of six verses, with eight lines to a verse. The preachers would read slowly and distinctly the first four lines, and the congregation would then sing them. The preacher would then read the second four lines, and the congregation would sing them. This would be repeated until the whole hymn had been sung. That meant twelve separate readings and twelve separate singings. I distinctly remember that in many of the hymns two lines only were read and then sung. The congregation, of course, standing the whole time. In process of time conditions changed, and the custom was to read and sing verse by verse. Later there came the present custom – that of reading the first verse only, the hymn then being sung through.

Of course it must be remembered that the arts of reading and writing were not so universal an accomplishment as to-day, especially among the older members of the congregations. Compulsory education came into force in 1870, when Board Schools were established. But the education of those days was of a rather lax order. In 1889 free education was brought into being and some improvement was made. It was not, however, until 1899, when the Board of Education became the educational authority, that the public conscience was awakened to the needs of making education really and vitally compulsory.

During the transition period the lack of reading powers was felt by all sections of the community. It was no less felt in the exercise of public worship. Hence the necessity for the preacher of reading each hymn in easy stages so that the people could follow, more or less, by memory. Happily those conditions no longer obtain, and the whole congregation can now enjoy a hymn unrestricted by its reading in stages.

Lessons of Harvest
By George E Hobbs
(First published: October 9, 1936)

This is the season of harvest festivals following that of fruit, vegetable and flower exhibitions under the heading of "flower shows". But there is a difference between the two.

In flower shows the exhibits are competitive. The best of a particular variety is shown, not so much because of the intrinsic value of the prizes awarded, but for the personal satisfaction and honour of having those magic words, "first prize," attached. After all, there is nothing selfish in this attitude of mind. Rather it is commendable, for, often in the search to produce the best, new discoveries are made in soil mixture, feeding, etc, which prove of great utilitarian value.

Some cottage gardeners set aside a certain plot of land for the special cultivation of flowers, fruit or vegetables for competitive exhibition. Exceptional care is exercised in the cultivation, and when, in due course, the particular exhibit obtains a "first" there is natural pride in the event.

* * *

In harvest festivals there is a difference. The comparison, however, is not of the odious type. The comparison is given for a specific purpose which will reveal itself as this article develops.

The best of the produce is sent in, as in the case of the flower show. There may be even a "competitive spirit", which, perhaps, is all to the good. But those who send in their produce are donors, and not exhibitors. That is, the produce is a gift. Afterwards it will be given either to the hospitals, or to the sick at home, or sold for the benefit of a particular organisation. Perhaps the ideal is to give the whole of the produce to the hospitals. In some cases this may be a delicate and difficult suggestion, as the individual organisation may be sorely in need of funds. The produce is then sold to this end.

Harvest festivals may or may not have originated in pagan times. Without detracting from the principles governing modern festivals, it is possible that, long before the conception came of the one God, the people of antiquity paid their respects to the gods of cultivation and of harvest. The mystery of increase, following the planting of one seed, must have been profound to them. And it is quite conceivable that the "festival" originated in a placating rather than in a thankful spirit.

* * *

But what is the spirit which underlies the modern harvest festival?

Let me first believe that the whole of the produce is from the hands of donors, and not exhibitors. Then I think the spirit is one of a tacit acknowledgement of man's limitations. Man can assist materially towards the end, but he cannot produce the end. I am aware that under modern scientific methods agricultural experts may proclaim a two-fold or a three-fold abundance. And in many cases what they proclaim has come true. But it is still true that, while man can assist, and assist very materially, he can no more produce the harvest than stay the sun in his course.

Away back in the late fall or the early spring the ground was prepared and the seed sown. In many cases nothing more can be done except a patient wait for results. Mother Earth begins her miracle. She broods over the tiny seed until she has changed its dead coldness into the warmth of living, so she caresses it with her sun-laughter and her rain-tears until it is sturdy and strong. And then she may forget herself and take on a wayward mood. She may house in her bosom the wireworm, and a hundred other enemies of the seed and the tiny shoot. Her tender caress may change into malignant hatred. And if she does this the harvest is foredoomed to be a lean one.

But the contrary may be true. Mother Earth, assisted by the genial sun and the refreshing rain, may produce a bumper harvest. And if the long view be taken it is found that there are infinitely more good harvests than bad ones. But, whether good or indifferent, the produce presented at the harvest festival is an acknowledgement of man's limitations.

Dare I suggest that the real spirit underneath the festival is that of gratitude? I am not quite so sure. I am all too conscious that in many of us it is a quality conspicuous by its absence, so prone are we to grumble and complain, so tardy are we to express gratitude. We take the things of life as our due and our right. Too often we forget to be grateful.

I am writing this on Sunday night. Even as I write, there are thousands who are praying that they may never see to-morrow's sunrise. Life, to these, has become wearisome and a burden. The pains they are enduring are excruciating and well-nigh unbearable, and they long for the release which will give them rest. There are thousands more who are lonely and friendless, with hearts that are hungry for love and sympathy and understanding. Yet they long for these in vain – hearts that would give their all for one kind word, one loving look, one friendly gesture. But the world, lusting for individual pleasure and self-satisfaction, forgets the lonely and friendless ones, and they are left to their misery and sorrow.

* * *

And yet, for every one who is sick with pain, there are thousands who are in the pink of health. For everyone who is lonely and friendless, there are thousands who have an abundance of friends. For everyone who is hungry for food, there are thousands who are prosperous and well-fed. The proportion of the healthy, prosperous, and well-fed, and of those who have friends, is many, many times greater than the pain-wracked, lonely and starving. We are among the number of the former, yet it is exceedingly rare that we even think grateful thoughts, let alone express our gratitude audibly.

That is why I want to read into the giving, at harvest festivals, of an expression of gratitude. A Benign Creator, operating through His laws, has given humanity of His best. He has withheld not one essential thing. In the ages that are past, an assurance was given to man that "seed-time and harvest should never cease". And never once has that continuity been broken. A drought, an overplus of rain, a premature or late frost, or a pestilence have all taken toll of harvests in localised areas, but never once in the long sequence of seasons has there been a world shortage. If famine has been in Canaan, there has been abundance in Egypt. The fault has not been in the Creator's supply, but in man's method of transport and distribution.

* * *

The tragedy is that this method is measured and expressed in terms of personal gain, and not in terms of human needs. If it "pays" to transport and to distribute, then it is done. If it does not pay, no matter what human needs may be, it is simply not done. It is a ghastly fact, but it is true.

Where foodstuffs are commercialised in such a way as to restrict their easy and cheap distribution to the needy, it is one of the worst crimes of which a human being can be guilty. Such utter selfishness is nothing short of devilishness, and should be sternly punished.

A generous Father has given to His children an abundance of the essential things of life. Can we do less than cultivate the grateful spirit?

The Present Menace [extracts]
By George E Hobbs
(First published: February 26, 1937)

This week I want to break upon my series of articles on "Light" and deal with something profoundly topical. I do not intend to hide the pill in a spoonful of jam. This has been done so skilfully, in times past, by "those in authority over us" that the pill has not been detected until too late. It is by far the best that we know the pill is made for our taking, and that if we take it we are in for a period of excessive vomiting.

Some time after the Great War ended, I was standing outside the factory gates. Two other men were with me. One was in a contented frame of mind, but the other was not so contented, for having lost an arm in the war, he could not return to his trade. Said the contented one, "You know, I bought two houses during the war. I should have bought a third if the war had only kept on a little longer." I need make no comment upon this statement, and there is little need to print the other man's observations. A little imagination and a limited acquaintance with a standard dictionary are all that is needed.

Surely there is another way out. But apparently that way seems impossible, because those who should stand four-square for this way out are divided among themselves. The time has come when plain speaking should be indulged in.

* * *

The stability of a nation stands unquestionably upon a foundation of moral and spiritual integrity. However "grandmotherly" and "soft" it may appear, the fundamentals of that foundation are not the forces of military display, but righteousness, truth, peace, tolerance, brotherhood, love. Yes, I am quite aware that these things do not produce the thrill and excitement which bands, and bugles, and flags, and uniforms produce. Nevertheless, the virtues herein enunciated are the virtues which produce stability and solidarity. The sponsors of these virtues should be the personnel of the Christian Church – the Church, which, by its very name and constitution, constitutes the followers of "The Man of Peace".

Just as I have tried to state the case dispassionately for the militarists, so let me be faithful to what I conceive to be the case for the Christian Church. That the Church, as a body, has failed its Lord is a statement which cannot be denied. And that failure is due to the fact that the Church is afraid – literally afraid – to face up to the issues involved. The Church is rich in Archbishops, Bishops, ministers, lay preachers, and in "members", but she cannot boast of a Paul or a Peter; she cannot boast of a membership willing to tell Caesar to his face that they are Christians. Christians to-day have not the backbone and stamina to stand up to scorn and abuse and suffering for the sake of principle and "for His sake". And because of this lack the Church is impotent and a ghastly failure.

* * *

Those of us who believe that the way of peace is by piling up armaments, that we believe in the present method of spending millions of money upon that which will destroy our fellow men, ought in honour bound to leave the Christian Church. To remain in an organisation when once we have denied its principles is to be false to our vows. Either we must follow Him who went to His death rather than pander to the forces of materialism, or we must deny and forsake Him. We cannot do both.

One last word. If the nation is to respond to the Archbishop of Canterbury's "Back to religion" call, then, from the Primate downwards, there will have to come a conversion from a belief in materialism to that of an implicit faith in the Lord we profess to follow.

Gleanings [4, extract]
By George E Hobbs
(First published: May 28, 1937)

In this country we have a State Church known under the name of the "Established Church", or "The Church of England". Twenty-four Bishops, by virtue of their high office, have the right to seats in the House of Lords. It is all to the good when State and Church run hand in hand. The influence of men trained in the highest service to mankind ought to have a beneficial effect upon the laws created for man's guidance. The snag is that a monopoly occurs in one section of the community. And where a monopoly exists there always lurks a danger to freedom.

The only figures I have by me are those for 1931, where the Anglican Church reveals a membership of 65 per cent of the total population. This is a majority, I grant. But if the principle is laid down that 24 members of one Church should represent 65 per cent of the population, it is logical to suggest that the other Churches should have nine or ten members to represent the other 35 per cent. In order to maintain a religious balance therefore, the governing heads of Non-Conformist Churches such as the Presidents of Conferences etc, ought also to have seats in the House of Lords, such seats to be held during their term of office.

* * *

In the early part of this article I stressed the fact that Britain is a democracy, and that democracy means "Government of the people, by the people, for the people". Also that "The majority shall rule by the will of the people". This is the true spirit of democracy. But such meaning breaks down where, in any section of its law-making machinery, a monopoly exists which does not exist by the will of the people.

I certainly do not suggest, neither do I wish, that the Bishops should be withdrawn from the House of Lords. What I do suggest is that there should be equal rights to representation by the other religious bodies. Then, and then only, should we interpret in spirit and in word the true meaning of democracy.

To put it bluntly, there is too much power vested in the office of the Archbishop of Canterbury. I do not suggest that the present holder abuses his office, but I do suggest that the possibility exists.

There is but one safeguard, and that is the inclusion in the Upper House of the heads of Non-Conformist Churches, Salvation Army, etc.

Gleanings [13, extract]
By George E Hobbs
(First published: July 30, 1937)

Now let us look the matter squarely in the face, and in so doing we shall have to face up to some ugly and unpalatable truths. Sunday speedway racing at

Wroughton is not so much a symptom as it is an eruption revealing the presence of a malady which is deep-seated. The sport itself is on a par with golf, tennis and cricket, all of which are played on Sunday. They are all eruptions revealing the same malady. Sunday speedway racing is not a menace because of its name, but because it violates a principle held sacred by teaching, custom and usage. The malady exists because it had a beginning conducive to growth and development. It grew and developed because the Church had not the foresight or the courage to arrest its growth. However unpalatable it sounds, let us who are in the Church admit an undeniable fact. The Church has long since not only lost its grip upon Mr and Mrs Everyman, but has utterly lost its grip upon their children. The latter fact is more tragic than the former. And in this lamentable admission, scarcely a minister, lay preacher or Church member is free from blame. The causes of the Church's lost grip are manifold.

* * *

Into a world of intellectual doubt and of political upheaval the Great War came. That war not merely changed the geographical markings of the world; it changed the outlook upon life – mental, moral and spiritual. Thinking, action, feeling underwent a revolutionary change. Added to this change there came the tremendous strides in educative knowledge. Education – academic learning – became a fetish. Standards of examinations were raised, and numbers of jobs, hitherto exempt, were conditioned by matriculation. It followed that the younger generation became academically wiser than their parents. The younger generation became more independent, and in their new-found independence they began to think for themselves.

It was at this stage of the new youth development that sage counsel should have been displayed. The new education gave to youth analytical minds. They began to sift, explore, experiment. But along each new line of thought they found the doors barred and marked "Forbidden". The older minds, standing aghast at youth's onslaught upon what had been the teaching of years, whipped and lashed them back again into their own dark and dusty modes of thought. There could be only one ending to such a condition. It has long since broken upon the Church. It has been a huge revolt of youth, misguided – or, better still, unguided – and tragic.

* * *

It is not true to say that our youths are indifferent to spiritual influence. This is another mistake older folk make. Many of those who constitute the competitors and crowd at Wroughton have passed through our Sunday Schools. From there they passed into the Church and that, in thousands of cases, was the beginning of the end.

They asked that religion should be explained to them in terms they understood – terms which a higher education had taught them. It was not that they did not believe the central truths of Christianity, but they asked that these should be presented less crudely. They demanded that a line be drawn between folk and tribal lore, symbol and figure – and that of actual history. Almost entirely their requests were met with indifference – in some instances with hostility and threats of expulsion. As I have already intimated, the result was a foregone conclusion. Youth has revolted! The profound indifference of the Church to the changing need of the times has cost the Church its virile youth. And this has reacted upon religious activity generally.

The lamentable fact is that the average religious person of to-day suffers from spiritual anaemia. Go to almost any church in Swindon on a Sunday morning, and the best congregation but half-fills the building. Many of the churches, with seating accommodation for between four and six hundred, have between 20 to 40 in the congregations. Some congregations average about 12. In many of the churches the same tale can be told on Sunday evenings – churches sparsely filled. Especially is this true during the summer months. I grant that the open air may be more healthful than a stuffy church – although most of the churches are well ventilated to-day. But even in this we may as well be honest. The old pious tale that we can worship God under the wide canopy of heaven as well as in church is quite true if carried out. But how many who absent themselves from church under the above plea worship as they walk the fields and lanes? They may admire Nature and revel in the bliss of its charm and beauty, but that is not worship. How many, pleading that pious reason for non-attendance, think of the Giver of that beauty and charm? Very few indeed.

* * *

I have come to this conclusion – a conclusion from which I cannot escape. If Sunday speedway racing is menacing the spiritual life of the people, the apathetic response to spiritual stability in the Church itself is more menacing. And the Church will never stop the former until she has purified and cleansed herself from the worst sin of all – sleep. When she becomes awakened, alive, virile, strong, she will be able to answer youth's great need – a reinterpretation of the great truths of Christianity.

Gleanings [73, extract]
By George E Hobbs
(First published: October 14, 1938)

When I have to talk to children – which I have to do most Sundays – I prepare for them with as much thought and care as I do for the adults. In point of fact, I love talking to youngsters even more than addressing an adult audience. I try to get my stories down to the youngest child present. I do so because I see there – if I may use the figure of speech – the acorn and the spark. I see the little tiny things which can produce beauty and grace and strength. And I see the evidence that the spark is there – the spark which can mean trouble and ultimate dismay.

I look at my little friends and see the buds of a glorious future if the training is but conducted rightly. Here is the material for the new earth, the very salvation of civilisation. I contrast the muddle we adults have made of things – we, in our boasted wisdom and cock-sureness – and I strive in a very agony of effort to nurture the acorn seed and stifle the activity of the "spark". And, believe me, the youngsters are responsive. It is just a matter of the right approach and the right application.

If the world is to be made brighter and saner, it is to the children of today we must turn. They are our only hope. Small and insignificant they may appear, but they are nevertheless the lords of destiny.

Gleanings [87, extract]
By George E Hobbs
(First published: January 27, 1939)

We live in a time of great personal strain and stress. Many things go towards the trying of tempers and the fraying of nerves. Most of the news, Press and wireless has reference to the selfishness and stupidity of man. The results are apparent.

I suppose no age has seen the equal to the present age for the prevalence of neuraesthenia. Nerve tonic seems to be the only medicine dispensed. Business and domestic worries come – unemployment, with lack of food and fuel. And during such times it is so easy to lose one's grip.

I wonder if I am writing to one who is fast losing grip? You are so weary and sick in body and in mind. Life holds no joy for you, and the sooner the end comes the better. To use our narrative, the boat is full of water and the wind blows mercilessly upon you. There is no escape.

I know, my friend, for I have been through it.

My own little boy, aged three, a lively little lad at nine in the morning, died in a terrible manner at three of the same afternoon. And I nearly lost my grip. This is one of other experiences.

To you, my friend, I say: 'Keep your grip.'

In that rocking boat, amid the howling of the wind and the roar of the thunder, there is one who knows all about it. Believe me, He does. And He will not let you down if you will but keep faith with Him. He will stabilise your mental balance, and bring you to a great and wonderful freedom.

Chapter 7

The Life of Reuben George

"His works do follow him. We may bury his body in peace, but his name liveth for evermore."
(From the funeral oration given by Dr Albert Mansbridge MA, founder of the WEA)

'He was essentially a fighter. He was happiest when championing an unpopular cause.'
(George Ewart Hobbs, September 10, 1937)

George Ewart Hobbs got to meet many people through the course of his work and as a consequence of his preaching duties throughout the locality. Occasionally – very occasionally – you come across a tribute that he had written about an individual who was dear to him.

Looking back through the records, there is only: war hero and fellow Methodist Lance-Corp Gee (1915); another fellow Methodist, TR Bray (1918); his former headmaster, Henry Day (1919); musical director and former school friend Mr Percy Lewis, of "Laughter (Un)Limited" (1923), and one more fellow Methodist, John George Wise (1939).

And then we come to Reuben George, a key figure of life in Swindon in the early 20th century. For around two decades you could find articles by George and Reuben occupying the same page in the *Advertiser*. Both of them liked to use the paper as a platform for preaching their own beliefs and world view, with Reuben probably the more verbose out of the two of them.

He was born in 1864 at 1 Highfield Cottages, Lower Barton Street, Barton St Mary, Gloucester, to Bristol-born bootmaker Stephen and his wife Elizabeth. At the age of 16 he joined the workforce at Gloucester Wagon Works, where, six years later, he was to lose parts of several fingers in an industrial accident.

He later became an agent for the Wesleyan & General Insurance Company and it was in this context that he moved to Swindon in 1890 – initially occupying two rooms in a shared house at 97 Princes Street, before settling at 132 Goddard Avenue.

In 1894 he was first elected to New Swindon Urban District Council, later becoming an Alderman in 1900.

He helped found the Labour Party's first branch in the town, and he sought election as a Labour parliamentary candidate for the Chippenham constituency during the 1918 General Election, albeit unsuccessfully. However, despite this setback, he went on to serve as an elected representative of the party on Wiltshire County Council and on the Municipal Borough of Swindon (aka Swindon Corporation) – even becoming Mayor of Swindon in 1921-22. In line with his lifelong mission to promote knowledge and enlightenment among working men, he also served on the education committees of both authorities.

His political views were such that according to the late historian Mark Child, 'the local Wesleyans disassociated themselves from him on the grounds that his views were 'incompatible with Christianity'; it was certainly the case that he couldn't reconcile his conscience with the policy of the mainstream churches and their support for the Boer War.

Thereafter harbouring a dislike of organised religion, he was later to find an alternative 'home' with the Religious Society of Friends (Quakers).

He famously refused to take up the rôle of ex-officio Magistrate (to which he was entitled during his year of office) and similarly notoriously 'opened a wooden diving board at Coate Water by jumping from it into the lake' – having stripped down to just his underpants!

He raised three sons with his wife Clara, the eldest of whom, Herbert Gladstone George, died in May 1917 while on military service in India with the 6th County of London Brigade, Royal Field Artillery.

A lifelong idealist, socialist, social reformer and pacifist, Reuben George is regarded to this day as a champion of the underprivileged and urban poor – making it his mission to improve the lives and life chances of working-class Swindonians through walking visits to the countryside and through education.

He co-founded the Swindon branch of the Workers' Educational Association in 1907 and stayed involved with the organisation until his death. He was a member of the Wiltshire Archaeological Society and an ardent supporter of the Richard Jefferies Society. In fact, he was instrumental in securing the purchase of Coate Farmhouse (now the Richard Jefferies Museum) by Swindon Corporation in 1926.

So it is no wonder that he was also a loyal supporter of another great Swindon writer, Alfred Williams, who intended to dedicate his great work, *Life in a Railway Factory*, to his friend when it was published in 1915, but changed his mind; the book was controversial enough because of its (albeit honest) criticism of working conditions and attitudes in Swindon's Railway Works, and Williams didn't want the dedication to come across as a political statement. He saved the dedication for a later book, *Round About the Upper Thames*.

Reuben's own thoughts and ideas were set out in his own book, *Unconventional Approaches to Adult Education: Our School Among the Hills and Hedgerows* (National Labour Press, London) published in 1919.

He loved his adopted county, and through his commitment to self-education he became an authority on its history and culture. A modest and humble man, Reuben was known for only striving for the betterment of others – not for his self-aggrandisement.

He died at the Victoria Hospital in Swindon on June 4, 1936, aged 71. News of his death was even reported on national radio by the BBC. His funeral service was held at Christ Church, Old Town and he was subsequently buried at Radnor Street Cemetery.

In 2014, former *Advertiser* journalist Barry Leighton wrote: 'No man had more friends among both Swindon's ordinary people, and its great and good, than Reuben George.' Quite an epitaph.

And to all those budding historians out there. If you fancy a project… well, all of Reuben's articles in the *Advertiser* have yet to be researched, catalogued and published, and his life story remains largely untold, which is one reason why George Hobbs's and the following other insights into this inspirational man are so valuable.

We commence the chapter with an open letter in which our George takes issue with Reuben's stated belief in an impersonal God, followed by two contemporary, uncredited articles (although they may well have been written by George) that appeared in the *North Wilts Herald* on June 12, 1936 – one is an account of his life and the other a report on the funeral of two days earlier.

Our George remembers his late friend in a piece from the *Swindon Advertiser*, also dated June 12, 1936, and we also reproduce a letter he submitted to the same paper on the death of Clara George, Reuben's widow, who survived him by just over two weeks.

And finally, there is a wonderful tribute to Reuben, just ahead of what would have been his 73rd birthday.

An open letter to Mr Reuben George
By George E Hobbs
(First published: January 20, 1933)

My Friend, – You have the powers of writing, not merely thought-provoking articles, but articles which are made articulate by discussion. When I read your Christmas article or, to be more precise, that of 30 December, I had no hesitation in believing it would not pass without criticism. That criticism has come. Now you have supplemented "Has Christ Failed?" with "My Religion: The God I want to serve".

Almost invariably I have enjoyed your contributions to the Swindon Advertiser. With regard to many, even though I were pugnaciously inclined, no criticism would I dare. I must confess – alas – that "My Religion" is so difficult to understand in some of its aspects, so much at variance with your usual philosophic logic, that I am baffled to know your true position.

I have the profoundest sympathy with those who have a real intellectual difficulty in believing in a "personal" God. The idea of a personal God is so awfully tremendous that the human brain is utterly incapable of formulating even the haziest constructional thought of what it means.

Theologians talk and write of the attributes of a "personal" God – of "Omnipotence", "Omnipresence", "Omniscience"; of "Pure Spirit", of "The Trinity" and the like. Yet they know just as much – and no more – of what these terms mean at 60 years of age as they did at twenty.

To the man who sees nothing but chemical action in the world, who sees that the basic principle of all existence is the atom, the attributes and nature of a "personal" God is mere jargon. Hence it is not to be wondered at that thousands of folk with high intellectual attainments find a "personal" God an impossible conception. There, for the moment, I will leave it.

Difficult to Square

Now, my friend – had you but stayed at your belief in an impersonal God; had you but said, "Do I believe in a God? Yes... but an impersonal God," this letter would not have been written. But you do not stay there, and therein constitutes the difficulty of squaring your logic. You say, "In a personal God? No!" Yet in the same paragraph, consisting of twenty-seven lines, you clothe the impersonal God of your belief with almost every personal virtue known to the English tongue.

I may have misread you. I may have misunderstood the point at which you aimed. But if I read you correctly, and have placed the only interpretation possible upon your article of belief, then I can only say your logic is difficult to square.

You are not an impersonal unit. You are a "person" in the accepted sense and meaning of the word. You have your own peculiar individuality, and through that individuality you express your desire by acts of your own volition. You are far from a mechanical robot or an impersonal unit when you are in session at the Town Hall, or engaged in educational work.

You have individual opinions and convictions which are so deep-seated that you propagate them assiduously. You do not care a brass farthing about the opposition involved. That, my friend, is "personality".

Impersonal and Personal

Hence, when you say that you "find God in every good desire, every act of unselfishness, every kind word, every act of forgiveness, every movement towards love, the kiss of a child, the love of a mother, in the work of the reformer, in the path of the pioneer," etc, you translate your impersonal into a personal God.

It is altogether impossible to divorce thought, desire, action from any personality. Every act, whether it be the kiss of a child, the protection by the mother, or in fact, any and every volitional act, is the culmination of a definite process – thought, desire, act. There is no such thing as an act without thought. There may be, and often is, action with insufficient thought, but no act is ever performed without thought. And in thought, desire and action there is the indisputable fact and proof of personality. If, therefore, you see God in those processes which are the evidences of personality, then God (to you) must be a personal Being.

Later you speak of John Burns and John Morley refusing to accept the Divinity of Jesus Christ. That, of course, has nothing to do with the personality of God. Unitarians do not believe in the Divinity of Jesus, but they hold tenaciously to a belief in a personal God.

And now, my friend, will you pardon me if I indulge in a simple parable? A man was told that mountains could be seen upon the moon. He looked, but failed to see them. With naked vision he saw the wonder, the glory, and felt the inspiration of that peerless Queen of Night, but her greater wonder, the wonder of which he was told, was hidden. He purchased a telescope, and with this help sought to see the lunar ranges. He failed again.

He was about to decide that the whole thing was a fable when he discovered that the eye-piece shutter had fallen. He lifted the shutter and there, exposed to his delighted eye, were the ranges he sought.

You are an enigma my friend, that seems to baffle solution. You are a better Christian than most of us who make a profession of it, but you persist in keeping the eye-piece shutter down. What would you be, what could you be if you would but lift that eye-piece shutter!

You find God in the virtues of your fellows, yet you lose Him in a vague impersonality. God is real, my friend, more real than the kiss of a child and the love of a mother. He is the greatest reality in life.

With my best wishes,
George E Hobbs

Swindon Pays Tribute to the Late Mr Reuben George
All Phases of Public Life Represented at Funeral: Bareheaded Crowds in Streets

(First published in *North Wilts Herald*, June 12, 1936, writer uncredited)

Idealist, democrat, champion of the under-dog yet, at the same time friend of peers and foremost men of the day, Ald Reuben George, outstanding figure of the century in the public life of Swindon, died last Thursday night.

He died in the Victoria Hospital, Swindon, just before midnight, after a gallant fight against the ravages of a malignant disease. He underwent an operation on 26 May, the day following his admission to the hospital, but it gave him only temporary relief.

For some days past his condition had given cause for anxiety, and it was known that the end was near. Since the previous Tuesday he had been in a state of coma, and his son, Mr SS George, was with him when the end came.

Mr George was in his 72nd year. In many respects Mr Reuben George was a remarkable man. To say that he lived 100 years before his time is not such an exaggeration as it may sound. Perhaps he realised it himself, for his every action, thought, and word was directed to the future. He was an idealist of a type who sees Utopia ahead, and strives to realise it, refusing to recognise how forlorn is the hope of success.

With his idealism was bound up a craving for true democracy. Snobbery, of any description he heartily loathed, for he was probably the democrat of all democrats; he was just "Reuben" to dustman and duke alike, the champion of the underdog, and yet the personal friend of peers.

Champion of Socialism

Before Socialist politics had properly gained an organised footing, he was propagating Socialism from all manner of platforms. He was one of the first Socialist members of the Wilts County Council, and there he was for many years a lone hand – his company, as a Socialist, almost resented. But though his views very seldom obtained support, he slowly commanded respect. Eventually one and all were ready to give a fair hearing to this member who was the friend of all, for, though perhaps his views were sometimes incapable of attainment, there was always a commendable object behind them.

Sometimes, even he failed to see eye-to-eye with those holding Socialist views. But Reuben was unswerving; he had marked his course on the chart of his life, and neither coercion, argument, nor appeal, would tempt him to falter or waver from that course.

Claims of the Children

On the County Council his membership went back to pre-war days. He served on many committees, and throughout its existence, the Council has never had a more regular attendant at its committee meetings, nor a more active one.

On this authority as on all the others of which he held membership, Reuben's efforts were always directed towards bettering the lot of the underdog. The roadmen and other lower-paid employees of the Wiltshire County Council have much to thank him for; the teachers never had a complaint but what their point of view was supported by him, and the schoolchildren were ever in his thoughts, for he realised the truth of the old adage that "all work and no play makes Jack a dull boy". On every occasion when a special holiday might be granted, Reuben came forward to back the claims of the children.

He was in every sense a reformer; he always looked for the bright side of things, and always saw it, but his vision went far beyond things superficial. He saw the drab interior, and the black spots that did not meet the common gaze.

Then, while not disregarding the good things, he would strive his utmost to remove the bad things.

For a long time he had been an Alderman of the County Council and he was primarily responsible for the movement on that authority that ended with the provision of travelling expenses for County Council members – for he must have spent scores of pounds on fares to and from Trowbridge.

The Primary Factor

In the search for the betterment of the lot of all classes of society, and notably for the "lower orders", Reuben George long ago realised that education was the primary factor. In his idea, no money spent under the head of education, however, and whenever spent, was wasted.

On the General Education Committee of the Wilts County Council he was always one of its keenest members, and through him many, perhaps minor, reforms in the school curriculum, and the general educational system, were brought about.

Occasionally he would advance a scheme which met with no support; he always got a hearing, but frequently there would be no seconder to his proposition. Reuben was courageous, and never gave up hope, for there are many instances where he was persisted from time to time in raising the same matter, and at length, though it might not be till years after he has carried his point.

His ability and interest in education have long been recognised in Swindon where, for many years, he has been a member of the local Education Committee.

In view of his prominent connection with everything Wiltshire, it seems strange that Reuben was not a native of the county. He was born at Gloucester and spent his early youth there. He was never ashamed of the fact that at one period in his early life he sold papers on the streets. Later he was employed at the Wagon Works at Gloucester, and came to Swindon while in his later teens. Here he became an agent for the Wesleyan and General Insurance Company, with whom he remained for a long period, retiring when holding the position of Superintendent when he was a little more than 60 years of age.

Reading and Study

Reuben practised what he preached. Realising that education was to play such an important part in the improvement of the lot of the classes, he set himself to obtain the best education possible – by the expedient of self-education.

He succeeded to a remarkable degree, for there was scarcely a subject on which Reuben could not converse fluently and freely.

Much of his knowledge was gained by reading and study, for he was an assiduous reader, with plenty of material ready at hand. His collection of books has probably no peer in Wiltshire. In his "den" at his home in Goddard-avenue, Swindon, is one room devoted to the purpose of a library. There is accommodation for roughly a couple of chairs, and every scrap of available space in the room is literally crammed with books.

Ald Reuben George

If Mr George had been asked to name his hobbies, he would probably have been unable to define them. Yet, broadly speaking, his hobbies could closely be identified with his principles and beliefs. Primarily, the Workers' Educational Association held his life's interest.

He was one of the pioneers of the movement, and for many years was responsible for the spark of vitality in the Swindon branch.

He was one of the few living authorities on Wiltshire, on its rural life, and on its dialect. He knew practically every inch of this county, in its urban and rural areas, and offhand could relate incidents of local history applying to almost any town or village in the county.

Much of this knowledge was gained through assiduous reading, and a good deal more by actually visiting the places, while no small amount was gained in the course of rambles with the WEA, which he founded, and by taking part in the meetings and outings of the Wiltshire Archaeological Society, of which he had long been a member.

Leisure was a word that was constantly on his tongue. He wanted the working classes to have more leisure, and, more important still, to know how profitably to employ that leisure.

It was seldom he talked of his boyhood, except to say that as a lad he was the worst boy in his class. While other boys patiently worked out the difficult sums that the schoolmaster set them, Reuben's thoughts were drifting out to the countryside. It was not unknown for him to play truant. Sometimes he led a blind man out for a walk, and other times he sold papers, not because his parents were poor, however, for they would have stopped him if they could. It was perhaps in realisation of what his inattention at school had cost him that he sought always to make education more palatable to the children, and endeavoured also to educate himself by intensive reading and study.

Christian Idealist

Dreamer and visionary, his philosophy of life was born from reading Ruskin, Bellamy, William Morris, and others, whose works were contained among the 3,000-odd books that composed his own library. And thus was founded his firm belief that the future lies in an educated democracy.

His place in organised religion was with the Wesleyans, for whom he was an enthusiastic member for years. But latterly he had occasionally worshipped with the Quakers. Yet, his Christianity, which was based on kindness and consideration to his fellow creatures, was probably nearer the ideal than that laid down in orthodox creeds.

He was, of course, a pacifist, and opponent of militarism in any form, and to him, the Boer War revealed that the churches were on the side of the big battalions, and thus he refused to accept their doctrines. Though at times it might seem paradoxical, he was the friend of bishops, deans, archdeacons, and all manner of ecclesiastical dignitaries.

Among his personal friends were some of the foremost brains in the country – scientists, writers, professors and thinkers of all types – for the character and name of Reuben George were known and appreciated in a circle far wider than that of the town in which he lived. Evidence of this was to be found in the letter, which he received shortly after he had gone into hospital, from the Archbishop of York.

An Election Fight

Though there were aspects of politics that he never liked, he once stood as Parliamentary candidate. It was a forlorn hope, and he only entered the field a fortnight before polling day. This was at Chippenham in 1918, and Mr George stood as Labour candidate. He was the first candidate of this colour in the town, but, to use his own words he was "The proudest candidate in England".

He opened his campaign with an empty pocket, a bicycle and a bell! But Reuben had fighting spirit and personality – his attributes to compensate for lack of funds, and, within a very short time Lady Gladstone, the Archbishop of York, Lord Sanderson, Professor Zimmern, and three lady friends each contributed £25, thus providing his deposit.

The division was a large one, and during the first week he cycled hundreds of miles to address constituents in various remote parts. Twice he was lost in the country, but the next week he secured a wagonette, and finished up with a motor-cycle.

He saved his deposit by a few hundred votes, repaid the money advanced, and finished up with £10 in hand! Since that date two Labour candidates at Chippenham have forfeited their deposits.

He had been a member of the Swindon Town Council since its incorporation as a borough council, served at least two periods as an Alderman, and became Mayor of Swindon in the year 1921-22.

Mr George's broad humanity, and stout adherence to his convictions made his mayoralty quite unlike anybody else's. He declined to sit as a magistrate – a position that is always given to the chief citizen of the town – because he believed that man should not judge the creatures of God. It was his boast that he was not invited to open as many bazaars or lay so many foundation stones as some of his predecessors, but he was always to the fore when the welfare of children was concerned.

During his mayoralty he first assumed, at Christmas 1921, the mantle of Father Christmas and toured all the schools in the town, bringing joy and gladness to hundreds of children. Of course, there were those who contended that the sight of the Mayor of Swindon, in scarlet cloak and hood, and with a false beard "lowered the dignity of the chain", but he started a practice that remained unbroken until 1934, when ill-health prevented him from going his usual rounds.

His views on organised religion were prominent, for he was the only Mayor who did not attend a civic service at the Parish Church the Sunday following his institution. Instead he organised a great meeting at the Baths Hall, at which an address was given by Archdeacon Talbot.

Before the Microphone

Reuben George suffered from no high-flown ideas of dignity. While he was Mayor, he inaugurated the new diving stage at Coate, and by way of celebration, plunged from it into the water – no mean feat for a man of 56. Then, only a few weeks ago, he made his first debut before the microphone, in a broadcast from West Regional on a Wiltshire topic. On this occasion, he sang a couple of folk songs – probably the first time he had rendered a solo in public.

Besides Mrs George, who was his firm companion in all his rambles, and WEA activities, Mr George leaves two sons. A third son died while on military service in India; one of the surviving sons is an architect in Manchester, and the other is Mr SS George, of "Glendowan", Avenue Road, Swindon.

Another two months, and Mr George would have completed 30 years with the Swindon WEA. At the last meeting of the winter session he was present, and, referring to his illness which would prevent him from accompanying the members on the summer rambles, begged them to carry on their summer activities as enthusiastically in his absence as they would have done under his leadership.

Broadcast Tribute

The news of the passing of Ald Reuben George was broadcast to the nation in the second news bulletin of the National programme on Friday night.

"Mr George," said the announcer, "rose from a humble origin to a unique position of respect and affection in Swindon, where he will be remembered for 40 years' unremitting public service. He was Mayor of Swindon in 1922, and was one of the Aldermen of the Wiltshire County Council for many years.

"He will chiefly be remembered for his invaluable work in adult education, especially as one of the pioneers of the Workers' Educational Association.

"The weekly summer lectures and rambles which he organised on behalf of the WEA have been a feature of the life of Swindon for the past quarter of a century.

"Few men could have done more than he to bring pleasure into the lives of the working classes of a large industrial town. The nobility of his mind and the simplicity of his character endeared him to all his associates, whatever their walk in life, and his passing will be mourned, particularly by all who knew him in Swindon."

Thirty Years Ago

Mr WP Bullock, of Waddesdon, Aylesbury, Bucks, sends us a copy of a little booklet, entitled "Reuben and I," written 30 years ago by the late Mr William Davidson. Here are a few extracts which, we think, sum up admirably the man, his character and aspirations:

"I always consider he (Reuben) is at his best and the nearest to himself when he is among the green fields or by the still waters, or careering on wheels over dusty roads, or through a leafy country lane, shouting, as he only can shout, about the birds and the beasts, ejaculating philosophic remarks about anything that for the moment absorbs his attention in nature or nature's panorama, reciting poetry of a sentimental character, like Cowper's *Mother's picture* or Burns' *Man was made to mourn*, or in the fullness of his soul bursting forth into a joyous song, loud and lusty, in a voice that would have never made a fortune for a Patti or a Melba.

"Is it any wonder that Reuben, with his love for the fresh air and the green grass, should have taken our recreation grounds under his particular care and made them peculiarly his own? His heart is in that part of municipal life, and I question if it will ever be known to what extent the Swindon public, who are justly proud of their splendid parks, are indebted to Reuben for the amount of time and care and labour he has expended on that part of his municipal career.

"The country always suggests to Reuben the stern necessity of the Government bringing the thousands of unemployed men and the thousands of unemployed acres together. The betterment of his fellow human beings is a passion with him; his great big heart is full to overflowing with love for the human derelict and the submerged. Gain for himself has no place in his thoughts; he is above that and beyond it. First, for the poor, second for his friend, and last for himself.

"Reuben may not be orthodox, the promises of 1,900 years ago may be to him very low and far away, and the stern realities with all their cruelties and injustice may be to him very loud and near at hand, but, if I read my Bible rightly, of this one thing I am sure and certain: That if Reuben holds firmly to that faith, if he continues to be guided by the Divine light of love for his fellows, then when he goes to that undiscovered country from 'whose bourne no traveller returns', he will hear coming from the thick mists of the other side the voice of Him who when on earth went about doing good, saying 'Well done! As ye did it unto one of the least of these, ye did it unto me.'"

Impressive Funeral [extract]
Mayor and Corporation Among the Mourners
(First published in *North Wilts Herald*, June 12, 1936, writer uncredited)

Long before the time appointed for the funeral service in the Swindon Parish Church on Wednesday, hundreds were waiting for admission and crowds stood bareheaded as the cortège passed through the town. Everything was at a standstill. The sadness of the occasion was relieved just a little by the mass of beautiful flowers. On the coffin were four family wreaths, including a touchingly-inscribed wreath from his baby grandson, Alan.

The cortège was met at the church by the Rt Rev the Lord Bishop of Bristol, who conducted the service, the Vicar of Swindon, the Rev J Gilbert, MA, and Dr A Mansbridge, MA, who delivered an oration.

Against the wish of medical advisors, the widow attended the service, although she was unwell. It was only on condition that a doctor accompanied her and that she went to the hospital immediately after that she was permitted to attend.

The Mayor and Corporation attended the service in a body, and next came representatives of public bodies, social organisations, and then friends and associates from notable and titled country people to ordinary men and women whose names meant nothing, but whose love and affection for Reuben were equally sincere.

The hymns sung were "Praise My Soul" and "Abide with Me", and Dr Mansbridge gave his address before the final hymn.

Every seat in the church was filled and heads were bowed as the sorrowing widow, supported by her sons, followed the coffin up the aisle. The organist, Mr AV May, played "O Rest in the Lord" as the mourners took their seats and the Dead March from Saul at the conclusion of the service.

"His Name Liveth"

Dr Mansbridge spoke from the pulpit. He was greatly overcome as he trembled with emotion, and when he had finished, men as well as women were sobbing audibly, and there were very few dry eyes among the congregation.

He began with the quotation: "For though a man be never so perfect among the children of men, yet if Thy wisdom be not with him, he shall be nothing regarded. If Thou seest a man of understanding get Thee betimes unto him and let Thy foot wear the steps of his door. Behold, I have laboured not for myself only, but for all them that seek wisdom."

Dr Mansbridge went on: "In sorrow we, who knew and loved Reuben George, take our leave of him, comforting and cheering his stricken wife and children as we do so. Our sorrow is shot through with joy and transfigured with triumph... His works do follow him. We may bury his body in peace, but his name liveth for evermore.

"His seed shall constantly remain a good inheritance. Reuben was a passionate lover of his fellow men. He was incapable of making distinctions between them, whether labourer, employer, professor, Bishop or Lord. They might oppose him, they might hinder him, they might live in ways foreign to him, but in the light of that brotherhood which shone in his clear and unafraid eyes, he saw straight through to a reality in which all are members one of another. He was an intense lover of beauty.

Poet and Prophet

"He was imbued with a deep sense of the meaning of history which distinguished him among the men, even the scholars, of his time. The hey days of his delight were when, week by week for over 30 years, accompanied by some great interpreter, he led the men, women and children of Swindon out to historic or notable places. Amid beautiful surroundings he rejoiced with them in fellowship, and crowned the happy days with worship in the House of God.

"Reuben was both poet and prophet. He sang with all his power the song of manhood. His song cheered men mightily for as he sang he strove to banish ugly and vicious forces from the pathways of life. With beloved books in his pocket he sallied forth, day by day, joyously, to battle with forces which tended to sap the health, strength and power of the children of his time and place. He fought for all children everywhere.

> "Often baffled, he never gave up.
> He fell but to rise – a happy warrior.
> Who through the heat of conflict keeps the law,
> In calmness made and sees what he foresaw."

"The tale of his public service is long – Councillor, Alderman, Mayor. He was the good citizen. Education, which he served in the WEA and on the Councils of Wiltshire and Swindon, was to him a power, refreshing and strengthening the minds and spirits of men, destined to work in and through all, even as sap rises in growing trees.

"The chair he loved to sit in stands empty in the room lined, even crowded, with books, where Reuben gave his overflowing sympathy, his kindly advice, and all the help he could, to those very many who 'wore the steps of his door', whether young or old, rich or poor, learned or unlearned.

"In Swindon streets his cheery greetings to all and sundry will be but cherished memories. His face, which 'in ripe age was as the bright light upon the Holy candlestick', will never more look in love at the little children as they pass him or playfully greet him, but it may well be that beholding the face of his Father in Heaven, he will continue in full power to serve and protect them in all their ways.

"Citizen of Swindon – these years that are past.

"Citizen of the Holy City – throughout timeless Eternity.

Rest to His Soul

"Reuben, who laboured to increase light and learning, who strove to banish sadness and oppression, who wept with them that weep, and rejoiced with them that rejoice, now finds rest to his soul. His tired spirit recreated, moving within the light of God, knowing even as he is known, will rejoice for evermore, his gentle and loving heart comforted in that Holy place, for he will ever be where God has wiped away all tears from their eyes, where there is no more death, neither sorrow nor crying, neither shall there be any more pain; for the former things are passed away."

At the conclusion of the address every voice was raised in the singing of the impressive hymn "Abide with me", and the congregation left the church as the last notes of the "Dead March" from Saul died away.

At the Cemetery

Slowly the long procession – at times a quarter of a mile in length – wended its way to the Radnor-street cemetery. All along the route the streets were lined with people of all classes, rich and poor, workmen who had sacrificed part of their lunch hour to pay a last tribute, sobbing women, and business people who had closed their shops. Everywhere blinds were drawn.

It was the greatest public demonstration of spontaneous affection for a public figure that the town of Swindon has seen for very many years.

In the cemetery, where the Bishop read the committal service, there seemed to be thousands of mourning townspeople. From every vantage point they watched the concluding portion of the service and saw the earthly remains of Reuben lowered into an evergreen-lined grave, in which were small bunches of irises. Many people sobbed and broke down. Reuben George, having served his generation faithfully, had entered into rest.

Members of the family, the Mayor, and members of the Corporation and then the rest of the public, filed past the coffin, on which reposed a tiny bunch of buttercups and daisies with the poignant inscription, "From baby Alan to Grandpa."

In Remembrance
By George E Hobbs
(First published: June 12, 1936)

Other pens, more able than mine, will record the life-work of one who for many years was prominent in the varied life of our town and county. But while other pens will more adequately describe that work, none will record more sincerity in the sorrow of his passing than mine.

Everyone in Swindon knew Reuben. Some knew of him; some knew about him; some knew him. Those who knew him best will best write of him.

Reuben was known to more than a mere local public. His activities with and for the WEA took him far afield, and many new friends came to him through that organisation. Also through the columns of "The Swindon Advertiser" he was known in America, in India, in Australia and in New Zealand.

It has been said that Reuben hadn't an enemy in the world. This I believe to be true. There were, however, many who misunderstood him. It was said he was unstable and vacillating. He was anything but that. He was of that type of individual who was ever on the alert to discover the highest expression of truth and justice, and beauty, and to find the best and most effective avenue through which these qualities revealed themselves.

* * *

He loved the beauty and inspiration of "Jesu, lover of my soul", but he found little help or inspiration in organised religion. He was honest enough to say so, and was prepared to shoulder the criticism entailed. He may have changed from one religious denomination to another, and from one political creed to another – not because he was unstable, but because what he found did not satisfy his craving for truth, and right, and beauty. He probably found an element of what he craved in each. But in all things he was true to his great ideal. If he found dissatisfaction in that which he tried, he left and sought it elsewhere.

It is not difficult to understand why, during his Mayoral year, he refused to take his place upon the judicial bench. Such a gesture was not a pose, but the expression of his deep-seated conviction. Was he not weak? Was he not liable to fall? Then how could he sit in judgement on those who did fall?!

I think he agreed that some sort of penal code should obtain, but as far as he personally was concerned, he felt himself unwilling to sit in judgement. To himself he wished to be true, and to himself he was true, irrespective of applause or criticism.

※ ※ ※

Through the columns of "The Swindon Advertiser" he revealed that peculiar genius for which he was known and loved. From the treasury of his wonderful and extensive library, he was able to cull the best of the world's thought and pass it on to his readers. His phrasing was simple and effective. What he wrote could be understood. Who but Reuben could write this:

> "I feel entranced as I hear the bells, and I travel on, my mind fixed on the picture of Bethlehem. I abandon myself to the spirit, and let my thoughts go to Him, and His great life. My faith is not that of the orthodox Christian, but the picture is mine and the ideal one I would like to live up to. They called his name Jesus – the Christ of the workingman."
> ("Swindon Advertiser," 20 December 1935)

Or this:

> "We pride ourselves on our sham culture and grammar and the beautiful modulation – so very essential, we say. The ploughman asks for nonsuch. He eats hearty, sleeps well and, above all, can count himself as one of the most honest and necessary workers in supplying the world's needs. He has no need to apologise; others should apologise to him. He is a producer, a carrier, a lifter and not a learner; a worker and not a parasite."
> ("Swindon Advertiser," 17 January 1936)

No, friend Reuben; you may not have been an orthodox Christian, but you exemplified His spirit more than some of us who call ourselves by His name. Your great heart was touched by His love and life, and oftentimes you must have heard His voice saying "You have found Me in your service to others."

I think no greater tribute could be paid to him – the children loved him. He was a friend to all children and he loved them. He was happy in his role of "Father Christmas", and he saw no loss of dignity in robing himself in the gown of "Santa".

※ ※ ※

The "Poor Kiddies' Outing Fund" was dear to his heart, and he laboured long and well for their day at the seaside.

In his last illness the children waited for news of him. "Was he better?" "Was he better?" And when the end came, the children in the schools were told – and they sorrowed for their friend.

In a letter sent to the Editor of "The Evening Advertiser", Dr Cornelius subscribed a personal tribute which I think may be termed a beautiful epitaph. He wrote: "In four years of close contact with him, I never heard a word from him that was unkind or ungenerous. Charity filled his heart and expressed itself in all his actions."

And now his big, generous heart is stilled forever. But the awful majesty of death cannot stay the continuance of his influence. He has not lived in vain, for in all things essential he knew he was his brother's keeper. He set his life for the betterment of his brother man.

He loved life and all that was beautiful in life. In the "life more expansive" he will find a more glorious beauty – a beauty and calm undreamed-of by him. Oft and again has he given us word pictures of the things that touched him most deeply: the rolling downs; the countryside in its spring and autumnal glories; the little wayside church with its charm and tranquillity; the beauty of the poet's touch and the artist's. All these things he loved and venerated. And now the shadows have gathered him in. But beyond the shadows will be found light.

> Sunset and evening star,
> And one clear call for me!
> And may there be no moaning of the bar,
> When I put out to sea.
>
> But such a tide as moving seems asleep,
> Too full for sound and foam,
> When that which drew from out the boundless deep
> Turns again home.
>
> Twilight and evening bell,
> And after that the dark!
> And may there be no sadness of farewell
> When I embark;
>
> For though from out our bourne of Time and Place
> The flood may bear me far,
> I hope to see my Pilot face to face
> When I have crossed the bar.

Readers of "The Swindon Advertiser" bid you "Goodnight", friend Reuben. We shall meet again in the morning.

The Late Mrs Reuben George
(letter to the *Swindon Advertiser*)
(First published: June 26, 1936)

Sir – How often do we associate death with the idea of inexorable cruelty? Yet how true it is that sometimes death is kindly and compassionate. I could not help but feel the truth of the latter when I read of the death of Mrs George.

I saw her at the graveside of the one she loved so much, and my heart went out to her in sympathy and pity. But all unseen by those who watched, a kindly face smiled down; a kindly voice whispered a message of love – "Only a few more steps, only a few more steps."

A few short days and the morning broke for her even as it had broken for him. Death had divided them but for a moment. In its compassionate embrace, death has reunited them.

I send this letter through the "Forum" of the "Swindon Advertiser" as a tribute to the memory of a wife who inspired her husband in his life work for the uplift of his town.

Yours etc,
George E Hobbs

Gleanings [19]
By George E Hobbs
(First published: September 10, 1937)

This week it is my privilege to write of one who for many years laboured hard for the good of his fellow men – the late Ald Reuben George. He was an outstanding personality in the public life of our town, and there were very few but what knew him. He was loved by many, misunderstood by many, hated by none. He was one of those rare individuals who seemed never to have an enemy in the world.

Many overseas, through articles in "The Swindon Advertiser," knew him, though they had never seen him. The appeal of those articles, written in that style peculiarly his own and written so that all could understand, brought more than one tribute to Newspaper House from distant lands. It is therefore of the late Ald Reuben George that I write.

It is fitting I should write of him this week. Tomorrow, 11 September is the anniversary of his birth. The Workers' Educational Association – the association he had so much at heart, and to which he gave of his best – will journey to the city of Gloucester and visit the house in which he was born, 73 years ago. Afterwards, in the Guildhall, Dr Mansbridge MA, the founder of the WEA, will deliver an address. Tomorrow his memory will be honoured by a distinguished company from far and near.

* * *

Ald Reuben George's life was a triumph over severe handicap. Who would have recognised a future Alderman and Mayor of a large industrial town in the small-sized lad of eight selling "The Gloucester Citizen" in the streets of the city? Yet that lad was destined – I use the word advisedly – not only to be a future Town and County Councillor, but a power for good in the town and county of his choice. He became a man whose word was listened to with respect.

To the very end, he remained a man of the common people, yet among his friends were men of the highest intellect and worth. They knew him for what he was – honest, fearless, intellectually sound, and with a great love of the underdog.

* * *

Reuben was born on 11 September 1864, in the city of Gloucester. At eight years of age his day was very different from that of a lad of that age in 1937. Before breakfast his job was to clean and polish the boots. After breakfast he attended school from nine to twelve. In the afternoon he took charge of a blind man and conducted him in his walks. In the evening he was out upon the streets, selling papers. At 12 years of age his "education" was complete – he having mastered the curriculum of the Second Standard.

From 16 years of age until he was 23, he worked for his living in the Gloucester Wagon Works. In 1886, when he was 22 years of age, he married Clara Acton of Gloucester, and through all the subsequent years the married partnership proved ideal in its perfect understanding and comradeship. No man could have accomplished what Reuben accomplished had he had a wife unsympathetic to his aims and ideals. A good wife is indeed a treasure from heaven itself.

* * *

It was about this time that the young married man began to feel the urge of some indefinable impulse. Just as it was for so many in similar circumstances, a lack of education produced bewilderment and confusion. It caused him to flounder about in an endeavour to discover the direction the urge would lead him. Was it a political or religious urge? In either case he felt himself to be a misshapen vehicle of oral expression or of the written word. Certainly he felt he was not equipped for deep thinking or for clear reasoning.

The religious urge was encouraged by his old class leader, Mr Colwell of Ryecroft Wesleyan Church. The political urge was fruiting from seeds sown by his father, a staunch unbending Liberal of the old school. It was the political rather than the religious atmosphere he had breathed in at home.

It is rather interesting to note that Reuben's grandfather (known as "Pipey George") and two of his grand-uncles were engaged in the sale of clay pipes in the city of Gloucester. When eventually the French briar displaced the clay, they continued business as retailers of the briar pipes. One of the grand-uncles, tiring of this business, went to Bristol and founded the famous firm known as the George's Bristol Brewery. Reuben remained a total abstainer throughout his life.

* * *

In process of time Reuben left Gloucester and took up insurance work at Hereford. In 1891 he came to Swindon in a similar capacity, and eventually he rose to the position of Superintendent. Meanwhile he had read extensively and studied hard in order to take up his life's work – the betterment of conditions for the worker. For this purpose he sought to become a member of a public body, and succeeded in being elected to the New Swindon Urban District Council. When incorporation came about he was elected on the Town Council.

In 1919, he became a member of the County Council, and at one period he was an Alderman of the Swindon Town Council and of the County Council at the same time. In 1918 he fought the Chippenham Division in the Labour interest. It seemed a hopeless proposition and he was laughed at for his temerity in attempting such a task. He never succeeded in becoming a member of Parliament, but he saved his deposit by a few hundred votes. Two subsequent Labour fighters in the Division lost their deposits.

In 1921 Reuben became Mayor of Swindon and his year of office was characterised by one peculiarity. The Mayor of a borough has a seat upon the Bench, but Reuben refused to accept such a position. It was not that he wished to assume an eccentric pose, but because he felt deep down in his heart that he had no right to sit in judgement upon his fellow men. And where Reuben believed himself to be right, he gave way to no man or to any conditions.

∗ ∗ ∗

I think it is true to say that Reuben's bent was politics in general and social reform in particular, rather than adherence to any religious creed or church. He often called himself an atheist but this was a pose rather than a fact. He certainly broke away from organised religion, but at no time was he irreligious. He was opposed to force in any guise, and when the churches gave their consent to war in the struggle between Briton and Boer, he cut adrift from the Wesleyan Church and gave his allegiance to the friends of peace – the Quakers.

That he was a "Freethinker" is true, but not in the sense that the stupid religious isolationists of a decade ago interpreted the term. He believed intensely that man should be free to use the greatest gift he possessed – his intellect.

If he had a religion, then it was that of freedom. His was a religion of free speech, a free press, and untrammelled expressions of religious freedom.

It was this great heart-throbbing for freedom which breathed through all his activities. His articles in "The Swindon Advertiser" were permeated with such ideals – freedom, liberty, the soul's self-expression. Perhaps it was because he carried this to excess that he was so frequently misunderstood. His doctrine of freedom was interpreted as licence, and his doctrine of leisure was interpreted as supreme laziness. Yet in all things he was true to the ideal before his vision, and worried but little about the criticisms levelled at him.

∗ ∗ ∗

He was sincere in his love for his fellow men – especially those who found life difficult. I remember on one occasion we debated before an audience the problem of Foreign versus Home Missions. I took the foreign and Reuben the home aspect. His plea for the unfortunates in England, for a more sympathetic understanding of their needs, their hopes and aspirations, better housing, more leisure, etc, was something worth listening to. His very soul was in his theme. It was not book knowledge he gave to the audience, but life's tragedy as he had encountered it.

He was essentially a fighter. He was happiest when championing an unpopular cause. There were times when he plunged into the fray, not because he believed heart and soul in the particular cause at issue, but because he believed in the free right of a free people.

It was to him not so much the details of a cause, but the principle of individual self-expression. The individual should be free above all things. Often misunderstood, often misrepresented – generally he got a hearing. His sheer personality compelled attention. His sincerity was admitted even by those who misunderstood him.

And now my allotted space is gone. There was so much more one would have wished to have written about this remarkable man. This brief sketch does not bring to the reader an unknown personality. It is [a] true record of a man every Swindonian knew.

If we can but give ourselves to service as he did, then like him, we shall hear the "Well done, good and faithful servant! Enter thou into the joy of the Lord."

Chapter 8

Freedom, Liberty and Aspects of Britishness

He took the sword at duty's call,
In freedom's cause he fought and died:
For Britain's sake he yielded all -
E'en life itself he ne'er denied.
From the poem In Memory of 2nd Lt WGC Gladstone
by George Ewart Hobbs (April 23, 1915)

If I see order and beauty and meaning in the expression of human life,
then I want to believe that every human life has the inalienable
right to express itself in unfettered freedom.
From Personal Freedom [3] by
George Ewart Hobbs (February 22, 1935)

For almost the whole of George's life, London had been the capital of the world's only, true military and economic superpower, and when he died, towards the end of 1946, profound change, as we now know, was just around the corner, with the decline of empire and the relegation of the United Kingdom to the status of 'former imperial heavy-hitter steadfastly punching above its weight'.

Like many of his fellow citizens, he would have been forgiven for thinking that the United Kingdom could do no wrong; after all, how could you possibly find fault with a country which had produced Magna Carta, Habeas Corpus, the Bill of Rights 1689, the rule of law, Common Law, parliamentary democracy and constitutional monarchy, let alone William Shakespeare, the abolition of slavery, the Tolpuddle Martyrs, the Industrial Revolution, the jet engine, and the British sense of fair play – exemplified in the game of cricket?

Despite all the checks and balances designed to rein in the power of the state and promote the rights of the individual, adverse criticism of your motherland and its government's policy in the colonies was unlikely to be well received – an act of disloyalty keenly felt by those families who had lost loved ones in the Great War. And it is perhaps significant that you won't find anything like this in the columns penned by George either, although having said that, he was critical of foreign policy when it came to the rise of fascism and the advent of war in Europe in the 1930s; the times they were a-changing, but even radicals like George found it hard to jettison the Empire that easily.

Interestingly, a number of individuals, other than Biblical characters, have been referenced by him in standalone articles over the years. Apart from his ongoing fascination with Charles Bradlaugh, the list includes British heroines, Grace Darling, Florence Nightingale and Boadicea, and Christian missionaries Mary Slessor and Dr David Livingstone, alongside more traditional 'Boy's Own Paper'-type figures, such as Lord Kitchener, Captain Scott and Major-General Sir Henry Havelock.

To the average British working man and woman, the British Empire was an overwhelming force for good, bringing civilisation, culture, prosperity, the Christian message and the Protestant work ethic to all four corners of the globe.

Even George had become swept up in its majesty. You only have to read through some of his Great War poetry to appreciate how he perceived Britain to be on the side of good – ie, doing God's work – in the fight against the evil of Imperial Germany. Although by 1936, in his summary of the life of Major-General Sir Henry Havelock KCB, he wrote:

> It is possible for a soldier or sailor, or anyone in the fighting services to be a Christian, and indeed many of them are. To these men, fighting for their country may be as much an article of their belief and faith as pacifism is mine... While it seems not inconsistent with a certain method of reasoning that God does aid physical force in a righteous cause, there is a difficulty in understanding Havelock's idea of prayer. In a letter to his wife, this remarkable passage occurs: "One of the prayers oft repeated throughout my life has been answered, and I have lived to command in a successful action." To pray for help in the fight is one thing. To pray that you may fight is altogether a different matter.

But George is anxious to place a caveat on his expression of patriotism. Although he agrees with Dean William Inge that it is 'an emotion which is the purest and noblest of which the ordinary man is capable', he goes on to confirm that this is on condition that 'the expression of that patriotism does not mean insularity, aloofness or a mistaken belief that Britishers are the chosen people of Jehovah'.

However, one man's freedom is often stated to be another man's prison. You hear little if anything of the plight of the indigenous peoples subjugated and persecuted in furtherance of the aims of the British Empire. Indeed, in the piece relating to the life of Havelock and the Indian Mutiny, we hear only of the glory of the victory at Cawnpore and the relief of Lucknow, but only of the barbarity of Nara Sahib.

And this comment, in relation to Lord Kitchener, is also quite telling – when he was recalled from Egypt in 1914 to become War Minister in Asquith's government: 'A European War was altogether a different proposition to that of the subjection of native hordes.'

Many would also regard the dispatch of Christian missionaries to Africa as simply another cynical arm of British colonial expansion during the 19th century. And as distressing as it sounds today, George wasn't averse to using words that would be wholly unacceptable today when writing about the recipients of missionary and charitable relief overseas.

The following is an extract from the Story of Sunday Sport, a piece written by George, which appeared in the *Advertiser* on July 21, 1922:

> Up to the – of August 1923, Johnny Bilson had caused his parents no anxiety whatever. He was a fine, manly lad of 14, clean of limb and of mind. A splendid athlete, he led his school in swimming, football and cricket; while in general knowledge his master was often heard to declare that he was the best boy he had ever handled.
>
> He was thoughtful above the average, and had a distinct bias towards the deeper things of life. His thoughts in this direction began when, as a lad in his eleventh year, he attended a foreign missionary meeting.
>
> The "deputation" gave a vivid description of the lives and customs of the heathen and, his heart warming within him, Johnny registered a vow that he would fit himself for missionary work.
>
> Two years later when he was 13 years of age, he accompanied his father to a "Home Mission" meeting, where a mission worker gave a synopsis of his work in the slums of Manchester and London. Individual cases were cited which proved to Johnny's thoughtful mind that the acts of civilised Christians could be worse than the acts of the savage.

> This revelation had two effects upon him. One was of distinct nausea to think that white men and women could so act. And then surging through his mind came a deep conviction that his life's work must not be to the heathen, but to the unhappy and sad of his own land.

But please don't get the idea that George acquiesced on the subject of slavery – despite his questionable choice of language. The next extract is from *A Nature Note*, written by George in 1923:

> Sandwiched in between the many good traits found in ant society, there is one trait that is exceedingly bad. In the human order we should term such as anti-social, because it hinders social development, and therefore hurts society. Ants not only follow all the arts of warfare, but to this they have added the detestable institution of slavery.
>
> LeTourneau tells that two species of ant… have subjugated a negro species, "Formica Fusca" and enslaved them. "But," says LeTourneau, "whilst behaving like men, ants have never allowed themselves the abuses of force to which men are accustomed." In this Professor LeTourneau means that the raiding ants never enslave the adult negro ant. It is the pupæ they seize upon, carry them away, and bring them up as slaves.

However, there's no doubting that George was a fan of the Wild West, in particular the historical novels of Zane Grey. He quotes from the book The Spirit of the Border (first published in 1906), which features the fictional exploits of the real-life character Lewis Wetzel – a man dedicated to the 'destruction of Native Americans and to the protection of nascent, white settlements' in the area of the Ohio River Valley. The following extract, written by George in 1937, and containing passages which glorify the killing of native peoples, makes for uncomfortable reading today:

> I remember reading in one of Zane Grey's books of the implacable Wetzel – the sworn foe of all Redmen – how he felt in the evening twilight. It was evening, and he and his companion were resting after an exciting day in the woods. Wetzel made this comment: "I've scalped Redskins every hour of the day 'ceptin' twilight." Zane Grey comments upon this attitude of mind in this way: "That hour which wooed Wetzel from his implacable pursuit was indeed a bewitching one."

If there was one trait about George that might be considered unusual for the period and perhaps somewhat un-British, it was his dislike of convention. In one of his Gleanings series of articles, which appeared on June 4, 1937, he made the following comments:

> When the National Anthem is played or sung well, there is much to inspire one in its beautiful melody. The harmony is delightful, especially

when played sympathetically by a military band. As to the poetry, I'm afraid it leaves much to be desired. But apparently it is neither the melody nor the poetry which counts. It is rather the visible attitude by which it is received.

Human values and standards are the funniest things imaginable. One bows before a Crucifix – and one is devoutly religious. One passes the Crucifix without a gesture – and one is thoughtless and irreligious. Yet the second may be the more religious.

If I stand up and stand still while the National Anthem is played I am neither showing loyalty nor respect nor patriotism. I am simply bowing to convention. Convention decrees that I conform to a certain standard of conduct, and that standard is that I stand straight and still. If I do not then I contend I am not showing disloyalty or disrespect. All I do is that I refuse to bow to convention.

And he expands his thoughts on this theme, two weeks later:

What then do we mean [when] we use the term "Convention"?

An old dictionary defines it as "arbitrary custom", and the adjective "conventional" to mean "growing out of, or depending on custom". Also "sanctioned by usage". The "Twentieth Century" dictionary defines it as "established usage and fashion".

Convention becomes tyrannical – or slavish to the individual and community – when it refuses to leave the old (which may be good) for the new (which may be better). An adherence to something which has outgrown its utility in preference to something which is as yet untried, but which augurs a higher grasp of truth and usefulness, is to my mind foolish. It is this very factor which has been the stumbling block to every reform and to every mode of progress. It is this blind, unreasoning adherence to outworn conventions that has made possible such beings as "diehards" and "last ditchers" in politics, religion, education and the like.

Nothing can stop ultimate progress. Progress may be delayed, thwarted, and even retrogression may set in. But in process of time, retrogression will be arrested, turned and the lost ground recovered. And I say again that one of the greatest hindrances to progress is convention.

Some kind critic will say I am mixing up convention with prejudice, and that it is prejudice which hinders progress. I would simply say I cannot mix what are already parts of a whole. Convention and prejudice are inseparable companions.

While it would be the height of folly – rather, the height of imbecility – to defy convention for the sake of a cheap notoriety, yet it is true that every reform and every advancement in human knowledge and for human happiness has begun with the "un-conventionalists". Every political and every religious emancipation has so begun. It is not that one wishes to defy convention for the sake of defying, but rather that one appreciates the light ahead more clearly.

And in relation to the coronation of King George VI, he had the following to say (in Gleanings [3]):

> Taking a retrospect of Coronation Day, we may say that we gave way to our feelings because it was generally in the air. To us, possibly, it was just a day's holiday with fun, according to our mood and fancy. We viewed the decorations – elaborate and otherwise – and thought them all very beautiful. But now the "daily round and common task" is again our portion and, so far as we personally are concerned, that ends our stocktaking of the Coronation and its significance.
>
> But this cannot be mine. And here let me say that, while I cannot be of a demonstrative nature – that is, I cannot personally express my reactions to the great national spirit in flags and bunting – nevertheless I do feel tremendously in sympathy with that spirit.
>
> I am glad and proud to be a citizen of the British commonwealth. Even with all her manifest sins she is, to me, the most wonderful nation-empire in the world. Of Britain herself, I believe that deeply embedded in the materials of her foundation there is the desire to "do justly and love mercy".

Later in the same piece, he reflects upon the ceremony itself and the fact that the king had dedicated himself to the service of his country and countrymen:

> But that dedication leaves us – the citizens of King George's kingdom – no less involved. We are all the partakers of a great heritage – a heritage of freedom in politics, speech, press and religion that no other country enjoys. And the call to all of Britain's sons and daughters is the call to dedication – dedication of powers, of service, of intellect and of capacities.

In the same 'mini-series' of articles, the British constitution also comes up for scrutiny on May 28, 1937:

> The heritage into which our British people have come is one of priceless worth. It is a heritage into which no sinister hand must be permitted to enter. For while this treasure is not ours by civil war or revolution, it has not been won without supreme sacrifice, the blood of martyrs [or] the broken spirits of the pioneers who saw in their dreams a better age.
>
> In translating what they saw into action, they were crushed under the wheels of convention and custom. Blood, tears and untold anguish were all in the price paid for the freedom of the present British constitution. That freedom is far too precious to lose.

More insights into George's thoughts on freedom and liberty, as well as those attributes of British society that he cherished – all from the perspective of a middle-aged working man in 1930s – can be found in the following articles, starting with **Freedom** (February 24, 1933), in which George examines the concept of freedom of choice and its practical limitations as evidenced by the phrase we all utter in exasperation from time to time – "If only I had my way!"

Then follows a three-part series entitled **Personal Freedom**. Part one (February 8, 1935) finds George seeking a workable definition of the subject in hand, and exploring the Theory of Determinism – the philosophical view that all events are determined completely by previously existing causes – and then astrology. And finally the theory that all acts by man have been predetermined by a supernatural deity.

In the second part (February 15, 1935) he enters the 'nature versus nurture' debate, including some discussion on degeneracy and parents' overall fitness to bear children – matters which stray uncomfortably into what sounds like eugenics.

In the concluding piece (February 22, 1935), George continues to show his fascination with the emerging science of psychology, examining the extent to which children acquire a sense of responsibility – and thereby, become accountable for their actions or inactions.

This short series of articles certainly caught the ire of a reader who would only identify as "Believer". His/her opening letter, dated March 1, 1935 argues:

> Sir, – It is certainly revealing that a teacher, and I believe a preacher of a certain Christian church should write as Mr Hobbs has done on several occasions. I think perhaps we follow some of these modern teachers at our peril. St Paul says, "If any man preach any other Gospel to you that I have preached, let him be accursed."

and, later:

> Mr Hobbs questions the point of "personal freedom". Of course we are free to decide what we shall or shall not do.
>
> He has evidently turned down Christianity. By this I mean that he has adopted the Modernist standpoint. Modernists depart from the faith, but not from the outward profession of Christianity.
>
> Paul says, "Such are false teachers, deceitful workers transforming themselves into the Apostles of Christ, and no marvel, for Satan himself is transformed into an angel of light."

After this stinging rebuke, we reproduce George's response, which appeared in the *Swindon Advertiser* a week later – a fantastic letter in which he declares his attitude to faith and dogma – renouncing his belief in a literal interpretation of much of the Old Testament's contents.

And finally, we reproduce in full one of the **Gleanings** series (September 2, 1938). In this article, which is on the theme of freedom and liberty, George reveals that he was proud 'to be born a Britisher' and references the 'many, many sacrifices that were made over time in order to win the cherished freedoms that we still enjoy today'.

We also get to hear of the conference held in London in September 1938, by the World Union of Freethinkers – nicknamed "the Godless Congress" by Protestant and Catholic conservatives, who opposed its very premise and sought to have it banned from ever taking place. George, on the other hand, came to its defence as a matter of principle and conscience.

Freedom
By George E Hobbs
(First published: February 24, 1933)

Theologians tell us we are creatures endowed with this wonderful quality, "choice". This would appear to mean that man is free to choose what he wills to choose. Above the rest of mankind, Britishers seem especially to be endowed with [this] wonderful quality. Britishers are free – free as the air that blows, free to will, free to choose, and free to act.

Catching a glimpse of this moral and spiritual verity and being inspired thereby, one of England's poets enthused thus:

> Rule, Britannia! Britannia rules the waves!
> Britons never will be slaves!

Undoubtedly, Thomson believed that one "never" was sufficient to show what was in his mind – that Britons would enjoy all the ramifications of freedom for all time. He wisely thought that with the cessation of time, it would not disturb the rest of mankind what happened to Britons. We, however, think differently. We insert "never" three times, in order to show a threefold emphasis. Time may come and time may go, but Britons go on being free for ever.

In order to clinch the argument we may say with elegant finality, "And that's that!"

Unfortunately, that isn't that. Both theological argument and national sentiment take us from facts and beguile us with fiction. So contradictory are facts to argument and sentiment that, like the character in the old-time song, man (especially the Britisher), "dunno where 'e are".

What The Law Demands

For instance (and more to follow), the Stork does not go into the Dreamland

and ask prospective "free-willers" if it is their pleasure to visit this planet. Not so. He just bundles them down, willy-nilly, whether they wish to come or not. At times the Stork is not even considerate of those into whose charge the little "free-willers" will come. That is to say, he often brings the wrong sort. So that right from the first peep into this topsy-turvy world, the fiat seems against any suggestion of a free choice.

When the Stork has left for other shores, the "present" he has left behind must not be treated as was Moses. The majesty of the law demands that it must be registered, weighed, measured and classified. And the "must" of the law is but another name for lack of freedom.

The child, having been classified, reaches the age of five years. Even now, freedom has not come either to mother or child. It is possible the child has "willed" not to go to school, and if the child has not played "Old Harry" with the mother's nerves, it is possible that she too has "willed" the child not to go. But let the mother exercise her "free-will" and "free-choice" and she will find her will redirected, and her choice reconditioned by those who would have us sing, "Rule Britannia!"

How often do we hear the expression, "If I had my way", etc? The "if" is the answer proving "free-will" and "free-choice" to be non-existent.

Like One-Way Traffic

"The Stroller" and "Commentator" can no more bring their free-will and free-choice into effect than the rest of us. "The Stroller" has a large tome in which names are inscribed of those he would wish to shoot. "Commentator", like the writer, fell over a dustbin. "Commentator" went home and began a book for future killing. Both, however, will have to fall back upon the inane expression, "If only I had my way". What on earth is the good of a free-will if its expression – free-action – is not possible? Let us assume it is possible, and that both of my good friends balanced theory with practice. What would result? One fine morning they would both rise from their beds with freedom to dress without a collar. The gentleman at the lever end would exercise his free-will even if his free-choice was a little at variance to his will.

And yet with all these contradictions, Britishers ARE FREE! The country that "...at Heaven's command, Arose from out the azure main" has given to her sons and daughters freedom – freedom of will and freedom of choice. Granted, the freedom is like one-way traffic; still, one cannot have it both ways.

What More Is Wanted?

When one makes the journey to pay his or her income tax or rates, one is expressing one's heritage of freedom. Not merely is free-will and free-choice expressed, but something more. On many a gory field, with wonderful self-sacrifice, have our forefathers fought for this freedom to be their children's. And we have come into this heritage. Even should the authorities refuse our expression of free-will and free-choice and demand that we keep our dues, nobly would we rise to the occasion and stand upon our rights. We would, with one voice say, "We will not be oppressed by any Tom, Dick or Harry. We are free to pay, and we mean to pay." Such a determined front would be bound to win the day for freedom.

And if we are not in such a position as to be able to yield up our free-will offering, we are still free. No-one can make us take the dole if we "will" not. We can be hanged for murder, get six months for kissing the wrong girl, fined for having a fire at the top of the chimney instead of at the bottom, but no penalty is attached to the refusal to take the dole. What more freedom could one wish for?

There is but one place where a mere man is without free-will and free-choice. And that is…

Sorry, I've given my name at the top!

Personal Freedom [1]
By George E Hobbs
(First published: February 8, 1935)

The thoughtful adult lives but a few years before coming up against one of the subtlest problems known to intellectual research. It is the problem of personal freedom. Are men free to think, free to will, free to act?

The answers to such questions are not easy to tabulate. Pitfalls abound, as they must abound, in every problem where the pro and the con seem to cancel each other. On the surface every "Yea" can be met with a "Nay", and every "Nay" with a "Yea". It is only as one digs beneath the surface, and patiently analyses the strata of human constitution, as they impose and superimpose one upon the other, that one is able to suspect something of a working hypothesis.

So that we may clearly understand the point at issue, it will be best, first of all, to obtain a common agreement upon terms. What is meant by personal freedom?

I suggest that it means the unrestricted power to select for one's self what one believes to be the best for one's self.

So that there may be no misunderstanding, let me concede that this definition will have to be modified later. At the moment, however, the problem before the court is that of personal freedom – the unfettered thought, will and act processes of the individual.

The constitution of the human contribution in the scheme of things must ever remain an enigma. The emergence of mind out of a blind, unreasoned instinct is the most profound problem in the phenomena of creative development. "I am fearfully and wonderfully made," was the verdict of the Psalmist. I do not think an improvement upon this dictum could be made.

Valuable Data

The biologist and the physiologist have tabulated valuable data in the classification of organic beings, and in the specialised science of life structures and developments. To this mass of accumulated data, rising higher and higher in the scale of development, comes the activities of the psychologist. The comparatively new science of psychological research aims to explore the ultra-physical realm of human experience, as evidenced in the operations of the mind – thought, desire and will, leading on to the act, which is the culmination of thought through desire by the will.

I have introduced the biologist and the physiologist in the problem, and have used the term "ultra-physical", instead of "non-physical", for a purpose. The tendency – which I contend is fatal to a proper solution of the problem – is to separate *from*, rather than connect *with*, the physical and the psychical. Whatever opinions we hold, whether it be that the mind is an evolutionary development or – as some contend – a separate creative act of the Creator, we cannot deny the fact that the psychical functions through the physical.

We may place the realm of the mind, the soul, the spiritual, if you like, on a higher plane, but it cannot be separate from the vehicle of its expression – the physical. The brain is physical, the mind is psychical, and the mind functions through the brain. "No brain, no thought processes", is a dictum that none can deny. Therefore, we are to take man in the normal expression of his physical completeness, with a fully functioning brain, and ask again: Does normal man possess personal freedom in thought, will and act?

An Intriguing Question

It is quite natural to find that this question has intrigued the philosophic mind of man, and that schools of thought have pronounced upon it.

In one form or another the theory of determinism has been advanced as an answer. Such answer, of course, is definitely opposed to the theory of personal freedom. At its lowest level the theory is that the acts of men are pre-determined by conditions over which they have no control. Robert Blatchford, with the sledge-hammer method that characterised his writings and speeches, once wrote: "The actions of a man's will are as mathematically fixed at birth as are the motions of a planet in its orbit." Yet, when the great world war raged, Blatchford contributed a weekly article to a London periodical in which the full force of his powers were directed to laying the blame upon the Germans. In doing so Blatchford made the pro and the con cancel each other. If the acts of men are "as mathematically fixed at birth as are the motions of a planet", then there can be no blame fixed for subsequent actions. The Germans, as everyone else under such conditions, must be blameless. It is illogical to argue both ways.

Another form of the argument – the astrological – is not so drastic. Ultimate pre-determined fate is not suggested. It supposes that dispositions and characteristics are determined by the position of the planets, etc, at birth. It is conceded, however, that these dispositions and characteristics may be modified by the sympathetic understanding of one's horoscope. By this knowledge the good tendencies may be fostered and the evil disciplined. Without this knowledge, or by a refusal to obey its behests, the dispositions and characteristics will determine the fate of the individual.

No Blind Chance

Here we have an acknowledgement of some kind of control over the expression of the individual personality. Granted it is a limited control, still, it goes much farther than the previous conception of blind chance.

To carry the idea a further stage, there is the theory, held by many folk, that the Deity has planned the life of every one of His intelligent creatures; that acts are certain because they are predestined by Omnipotence to occur. Some affirm that wrong acts, as well as right acts, are pre-determined, citing such an example as that of Judas, whose act of betrayal was part of a pre-determined scheme. The words used by Jesus are taken as being indicative of that acknowledged plan: "And none of them is lost, but the son of perdition, *that the Scripture might be fulfilled.*" I have italicised the last clause in order to show the basis of the claim that immoral acts are predetermined as well as moral acts.

Now it must be conceded that, whichever view is held of the three tabulated, it must of necessity come under the general heading of determinism. Whether thought, will and act are governed by a blind, unreasoned necessity, or by astral influence or by a predetermined plan by God Himself, personal freedom must be negatived.

Just as we saw Blatchford taking the illogical role of "Mr Facing-both-Ways", so we shall be guilty of the same faulty position if we agree to any form of determinism, and, at the same time, agree that man has personal freedom.

(To be continued)

Personal Freedom [2]
By George E Hobbs
(First published: February 15, 1935)

I have said that the physical is introduced into our problem of personal freedom for a specific reason. I had in mind that, as the psychical functions through the physical brain, perhaps immediate and less immediate ancestry may have some influence upon the thought, will and action of the individual. There is little doubt that parental teaching, by precept and example, would have some influence in moulding and directing the expression of the child's personality. But would some directional control come from pre-natal sources – sources which the child inherits, and for which the child cannot be held responsible?

I am not now harking back to the blind and dark avenues of a chaotic Determinism, but of transmission through the parents, grandparents, etc.

It has been declared that instances have occurred where characteristics in the parents have been repeated in the child – not only mannerisms and gestures, which may be termed physical transmissions, but also those subtler characteristics which must, by their very nature, influence thought, will and act.

Viewing life reproductively, and judging the circumstances from the physical aspect only, it would seem that this must be the law in all cases – that every child born must be somewhat of a replica of the father, or the mother, or a modified combination of both. There is an anxious query often put by newly-made parents to visiting friends as to whom the little one features. When the tactless one volunteers a blunt denial that the little one features either, there follows a lull in the conversation. But when, as is usually the case there is enthusiastic agreement that eyes and ears feature mother, and nose and chin feature father, there is contentment and joy.

More Than Physical

But external features are only the visible expression of transmission. Are there internal features which lead to a suggestion of a subtler transmission? It would seem that such often is acknowledged in humorous vein – or non-humorous, according to the point of view. It is sometimes said of a child that it has its father's temper, or, conversely its mother's sweet disposition. Of course, as I have intimated, such a remark may have been made facetiously, and may have no biological significance. But if this is true in substance and in fact, and knowing the child could not have cultivated a temper or a disposition, then we have agreement that parents can transmit more than physical qualities to their children.

In this connection there is a very striking passage in Gerald Leighton's book, "The Greatest Life". He writes: "Man is composed partly of characteristics, which are derived from pre-existing germ-cells, and over the possession of which he has no control. Be they good, bad or indifferent, these characteristics are his from his ancestry, in virtue of his inheritance. The possession of these characteristics is, to him, a matter of neither blame nor praise, but of necessity. They are inevitable."

And there is worse to follow!

Eugene Talbot, in his book, "Degeneracy, its causes, signs and results", has this striking passage (italics are mine):

> "Thirdly, there came a class whom no kindness could conciliate, and no discipline tame. They were sent into the world labelled 'incorrigible' wickedness, as it were, being stamped upon their organisation."

The Decalogue, it would seem, takes a physical, rather than a psychical, view to this difficult problem. "Visiting the iniquity of the fathers upon the children", etc, is the result of the violation of natural law – the transmission of disease, etc, through unnatural living. But Leighton and Talbot take us into a deeper strata, and, in consequence, make the problem of personal freedom more difficult of solution. Even so, we have at least reached one vital issue in our search.

Whatever may be our subsequent solution of the problem, we have found that the office of parenthood carries a much greater responsibility than what appears upon the surface.

The rapture of love between man and wife inevitably leads to its normal consummation. But, probably too often, little thought is given to the vital issues at stake. The bringing of a child into the world is considered an event too ordinary to occasion anything but the thought that it is as it should be. It is natural according to the dictates of the physical law of reproduction.

But the mere fact that natural law has manifested itself is by no means the only thing that matters. A vital and far-reaching sequence has been brought about. A separate entity, which must bring its quota to the weal or woe of its fellows, has been born into the world.

Now, if the theory of a blind Determinism be true, there can be no question of responsibility either upon the part of the producers or upon that which is produced. The question would resolve itself into matter of automatic cyclic activity. The cycle of production and of reproduction would be that a sensitised, mechanical robot would produce by mechanical law a small, sensitised mechanical robot of like kind. There could be no more in it than this. I think we shall have no hesitation in ruling out such a theory as altogether illogical and foolish, and certainly contrary to the facts as we find them.

A Grave Responsibility

That there is a responsibility in this matter I think cannot be denied. And if the findings of Talbot and Leighton are as stated – that parents can and do influence those factors in the subsequent child that shall have some control upon its thought, will and act – then that responsibility is of the gravest. It would seem that not only should physical fitness be incumbent upon prospective parents, but also normal mental and moral fitness. By "mental" fitness I do not suggest an academic static, but a fitness in the proper understanding of the responsibilities involved.

It seems a terrible thing to contemplate that it may be possible to bring a child into the world damned at its very birth. Even, further, that it may be foredoomed to failure before it is born. One remembers the words of the Great Teacher – ever a lover of children – in this connection. Said He: "He that harmeth one of these little ones, it were better that a millstone be hanged about his neck and that he be drowned in the midst of the sea."

But does pre-natal influence (assuming such to be true) exclude the possibility of personal freedom in the child – the freedom to think, will and act of its own volition?

Before this question can be answered satisfactorily there is one other avenue we shall have to explore. There is the aspect of accountability. Each normal individual becomes conscious, at some time early in his or her life, that he or she is accountable to someone for the visible expression of thought and will.

Is this sense of accountability a final proof that the individual has personal freedom? This aspect we shall explore in our next week's article.

(To be continued)

Personal Freedom [3]
By George E Hobbs
(First published: February 22, 1935)

We now reach a very important factor in our investigation of personal freedom. The avenue of research will be that of the sense of accountability.

We live but a few years before we become aware that our actions – the visible manifestations of our thought and will – carry with them certain responsibilities. That awareness, within ourselves, is, at first, vague and difficult to define. The reason is that our immature minds are incapable of that analysis which will yield values in their proper perspective.

Our first "sense" of accountability – or, rather, our conception – comes through the punishment meted out for childish pranks, or through constant cautions of "you must not!" It may be said in passing that, under the newer and better understanding of child psychology, we appreciate that the positive "this do and thou shalt live" is a far better plan for guidance than the negative "Thou shalt not".

The sense of accountability which is derived from punishment or caution, of course, is purely the result of teaching or discipline. It operates from without to within; from the act to the consciousness.

A Glimmer of Truth

There is another sense of accountability which is deep-seated in the constitution of every normal human being. I claim that it is not true to say the latter is a growth or a development of the former. The latter is not the result of teaching, but is innate. It is innate by virtue of that higher self in man which we term the divine. In other words, in contradistinction to the former sense which operates from without to within, this latter sense operates from within and works outward to the act. It is seated, or centred, in that mystic core of personality we term the soul. From this source springs an urge which, operating through the thought to the will, will determine the act.

It is, then, in this sense of innate accountability that I begin to see a glimmer of the truth. I see that, instead of this sense negativing personal freedom, it yields to it a positive place in human affairs. I see that man in his normal state has personal freedom in thought, will and act. He is free to think, free to will, and free to act by the dictates of that higher self which is the possession of every human being *at the period of normality*. I have italicised these words because I feel that the whole case of for and against must rest upon the normality of the individual.

It would be absurd to reason that a drink-soddened mind is free to operate the divine gift of freedom when another glass of whisky is placed in front of him. It would be equally absurd to reason that a gourmand is free to refuse a perfectly-turned breast of a chicken. The thought and will are already enslaved and held in bondage by the desire to satisfy the craving of their being. Therefore the period of normality has passed.

The Directing Factor

Before this matter is further stressed there is one important aspect I should like to mention. When I suggest it is in the consciousness of accountability that I see freedom, I am not thinking of the idea of "rendering an account to God". I feel that too often 'fear', or a desire to placate, forms part of our personal creed. And when this happens I have no hesitation in saying that such an attitude of mind is not an expression of freedom.

I think it more true to say that the free individual is the individual who recognises he is accountable to *himself* or to the highest moral expression of himself of which he is capable.

The inward urge to respond to the highest moral expression of which one is capable is a directing factor which ever pulls gently upwards. There is nothing of bond-slavery in permitting full scope to its sway. On the other hand, the urge to respond to a low moral expression of one's self is attended by the enslavement of thought and will. The act which follows will be visible proof that the individual is not free.

In course of time, the net of habit will close round the unfortunate one and render him helpless against any and all expression of freedom. Only a miracle of Infinite Power, outside of himself and operating back to the source of his personality, can rehabilitate such [an individual and once again establish his expression of freedom]. It can be done! It *has* been done!

[Therefore, freedom comes to the individual who, when standing before the tribunal of his highest moral achievement, has no case to answer to his own conscience]. To fall below this standard is to admit that the thought and will are not free.

No Choice Without Freedom

That real personal freedom is a rare achievement is no proof that the deductions I have submitted are not generally possible. I cannot say at the moment I believe, because I am still wrestling with the ultimate problem: But I want to believe that many of the old-time arguments upon what I term "physical heredity" are not logically sound. If I see order and beauty and meaning in the expression of human life, then I want to believe that every human life has the in-alienable right to express itself in unfettered freedom. If this is true, then the period of expression must be the period of normality. It is at this period when:

"Once to every man and nation comes the moment to decide
In the strife of truth and falsehood, for the good or evil side."

Once! For good or ill, in the hand of every normal individual is the dynamic of choice. If the dynamic of choice is admitted, then freedom must also be admitted. There can be no choice without freedom.

That the critical period of choice is of short duration I think must be true. I think it must be that supreme moment of crisis when one arrives at one's full soul consciousness. It is then that the challenge comes to express freedom in thought, will and act. It is the vital moment of decision. The parting of the ways begins here.

"To every man there openeth,
A high way and a low –
The high soul take the high way,
And the low soul takes the low."

When man is normal, he is free to choose. Free to choose the highest and best – or lowest and worst.

Personal Freedom
(letter to the *Swindon Advertiser*)
(First published: March 8, 1935)

Sir – One consideration only prompts me to reply to "Believer's" criticism of my articles. His sincerity has appealed to me, though his *nom-de-plume* irritates me.

"Believer" hits hard, but he is reluctant to wound. Even when he declares I have turned down Christianity and departed from the Faith and that "as Satan himself, so Satan's ministers must be…" etc, I still see the reluctance to wound.

I welcome criticism provided it is constructive. I have never yet feared adverse criticism. But "Believer" could never have read the last article of the "Personal Freedom" series, or he would not have written what he did. I definitely stated there that men could be and were held in bondage by their baser appetites, and that only a miracle of Infinite Power, outside of themselves, could give them freedom again.

No, I have not renounced Christianity. I have simply renounced my belief in a literal interpretation of much of the Old Testament's contents. I do not accept what pleases me – I accept what convinces me even though it does not please me. I teach and preach truth as I see it. To tell me I am wrong is either the attitude of a spiritual know-all (which is tantamount to personal arrogance), or the attitude of one who is held by fear.

For me to tell a Roman Catholic, an Anglican, a Baptist, a Salvationist, a Spiritualist, or any other participant of religious formulæ that he is wrong simply boils down to the ridiculous.

The freedom I possess is the freedom of the Christ working in and through my being. It is because of this I fear no man's condemnation where my personal belief is concerned.

What an infinite pity it is that folk are still being led like lambs to the slaughter, unthinking and unreasoning – creeds and dogmas, dead as the dodo and as mummified as an Egyptian corpse, still being fed upon! What spiritual vitamins there are in those mummies, to be sure!

I do not say anyone differing from me is wrong. All that I am thankful for is that fear no longer holds me in thrall.

Yours etc,
George E Hobbs

Gleanings [68]
By George E Hobbs
(First published: September 2, 1938)

There seems to be no lack of material upon which a ready pen may work. News items and articles, both grave and gay, fill the columns of our daily and weekly journals – news which touches life not only at its centre, but also at its extremities. Correspondence columns reveal how the public react to these things – sometimes giving food for thought by the perfect balance of a weighed judgement, sometimes giving rise to a sense of irritation by the bias of creed and the narrowness of individual thought and outlook.

We continue to read of wars and rumours of wars – part of a dictum which should have been eradicated from our vocabulary long since. We read of deeds of heroism and of selfless devotion which stir the heart by the revelation that man can be Godlike. We read of deeds of ignoble treachery and of selfishness which sadden the heart by the revelation that man can be Satanic. And so from these two extremes, with all the thousands of happenings which stretch between them, we have "news" – the record of what man thinks, plans and does.

* * *

And this leads me to my theme for this week: "Freedom and Liberty".

One of the greatest of our possessions is that of freedom. To compound that possession, let us call it the freedom-liberty heritage. In prose and poetry, in oral speech and in song, we proclaim our joy in a heritage which is beyond price.

On more than one occasion I have felt bound to criticise some national trait which lowers our country from the standard of national greatness. Even so, I thank God that the "accident of birth" caused me to be born a Britisher. I have never been a flag-wagger, and, whatever the consequences, I never intend to be. In all things I shall reserve to myself the right of conscience. But truth demands the admission that liberty and freedom are expressed within the shores of Great Britain more royally than anywhere else on earth

* * *

I know there are conditions and circumstances which chafe and vex the individual. And only those who are the victims of these vicious conditions know how sore is the chafing and how heartbreaking is the vexation. But this, unfortunately, is due to the fact that nothing which man formulates himself is or can be perfect. Perfect law is not yet an attribute of the Legislature. But if the long view is taken, or, as we sometimes inelegantly say, "take it on the whole", freedom and liberty are expressed more fully in this country than elsewhere.

And such a heritage dare not be limited or restricted. In no way dare a hand be laid upon it to interfere or derange. The price paid has been too heavy, too costly. Bound up in the cost of freedom there is suffering of a degree no word of the English tongue could adequately describe – burning at the stake, floggings, deprivation of status and of rights, transportation, with cruel acts of inhuman conduct upon loved ones left behind. In fact, the tortures invented to suppress liberty were legion. Yet men dared the tortures, visualising through their agony a better England.

* * *

To show the stuff of which these heroes were made let me quote one example which is before me at this moment. It is from Harry Brooks' little book, "Six Heroes in Chains".

George Loveless, one of the "Tolpuddle Martyrs", had just heard sentence passed upon himself and five of his companions – seven years' transportation. He says, "I took a scrap of paper and wrote the following lines:

> God is our guide from field, from wave,
> From plough, from anvil, and from loom;
> We come, our country's rights to save,
> And speak the tyrant factions' doom;
> We raise the watchword 'Liberty'
> We will, we will, we will be free.
>
> God is our guide – no sword we draw,
> We kindle not war's battle fires,
> By reason, union, justice, law,
> We claim the birth-right of our sires,
> We raise the watchword 'Liberty'
> We will, we will, we will be free."

* * *

This is the spirit which has won for us freedom in thought and speech; freedom of the Press; religious and political freedom. It was this spirit which compelled social reform. All the privileges we enjoy to-day were bought and paid for by the pioneer martyrs. To say that we raise our hats to those is oftentimes but the gesture of a meaningless ritual. We can best honour the pioneers of freedom by dedicating ourselves to the untrammelled continuance of freedom; to see that no encroachment is made upon any one aspect of present-day liberty.

To use a rather crude expression, efforts have been made to "muzzle" the Press. In no circumstances must this be tolerated. The Press is the greatest uncensored vehicle by which the public learns of world affairs. It would be nothing short of a betrayal of liberty and freedom if the Press were censored.

I must admit that sometimes details are given which could better have been omitted. I do not mean of public policy, but the crude morbid details of some atrocious act. In a London Daily the other day I read a most revolting story of a person who [was] carried into literal execution, "If thine eye offend thee, pluck it out. If thine hand offend thee, cut it off." It may have been true, but it did no-one any good to read of it. It is items of this nature I should like to see eliminated. Still let us have a free, untrammelled Press in any circumstance.

Speaking of one aspect of freedom – that of toleration – one has only to remember the correspondence in the columns of "The Evening Advertiser" of the past week or so. Correspondents have been given the greatest freedom of expression, even to the hardest of hard hitting. And this is all to the good, for it compels a correspondent to think twice, and think carefully, before giving expression to opinions for public perusal. Personally I have enjoyed the correspondence column of the past few weeks.

But to return to our theme. Liberty and freedom are not complete in any community unless they are the common right of every section of that community. To condition one section where another section of the same social order is not conditioned is tantamount to tyranny. True freedom is indiscriminate freedom. The freedom enjoyed by one section must be the freedom enjoyed by all. And now to the point.

This month, in London, a Free-thinkers' Congress is being held, and petitions are already out for signature praying the Home Secretary to ban the Congress. Personally I think this is a most illogical and thoughtless action.

Probably there will be many signatures recorded, but I am inclined to forecast that quite 50 per cent will sign from the standpoint of a mistaken sentiment rather than by thought.

I have no wish to discriminate, but I imagine that no thoughtful Christian dare sign such a petition. I said "thoughtful" Christian. Every signature involves a two-fold declaration. One is a declaration against freedom of thought and speech, and one is a declaration of fear. I was almost inclined to write that it is a declaration of defeat. When one fears a thing it is an admission that one's convictions are less strong than the thing feared.

These folk – whoever they may be – have as much right to explain the Universe without God – if they can – as I have the right to explain it by Him. I concede the right to them to hold their opinions, pessimistic, hopeless and gloomy as they are. And I claim the right to hold my opinions which are optimistic, hopeful and bright. I would not sign the petition under any consideration. I should be false to my great love of freedom if I did. Not only so, but I should hate to feel afraid of possible arguments against my convictions. If I were afraid it would prove they were not convictions.

All I hope is that Congress will meet in open session and that the Press will give good space to their deliberations. I would far sooner fight their arguments, if I found them contradict my convictions, than bar them from meeting.

Chapter 9

A Call for Peace, Brotherhood and Internationalism

Those who make war do not fight. They engage others to do this for them.
Anon

All new thought is revolutionary. In course of time the revolutionary becomes the evolutionary. This is the vision of the new thought, the new world order, the new commonwealth of nations. And it will come into being. The world is soul sick and weary of the present order of things. The world longs for peace and for a greater security. It can only lie along the pathway of Internationalism.
by George Ewart Hobbs, from Gleanings [8], June 25, 1937

George was aged 31 when Great Britain declared war on Germany at the start of the First World War, on August 4, 1914 – by which time he was a time-served fitter and turner in G Shop (Millwrights) in Swindon's GWR Works. In April 1915, when the British Government was still recruiting for an exclusively volunteer army, he declared that he was 'debarred from going out there to fight himself, or he would have gone'.

Presumably, he was referring to the fact that his job in the Railway Works was deemed too vital to the war effort for him to be released. Notwithstanding all the millions of troops that needed to be moved to and from the Channel ports via the GWR and other railway companies, civilian passenger traffic also increased during the years 1913 to 1916. It is not surprising then that the GWR were anxious to retain their skilled labour where possible.

The British Government wasted no time and had already placed the railways under the control of a Railway Executive Committee, the day after war was declared. Swindon Works was effectively commandeered to assist the war effort by producing military hardware and munitions for the Western Front – something that caused George deep distress – given his revulsion at the loss of so many lives and his nascent interest in the cause of pacifism.

In January 1916 The Military Service Act was passed, which imposed conscription on all single men aged between 18 and 41, and in the following May this was extended to included married men. George's trade union, The Amalgamated Society of Engineers, helped secure exemption from conscription for craft union members in late 1916.

With a second conflict looming, George's knowledge of the carnage of the First World War, the loss of friends and his witness to so many bereaved families in his work for the Wesleyan Methodist Church doubtless informed part of a piece he wrote in 1937 on the subject of marriage, and the wider implications for the relationship in the event of starting a family. He raises the subject of economic considerations and affordability, the likely impact on one's social life, the fear (or lack of understanding of) childbirth and then, poignantly he adds a fourth consideration:

"Will my boy become cannon-fodder? Have I (a potential mother, fit healthy and strong) to agonise for my son, sacrifice for him, train him to be good, upright and manly, and then hand him over to be the victim of senseless national jealousies? If I bring him into the world, I would wish him to live for his country, I would wish him to help make his country pure and true and wholesome. But under the present system of individualism, I fear. And I greatly fear."

So the potential mother may argue, and has the right to argue. And by that argument may rest her decision to refuse the state of motherhood. Her child may prove to be a son.

And as the nation continued its seemingly inevitable slide towards conflict, George continued to 'bang the drum' for pacifism. Appearing in the *Advertiser* on October 14, 1938, he wrote:

This week I want to get right away from wars and threats of war. Most of us have our pet ideas of cause and effect, and have spared no pains in airing them. Some of us too have shared no effort in offering solutions to the grave problems that confront us. Some of us believe in Pacifism, either in a mild or extreme form. Some believe in the establishment of an International

Police Force and in an Equity Tribunal. Some believe in force as vested in armies and navies. And some of us believe in the utter futility of armaments and see the only possible solution in faith in God. Most of us try to give the other fellow credit for his opinions, but, at the same time, we continue to thrash out our own pet convictions. Controversy is ever good and beneficial provided sincerity of thought and purity of motive be behind it.

By the time war was declared on Nazi Germany on September 3, 1939, the National Service (Armed Forces) Act imposed a liability to conscription on all men aged 18 to 41, with some exemptions, although by 1942 the upper age had been increased to 51. George was at no risk of being conscripted under any circumstances; he had reached the age of 58 on January 16, 1941.

We have selected 14 items for this chapter, one of which is an open letter and, for context, we have also included two news reports that appeared in the *North Wilts Herald*.

We commence this chapter with **Wireless Talks [1]** (October 26, 1934), an extract from a review of a radio programme: in this case, a talk given by the then Dean of St Paul's Cathedral, William Inge (1860-1954). We hear not only of the 'utter stupidity of war' but also of the dilemma facing every pacifist.

In **"Rules" of War** (January 17, 1936), George hints at 'A rich man's war but a poor man's fight', and while he does not mention the Hague Conventions, nor the 1925 Geneva Protocol by name, he draws the somewhat ironic distinction between similar-looking weapons that are legal and those that are outlawed.

An example of the perceived flouting of international law is provided by the sinking of the Cunard liner Lusitania by a German submarine on in May 1915 with the loss of 1,198 civilian lives (including, incidentally, one from Swindon). So while the British press were eager to condemn the Germans as evil-doers, the chilling footnote in George's newspaper was that 'she was armed with six-inch guns and quick-firers' and that by implication, the British Government was indeed partly culpable for the tragedy.

In fact, although the suggestion at the time was that the Lusitania was armed, this was wide of the mark. It is true that the vessel was officially listed as an Armed Merchant Cruiser (and therefore fitted out with gun mounts), but deck guns had never actually been deployed. However, it is now known that she was carrying a cargo that included .303 rifle cartridges, fragmentation shell casings and percussion fuses.

Pubic opinion – or at least pacifists' like George's attitudes – in 1936, still nearly three-and-a-half years from war, can be gauged in **An Open Letter to Mr WW Wakefield MP** (*Evening Advertiser*, April 8, 1936), reproduced along with **Government's Armament Policy: Mr WW Wakefield's Defence** (*North Wilts Herald*, April 24, 1936).

They refer to Swindon's Conservative MP, Wavell Wakefield and a speech he gave at the Oxford Hotel (now The Merlin), following an earlier one at Victoria Road Congregational Church.

Notice a somewhat surprising viewpoint by George about which country – Germany or France – constitutes the greatest threat to world peace.

Another two articles that should be read together are **Swindon Peace Demonstration** (*North Wilts Herald*, September 4, 1936) and **Peace** (September 11, 1936).

The report (uncredited but probably *not* written by George) of the march that took place on September 2, 1936, to the GWR Park in Faringdon Road, provides some useful background and contextual information, ahead of George's own article, his personal 'take' on the same event.

Internationalism (October 23, 1936) and **Internationalism (continued)** (October 30, 1936) see George voicing his regret that the League of Nations – formed out of the ashes of the Great War – had failed to live up to its promise to turn nationalism into internationalism. He lists the organisation's failure to prevent the Japanese invasion of Manchuria (today lying almost exclusively within the People's Republic of China), as well as the Italian occupation of Abyssinia (present-day Ethiopia) and, by implication, its impotency in the face of the Spanish Civil War. He goes on to expand his view that security can only be found in Internationalism via a strengthened League of Nations.

In *A Swindon Wordsmith* we lamented that the article entitled The Virtue of Gratitude was likely to be 'the closest we will ever have to one of his own sermons'. Well, subsequent research which took place in March 2020 has allowed us to go one better.

In **World Peace** (27th November 1936) we have the actual text of an address that was delivered by George to the Wootton Bassett Brotherhood, only a few days before, on Sunday, November 22, 1936, at the High Street Methodist Church, Wootton Bassett.

Built in 1855 for the Wesleyans, it suffered from decreasing numbers in the years following the First World War, but survived as a place of worship until around 1965. Then the two Methodist congregations in Bassett were merged and found a base at the former Primitive 'Hillside' Chapel, and the High Street chapel was subsequently demolished as part of a road-widening scheme.

There is evidence that George was involved with the non-sectarian Brotherhood movement going back to at least 1930 – which would certainly tie in with his growing reputation as a Zoon Politikon. Evolving out of the Adult School Movement, the Brotherhood and Sisterhood groups promoted Protestant evangelism, and drew much of their support from the Free Churches. Holding informal services with hymns and talks, often taking place on a Sunday afternoon, the movement sought to reach lapsed Christians.

The National Association of Brotherhoods was founded in London in 1906 and the movement went on to become an enthusiastic supporter of the League of Nations – holding a huge rally in the Royal Albert Hall in February 1919, following the approval of the proposal to create the League on January 25.

Ostensibly non-political, the meetings were often the forum for debates and discussions on live political and social issues, although 'the long-standing relationship between political Liberalism and Nonconformity brought active Liberals into the movement'.

Membership peaked in 1913 with more than 300,000 members, but had declined to around 100,000 by 1919, although 'it still claimed 115,000 members in the 1930s'.

George's address sets out a shared belief in 'Brotherhood, Fraternity and Comradeship' as a blueprint for a new society, and as a vehicle for world peace. Once again, we get to hear that the way to this objective is through the concept of Internationalism – a commonwealth of nations – and we learn that George is a member of The New Commonwealth Society – whose visioned ideal is a world federation.

This society was formed in London in 1932, and advocated pacifism, disarmament and multilateral conflict resolution through the creation of an international tribunal, an international police force and later, an international air force. Indeed, it was said by Winston Churchill to be one of the few peace societies that advocated the use of force, even overwhelming force in support of international law.

We also know that George had some deep sympathies towards the LNU (League of Nations Union). Formed in London in October 1918, it sought to lobby mainstream British society in favour of the League of Nations and, among other things, advocated the creation of a new and transparent system of international relations and the establishment of world peace through collective security and disarmament. Reported to have enjoyed close relations with the Liberal Party, it is said to have played an important role in interwar politics.

If the piece throws light on George's and others' intellectual efforts to find a solution to the darkening clouds spreading across Europe in 1936, it also includes a chilling prophesy of "a war of extermination".

In the following year, George points out, in **The Problems of Defence** (April 23, 1937) the spiralling costs to each nation involved in an international arms race and, in the process draws the attention of the reader to the question of whether fighting to retain the occupation of territory stolen from indigenous peoples is in itself 'defence'.

But the logical conclusion, he argues, is still the same: a true Commonwealth of Nations.

Gleanings [27] (November 12, 1937) laments what George describes as a 'change of emphasis' in respect of Armistice/Remembrance Day, to one increasingly dominated by military parades, and in **Gleanings [32]** (December 17, 1937) George takes as a starting point a radio broadcast made by Sir Fabian Ware (1869-1949) who was the founder of the Imperial War Graves Commission (now known as the Commonwealth War Graves Commission) in 1917.

George references Sir Fabian as one of the foremost advocates of "New Internationalism", given that he sought to set up 'a joint body to conduct and plan in common cause for the remembrance of the dead'. The hope was that uniting the British Empire, France and Germany in such an undertaking would advance the cause of peace and avoid another conflict. Indeed, such an agreement was made in November 1935, and it has been said of Ware by historian Philip Longworth that he intended to "use the Commission as a sort of minor League of Nations to forward the work of international understanding".

This article also sees George take a flight of fancy by writing a fantasy piece for 20 years in the future, the contents of which amount to a 'wish list' for world peace. Interestingly, it only comes about following a fictional war (said to have taken place in 1947) which resulted in 'thirty million dead' – a figure for a future world war which was to sadly prove a massive underestimate.

Gleanings [84, extract] (December 30, 1938) is a worldwide 'moral' stocktake of the previous 12 months, in which George laments how the leaders of Germany, Italy and Japan have chosen the path of world domination – and their peoples in turn have chosen to place their trust in evil strongmen rather than the Christian Church.

But if all hope seems lost at this point, **Gleanings [85, extract]** (January 6, 1939) sees George still believing that concord might yet prevail among the nations of Europe. The call is for all individuals to make good on their New Year resolutions to become men and women of peace.

Before the year was out, of course, it would become all too clear.

Wireless Talks [1, extract]
By George E Hobbs
(First published: October 26, 1934)

The utter stupidity of war was emphasised by the Dean. The romance of war has departed, he said, leaving the stark reality more ugly and cruel than words can describe. The rank and file of the armies hurled against each other have not the slightest cause of enmity, and often have no notion why they are fighting.

I did not get the drift of the Dean's meaning when, speaking of armament firms, he said that the shareholders have no interest in promoting war. If this is true it is more than passing strange how quickly interest is stimulated when two little states, thousands of miles away, begin to growl at one another. I imagine that the salesman who deferred getting quickly to grips with the situation would not be looked upon with favour. Folk do not buy shares in armament firms because those firms supply sporting guns.

Dean Inge agreed that the case against war was not always clear. Questions sometimes arise which are difficult for the consistent pacifist to answer. Are Americans and Australians right in keeping Asiatics out of their countries by force? What of the American Civil War? Was the abolition of slavery worth the four years of war and the loss of thousands of lives? In other words, the Dean asked, "Was war and subsequent loss of life justified to effect the abolition of slavery?" What answers will extreme pacifists give to such a question?

Dean Inge touched the crux of the problem when he said that the main cause of modern war is unquestionably 'Fear'. The causes of fear must be removed or… these causes will some day repeat the same awful tragedy.

In patriotism Dean Inge sees an emotion which is the purest and noblest of which the ordinary man is capable. One agrees with the speaker, providing that the expression of that patriotism does not mean insularity, aloofness or a mistaken belief that Britishers are the chosen people of Jehovah. Some of the world's best patriots have declared against the policy of their own country.

"Rules" of War
By George E Hobbs
(First published: January 17, 1936)

Nineteen hundred years ago, in the same empire in which the Babe of Bethlehem was born, gladiatorial sports were held. Bands of men, or in pairs, fought to the death in the arena before an audience of men, women and children. The contests were governed by rules. One rule, among others, was that each combatant pledged himself to fight "to the death". As they entered the arena their reckless defiance of death was, "Ave, Caesar! Morituri te salutant!" ("Hail, Caesar! Those about to die salute thee!"). Provided they fought, and one was slain, the audience was satisfied.

But, of course, the people of whom I write were barbarians. They had not that fine sense of moral values which modern civilisations possess. So delicate is our sense of the fitness of things that we say "all-in" wrestling is barbarity, that women boxers are unsexed, and that murderers should be hung by the neck until they are dead. Which shows, as I have already intimated, that our ethical standard is miles higher than that of the poor benighted Roman.

This standard is seen more clearly when we study the "rules" governing the killing of men. The mere taking of a man's life is immaterial – almost a side issue. It is the manner by which he is killed which constitutes compliance with, or a breach of, the rules. If the killer obeys the rules, he is said to be civilised. If he disobeys the rules then he is said to be uncivilised. He certainly cannot be a Christian, because he has killed contrary to the rules.

"Civilised Warfare"

Now let us examine a few of the "Rules of Civilised Warfare" (what a travesty of logic and sense!). In studying these rules we must first indulge in a trite saying. It is as old as the hills and long since worn threadbare. Nevertheless, it has the hall-mark of truth and sense. It is this: "Those who make war do not fight." They engage others to do this for them. Those who are engaged on the one side have no quarrel with those engaged on the other side. But, like the uncivilised gladiators of old, they are engaged to kill, and kill they must or be accused of possessing that queer commodity called "cold feet", "funk", or "cowardice".

When the stage is set, each side is encouraged by those who have made the war to "Go in and kill the –s!" (Oh, yes, my masters, there is a cessation or suspension of the rules in the preliminaries of "cussing"). After that the "rules of civilised warfare" begin to operate.

If the killer kills his man at a distance with a bullet, such bullet must be of the pattern approved by the civilised powers. If the right pattern bullet is used, then, when the killer sees his opponent throw up his arms and fall to the ground, dead, he can justly exclaim: "Thank God I am a civilised man!" But if the killer should use an expanding bullet – a "dum-dum" bullet – then he cannot think of himself in such high terms. The same end has been reached – death. But in the one case the dead man looks clean, while in the other he looks a bit of a mess. You see, my masters, the killing of the killer's brother does not matter one brass button. It is the method of despatch which is apt to raise Cain.

The killer may slay his brother by being quicker with his bayonet in a hand-to-hand struggle. He may knock out his brother's brains with the butt-end of his rifle. He may drop a few bombs and blow men to pieces. He may disfigure his brother so much that the girl to whom he is betrothed flees from him in horror. He may take away his brother's sight and leave him a hopeless wreck, praying the heartbreaking prayer, "Oh, God! Why did not that bullet go through my brain and finish me?" The killer may leave his opponent a hopeless and helpless imbecile. But, as long as the killer has kept within the rules of "civilised warfare", he still retains his status as a civilised man, and the killer's "hirers" can go to bed and dream of heaven, satisfied that all's well with that wonderful civilisation of which they are such shining lights.

But, if the killer uses a "saw-edge" bayonet, or indulges in any practice outside those prescribed in the "rules", then he is deemed not to be civilised, but to be a savage and a barbarian. When this happens, all the rest of the civilised world lift their hands in horror to think that after two thousand years of Christian teaching, a man should slay his brother man by a method not laid down in the rules. Again let me emphasise the indisputable fact. The death or mutilation of the individual being does not count by the "rules". It is the method by which that death is brought about which counts.

As I write I have a newspaper in front of me. It is dated Saturday, 8 May, 1915. On the font page is a picture of the ill-fated "Lusitania". A headline runs: "German pirates sink the Lusitania; 1,978 on board." One passage makes intriguing reading. Here it is:

> "They (The Germans) have been willing to incur classification as evildoers acting outside international law – as pirates and murderers from the point of view of those who believe that *warfare should be conducted in a humane and civilised manner*" (the italics are mine).

From the same publication I gather that the "Lusitania" was "the fastest Atlantic liner, and she was armed with six-inch guns and quick-firers". I leave it at that.

Jungle Instincts

Why not let us strip ourselves of humbug and cant and sanctimonious vapourings? THERE CAN BE NO RULES TO WAR, and "civilised warfare" is a misnomer. War is the release of jungle instincts and passion, and jungle instincts and passions know no law, save one – kill or be killed, maim or be maimed.

A friend told me that as he awaited the order to go "over the top", his heart pounded madly. He was nervous and afraid, and near to tears. The moment he sprang from the parapet there came to him a strange reversal of feeling. He was no longer afraid, but exulted; no longer nervous, but confident; no longer near to tears, but filled with a wild passion. It was to kill! kill! kill! The psychology of his mind was changed from the human to that of the beast. It was not that he hated the foeman in front of him. He had no cause to hate him as an individual, but he desired to kill him. The law of self-preservation will not fully explain the circumstances. It was a definite passion – not born, but released under the abnormal stress.

The "abuse" of the white flag, the sinking of non-armed ships, the bombing of a civil population, the bombing of a Red Cross hospital, are all contingencies of the same primal cause – human or inhuman passions released under stress of "civilised warfare".

I am aware of the heroism, the devotion, the self-sacrifice that have been shown during periods of war. But these can never offset the madness and futility of war.

"Rules of civilised war" is a stupid phrase, and ought never to be used by anyone who boasts an intelligence. Scrap war and then the rules will go to where they belong – to blazes!

An Open Letter to Mr WW Wakefield MP By George E Hobbs
(First published: April 8, 1936)

Dear Mr Wakefield, – I have the honour to address you upon a matter of public interest. Both the evening and weekly issues of the "Advertiser" report a meeting which took place between the members of the Victoria Road Congregational Church, Swindon, and yourself. This meeting resulted from a resolution sent to you by the members upon the Government's plan for rearmament.

You are reported to have expressed the opinion that "it is an absolute tragedy that, in the civilised world of today, we have to spend money on armaments which might be spent on furthering the welfare and interests of our citizens".

By ordinary standards, this opinion may be said to be commendable. I give you the credit that this opinion is not so much a party, as a personal one. You, personally, believe that "we have to spend money on armaments" which "ought" to be spent on furthering the welfare and interests of our people.

Profoundly I agree that it is a tragedy spending money on that which can give no returns but suffering and misery and renewed hatreds – instead of that which can give returns of happiness and joy. But I have the temerity of saying that just as profoundly I disagree with you when say we "have to" so spend the money.

We "have to" do nothing of the sort. Let us cut out all fancy trimmings and face the unpalatable truth. We do so because we are as mad and unbalanced as the rest of the "civilised" world.

You, sir, are not the only one who has expressed such an opinion. Some of the leading statesmen of Britain have so expressed themselves. But it is the expression of weakness – of pitiable and abject weakness.

I yield to none my love of country, but that love of country will not permit me to gild over the ugly truths which lie open to an unbiased mind.

In stating that Germany formed a menace to world peace, and that a spirit of fear was to be found in all the little states surrounding Germany, you are reported to have said, "These little states were viewing British rearmament with thankfulness in their hearts, for they knew that ours was not an aggressive rearmament."

Sir, you have but recently taken upon your shoulders the responsibilities of Parliamentary duties. I congratulate you that so soon you have learned the artistry of your job. The phrase I have quoted from your address expresses the art of diplomatic oratory. While the two clauses are separated by a comma only, a sharp transition of thought occurs. "The little states are viewing British rearmament with thankfulness in their hearts."

Why? Not because they know such rearmament is for their protection (which would have been the logical sequel to the former clause, but would have involved commitments), but because "they knew that ours was not an aggressive rearmament". As we never have and never shall (I trust) menace the "little states", just how a non-existing supposition can give thankfulness is not for me to postulate.

I further suggest, Mr Wakefield, that it is not Germany who forms a menace to world peace – but France. France is the overgrown schoolboy of Europe and it is about time that Britain ceased to be the big brother of one nation only. Anyone who has read the first edition of "Haig Speaks" will know the trouble the Allies had to endure from petulant France. And the characteristic displayed during that period is still part of that nation's make-up.

If the same consideration had been extended to New Germany as that always given to France, and had the right hand of fellowship been given to her, the present unfortunate circumstances would never had occurred.

You are further reported to have said "First, one had to get rid of the spirit of fear and the spectre of war which overshadowed us." Here, Mr Wakefield, you score a bulls-eye. The saying may be trite, but it is still true. The "spirit of fear" is the great barrier to world peace. But frankly, increased armaments can never assuage fear. It creates fear and makes it more insistently alive. And that fear is at present very real because of the inconsistencies of European statesmen. Lord Davies said, the other day, "At the moment the statesmen of Europe are loud in their protestations of peace [yet] simultaneously they are feverishly preparing for war." And such attitudes engender fear.

Mr Wakefield, I believe that Britain can be a power for good in the world. I believe that in her inmost soul, she abhors tyranny and injustice. I believe that deep in her foundations there is a belief in God – The God of Peace.

At this period of "victory through sacrifice" Britain can make history in one great and glorious gesture. Let her go to the League of Nations and say: "Gentlemen, you as free agents, may do as you please. We in Britain believe that example is better than precept. We are going to stop our rearmament plans at once."

That is the way to eliminate fear. And that is the way to wipe out the disgrace of the last few months.

Yours etc,

George E Hobbs

Government's Armament Policy
Mr WW Wakefield's Defence: Swindon Speech

(First published in *North Wilts Herald*, April 24, 1936, writer uncredited)

A vigorous defence of the Government's armament policy, as being wholly justified and in every way consistent with its defence of the principles of collective security, was made by Mr WW Wakefield, MP for Swindon, when speaking at the East Ward "A" Conservative supper, held at the Oxford Hotel on Saturday night, under the chairmanship of Mr HC Preater. He bitterly decried that section of public opinion that advocated the beggaring of our Forces and the consequent betraying of everything for which the League of Nations stood.

To those who chose to face stark facts, it was quite evident, by the European situation of to-day, the League of Nations had failed; that did not mean that the League was doomed, but it did mean that its ideas would have to be developed on different lines.

In his view, the only way to give real effect to the influence of the League of Nations was to build up, particularly in the "danger-spots" of the world, pacts based on the lines of the Locarno Pact.

Situation In Europe

In this way they might hope to link up the nations of the world through the different collective security pacts of non-aggression based on the ideal of the League itself. With such an arrangement, the League and the governments concerned would be ready to deal with an emergency immediately, if it arose.

The very complex and critical situation in Europe to-day reminded him of the story of four old gentlemen who sat down to a reunion dinner and went on to engage in a rubber of contract bridge. The bidding went as follows: North called "one, no-trick", East, "two no-bids", South, "three blind mice", West – throwing in his hand – "To hell with all these modern conventions, I'm not going to play."

That about summed up the position between Germany, France, Italy and Great Britain.

But while there was rare humour about the experience of these four old gentlemen, there was terrible tragedy about the experience of the nations, which at this stage of humanity and civilisation, were having recourse to the ruthless methods of war.

Reply to Critic

In effect, Mr Wakefield's address was a reply to an open letter addressed to himself by Mr George E Hobbs, through the columns of "The Evening Advertiser".

At the outset he declared that while standing by everything which he had said on the subject at a recent meeting at the Victoria-road Congregational Church, he pointed out that a newspaper could not afford the space to record the whole of his arguments; otherwise the points contained in Mr Hobbs' letter might not have been raised.

This correspondent had expressed his profound agreement with the speaker's opinion in that "it is an absolute tragedy that, in the civilised world of to-day we have to spend money on armaments which might have been spent on furthering the welfare and interests of our citizens".

Mr Hobbs went further; he said he profoundly agreed that "it is a tragedy spending money on that which can give no return but suffering, misery and renewed hatreds, instead of that which can give returns of happiness and joy".

Unfortunately, observed Mr Wakefield, it was necessary continually to reiterate the very sound and logical reasons that actuated the Government in its present policy.

Bloodshed Saved

He emphatically denied that the money spent by Great Britain on armaments and the Forces in recent years had brought suffering, and misery and renewed hatreds. It had done the opposite and helped, in considerable measure, to preserve the peace.

He instanced the Quetta earthquake where, in the absence of troops and tanks, there would undoubtedly have been pillage and murder; and the Shanghai Expeditionary Force which, also, had saved bloodshed.

In such ways as these, our troops were fulfilling the functions of police, and were essentially a defensive force.

"What I am distressed about," added Mr Wakefield, "is that we find it necessary to increase our armaments in the same way as other countries are increasing theirs, when such increase is not necessary for 'policing'."

In the past Great Britain had given full support to the system of collective security and to the League of Nations, and yet to-day its obligations were wider and weightier than ever. Was it expected now, he asked, that Great Britain should renounce her responsibility and leave the world to the mercy of a few nations that chose to remain outside the League; that she should blind her face to the facts and leave herself powerless to enforce the great principles for which she stands?

On the one hand, there was a cry for more extensive sanctions against Italy and the "closing of communications" between that country and Abyssinia. That, without the slightest doubt, would mean war for England, and yet, on the other hand, the Government was being urged by equally irresponsible and thoughtless critics, to disarm. It was high time that these people came down from the clouds and planted their feet on firm ground.

Answering further criticisms in Mr Hobbs' letter, he pointed out that, in addition to what was reported of his (Mr Wakefield's) speech in "The Evening Advertiser", he also stressed the fact that smaller nations appreciated that we were not embarking upon an aggressive re-armament, but that our sole intent was to give the necessary support to the idea of collective security.

Great Britain was not "the great brother" of any one nation. That fact had been made abundantly clear by Mr Eden in a recent speech in the House of Commons, when he declared that we were tied to nobody's tail, and that our earnest desire and endeavour was the creation of friendship between Germany and France.

France's Safeguard

France, it should be remembered, had twice been invaded during comparatively recent years, and it was not surprising, therefore, that she had built up for herself a strong line of fortifications. But there was nothing mobile or ambiguous about this great defence work, it obviously was a safeguard against the danger of another invasion.

Mr Wakefield was responding to the toast of "The Member", proposed by the chairman.

"Swindon Division Conservative and Unionist Association" was proposed by Councillor TC Newman and Mr TN Arkell replied.

Swindon Peace Demonstration Over 300 People Take Part in March to the Park: A United Front

(First published in *North Wilts Herald*, September 4, 1936, writer uncredited)

Between 300 and 350 people "peace marched" through Swindon on Wednesday night, from Regent Circus to the Park – these were joined by another hundred to participate in a mass, open-air peace demonstration.

Representatives of all sections of the town's religious and political thought were present in this united effort to further the cause of peace. The crowd stood in the Park, listening to speeches, until darkness fell, and a resolution was passed, urging the Government to continue a policy of co-operation with other countries.

Mr Gladstone Cox was in charge of the arrangements. The procession, which marshalled outside the Town Hall, included representatives of all the churches and other organisations. The Mayor (Ald Mrs May George) was present at the assembling, but she went to the Park in her car.

Swindon Salvation Army Citadel band led the way. Immediately behind the big drummer walked Mr WW Wakefield MP, and following him was Mr WG Hall, Swindon's prospective Labour candidate. Then came the rest of the peacemakers, and Gorse Hill SA band brought up the rear. Crowds turned out to see the spectacle, and to listen to the bands.

Arriving at the Park, the speakers assembled on the platform of the pavilion, while the crowd gathered in front. The Mayor presided, and also on the platform were the Rev W Kingsley Martin, the Rev CH Cleal, Canon Narborough of Bristol, Mr WW Wakefield MP, Mr WG Hall, Councillor AM Bennett, Major Daysh (Swindon Citadel) and Adjutant Bourne (Gorse Hill) of the SA.

"War Morally Wrong"

Before the procession left the Town Hall, a number of youths – many little more than schoolboys – began to distribute Communist literature. They were asked to refrain from doing so until after the meeting, so that there should be no trouble, and they readily agreed.

After a prayer and a hymn, the Mayor introduced, very briefly, the speakers. Her presence, she said, signified her very great interest in the cause of peace. "We women," she continued, "know what it means to give up everything for peace. It is far greater than giving up everything for war. I am very pleased to see so many women here."

She then read the resolution, which was ultimately carried unanimously. It was: "This meeting of the citizens of Swindon declares its belief that war is morally wrong and economically futile; it rejects the idea that war is inevitable, and believes the majority of the peoples of all nations earnestly desire peace. The meeting is of the opinion that the trend of the world race in armaments is detrimental to world peace, and requests His Majesty's Government to continue a policy of co-operation with other nations, based on the principle of the sacredness of human life."

Religion's Place

Canon Narborough of Bristol then spoke, and at the outset dealt with religion's place in the matter of peace. From the Christian point of view he was convinced there was a great place for such mass demonstrations as this one. Religion should be a foundation and not an ornament. It's true function was to under-lie all thinking; it should not be just brought in here and there for garnishing. In this world it was not expediency but moral law that won and ruled, and the only real security of peace was, in the long run, not might but right; not armaments but justice. If anyone tried to persuade him otherwise, and convince him, he would have to give up his ministry and his faith.

The only alternative course to re-arming was a very bold one – it was the policy of calling an economic conference for the more equitable distribution among nations of the material resources of the world. That path was beset with difficulties, and for this country beset with sacrifices, but there was no other path open to us.

"We of the churches have got to try our best to give some lead in applying Christian principles to the problem of the present day, and give up simply harping on the principles themselves. If we don't try and give some application to them, they degenerate into platitudes which everyone ignores."

United Front

Describing the meeting as an attempt to produce a united front on the issue of peace, the Rev CH Cleal of the Baptist Tabernacle said that in a world which had been created by one God for one purpose, it followed that what [was] morally wrong must also be economically futile.

It was the business of those who believed in peace never to fall into the mood of thinking that war was inevitable. He was surprised how many young people were more or less resigned to the idea of another war; the reason for the present race in armaments was the fact that so many people were resigned to the inevitability of war. The fact that a minority of folk had a vested interest in the finance of armaments involved a temptation which was overwhelming, and he was absolutely opposed to the private manufacture of armaments.

The speaker agreed with the idea of a world conference. There were many difficulties as to a peace conference as there were so many divergencies as to method. There had to be a united front, and if there was to be a rearmament programme, it should be related to a peace policy, and unless men and women were prepared to find out God's will and do it, there could be no peace on earth.

Economic Conference

When Mr WW Wakefield rose to move a vote of thanks to the speakers and organisers, "the shades of night were falling fast" and he could not read his notes. He said the great problems which faced the world today had to be discussed freely, and we should not turn to arms and war to settle our differences.

At this stage in civilisation we should be able to settle our differences by popular vote and to discuss freely our problems without resorting to war. For that reason he welcomed the suggestion of an economic conference. The unanimous way in which the resolution had been accepted showed they were all pacifists. Everyone desired peace, and it was with some misgivings he heard Mr Cleal say that young people were resigned to the prospect of war. Every means in our power had to be used to prevent a conflagration like the last war. Peace was only an absence from war. Something more was wanted – a positive peace, not just by being 'at peace', but by all being friends one with another, individuals and nations.

No Platitudes

Seconding the vote of thanks, Mr WG Hall, the prospective Labour candidate for Swindon, said he was afraid the speakers would deal almost exclusively in platitudes, but he was delighted they had had the courage to give some idea of what was in their minds.

"We don't all think alike," said Mr Hall, "but on this issue I am sure between us we can arrive at the right conclusion. It is fatal to think you can achieve security or peace through armaments.

"The world was armed to the teeth in 1914, but it did not give us peace. Unless we get together, we shall drift to another war. We have to get a change of heart in this country and then get a change of heart in others."

Save for the faint reddish glow of the rising full moon, which fell on the bared and bowed heads as Canon Narborough pronounced the Benediction, the Park was now almost completely in darkness. The National Anthem was sung and then slowly the crowd made their way to the gates.

Peace
By George E Hobbs
(First published: September 11, 1936)

At last week's peace rally in Swindon Park, practically all sections of the community were represented, and the meeting was of an enthusiastic character. One common desire brought the people to the rally, and that was a sincere desire for peace.

The resolution moved was in the nature of a declaration of the belief: "That war is morally wrong and economically futile", and that "it rejects the idea that war is inevitable and believes the majority of peoples of all nations earnestly desire peace".

There was a further clause to the resolution: "The meeting is of the opinion that the trend of the world race in armaments is detrimental to world peace, and requests His Majesty's Government to continue a policy of co-operation with other nations, based on the principle of the sacredness of human life."

An excellent resolution and very comprehensive. There is a very real desire for peace in every country of the world, and the emphasis in the above resolution is the emphasis of every thoughtful person of every civilised country. War is morally wrong, and war is not inevitable. But this is by no means a unanimous opinion.

I have not to stretch my imagination far before I can conceive of a mind that still desires the "glamour" and "glory" of war. Such a mind may not openly express this desire, but deep down it is there. War, to such a mind, is the "manly" way of settling disputes, and, if disarmament should be realised, the nation that should adopt it would become soft and effeminate. The strong right arm is the means of showing one's foe – contemptuous foes at that – that one cannot be trifled with.

In our own country's history, war has brought to us the richest possessions the world could offer. We have only to look at the structure of the British Empire to realise this fact. By conquest – which means war – we obtained a greater part of the Indian Empire. In Africa we obtained the South-West Protectorate, Basutoland, Bechuanaland, Swaziland, Southern Rhodesia, Kenya, Nyasaland and the Sudan. In the American Continent we obtained by conquest Ontario, Quebec, Nova Scotia, Prince Edward Land, Jamaica, Trinidad and Tobago. In the Southern Seas we obtained parts of New Zealand.

By conquest and annexation – the latter again meaning war, because by annexation we obtained Natal, Transvaal, and the Orange Free State – nearly five million square miles have been added to British imperial power. The story of these conquests is in our history books. They are retold with the horrors left out, and they make a positive appeal to thousands of our present-day youth.

When the Rev CH Cleal said he was "surprised that many young people were more or less resigned to the idea of another war", he was not misinterpreting the signs, the only difference being that "resignation" is passive, while the "call of past glories", and the desire to see Britain ever in the forefront, yields not a passive resignation, but a desire for positive action.

It is to the youth of the country the appeal must be made. It is to force home upon their growing minds – in day and Sunday schools – that "war is morally wrong", literally that war is a crime against humanity. Such teaching, to have the desired effect of world peace, must begin at the cradle.

In Inez Scrivener's declaration of creed which was published in the evening and weekly issues of "The Advertiser", and is worth retaining, there is one which every mother should take to heart. This is what she wrote:

> "I believe that the peace of the world is mainly dependent on good mothers, by sowing seeds of anti-war in the minds of growing children."

Every mother has in her grasp this great responsibility and glorious privilege. Too often she feels that politics and world affairs are much too complicated for her. She feels probably that it is too utterly absurd to imagine that she can influence England's future destiny. Inez Scrivener has pointed the way which, if followed, will make the absurd practical and logical.

Coming back to the peace rally, I think Canon Narborough touched the vital spot when he said, "In this world it was not expediency, but moral law that won and ruled, and the only real security of peace was, in the long run, not might, but right, not armaments, but justice."

Mr WW Wakefield MP, backed up this statement of faith by saying, "We should not turn to arms and war to settle our differences," and Mr WG Hall reinforced both by declaring that "it is fatal to think you can achieve security or peace through armaments". Mr Hall clinched the issue with a concrete example. Said he, with telling emphasis, "The world was armed to the teeth in 1914, but it did not give us peace."

Here we have three considered expressions of faith and belief – one from the church, one from a member of Parliament, whose allegiance is to the existing Government, and one from another political party whose allegiance is to the Opposition. Yet with one voice they acclaim the futility of war as a means to peace. And such is the considered judgement of every individual who will face sanely up to the issue.

Then if war be futile, and the race for armaments a menace, where lies the solution? Which is the way out?

The way is not to deride, but to strengthen the powers of the League of Nations. The strengthening process should first involve a reconstitution. There is an urgent need that public opinion should be educated up to the desirability of establishing an international force. This is a vital necessity if the peace of the world is to be maintained. By "force", I do not suggest menace or aggression, for that would be contrary to the peace we so ardently desire.

The recent failure of the League is not disheartening when we remember that it was due to lack of experience and of immaturity. That failure taught the urgent need of reconstitution, which can be accomplished if sanity but prevails.

The success of the League depends upon the immediate formation of an International Police Force, under the positive control of an international authority. A permanent international tribunal should be set up, and the misdemeanours of nations should come before that court and be dealt in the same way as before civil court.

The constitution of this International Police Force, however, must be of such a nature that it can and must enforce the decisions of the international courts and tribunals.

It is desperately imperative that some such objective should be arrived at, or the end will soon be anarchy and destruction.

I had reached this point in this article when, on Sunday morning last, I had the pleasure of listening to a young friend preach a very forceful sermon. His theme was "Perfect love casteth out fear". As I listened, I felt that his message would be a fitting end to this article. With consummate skill he traced through those eccentricities which so often assail otherwise normal folk. One case quoted was of a Doctor of Medicine who was uneasy if he sat on an end seat. He must have people on either side of him. Every case quoted could be attributed to that mental distress called "fear" – fear of heights, of entering public buildings, or, as in the case of the doctor, fear of the empty space by his side. In most cases the causes could be traced to childish fears that were never fully overcome.

And then my young friend went out into the world of present-day affairs. He traced the malady of unrest to its cause, fear. Nations fear each other, and because of that fear there is the present mad race for armaments. "Perfect love," concluded my friend, "love to God, and for God, love to our fellows and for our fellows, casteth out fear." I am indebted to my friend, Mr SH Gee, for the fine thoughts he gave us.

Internationalism
By George E Hobbs
(First published: October 23, 1936)

Upon every question of major importance there must be, of necessity, diversity of opinion. When a question is first raised the issue usually appears to rest between two directly-opposing forces – that of the direct positive and the direct negative. If it were possible to isolate all controversy within these limits, much of the confusion would automatically vanish. In a world where freedom of thought obtains, however, it is far too much to expect that controversy can be so limited. Individual minds think individual thoughts, and individual opinions and convictions are the outcome. In consequence there eventually emerges from the direct positive and direct negative, modifications of both. Every modification sets up new machinery until we have a mass – a confusing mass – of organisations, societies, guilds, camps, etc, each differing from the other, either superficially or fundamentally.

In the realms of religion and politics there is a constant setting-up of new machinery. It indicates that the avenues through which human thought expresses itself is well-nigh unlimited. In the religious world it is seen in the multiplicity of denominations and of sects. In some instances the difference is nominal, consisting of a mere matter of church government. In other cases the difference is so fundamental as to be rigidly exclusive. One may not feel sympathetically disposed towards the exclusive denomination, but whether exclusive or inclusive, the multiplicity of religious denominations is proof that the human mind can explore and declare upon many aspects of the one central idea.

* * *

It is so in the world of what one may mass under the general heading of "politics". Political systems of thought are constantly multiplying themselves. In every party are to be found the advanced and revolutionary thinkers. In process of time these advanced thinkers weary of the slow progress made by the rank and file of their party, and they strike out along new paths of discovery and adventure. New organisations are formed and new machinery set up until, like religious organisations, their name is Legion.

And here we branch out into another field of controversy – a field which literally bristles with snags and pitfalls.

It is not to be wondered at that intensive controversy should rage around the great problem of national safety and security. It is a problem of vital importance. There is not an individual in Great Britain but what desires greatly to feel safe and secure from the perils of war. We know what war can do. We feel with a sinking dread that the last war will have been but child's play to what the next may be. And because of that knowledge and because of that dread, we wish for and pray for peace. We want to feel that sense of safety and security, not merely for ourselves, but for our work, our homes, our country. We therefore begin happily, because we all have one mind and one purpose. We desire peace. We aim for peace.

Unhappily we do not progress very far. Immediately ways and means are introduced to bring about that sense of safety and security, trouble looms upon the horizon. Singleness of purpose is maintained because all desire peace. It is singleness of mind that disappears. It is the means, and not the end, which becomes keenly controversial. As we live in a land where each individual has the right to think his own thoughts, and to pursue the path he thinks right, the controversy becomes hydra-headed and exceedingly complicated. There are as many points of view as there are degrees in a circle, and they range from extreme militancy on the one hand to extreme pacifism on the other.

There are those who believe that safety and security can be obtained by and through an individual nationalism. This process of thinking prevailed for centuries. In point of fact it prevailed up to the time of the Great War. At times, under stress of expediency, concessions were made to this mode of thought, and alliances were formed. Even so, the ingrained principle of individual nationalism could not be obliterated. Even during the Great War, if we claim that victory came to the Allies, we must remember that the chances of victory were in serious jeopardy on more than one occasion. Victory was in jeopardy because, at times, individual national prejudices and national feeling were subordinated to the common cause only with difficulty. The Diary of Earl Haig, the bitter reply to that Diary by the son of the Earl of Ypres, and the recent "War Memoirs of David Lloyd George" all hint at the presence of this danger.

Following the Great War, and while the world lay prostrate before the horror of that recent carnage and destruction, there emerged a desire to weld nationalism into internationalism, and the League of Nations was formed. For a time it seemed that the ideal of a world federation had been attained. The abstention of the USA was unfortunate. Still, a federated Europe and Near East was something of which to boast. But, alas! Immaturity and the lack of experience revealed its weaknesses. Those weaknesses, instead of being met with sympathy and courage and forbearance, gave scope to the insidious activities of the enemies of peace. The lamentable truth must be faced.

A more intense nationalism was reborn. Japan left the League. She left because she wished to exercise her right to national independence. That desire to re-establish national independence, and her (at present) quiescence, will deceive no-one. The eyes of national Japan have been, and still are, towards the West, across the Ural Mountains and, eventually, a trial of strength with Soviet Russia. Her dream has been one of conquest. If this statement is doubted, one has only to recall the words of Baron Yanaka when he was Premier of Japan. Said he in an historic speech: "In our national programme of expansion, another war with Russia, to secure the resources of North Manchuria, seems inevitable. If Soviet Russia objects to our programme, as she certainly will, this will be the opportunity for open hostilities."

* * *

The fact that Japan eventually occupied Manchuria is to the credit of Russia. Japan's attitude was hostile and aggressive. Russia stood aside and permitted the occupation of Manchuria. She did this in order to avoid war. Just how long that spirit of toleration will be permitted, or whether Russia will presently tire of Japan's aggressive attitude, and stay her with force, is a matter for future history to declare upon. Certain it is that Japan is far from satisfied, even with the vast resources of Manchuria. Her lust is still the lust of conquest.

And Italy flouted the League. Before the League's helpless vision Italy tortured Abyssinia upon the rack. Italy sought no new territory, but went to war in "defence of her honour". But the fact remains that she has besmirched what honour she may have possessed, and she has added to her Empire many hundreds of square miles. The ineptitude of the League of Nations in the face of the bombast of the dictator, Mussolini, will stand as a matter of wonder to future generations.

And France and Germany face each other with claws barely concealed. At the head of the German nation is Hitler, who, at Nuremberg last year, said: "If I were going to attack an opponent, I should act quite differently from Mussolini. I should not negotiate for months – I should suddenly, like a flash of lightning in the night, hurl myself upon the enemy."

Spain is in the midst of horrors unspeakable. And Britain is working a feverish overtime upon war materials, and enlisting a gigantic war personnel.

* * *

Nationalism has proved in the past to be ineffectual to preserve peace and to give safety and security. This return to its re-birth is futile. It can lead again to but one thing. That is war, and war more horrible than the world has yet known.

In my next article I want to show that safety and security can lie in one direction only. It lies in Internationalism as expressed through a re-vitalised League of Nations.

Internationalism (continued)
By George E Hobbs
(First published: October 30, 1936)

In my article of last week I stressed the fact that Nationalism was ineffectual to preserve peace or to give safety and security. I also stated the indisputable aspect of Nationalism – that it would lead again to war, more terrible than the world has yet known. The reasons for this are hidden from no-one who will give but an hour's serious thinking to the problem. Nationalism must fail because it is built and maintained upon individualism.

Suppose, for a moment, that all the counties of England were governed and maintained upon a individualistic basis; that every county was a law unto itself; that each county could create and administer its own laws. There would be, there could be, but one end to such a state of affairs – confusion, disruption, extermination. The internal serenity and peace of England is possible from the fact that each county is bound by moral and economic obligations to every other county, and the whole by legal obligations to the central governing head.

It was this very problem of individualism which confronted America, 150 years ago, and which changed her from a Confederacy into a Federacy.

It may be argued that the illustration of English counties, or that of the USA, does not apply to world affairs. But I claim that it does apply, just as counties in the lesser sense, are parts of a whole, and each part is dependent upon every other part in order to preserve stability. Just as, in the case of the United States of America, it was found imperative to weld individualism into collectivism, so, in the larger sense, the same principle applies to world affairs.

∗ ∗ ∗

The underlying principle of Nationalism, that of each nation being the judge of its own cause, and the punisher of its own wrongs, utterly breaks down in a world where nations are dependent and inter-dependent upon each other.

Hitler, in trying to make Germany self-contained, is attempting the impossible. "Splendid isolation" in world economics is the dream only of a disordered brain. It simply cannot be done. At some point of her national life Germany is bound to find contact with the other nations, and because of that contact she cannot isolate herself.

I, therefore, claim that Nationalism, individualism, the building of a dense hedge about a nation and saying, "We are an entity; we pursue our own independent policy," fails utterly to preserve peace and to give safety and security. There is one royal road to this attainment – one only – and that road is Internationalism.

A layman would be presumptuous in claiming proprietary rights to methods of construction. But, at least, he can use his powers of thought to separate the wheat from the chaff in the policies already outlined. We have abundant subject matter at our disposal from which to construct the avenues through which Internationalism in its highest expression can be attained.

Usually reconstruction is best by a complete demolition of existing machinery and re-building from the foundation. But this is not the policy suggested here. There is no desire to destroy the League of Nations, for, in principle, the establishment of the league was a glorious and wonderful achievement. What is needed, and urgently needed, is that the League must be strengthened and re-vitalised. Give it these added powers and this new life, and the great Commonwealth of Nations can come into being.

That this need of re-vitalising the League is present is proved from a speech by Mr Eden, a short while since. Said Mr Eden: "Nations can only strive to maintain peace if they are confident that there are peaceful means by which a change can be effected. In the view of many, it is the principal failing of the League that it stereotypes a state of things which cannot be expected to last for all time. Article XIX shows the recognition that the present state of things cannot be expected to last always – we must strive for a balanced world in which justice is done to all, and where grievances can be remedied. Unless we can set up peace on this basis, our work is useless. His Majesty's Government do not deceive themselves on this point, and, without its being achieved, they cannot hope to re-vitalise the League."

Mr Eden is an authority whose words cannot be taken lightly. Peace, he says, must be set up on a basis of justice for all, or the work of the League is useless.

Just what are the implications underlying "a basis of justice"?

Someone has said that "In all human societies, experience has proved that, in order to obtain justice, three institutions are necessary – a tribunal to translate justice into terms of law, a court to interpret it, and a sanction to enforce it." Simply interpreted, it means this: a court in which the claims of aggressor and victim can be thrashed out intelligently to all, judges to judge the claims and decree verdicts, and a police force strong enough to see that the verdict, once given, shall be duly carried out and enforced.

* * *

In my article on "Peace" of 11 September, I ventured a suggestion along these lines: that a strengthening buttress should be built into the League of Nations by the establishment of a permanent international tribunal, where the misdemeanours of nations could be tried, as is the case in civil courts. Also that an International Police Force should be established [that is] powerful enough to enforce the decisions of that court.

It would seem that the New Zealand Government hold views similar to those of Mr Eden. They have declared: "We are prepared to agree to the institution of an international force under the control of the League, or to the allocation to the League of a definite proportion of the armed forces of its members to the extent, if desired, of the whole of those forces – land, sea and air."

And then follows this significant paragraph: "We believe it improper to enforce a system of preventing war without, at the same time, setting up adequate machinery for the ventilation, and, if possible, rectification of international grievances, and we would support the establishment of an acceptable tribunal for that purpose."

The general idea of the New Zealand Government's contribution to the League's reconstruction is not impracticable, although it is of a daring character. It is that peace should be based upon equal justice for all nations through "an acceptable tribunal", and that the League – presumably through an established International Police Force – should be the custodian of all means of death and destruction, of land, sea and air.

At first glance, and without adequate thought being given to the idea, it certainly seems altogether impracticable, almost bordering upon the absurd. But, if we get down to fundamentals, we find that it is impracticable and absurd only because we argue from the standpoint of Nationalism and of Individualism. As long as argument is retained upon that basis, world peace is impossible.

Individualism is based upon the old jungle law of "everyone for himself and the devil take the hindmost". That is no satisfying conclusion for a sane-thinking world to come to. If we really and honestly desire peace, we have to think in terms of Internationalism, and not of Nationalism. As DV Wallace said, in his letter in last week's "Swindon Advertiser": "Peace, real peace, lasting peace, is based upon the active (not passive) spirit of goodwill, righteousness, and justice." Such an expression goes beyond Nationalism. It broadens out into the ideal of Internationalism. Not "my country" only, but "the world", for peace, and safety, and security.

"World Peace"
An Address Given Before the Wootton Bassett Brotherhood
By George E Hobbs
(First published: November 27, 1936)

There is no sane, normal individual who does not desire peace. You who are assembled here, in the great movement known as the "Brotherhood movement", are in it because you believe that Brotherhood, Fraternity, Comradeship is the ideal state in which society should exist. It is, to you, even more than a belief, for sometimes beliefs are found to be impracticable and even erroneous. This, for which you stand, is a great ideal – a religion, vitalised by the fact that it is practical and can be lived. But like all other religious faiths it is effective only as it is unrestricted in its operations and it its scope. Brotherhood ceases to be such, and becomes meaningless, if there be a class barrier or a colour ban. It must be universal in its scope and application – or it utterly fails. We, therefore, take our stand boldly by interpreting the Brotherhood movement – the religion of love and service – to be a movement for world peace. That is the ideal for which we aim – the ideal for which we work to achieve.

We have to take into account, however, that there are myriads of people who do not think as we think. They argue that such beliefs as we advocate are effeminate and are signs of weakness, that they are not the beliefs which strong virile men should hold. They argue that a strong armed force is the best and highest guarantee of peace. Let us agree, for the moment, with our militant friends that such argument is sound in theory and practice, but who is to have this armed force at its disposal? Being Britishers, the answer is – Britain! Good! Britain it shall be.

* * *

But what is the attitude of the other countries in this matter? Have not these the right to answer similarly? Surely the old adage is applicable, "What is sauce for the goose is sauce for the gander." Other countries have the same right to arm as we have. There follows then but one logical sequel to this attitude. As each country will wish to arm to the top of its bent, and will use every endeavour to outstrip its neighbour, there follows a mad and unrestricted race for superiority. Rich countries will have the advantage, and if the poorer countries attempt the impossible, it will be at the economic expense and subsequent poverty and misery of those countries. This argument is based upon pure individualism. Instead of securing peace, it must inevitably lead to war.

* * *

In the "Swindon Advertiser" of a week or so ago, I stressed the fact that nationalism – individualism – utterly breaks down as a guarantee of peace in a world where nations are dependent and interdependent upon each other. Just as we, individually, are parts of the whole, so we as a nation, are but part of the whole, and, as such, we cannot act independently if we would desire peace. The royal road to world peace is that of internationalism – a commonwealth of nations. But how is this great ideal to be brought about?

Following the Great War, some effort was made to outlaw war by the establishment of the "League of Nations", and while the principle of the League is sound, its functioning powers are unsound because they are limited. It is not true to say that the League has failed. I again repeat that the principle of the League is sound, but that it functions badly because of its limitations. The League will function effectively when international authority has vested in the League supreme and unrestricted control. How this can be brought about our own history can show.

Our ancestors put a stop to fighting in this country by introducing and developing a system which ensured justice. Courts were set up and policemen were enrolled. If an individual, therefore, has a grievance, instead of taking the law into his own hands and committing an assault upon his neighbour, he makes application for his case to be heard before the courts. The policeman is there to prevent him from committing the assault, and to see that the decisions of the court are carried out. Only when some such system has been set up for nations, when the reign of law has taken the place of the present international anarchy, will war, as we have known it in the past, become impossible.

* * *

We have to acknowledge the fact that the League, as at present constituted, is not equipped adequately either to deal with those disputes which arise between nations or to maintain peace. To be fully equipped, the League must have vested in it supreme authority, and powers to compel that authority being upheld.

At the end of 1918, General Smuts gave some practical suggestions to aid the new charter which then loomed in sight. Said he: "We must carefully avoid the League becoming a mere debating society. The situation does not call for a new talking shop. We want an instrument of government which, however much talk is put into it at the one end, will grind out a decision at the other end. We want a League which will be real, practical and effective as a system of government." Smuts was far-seeing. He probably realised that while the "conference method" – the "talking shop" – was good in domestic politics, it was useless, of itself, in world politics. Conferences must give place to courts, and courts must have the power at their disposal to enforce the decisions given.

* * *

"But," you will say to me, "do not you develop into a mere talking machine? Please bring out some practical suggestion." Let me try. I am a member of a society known as "The New Commonwealth". I am a member because I believe they advocate the best policy yet postulated. We seek to educate public opinion up to the great need of a reconstituted and revitalised League of Nations. The visioned ideal is a world federation, a commonwealth of nations, a world Parliament. Such a revolutionary concept, however, is impossible for fruition until the "international mind" has been created and developed to a far greater extent than exists to-day.

There is a desire first, to set up an International Equity Tribunal, this tribunal to be empowered to deal with all disputes that do not come within the jurisdiction of the Permanent Court at The Hague; and, secondly, the creation of an International Police Force, under the control of the international authority. These are complementary. They cannot be divorced, and should be established simultaneously. The court or judge cannot be effective without the policeman, and conversely, the policeman cannot function without the judge.

But let us understand what is intended by a police force. There is a distinction between an Army force and a police force. The business of an army is to prepare for war, and when war eventuates, to fight against the enemy until victory is assured. On the other hand, the business of the police force is to serve as the arm of the law, to stop a brawl or quell disturbances – this as a preliminary to the case being taken before a magistrate. In the police force thus set up, they would function in a similar manner. They would act to compel, if necessary, the cessation of hostilities, if hostilities eventuated.

But how is this force to be equipped? We have said that the police force should be so equipped as to be able to deal effectively with the findings of the International Court. How can it be so equipped? Let us examine the two alternatives.

* * *

The next war (which God forbid!) will be a war of extermination. Under existing conditions there can be no rules of war. The first shattering blow will be directed against the civil population – its cities, ports and nerve centres. The most diabolical methods will be used for destruction. Armies and navies are no longer protective screens. The range of the bomber has now become the deciding factor. Europe may not be able to bomb America, or America… Europe. The same is true of Europe and Japan, but the nations of Western Europe can annihilate each other in a few hours or days. And Western European Nations are compelled to adapt themselves to these conditions – or perish. The annihilation of European civilisation is then the one alternative, an alternative, which under present conditions, cannot be denied.

* * *

The other alternative is revolutionary, but it is certainly not impracticable. We can speculate upon the effect of its achievement. Given the creation of the International Police Force, then, into their custody must be placed those super-weapons of destruction which scientists have given to mankind during the last 25 years – the super-land weapons, poison gas, the aerial bomber, and under the control of the international authority, the submarine, or its abolition.

On two occasions France has submitted a plan for an International Air Force to the Disarmament Conference, based upon the technical knowledge of its air experts. Whatever thoughts we may have upon this very difficult and complicated problem, we have to agree that nationalism has not solved the problem of peace. Nationalism cannot solve it. It is diametrically opposed to the solution of peace. Internationalism has not yet been tried. Why not, at least, think upon these lines as a possible solution? Things cannot be worse than the present condition of international anarchy. Why not think along the lines of international fellowship – a federation of nations, a world Parliament.

The Problems of "Defence"
By George E Hobbs
(First published: April 30, 1937)

Mr Chamberlain, the Chancellor of our national finances, in dealing with his Budget proposals, spoke of a "National defence contribution". The name he gave to this proposed contribution explains itself. He spoke of millions of pounds as glibly and as easily as the housewife speaks of pennies, but while the housewife – the chancellor of her household – speaks of her pennies as being expended upon food, clothing, rates, rents and a possible holiday, the National Chancellor speaks of his millions as being expended upon some object which he terms "National defence". The earnestness with which Mr Chamberlain pleaded for a ready acceptance of his plan proves that he, at least, feels that millions of pounds spent upon national defence is justifiable and needful. He may be right and he may be wrong. Let us see if we can find out what it is all about.

The dictionary defines defence as "protection" and "vindication". It is an abstract noun, and the sounds of its pronouncement and of its meanings seem good and virtuous. Emerging from the noun is the verb "defend", which again seems to have a wholesome ring about it. Its meaning too, is good, for it is interpreted to mean "keep off anything hurtful" and "to maintain against attack".

But just as that trite old saying is true, "There is more than one way of killing a cat", so it is equally true that there is more than one way of interpreting terms of human speech.

* * *

Settlers in wild regions build stockades around their possessions so that the cattle – their means of subsistence – can be driven in at night. The stockade is the means of defence against the marauding creatures of the wild, but should these creatures attempt to break through, then the settlers "defend" to "keep off anything hurtful", and "to maintain against attack".

Against the creatures whose only law is the instinctive slaughter to kill for food, the passive "defence" – the stockade – and the active "defend" – rifles to kill – are both natural and legitimate. But when we get into the world of men, the terms take on a slightly different meaning.

The pioneer who trespassed into the lands of the native peoples had also to build stockades, but this time not for defence, or to defend, against animals, but against his own human kind. The natives, resenting the intrusion into, and confiscation of, their territory, waged continual warfare against the pioneer; and the pioneer, in order to maintain what he had stolen, defended his possessions by force of arms. In these circumstances while "defence" and "defend" still retain the meanings given to them, both terms take on a deeper significance. The defence of the pioneer becomes really an attack of aggression, for they have stolen land from the rightful possessors, and, by the same argument, the attack by the natives becomes a defence, for they attack to defend their lawful territory.

Now it may be that some such idea may be behind the term "National defence" – that nations with aggressive dispositions and desires look upon Britain and her possessions with covetous eyes; that, if only they felt strong enough, they would challenge her to a trial of strength and attempt to beat her to her knees, in order to plunder and rob her of her possessions. If this is so, then a menace to Britain's life does exist and a remedy must be found, a remedy so powerful that it will stay the hand of any nation which has aggressive designs upon our land.

* * *

But it is not true to say that if this is Britain's meaning of the term "National defence", so also is it the meaning given to it by other nations; that just as we fear aggression and must, in consequence, prepare a force adequate to meet it, so other nations fear the same and must also prepare to resist it. If this supposition be true, then the remedy by any national individualism becomes an impossible one. The remedy becomes a new menace, and by its very nature must defeat itself.

The argument that the existence of a strong army, navy and air-force is a guarantee of peace may be true, but it cannot be true, from an individual standpoint. Every pound sterling spent by an individual nation upon armaments is at once countered by a similar amount spent upon a similar project by every other nation. Every scientist of an individual nation bent upon research work into poison gases for destruction, is countered by the scientists of every other nation bent upon the same dire objective. It is not merely futile. It is utter madness.

If "force" by armaments is to be the only guarantee of peace, then it should be an international force, internationally controlled, and under international authority. And this, I am convinced, will be the realisation of the near future. It may be somewhat tardy in its recognition and in its establishment, but it will come. It is bound to come. The rule of law is bound to supersede the present rule of anarchy.

* * *

Men of clear vision and sane thinking – the "sun-crowned men" of the present generation throughout the nations – are visioning a time when the Commonwealth of Nations will be an established fact. Before that time the machinery of the League of Nations will have been strengthened in its weaker parts. The force of the world will be concentrated into a pooled international Police Force, with all the major lethal weapons under its supreme control. A nation then daring to upset the peace of the world will do so with the knowledge that disciplinary measures will at once be instituted against its aggression.

If, instead of being insular in our thinking and in our endeavours, we would but expend our national energies and our national resources into an endeavour to create an international authority of power, we should then begin that glorious era of peace which the world so badly needs.

No one will object to taxation if lasting good is the outcome, but we do object to taxation when the outcome is waste, discontent and ultimate poverty. That way lies danger, and danger which is very real.

Gleanings [27]
By George E Hobbs
(First published: November 12, 1937)

This week our thoughts turn naturally to the significance of Armistice Day. Some prefer to call it "Remembrance" Day. Call it by what name suits the mind best, it must mean something to that mind – or nothing. The reader to whom it means nothing will probably read to this point, and cease to read farther. But may I beg one favour of such a reader? Will you please continue to read to the very end. I have never yet begged such a favour of any individual. I beg it now of you – you, to whom Armistice Day means nothing.

You see, I feel somehow that I know why it means nothing to you. It once meant something to you – something which brought to your vision an ideal towards which all your endeavours were directed. You have not abated one jot in your efforts towards that ideal. Simply, you have changed in your attitude towards Armistice Day. And the reason for your changed attitude is that you became nauseated by the change of emphasis given to that day.

The original emphasis – and the one you yourself gave to the day – was that of consecration and of dedication. In the original setting of that day there was evidenced a humility of spirit. The awful toll of life – life which could not be spared from the world, the physical and mental suffering of the wounded, the heart-broken agony of the bereaved, the indescribable misery due to the abnormal conditions under which the world lived for four years – brought not only a chastened, but a humbled spirit. On Armistice Day we bowed our heads in shame that we, made in the image of Divinity, had betrayed that Divinity, and made of ourselves less than men. A mental vow was recorded that never again should such things be.

Gradually, but surely, there came a change of emphasis to Armistice Day. The glorious dead were remembered because they had given their all. Under the call of supreme duty they had made the supreme sacrifice. And we must never forget that fact. The tribute to their courage, their bravery and fidelity to duty must ever remain green.

While this is as it should be, the unfortunate fact remains that a change of emphasis has come. No longer does the national conscience assume an attitude of consecration and dedication – an attitude which, in the earlier days, tended to a mental, moral and spiritual reconstruction. To-day such an attitude would be considered effeminate, soft and contradictory to the spirit of the nation. That is the key-stone – the spirit of the nation – and that changing spirit has made its presence felt upon Armistice Day. No useful purpose is served in blinding the eyes to this indisputable fact. The emphasis has changed from antimilitarism to militarism. Instead of it being a day set apart that the nation may re-affirm its determination to avoid even the semblance of war, it has become more and more a series of military parades. And the two spirits are not in harmony. By all means have military parades when necessary. But the one day of the year when the symbol of war should be absent is... Armistice Day.

* * *

I had written this far when, in Monday's issue of "The Evening Advertiser", I read the following in "Our London Letter":

> "In Regent's Park there is also being organised a service for those who wish to celebrate Armistice as a religious service rather than as a military parade. The late Canon Sheppard was to have conducted it. On reflection there is some justification for dropping the troops from the Cenotaph ceremony nowadays, when scarcely any of the men on parade possess war medal ribbons."

Now it seems to me that the suggestion contained in the letter is entirely wrong in principle. It matters not one iota whether the troops have war medal ribbons or not. The principle of Armistice Day is that war has ceased. And, in the spirit of rejoicing that the devilish horrors, so long experienced, are now things of the past, nothing should appear that day which symbolises that horror.

I can quite understand that military, naval and air units would wish to attend the Cenotaph ceremonies as a mark of respect to, and remembrance of, fallen comrades of the various units. This could be accomplished by, at the most, the wearing of uniform only. Even side-arms should be left in barracks.

* * *

And now let us leave the controversial and get down to what we feel to be the real implications of Armistice Day. By the time this appears in print the celebrations will be over, and therefore I must continue this article in the past tense.

Just why did we gather round the Cenotaph, or attend a service, or listen to the wireless broadcast of the London Cenotaph service? Were our actions guided purely by sentiment? If so, then we found the sentiment vanish with the conclusion of the service. So far as we ourselves personally were concerned, the service gave to us no stimulus beyond the emotion of the moment. Was our attendance merely the celebration of an anniversary? If so, then again all that was gained was an inspiration as short-lived as the day itself.

There must be more than sentiment or the date upon the calendar, to inspire one towards working for a better future. There must be the seed-germ of some great conviction, some great urge, which shall drive one, even to sacrifice, towards the fulfilment of one's ideal. There can be no greater ideal than the peace of the world. Not merely the peace of Britain, but the peace of the world – a peace in which, remembering that all nations are the children of one Father, shall be the peace of one common fraternity. That is the ideal for which one works. That is the vision one sees.

"When all the Earth shall brothers be;
The nations, one fraternity."

If this ideal is to be attained then, to me, Armistice Day implies a threefold necessity, a threefold obligation – a change of heart, a change of outlook, a change of purpose.

It seems to me very profoundly that to achieve the general we must begin with the particular – ie, oneself. In our own lives we have to cultivate kindness and tolerance, forgiveness and generosity. We certainly cannot hope to bring these qualities to the world in general unless we ourselves can show them in our own lives. If these are but travesties in our own lives, then we are hopeless as examples of them. We have to exhibit them, or fail.

Then there must be a change of outlook. We have to fix in our minds, with a sincerity that brooks no contradiction or compromise, that force, as contained in individual national armaments, cannot give security and peace – or alternatively face the prospect of wars created and made possible by nationalism.

If we honestly and sincerely believe that, in so far as our own country is concerned, national armaments are the only bulwarks of security and peace, then, at least, let us cease to be hypocritical about our convictions. We have to take our stand either on that side which believes moral and spiritual regeneration to be the only hope of humanity, or upon that side which believes material force, as rested in nationalism, to be the only hope. The two will not, and cannot, mix. That is one reason why I feel that all symbols of material force should be eliminated from Armistice Day services.

There must also be a change of purpose. A change of heart and of outlook are of no avail unless such changes produce results. And those results should be of practical utility – a change of purpose.

∗ ∗ ∗

HG Wells has declared that war on a grand scale is imminent. He has demonstrated this by means of a graphed war curve. If, by this demonstration, he infers that wars move in cycles, then he is profoundly wrong. Wars are not brought about by blind forces, nor by mechanical laws, but by the deliberate choice and determination of man. Man himself determines war.

Wells's picture of the immediate future cannot mature if man's purpose is changed and redirected towards peace. Our purpose, to have any practical effect for good, must be directed towards a reconstruction of moral and spiritual values. I trust we thought of this yesterday and determined upon our future activity.

Gleanings [32]
By George E Hobbs
(First published: December 17, 1937)

A short time ago Sir Fabian Ware broadcast a talk entitled "The Ten Million Dead". In that broadcast Sir Fabian said that "of the ten millions dead of the world's fighting forces, 1,104,000 were sailors, soldiers and airmen of our own British Commonwealth". He then went on to speak of the war graves, cemeteries and war memorials, how they were maintained, etc, and added: "These are the material memorials to our dead of the Great War, and through these memorials the dead speak to us and to posterity."

Sir Fabian recalled that King George V visited the war cemeteries in 1922, and spent four days among them. He was profoundly impressed, and he summed up his impressions in the following words:

> "I have asked myself whether there can be more potent advocates of peace upon earth through the years to come than this massed multitude of silent witnesses to the desolation of war. The existence of these visible memorials will eventually serve to draw all peoples together in sanity and self-control."

The speaker, in recalling these words, said that this hope "has begun to be realised", and this realisation he termed "The New Internationalism", which first was formed by the "independent nations of the British Empire". Next came a union with former Allies. Then, after some time had elapsed, the German nation also came into this amalgamation.

All this makes good hearing. Former enemies have now concerted together in common cause. In order that this common cause should be placed upon a solid foundation, a treaty has been signed between "all States of the British Empire, Germany and France".

* * *

Now just what is this New Internationalism? What is the common cause which has been ratified by treaty? It is "for setting up a joint body to conduct and plan in common for the remembrance of the dead". Since the treaty has been signed, "all three together have visited German graves in France and Great Britain, bringing the peoples of the three countries, slowly perhaps, and only one short step at a time, closer together".

Every agency by which the nations of the earth can be brought closer together should be welcomed with thankful hearts. And if the common remembrance of the dead and the interchange of visits to war graves can be the means of cementing nations together in the great cause of peace, then thank God for this one common approach to the solution of the problem.

But can we not advance a step farther? If Internationalism is a good thing in remembrance, and if this is a step to bring the nations closer together, then surely the same principle should hold good in the case of prevention. If nationalism was to be merged into Internationalism where regret of, and sorrow for, the foolishness of the past is concerned, then I suggest it can be merged in a constructive policy for the prevention of future foolishness.

To prevent a future cause for remembrance, then, must be the next step forward in the great quest of universal peace. With every credit given to the better understanding brought about by the planning in common for the remembrance of the dead, it must be remembered that this is not a policy of construction, but a gesture of courtesy. To internationalise constructively for the prevention of future wars demands a policy of boldness – a policy in which national isolation has no part.

* * *

I can best outline that policy by "gleaning" from the columns of "The Swindon Advertiser" of December 18, 1957 (20 years hence):

"At long last the Age of Reason has dawned. And it is fitting that the International Council of the Commonwealth of Nations should commence its first session so near to Christmas. The message of the Angels has at last been fulfilled in its literal completeness. 'On earth peace, goodwill toward men.' Perhaps we shall be pardoned if we give a brief resume of the steps which led to this great and glorious consummation.

"The war early in the present century was known as the 'Great War'– so named because it was the greatest war known to history. Upon its termination the world generally, realising the utter madness and futility of war, made a solemn vow that never again should war ravish the nations of the earth. Strengthened in this newfound virtue, the League of Nations was born.

"Looking back across the years, we can judge the depth of that virtue. The machinery set up to outlaw war became very complex. But even with its undoubted complexity, it would have functioned but for the fact it was housed upon a faulty foundation. The League became International in name only. Each member of the League, instructed by his individual Government, retained his insular national outlook. Every proposition coming before the League was first rigidly inspected from the national point of view. In consequence, it became a house divided against itself. And it is proverbial that a house so divided cannot stand. It was therefore not surprising that the 'Greater War' came 1947 – just ten years ago. Under the then existing national conditions, each nation built its armaments to the limit of its capacity. This race for armaments was known as 'Defence Schemes'. In our modern vocabulary we know them by another name.

"As we too sorrowfully know, the war of 1947 out-devilled that of 1914-1918. Thirty million dead against ten million in the previous war. But, thank God! – out of madness sanity has come.

"The dream of an International Court of Law, with Judges having supreme powers of administering international justice, an International Police Force, comprising Army, Navy, and Air units, and, above all, the free International territory from which these new powers could function, had become an experience of fact.

"Looking back, one can feel sympathy with those who strenuously opposed this scheme. It was too fantastic, too impossible. Where could a territory be found of sufficient size to work the scheme? Where could men be found to act as International Judges? What would be their own status relative to their own country? Not only so, but the greatest difficulty of all: Would the nations yield their age-long right (individuality) to the world's general good?

It was just nonsense, the dream of a mind diseased. How true it is that progress is never purchased cheaply! And the price paid to free the world for ever from the terror of war has been thirty million precious lives. This price, this terrible sacrifice, need never have been, had the statesman of the world faced up to the issue, boldly and frankly, 30 years ago. Theirs must be the responsibility.

"But now of the immediate future. It will be remembered that when the International scheme caught the popular imagination, and public opinion began to voice its demand for its inception, the vexed problem of territory settled itself. The whole world has expressed its admiration at the magnanimity of the Spanish Government. That in expiation for the profound suffering of her people through years of internal strife, the Spanish Government places it territory unconditionally at the disposal of the International Council.

"As our readers know, the Seat of the International Court is at Madrid. The International Police Fleet is divided into two squadrons. One operates from the southern Port of Málaga in the Province of Granada; the Northern squadron from a fairly wide, protected bay near to Santoña. The International Air Police Force are stationed at Jaén, while the International Military Police Force are located at Santiago. Hence, what was thought to be the dream of a mind diseased, twenty years ago, has now become the realisation of sanity.

"Our readers will also know that the Judges who are upon the Equity Tribunal automatically become denationalised, or perhaps it would be better to put it, Internationalised, during their term of office. Each has signed a declaration that during his term of office he will rigidly refrain from State politics.

"One important clause in the new Commonwealth Constitution is the entire abolition of submarines as weapons of defence or attack. Whether they will be used as under-water carriers of passengers and mail is still to be considered by the Council. Air-bombing machines, of course, are directly under the control of the International Police Force.

"The Doxology can now be sung. War, the despoiler, is dead. No nation or people dare now become aggressive. Law replaces anarchy."

Gleanings [84, extract]
By George E Hobbs
(First published: December 30, 1938)

First then, let us look into the "Retrospect" mirror. What does it show to us?

In general, it shows a world distorted and out of true alignment; a world which has lived unto itself, selfish and cruel; a world which can be truly summed up by a recent cartoon. A picture of Santa Claus was shown carrying two sacks. In one there were cannon, in the other were rifles. And Santa was pictured as saying, "Everybody seems to be wanting the same this year."

But I think our retrospect mirror reveals that, while every nation seems to want the same thing, they are not all animated by the same root cause. Some leaders of nations speak of peace with tongue in cheek, and these are out for aggression.

The mirror shows an undistorted view of rebels against civilisation. Some devilish spirit possesses the souls of these leaders, and they are out for world domination. The mirror records not so much the bombast of two men as it does the swirling torrent of a rising cult, uncompromisingly ruthless and cruel. Call that cult by what name you will, it is now the credal faith of Germany, Italy and Japan, and it aims at the overthrow of the world's stability.

And the mirror reveals no less the other side of the picture – the servility of "non-aggressive" nations to the same god (power), and to the same ritual (force). The ugly visage of Baal has put fear into the hearts of these nations – such terrible fear as to render them incapable of seeing the glowing presence of Supreme Justice, whose "mills grind slowly, but grind exceedingly small".

The retrospect mirror reveals all too plainly where faiths are placed – not in the power which can frustrate evil and bring to naught the schemes of ill-balanced minds, but in a power which in itself must destroy itself.

Mighty empires of the past have attempted to pull off similar tricks, and in doing so have believed the world [was] at their feet. Where these empires stood are now tractless wastes, forgotten save for the interest in them of archæologists.

There are thousands of folk today who fear very much more what Hitler and Mussolini threaten than what Supreme Justice can do. And in that fear they betray the weakness of their faith.

Oh, I know the old, old slogans which thrill the heart by their very phrasing. Literally they are "red herrings" which distract the thoughts and which rob the logical of their logic and the wise of their wisdom. "We must arm against aggression!" "We must be powerful to resist attack!" "Our defence is not defiance!" etc, and a good many more etcs. And they are all so pitifully futile.

No, among the people of the Earth the mirror shows not one strong nation; not one nation that is prepared to become weak, so weak that in that very weakness it may find itself superlatively strong. To undertake such a task would mean a people saturated in the truth that "Right-doing exalteth a nation". It would mean a people whose faith is steadfast in the only things that mattered. In the fact that:

"...behind the dim unknown,
Standeth God within the shadow,
Keeping watch above His own,"

This pen of mine is but a weak instrument. My voice is but one "crying in the wilderness". But, just as long as I can grasp a pen, and just as long as I can make my voice heard, so long shall I write and say: "O foolish ones. Who hath bewitched you that ye should not obey the truth?"

And the truth is that by armaments cometh Armageddon, but by a working faith in the All Wise cometh security and peace.

The reader may term the above "the vapourings of a mind diseased" if they so wish. But just as true as morning follows the night, so true will history record that security and peace can never depend upon physical means. The whole long history of the world is against it, and time after time has proved its futility.

"They that take the sword must perish by the sword" is a truism which no argument can refute.

And there I must leave it.

Gleanings [85, extracts]
By George E Hobbs
(First published: January 6, 1939)

New Year's Eve! The sands of the year are sinking fast as I write my last article in the year 1938. By the time this appears in print the new year will be six days old. One more lap of the journey ticked off; one more commenced. What has 1939 in store for us and the world?

But I anticipate. Let us look once more into the "Retrospect" mirror. In my last article I stressed with intent the darker side of the international picture—the world adrift in chaos like a ship without rudder, compass or pilot. It is indeed a tragic picture, and certainly one which will reflect little credit in the eyes of posterity. The banal jest of "What did you do in the Great War, Daddie?" will be changed into a searching challenge. "What did you do in the great peace, Daddie?" will be the query of posterity. And the reply to that challenge must be, "Prepared for another war, son!" Such is the correct interpretation of the present age...

And what is your attitude to the great call of peace? It is little good praying for peace if you yourself are not of a peaceful mind and heart. Just as charity begins at home, so does the desire for peace. And we have no right to pray for world peace until we ourselves are men and women of peace. Then we can work for national and international peace, but not until then.

The future hangs upon the present, and the present depends upon each one of us. If New Year's Day found us with an added zeal for Truth, and Right, and Peace, then the future is rosy with promise. And next year, please God, we shall find the world so advanced for these that "The new earth" will have dawned.

Chapter 10

The Long March to War

> *This is the true militancy – the militancy of intelligent thought and conviction, and action against wrong and oppression; the intelligent, sane thinking which must herald in the reign of brotherhood, of peace and of universal tranquility. Not shell and shrapnel, but the free choice of intelligence.*
> **From Gleanings [30] by George Ewart Hobbs (December 3, 1937)**

George was already aged 56 at the outbreak of the Second World War, and Foreman-in-Charge of X Shop at GWR works, Swindon. In the circumstances, he was never going to be required to take up arms, but we do know that he was enrolled as an Air Raid Precaution (ARP) warden.

In the previous chapter, you will have already read much of his barely-concealed panic that many of the world's major powers were sleepwalking into another global conflagration. As a preacher and an experienced public speaker, he was no stranger to emphasising his key points, many times over. Some might argue: *ad nauseam*. So passionately did he feel that the answer to international unrest lay in a more assertive League of Nations #2 that he almost comes across as over-invested in this solution – and unwilling to explore (or countenance) alternatives.

You get a real sense of his frustration with the political establishment and perhaps even more poignantly... with his apparent inability to influence events. You can almost hear him saying: "Why is no one listening to me?"

To George, the co-remedies of the Christian gospel, internationalism and disarmament seemed so blindingly obvious that for the ruling class to go on and ignore them must have hurt him badly. But it's fair to say that his belief in pacifism hadn't always been as well-entrenched as it was to become in the 1930s.

Even great thinkers are entitled to change their minds; their willingness and their ability to do so on fundamental issues may be why they *are* great thinkers.

Around the middle part of 1915, Morris Bros (then owners of the *Swindon Advertiser*) published a booklet entitled T*he British Soldier and Other Poems 1914-15* containing a selection of George's verses, almost all of which had already appeared in the newspaper from October 1914 onwards.

Inspired and informed by Britain's declaration of war on Imperial Germany on August 4, 1914, some of these poems might be described as 'heroic' at best and 'jingoistic' at worst. It's also the case that his use of the derogatory term 'Hun' sets a more bellicose tone which one might not find with the terms 'Prussian' or 'German'.

> O God of the Battles to Thee now we cry,
> Our forces to strengthen, and each brave Ally.
> They fight all for justice 'gainst tyranny strong,
> God give them the victory – they fight against wrong.
> (From *Britain's Response* by George Ewart Hobbs, October 30, 1914)

And look at the fifth stanza from his poem, *Don't Criticise*, first published on December 5, 1914:

> We will give our soldiers credit – may god bless them every one!
> From the Continental coastline they have kept the boastful Hun.
> But should that coastline be exposed, and its towns in Prussia's grip,
> There is still a potent factor in each British battleship.

The poem entitled *Britain's Need*, which appeared on June 25, 1915, is prefaced with the following lines, which relate to a Glasgow-based heavy-engineering and armaments conglomerate:

> Messrs Wm Beardmore & Co, with the consent of Lord Kitchener, sent a deputation of eight of their employees to visit our soldiers in the trenches. They returned with this message ringing in their ears, from all grades and ranks: "More shells are needed, and needed quickly."

The sixth verse leaves one in no doubt about George's feelings at that time:

> Would you prevent that cry of awful fear,
> From British lads with ammunition spent,
> Fighting for us, and all we hold most dear,
> Can you desert those lads and be content?

Indeed, by the previous April, the content of a number of the war-related poems that appeared in Poet's Corner in the *Advertiser* were on the receiving end of adverse criticism from a few in the wider readership.

In response, George wrote a letter to the paper dated April 8, 1915 (under the general heading of Poets and the War) in which he pointed out that wars are caused by the selfishness of man and that the then current war was no exception. He went on to state:

> This was, then, as far as England was concerned, a war of honour, and had England failed in her duty, she would forever cease to be an honourable nation. War is horrible, it is detestable, it is devilish, and the responsibility of this war rests, not upon the defender, but upon the aggressor. And there can be no two opinions as to who the aggressor was.
>
> This being the case, when I write my verses upon some particular phase of the war, I do not extol war. Nor do I not rejoice at victory, because victory means death to someone. But, in that victory I see what our brave lads are fighting for.
>
> They are fighting because the honour of England demanded it. They are laying down their lives in the defence of the weak. The cry of Belgium has entered like iron into their souls, and if I can pay a humble tribute to their courage, I want to do so, and shall continue to do so as long as the Editor consents to publish my verses.

However, by the following July, George had written a more reflective piece, entitled *Meditation*, and we thought it important enough to include the penultimate and final stanzas:

> When concord, peace and brotherhood
> Reigns o'er the world;
> When each will seek the other's good:
> Hate's banner furled.
>
> I pray: I rise a better man
> For this blest sight;
> And trust to do whatever I can
> To aid the right

We can only speculate as to what may have caused George to look again at his stance on the Great War. No doubt the increasing British casualties would have done more than anything to influence public opinion. But perhaps it was the death in action on June 15, 1915 of Lance-Corporal George Wilfred Gee, a friend and fellow Methodist Local Preacher that caused George to reflect more profoundly upon the war, its belligerents and its human consequences.

It is certainly the case that following Gee's demise, George never mentioned the Germans by name again. Instead of that you hear: 'This is the future. The Dragon is vanquished' (A Year of War, July 1915), 'Demons of the night' (Nurse Cavell, October 13, 1915) and 'our struggles 'gainst Satanic might' (Intercession – October 29, 1915) with the battle now condensed to one of good versus evil and of justice and liberty versus injustice and tyranny. There's no guessing which side George thought God was on.

The series of war-related and other poetry had effectively concluded by the end of 1916, although a further piece entitled *A Column of Verse – David & Goliath/The French Soldier*, appeared in 1922. Nothing more on the subject of warfare or bloodshed by George, either in the form of poetry or prose, appeared... until 1933.

In this chapter, we will set out to chart the events that, with the benefit of hindsight, lead up to the advent of the Second World War – all of profound concern to George in his articles in the *Swindon Advertiser*.

History and hindsight now inform us that the war was inevitable, years before, and that it was global, but if the world was sleepwalking towards it, George was different; he saw the signs, and his writings at this time tell us what it was like for those who knew what they meant.

We begin our examples with a letter, **World Peace in Peril** (March 3, 1933), in which George reveals his concerns about the potential for conflict involving the Japanese Empire, The Republic of China and the Soviet Union.

For background, the Japanese Empire invaded Manchuria in 1931 (an area rich in natural resources) under a confected pretext, and then established the puppet state of Manchukuo, six months later. Following the publication of the report on the invasion by the Lytton Commission of the League of Nations, a motion was raised to condemn Japan as an aggressor. This prompted Japan to withdraw from the League in March 1933.

In **One Aspect of the Incarnation** (December 21, 1934), he begins by highlighting how even the mighty Roman empire eventually slipped into terminal decline and then goes on to assert his master plan for a better world – themes that would become familiar in much of his subsequent writing.

The "Bombshell" (March 13, 1936) is a response to the actions of the previous week, when Hitler ordered the military re-occupation of the Rhineland – German territory from where it had been forbidden to station its own troops under the terms of the post Great War Treaty of Versailles and Locarno Treaties.

As far as George was concerned, the humiliation that Germany suffered at the hands of the Allies at the end of the Great War was entirely responsible for the current emergency, and a resurgent Germany was an entirely predictable event, representing not only a huge failure of statecraft, but also revealing a lack of understanding of basic psychology. It is fair to say that is also what we, with hindsight, would agree with him; the fact that he needed to point it out at the time suggests either that it was not so obvious to his contemporaries, but it certainly tells us much about his wisdom and ability to read situations.

But it is not just the actions of the Nazis in Germany that are ringing George's alarm bells. In **Victory & Annexation** (May 15, 1936), he references the Second Italo-Abyssinian War, which commenced with the Italian invasion of present-day Ethiopia in October 1935 – resulting in a declaration of its annexation on May 7, 1936. He viewed it as a further example of the aggressive expansionism that characterised the behaviour of the Axis powers, as well as the inability of the League of Nations to bring errant nations to account.

As a footnote: a resolution tabled at the League of Nations on June 30, by Emperor Haile Selassie – to deny recognition of the Italian conquest – was defeated, and days later, the League voted to end all sanctions against the aggressor. And somewhat shamefully, Britain and France recognised Italian hegemony over Abyssinia in 1938.

Gleanings [21] (October 1, 1937) could quite easily have been included in the previous chapter, Peace, Brotherhood & Internationalism. However, it rightfully takes its place here, given that George seizes the opportunity to highlight the Japanese bombing of Nanking (Nanjing) and Canton (Guangzhou), which took place on or around September 23, during the Second Sino-Japanese War. What shocked the world particularly was the targeting of densely-populated residential districts, as well as strategic targets, leading to huge civilian losses.

From a historical perspective, it is significant that he also references the bombing of the Basque town of Guernica on April 26, 1937, during the Spanish Civil War. Carried out by the Condor Legion of the German Luftwaffe and the Fascist Italian Aviazione Legionaria in support of Franco's Nationalists, it was one of the first aerial bombings to come to world attention because of its deliberate targeting of a civilian population.

Nevertheless, he does take some solace from the results of the Nyon Conference held in Switzerland the month before – particularly because it chimes with his own belief that the armed forces of various nations ought to work together to enforce peace in conflict zones.

In this instance, numerous countries including the UK, France, Turkey and the Soviet Union worked together to provide naval patrols in the

Mediterranean, to deter 'piracy' and to strengthen non-intervention in the Spanish Civil War. Indeed, the word 'piracy' was *de facto*, the unrestricted submarine warfare being conducted by Italy on international shipping and, interestingly, the Nyon Conference succeeded where the League of Nations had already failed.

Gleanings [44, extract] (March 18, 1938) makes reference to the Anschluss of Austria by Nazi Germany, which began on March 12, 1938, when German troops crossed the border to enforce the annexation of their near neighbour.

George also mentions the militarisation of the previously demilitarised Saarland, a German territory which was *de facto* controlled by France under a League of Nations mandate, in the aftermath of the Great War. The Saar returned to German rule following a plebiscite in 1935, and then, along with the wider Rhineland region, was subsequently re-occupied by Wehrmacht troops, the following year, thereby restoring full German sovereignty.

This piece is also notable for George's attempt to analyse Adolf Hitler's psyche.

In **Gleanings [45, extract]** (March 25, 1938) George returns to the ongoing matter of the Spanish Civil War, and in particular the aerial bombing of Barcelona, which was targeted by the Fascist Italian air wing and the Nazi Luftwaffe, in a series of airstrikes over three days, beginning March 16, 1938. Believed to be the first example of carpet bombing in the history of aerial warfare, it resulted in the deaths of 1,300 people, with around 2,000 people injured. It was also notable for the fact that there were few, if any, military sites in the campaign, plus the fact that the sporadic nature of the raids was designed to demoralise the civilian population.

Also mentioned is the blowing up by Republican forces of the five-storey Casa Blanca building, in Extremadura, near Madrid on March 19, in which 300 Nationalists died. It is said that it took Government loyalists six months to dig the 600-yard tunnel in order to lay the landmine that caused the explosion.

And George poses the question as to whether Hitler could yet be invited to join a caucus of nations in the interests of peace.

The issues surrounding the rebellious German minority within the borders of Czechoslovakia are uppermost in the mind of George Hobbs in **Gleanings [70]** (September 23, 1938).

At the instigation of Hitler, the Sudeten German leader, Konrad Henlein, terminated his dialogue with the Czech government about a possible constitutional settlement and, with tensions mounting, the state declared martial law.

Hitler had already demanded, in a speech on September 12, that the 'oppression' of the German minority must end, and it fell to British Prime

Minister Neville Chamberlain to fly to Berchtesgaden to meet with the German Chancellor and try to hammer out a solution that stopped short of war.

When George states that 'the consensus of opinion seems to point to the possible sacrifice of Czecho-Slovakia to the cause of world peace', he was, of course, correct – but only in the short term. All that the diplomacy achieved was to delay war, rather than to prevent it from breaking out. The Munich Agreement of September 30, entered into by Germany, Great Britain, France and Italy, provided for the ceding of the Sudetenland to Nazi Germany by October 10. The sovereignty of the 'rump' of Czechoslovakia would then be guaranteed by all the signatories, and Chamberlain's time in office would forever be associated with his policy of appeasement.

As history shows, it didn't end there. Whilst the Sudetenland was duly occupied by Germany in October, Hitler went on to invade the Czech portion of what was left in March 1939 – annexing part, with the remainder becoming the German Protectorate of Bohemia and Moravia.

With regard to **Gleanings [74, extract]** (October 21, 1938), we have to speculate that it was actually penned by George at least a week or two prior to its actual publication date, and although not mentioned by name, we assume that it refers to Chamberlain's meeting with Hitler and the signing of the so-called Munich Agreement on September 30, 1938 – considered at the time to be a concordat that would deliver 'peace for our time'.

Interestingly, some historians now believe that the BBC was indeed 'leant on' at the time, by the Government, to put a positive spin on the events, despite a huge protest in Trafalgar Square against the agreement. We assume that George is also referencing the universal day of prayer called by the Archbishop of Canterbury on Sunday, September 18, and the subsequent fluctuations in church attendances, culminating in a surge in the numbers on Sunday, October 2, as people wished to give thanks for the apparent resolution to the crisis.

He argues that it wasn't Divine intervention that brought about a peace agreement with Nazi Germany, but unashamedly simple, military pragmatism. And George, as ever intolerant of 'muddled' thinking, is happy to point out the sanctimonious nonsense of those ascribing Divine intervention to the emergency, particularly when he had consistently argued that conflict between nations is man's bailiwick alone.

Gleanings [75] (October 28, 1938) is a further example of where the article in question could have been placed either here or in the previous chapter. Once again, George bemoans the failure of the League of Nations to build a system of international collective security, something many hoped it would achieve when first established.

He quotes a correspondent to *The Listener*, who stated: 'The German annexation of Sudeten German regions will not be the end, but only the beginning, of German expansion eastwards'; very prophetic indeed.

Finally there is **The Root Cause of War** (December 8, 1939), a hard-hitting and reflective piece that appeared three months after war had finally been declared. George laments that the lessons of the Great War had all but been forgotten – despite much of the well-intentioned rhetoric designed to usher in a new world order of peace and selflessness.

The First World War was supposed to have been the 'war to end war' and was expected to herald a 'New Age' of reason and understanding between nations; instead, according to George, it was selfishness that had ultimately prevailed – with all sections of society having to bear their own share of responsibility for this moral malaise.

In what became his valedictory article, George signs off in typically robust fashion – probably leaving the reader frantically searching their own soul for any semblance of complicity in this sin against God and man (as George would doubtless have seen it).

However, above and beyond all of the above, you get a real sense of the sheer agony being borne by a pacifist at the advent of war, over eighty years ago – a final insight into the mind of a man who had been warning readers where it was all leading for more than six years, and now finally had to submit to the consequences.

World Peace In Peril
(letter to the *Swindon Advertiser*)
(First published: March 3, 1933)

Sir – The peace of the world is menaced by the threat of war in the Far East. The war-dogs are as yet in leash, but the leash is of the flimsiest material and may break at any moment, and when the mad dogs are let loose none can tell how widespread and far-reaching will be the results.

Looking back to 1914, who would have had the hardihood to suggest that the assassination of a Serbian archduke would alter the map as it has done? Who would have dared to prophesy that the scale of hostilities, the magnitude of the troops engaged, the hellish death roll would have been what it was. No one could have done. And just as the Great War had an insignificant beginning, so history may easily repeat itself.

The snarls and growls between Japan and China are not merely those of two mastiffs showing-off. They are real and menacing because between them is a luscious bone. It is the old, old story of expansion for possession. Manchuria is the bone, and it is not too much to assert that in the selfish struggle for [it], the whole world may be involved.

When Baron Tanaka was Premier of Japan, he made this momentous statement:

> In our national programme of expansion, another war with Russia to secure the resources of North Manchuria seems inevitable. If Soviet Russia objects to our programme, as she certainly will, this will be the opportunity for open hostility.

And so the menace will spread. The war spirit is by no means dead, even in enlightened England. There are still "glories" attached to the upholding of national prestige, and what is true of England is true of every country.

There is no time to lose. Every civilised country is upon its trial. The trial is the greatest of all – that of honour. If Japan breaks from the League of Nations, all the other powers who are signatories to the League's Pact must immediately pass a law forbidding, under extreme penalty, the manufacture and supply of arms and ammunition to either side. If Japan and China must go to war, let the supply of munitions come from their own resources.

There is another thing. Money should be stringently withheld. No loan should be permitted, whatever rate of interest is offered, to Japan or China.

Unless these laws are passed and tenaciously enforced, the League will prove itself a farce. Now is the time to prove the worth of sentiment. Will it be practical or mere sentiment?

Yours etc,
George E Hobbs

One Aspect of the Incarnation [extract]
By George E Hobbs
(First published: December 21, 1934)

So nations grew into Empires. They grew with their golden wealth, their silvered culture, their brazen laws of internal subjection and tyranny, their iron laws of external aggression.

But as each Empire grew, in process of time they fell into the dust – fell, not because they became less wealthy, or cultured, or aggressive, but because of moral dry-rot. The foundation upon which each Empire reared its head of gold was of clay, and therefore unstable. However costly and powerful the superstructure may be, if it be built upon a corrupt foundation, it must topple and fall.

And so we have the magnificent Empires of the past – Egypt, Assyria, Babylon, Persia and Rome – crumbling and falling to the dust. No Empire, however great its power, can long retain its supremacy if the foundation of its superstructure is unstable and faulty.

A New Moral Order

When Rome was tottering to a fall, there came by The Incarnation the conception of a new moral order. The plane upon which life circled was to be lifted into a higher and nobler conception. A kingdom was to be inaugurated which, like leaven, was to work silently through the races and unify them into one homogenous whole. Racial prejudices and colour barriers were to be broken down, and universal peace would come. A beautiful picture indeed, and we can review the progress made in the two thousand years which have elapsed since its inception.

It is not strange that for a time little progress was made. The idea was too revolutionary. But as the years came and vanished, one would expect to see a gradual change for the better. I think we ought to see the higher moral order taking root in the various national consciences.

To our surprise we find that, as nations succeeded great nations, they were still constituted as were the Empires of the dead past. The only difference was that they grew more and more stupid. Each reared its head of gold, and had arms of silver. Each grew more and more aggressive and intolerantly arrogant – the iron and the brass in their constitution.

But, just as the old Empires stood upon feet of unstable clay, so the modern Empires stood. But the clay was now consecrated clay. God became the "mascot" of each supreme nation. It mattered little how a nation was constituted as long as its priests could claim that God was pleased with its constitution. For this continued blasphemy, the Kingdom which was to operate its beneficence through the nations, broke them and ground them into dust. Their wealth, culture and armaments, their strategic positions of supremacy, were not proof against the fiat of an outraged moral order.

They fell into ruins because the foundations upon which they were built were corrupt. No law of evolution or biology was responsible, but moral dry-rot.

The purely physical was the be-all and end-all of power and achievement – and ruin resulted.

The Unlearned Lesson

In these later days there are similar signs of disaster and ultimate decay. The greatest military nation the world has seen now lies humbled in the dust. And still the world has not learned its lesson.

It is utterly futile to imagine that wealth, armaments, naval and military superiority are the bulwarks of national stability. The history of nations has taught that disintegration lies along this path. The greatest truism the world has ever known is this: the nation that forgets God is a doomed nation. National stability and national supremacy are possible only when the foundations are laid in Righteousness, Truth and Peace. This, and this only, is the condition of supremacy.

This, for the moment, will be considered merely the babbling of a diseased mind. But, unless sanity prevails, the world will yet be drenched in blood before the knowledge is gained that national wellbeing is better than wealth, and that international brotherhood is preferable to international strife.

The "Bombshell"
By George E Hobbs
(First published: March 13, 1936)

The action of Herr Hitler in sending troops into the demilitarised area of the Rhineland has been designated as a "bombshell", "startling", "dramatic", and various other terms of more or less equivalent meaning. Nothing could be farther from the truth.

A sixth-standard schoolboy specialising in post-war history could have told that, instead of being a "bombshell", it was the natural sequence of events. The kindest thing one can say is that the "big guns" of international statecraft have yet to learn the first principles of psychology. Unless this be the explanation, the "sequence" just brought to pass assumes an ugly inference. It is that Hitler has fallen into a trap which has been baited for him and into which it was intended he should fall. Personally I am inclined to the kindlier view – that European politicians, having their visions so filled with the physical aspect of force, have failed to appreciate the subtler powers of psychology.

The Spirit Survived

In 1918 Germany was beaten to her knees. In the subsequent peace treaty, every condition to which she applied her signature as the vanquished was physical in nature. She was not to "re-arm", she was not to re-occupy territory, and so forth. But there was one fundamental quality no power in the world could destroy. That was the "mind" and the "spirit" of Germany. Her war materials could be confiscated and destroyed. Her Navy could be shattered and her Mercantile Fleet pooled among the nations. But the "mind" and "spirit" could not be so handled. That spirit survived the biggest thrashing a nation ever experienced, and survived, too, the greatest humiliation a proud nation ever endured.

Like life in all its aspects, the body of old Germany died, and out of death and disruption a new Germany was born. The statesmen of the world made the fatal mistake of judging the infant by the parent. Heredity may or may not be an inflexible law, but at any rate we give every new-born child a fighting chance. If, in our social life, we followed the same principle as that applied to new-born Germany we should sterilise every new-born child of bad parentage. The child is watched and trained sympathetically, and is gradually allowed to exercise its self-expression as other children. To hedge such a child about with rigid bands of repression while it sees other children free of such bands is to damn that child to ultimate folly and wrong.

Isolated and Shunned

Just such an analogy holds here. With the re-birth of the nation her past history could not be forgotten. The parent was evil-disposed and a menace; the child must be evil-disposed and a menace. The rest of Europe was something like a confederacy. Germany remained "in Coventry" – isolated and shunned. The rest of the nations could arm to the top of their bent. Germany must not arm. If she made such an attempt it would be counted as an offence. Yet Germany saw the rest of Europe increasing their armaments and war materials, and the very natural sequence came last Saturday.

A people defeated and suffering under a sense of continual injustice revive a spirit that will become formidable to the peace of the world. It gradually grows into a sullen disregard of consequences. In a very real sense it was not Ishmael's fault that his hand was against every other man's hand. The lack of sympathy, the daily indignities, the constant reminder of inferiority, the hounding from pillar to post engendered at last that spirit of hostility and of revolt as, literally, to find himself against the rest of his fellows.

Humiliation of Defeat

Germany has been placed in such a position. All the hatred of Germany in the world cannot obliterate the admission that she has not had a fair and square deal.

Almost by common consent it has been agreed that Germany precipitated the Great War of 1914-18; and that she, being the aggressor, was responsible for the death and carnage which eventuated. Even so, it must be conceded that she, too, lost many brave sons, and fathers and brothers. And in addition to the sacrifice of the flower of her manhood was added the humiliation of defeat.

I do not pretend to excuse a crime, but I do suggest that the present ugly situation – and there is no disguising the fact that it is ugly – would never have arisen if Germany had been treated with more toleration. One believes that had toleration been extended the psychological effect would have been a desire to conform to the dictates of peace rather than the desire for aggressive self-assertion. A little tact, a great sympathy to help in the desire for reformation and an understanding of psychological processes, and there would have been no "bombshell".

"Victory" and Annexation
By George E Hobbs
(First published: May 15, 1936)

Anyone who can look upon the present state of world affairs with complacency must either be a loose thinker or a thinker of exquisite faith. The loose thinker will not care a brass farthing what happens until it touches his pocket or stomach. Then he will sit up and take notice – and ask a lot of silly questions. The thinker of exquisite faith may see in the present turmoil but a phase in the scheme of things. It will probably be to him a necessary piece in the jig-saw puzzle which will emerge eventually into a beautiful picture or structure.

Personally I cannot be a loose thinker, nor am I a thinker who sees in the present muddle a necessary part fixing into a picture already designed.

That a picture may have been designed I do not deny. But I imagine the Designer never intended each piece to be fitted in only through the pangs of hatred, and murder, and selfishness. If such were true, then personal responsibility ceases, and we become pawns in the game instead of reasoning beings.

If the "time-table" theory is correct then the Christ's denunciations of the cities of His day become meaningless. "It shall be more tolerable for Tyre and Sidon in the day of judgement than for thee," said he of Chorazin and Bethsaida. In other words, "You have greater light, greater culture, and a more advanced civilisation than had Tyre and Sidon, yet you are more gross than those cities of ancient times. You have failed in your greater responsibilities."

* * *

What responsibilities have we shelved? We who claim to be the most enlightened people the world has yet seen! We who prated of our desire to see that the right thing should be done for Abyssinia!

As one listened to the news bulletin and then read again in the press of the annexation of Abyssinia by Italy, one felt a definite sense of shame, almost of despondency.

A country forced to fight for its very life, appealing with pathetic expectancy, to the world for succour, only to be met by that which was worse than a blank refusal. Week after week came the parrot-like cry until it nauseated by its repetition. "The Committee of Thirteen has adjourned until next Tuesday, when a sub-committee will be set up to deal with the situation." I believe it was the one item in the news bulletin in which the BBC announcer did not consult his notes. He became quite word-perfect.

God knows I have no desire to throw cheap sneers at the League of Nations. Probably the League has functioned as far as "interested" circumstances permitted. There is little doubt that it functioned with the ever present consciousness of its limitations. And the fact remains that, with all its proud boasting, it will cease to function unless Italy is brought to book and Abyssinian independence restored.

* * *

The position could not be more serious. Italy has challenged the moral fabric of the world, and, up to date, Italy has won. She has ridden roughshod over every convention and ignored every plea of our common humanity. Not only has she won, but she is defiant in her victory.

In connection with that victory there is one little episode I think I shall not readily forget. I have never studied the Catholic faith, but when I do I shall study it sympathetically. I shall study it with the remembrance that, when the bells of every church in Italy clanged out its "rejoicing at victory", the bells of St Peter were silent. No greater expression of indignant disgust could have been given than the silence of the Vatican bells. I raise my hat to His Eminence the Pope.

The bombastic attitude of Mussolini would be truly comic were it not so tragic. Victory has gone to his head like new wine, and has made him more irresponsible than ever. If Mussolini was unable to appreciate moral values before, he certainly will not be able to appreciate them now.

Speaking of the victory over, and the annexation of Abyssinia, Mussolini said: "In all our 30 centuries of existence, this is the greatest achievement of all."

This may or may not be true. The saner part of the world will judge this in the light of the meaning of the word "achievement". And in this light of achievement there stands out one striking parallel. It is this:

Italy has crucified the Abyssinians just as much as her ancestors crucified the Christ. She has crucified Abyssinia with the same callous indifference and "damn the consequence" spirit as did her ancestors. But history has a habit of repeating itself in more ways than one. Just as she fell – as the Roman Empire – into inglorious ruin, so, as Italy, the belated child of that Roman Empire, will she fall again into the dust. She will fall, she must fall, if the saner part of the world is but true to itself.

* * *

If the annexation of Abyssinia be permitted to stand, then it means that a reign of anarchy will be begun among the nations of the earth. It will suppose a tacit agreement to exist that in the affairs of nations it will be a case of "every nation for itself, and the devil take the hindmost". The stronger will have its impetus to prey upon the weaker, and law and order will cease. It is therefore imperative and immediately imperative, to refuse Italy the right of annexation.

How can this be brought about? Militant spirits say: "By war." If this is the only answer, then the remedy is going to be worse than the disease. It can be accomplished without war. I shall be told I am presumptuous and foolish, rushing in where angels fear to tread. So be it. I have been told this before, so once more will not harm me. Here is how it can be done.

If all the peoples of the nations compelled their respective Governments to break off all diplomatic relationships with Italy, withdraw all Ambassadors, and expel from each country all Italian Ambassadors – that in all essentials, save that of food, Italy should be completely isolated – it would bring that country to her senses.

There is, however, an unhappy sequel. For some inscrutable reason, difficult indeed to postulate, Internationalism – as expressed by the League – has bred a more intensified Nationalism. It is this individualism which stands in the way of redress for Abyssinia and suitable punishment for Italy.

There can be no true world reform until Nationalism is lost in the truest Internationalism.

Gleanings [21]
By George E Hobbs
(First published: October 1, 1937)

I am writing this article on Saturday evening, 25 September. By the time this appears in print, almost a week will have elapsed. Much may happen for the better or worse in that short period of time.

It is an oft quoted phrase that the future is in the lap of the gods, meaning, of course, that as the gods are imaginary beings, the future is in the lap of chance. But such an interpretation is false. The future is controlled, and the controlling factor is the hand of man himself. Man fashioned past history. Man is fashioning present history. Man will fashion future history. Man individually determines his own destiny. Man collectively determines the destiny of his race and people. It is by agreeing to this principle that individual and collective responsibilities can be fixed.

However much the following may be thought to be provocative, calm thinking must prove its truth. A wave of emotion – I can only term it, hysterical emotion – has traversed the globe over the bombing of Nanking and Canton. The hysterical reaction is more pronounced than when Guernica suffered a similar fate, some months ago. In each case, thousands of folk were killed. Combatants and non-combatants, men, women, children, all were gathered in and ruthlessly hurled into eternity. Many died speedily, others died a more protracted death.

But they died, quickly or lingeringly, and that was that. Honour has been satisfied. Nationalism has triumphed, and human devilry has come again into its own.

Just why folk become emotionally indignant when the real thing begins I am at a loss to understand. I know it is devilish. I know it is horrible. I know it is inhuman. But surely this was known 23 years ago! For 51 months, war tore the world into shreds. It killed the best of the nation's manhood. It ruined hundreds and hundreds of intellects, and made them naught but babbling children. It wrenched out eyes from eye-sockets and rendered hundreds so unsightly that they must remain in perpetual seclusion until a merciful death releases them from their hold upon life. All this was known with a knowledge which seared the heart.

* * *

Nineteen years ago, that war came to an end. At the conclusion of hostilities the popular slogan was that it was "a war to end war". A great sigh of relief went up from the hearts of ravished peoples – "thank God it is all over!" But was it all over? And is it all over? And was it a war to end war? Looking back over the years, we know that a negative answer must be given to each question. We know that with all the protestations of diplomatic oratory for peace and concord, the fingers of nations have never been far from the throats of their neighbours. It is an ugly admission to make, but it is a true admission, and unfortunately, by the very nature of present-day national constitutions, it must remain true. A permanent peace is impossible so long as insular nationalism is paramount in world affairs. While this has been proved over and over again, the peoples of the earth seem unwilling to learn what history would teach them.

I have stressed this fact many times in the columns of "The Swindon Advertiser". Individual nationalism tends to retain all the vices engendered by a pent-up and continuous fear. Each nation must be in a constant state of preparation for defence, which, to put it bluntly, means to be in a constant state of preparation to attack. The assumed security is costly in the extreme, and millions of pounds sterling must be spent upon this phantom objective. And it is a phantom. The mightiest military, naval and air combination in the world cannot give security if it is based upon individualism.

* * *

That the position to-day is serious is but to play with words that never seemed so weak. The horrible slaughter at Nanking and Canton is but an expression of the madness that is in world affairs of to-day. It has been said that such things could never happen in Europe. Probably this remark was intended to convey the idea that Japanese and European civilisations were on differing levels. But Guernica disproved such a contention. Here were blood brothers of an equal civilised status. Even if it is conceded that Italians did the bombing, it must not be forgotten that the slaughter of Spanish women and children was directed by a Spaniard. And, after all, the Italians are Europeans.

Following the bombing of Nanking a leader writer expressed himself thus: "But at least millions of decent people are sick with horror to-day. Horror of pity first. Then, at the back of the mind, horror of fear. For whose turn will be next?"

There is no reluctance here to believe that Canton's fate may be the fate of any European city. To believe that European civilisation and culture would prevent a betrayal of manhood under stress of modern warfare is to believe in a fool's paradise. When the jungle spirit takes possession of intelligent manhood, it is at the expense of sanity and reason. No amount of cant will alter the fact that human nature is the same the world over.

During the Great War, aeroplanes as fighting units were just coming into being. Even in their imperfect state they were used upon occasions to perform the same duties as at Nanking – to break the morale, the spirit, of the enemy. Had they then reached present-day perfection, the horror of Nanking and Canton would have been experienced, 20 years ago.

I say again that as long as individual nationalism retains its present position in world affairs, there can be no permanent security or lasting peace. Rather, it must continue to fret the nations and keep the world in a constant state of suspense.

* * *

But there is a way out – a way which admittedly involves sacrifice. The sacrifice involved, however, would be more than compensated by the good results achieved. That way out is to replace nationalism by internationalism. This is bound to come. Pray God it may become practical world politics before Armageddon becomes the shambles of civilisation.

On more than one occasion in these columns I have suggested the establishment of an International Equity Court, under international control, also the creation of an International Police Force as an integral part of the Court, the Police Force to comprise of naval, military and air sections. That similar ideas have and are taking root in the minds of politicians a few brief extracts will reveal. The Nyon plan to check "piracy" in the Mediterranean is really the establishment of a policing force, established in order to eliminate the menace of contending national forces. At least, no less an authority than Mr Anthony Eden, sees it as such. Broadcasting from Geneva on 14 September, he said: "We have set up in that sea a police force." It is the acceptance of this ideal which is urgently needed. The development into practical world politics would then be a mere matter of adjustment.

And now an authority from a different political camp. The Rt Hon CR Attlee MP, published a book entitled "The Labour Party in Perspective". From that book I cull the following: "I can only say that I do not believe the scheme of an international air force is chimerical. I think that it is supremely practical. A start among a limited number of nations would be an immense advance. If the most powerful offensive weapon in the world were manned by men drawn from many nations, who would in their service create an esprit de corps, based on common service in the interests of humanity – a really constructive step towards world peace would have been taken."

The New Zealand Government is out for international control. France is agreeable to its inception. Some of the small central European states have signified their agreement to its principles. Public opinion needs to decide quickly for internationalism, if the world is to be saved from suicide.

Gleanings [44, extract]
By George E Hobbs
(First published: March 18, 1938)

Herr Hitler has been at it again. Without even a "by your leave", he has taken the law into his own hands and defied the world once more. Just as in his dramatic militarising of the demilitarised Saar, so again he has shown to the world the stuff of which he is made. Whatever opinions we may hold of Hitler, it must be conceded that he is the strong man of European politics.

Let us give the devil his due. Not once has Hitler acted slyly; not once has he been guilty of double-crossing. Like a rattle-snake, he has given warning of his intentions, and those intentions have been carried out, ruthlessly and without compromise.

Hitler's ambitions are scarcely personal. It is not that he wishes for himself a place in the sun. If I judge the man aright – and I honestly believe I do judge him correctly – he has lost himself in the needs of the nation. He is the super-patriot of the German nation. He has faith in the aims of Germany, he has faith in his country's ideals, and because of that faith he has ventured upon a policy of boldness which would have paralysed the initiative of half the world's political leaders.

But, while we cannot help but pay tribute to his boldness, such an attitude must not remain unchallenged. Boldness and stratagem must be met with equal boldness and stratagem. Goliath of old issued his challenge to the forces of Israel by oral speech, Hitler has issued his challenge to the peace of Europe by action, and the gage of battle must be accepted. There can be no compromise with the situation. To compromise now would be fatal.

Those who remember the domestic politics of Great Britain just previous to the Great War will recall how near we were to civil strife. Ireland, in particular, was proving a serious problem. The war came, and, in face of the common enemy, party quarrels were bridged and forgotten, and a united front was established. It is in the spirit of this simile that the present menace can be met.

The problem is one essentially for the League of Nations. And if, under their present constitution, they are impotent to deal with the menace, then the League must be given extra powers. Never has the time been more ripe for the establishment of those principles which I have advocated through this column on more than one occasion.

We believe in the principle of "United we stand", and that "Divided we fall". At the moment, even the nations who desire peace are not united with that essential unity which would secure peace. That unity is obscured by insular national interests which operate against collective security.

Now it seems to me that the League of Nations cannot function properly if it is merely an investigatory or advisory body, relying solely for its importance on the moral weight attached to its findings. There must be more than moral weight. There must be the weight of law – of law reinforced by a power adequate to vindicate its considered findings. Law is of little use unless it can be enforced.

It is therefore of urgent necessity to buttress the functions of the League of Nations with tribunal powers, capable, not only of adjudicating in cases of specific dispute, but of seeing that the findings of that tribunal are carried out into effect. This can be achieved only by the creation of some internationally organised force which is capable of enforcing the decisions of the tribunal and of preventing breaches of international law and peace.

It is just a question of whether the world wishes universal peace or is content with the present state of world anarchy. Hitler has thrown down the gage of battle. He is courageous in his attitude. Will the rest of the world be equally courageous?

Gleanings [45, extract]
By George E Hobbs
(First published: March 25, 1938)

The war in Spain is a reflex in miniature of what war on a grand scale can now be. Both sides are tarred with the same black brush. Both are fighting for their own individual, insular ideals, and both are out to kill and damn the consequences. If horror and disgust are to be expressed, then let it be expressed with indiscriminate impartiality.

Whether a spade can more properly be termed a garden implement or not, it is still a "spade". War may be termed a "punitive expedition", "the vehicle by which honour is vindicated", or by any other term. It is still "war" – devilish, inhuman, immoral and anti-social. No change of name can alter its character, and no excuse can vindicate its crime. War stands impeached before the tribunal of mental sanity and moral justice.

Barcelona is an open city. According to photographs, it has beautiful buildings, wide open spaces, ornate churches. The object of aerial bombings is to cripple enemy arsenals. Barcelona is not an arsenal city, neither is it fortified to resist aerial attack. It is therefore certain that aerial bombing has now taken on a new meaning. It is to break the morale of the non-combatants. And the morale (according to the new "rules" of "civilised" warfare) can be broken only by the slaughter of innocent victims – women and little children!

Oh yes. We always knew that war was no Sunday School picnic. What we did not know was that human beings could debase themselves into the character of wolves, starved and hungry for prey. Personally, I do not believe in a theological hell – eternal, literal fire, and gnashing teeth. I should insult my moral intelligence were I to believe in such a grotesque place. But when I think of Barcelona I am definitely convinced that some sort of retribution must follow the perpetrators of such a crime – those cold-blooded ghouls in human guise, swinging out over that beautiful city, not only doing their damnedest to efface the image of God within them by a single journey of destruction, but returning again and again to their enormity.

It seems to me sometimes that we must be living in a nightmare world – that the things of which we read do not really happen, and that soon we shall wake up to find that, after all, it has been naught but a dream. How one wishes this were true!

But Franco is not the only sinner in this tragic morass. Yet, one supposes that the Spanish Government troops which blew up the Casa Blanca acted according to the accredited rules of war.

In this building, situated in Extremadura, a suburb of south-west Madrid, 300 of Franco's men held it as a fort. For six months Government troops had been busy tunnelling to get beneath the building. They succeeded, and beneath 300 unsuspecting men 15 tons of dynamite was placed. One second, and the building was occupied with live, vibrant human souls. The next second – and 300 men ceased to live. Twisted, broken, smashed, a whole cargo hurled into eternity.

And now, out of all this horror, let me re-state my plea. It is that, while we know these things to exist, there shall be no thought or desire of rendering an eye for an eye. I have said already that I know the almost irresistible pull of this desire. It is in my nature. I "feel" I want to take some active part in bringing retribution to the inhuman devils who can so easily forget their humanity. But I recognise that retaliation – to plunge another nation into war in order to punish the violator of our common humanity – is the most futile of efforts to end strife. And because of this knowledge I stifle its insidious lure.

War can never end war. It was tried in 1914-18, and it dismally failed. The greatest war the world has ever experienced. A war to end war – the slogan that now is a hoary joke. It is just as logical to say that fire can be extinguished by fire, or that water can be evaporated by water, as to insist that war can be abolished by war. It is not sound reasoning.

In the years to come we shall have learned the virtues embodied in the Sermon on the Mount. We shall have learned that love, tolerance and brotherhood are the only bulwarks to a stable world peace. In the meantime, as we are not yet ready for this great ideal, we must establish the next best thing. That is the establishment of some code of international law. Surely, with the failure of every other method, this could be tried.

There is a strong combination of nations which, could they but sink individual feelings, would make the establishment of international law possible. The British Empire, France, the United States of America, Russia, Holland, Belgium, Norway and Sweden, Denmark and the Balkan States would be sufficient to form a powerful combination of international law.

The gesture of magnanimity could be extended to Hitler, and his co-operation invited. I imagine that, beneath the surface of world happenings, there is a rupture between the two European Dictators. And the psychological moment for the invitation to Hitler is now.

Italy could be invited to join the Commonwealth of Nations when she has purged her soul and returned Abyssinia to its rightful owners.

Gleanings [70]
By George E Hobbs
(First published: September 23, 1938)

At the moment of writing the whole of the civilised world awaits the result of the Chamberlain-Hitler conversation. The tension naturally is great, for much depends upon the outcome. Before this appears in print the die will probably have been cast, either for good or ill. Whatever the outcome may be, it will never be forgotten that the British Premier, in the name of humanity, made one last desperate effort to avert war – a war, which if once precipitated, would completely wreck civilisation and ruin the world.

The mission of Mr Chamberlain has won the admiration of the world. Apart from its ultimate objective, the circumstances attending the journey were of particularly outstanding merit. I have no knowledge of the Premier's previous reactions to the thought of air travel. As Premier, had he so wished, he could have flown scores of times. The best of the RAF pilots could have been his choice. Yet never before had he flown.

To a man of 70, nerves are less reliable than to a younger man. The weather report, too, previous to the flight, was certainly not a happy one. Yet, in face of possibly a thousand nervous fears, Mr Chamberlain, having seen in which direction his duty called him, obeyed that call without question. I imagine that the magnificent gesture upon the part of the British Premier, and his indomitable courage in facing such a journey and undertaking, must have had an influence for good upon Herr Hitler.

While it is agreed that the gesture was magnificent and the courage high, the virtue of the conversation can be appraised only by results. What, therefore, will be the outcome? No-one, as yet, knows. Conferences upon the visit have been held by the Cabinet and other responsible individuals. And another visit is contemplated – even now probably has taken place. Then there will be further conferences, and the outcome is yet to be.

But, while nothing definite is known, conjectures have been rife. Dame

Rumour may be a lying jade, but sometimes she hits the mark with remarkable accuracy. And the consensus of opinion seems to point to the possible sacrifice of Czecho-Slovakia to the cause of world peace. I am going to be bold to assert that even if this eventuates it will not bring about world peace. It may postpone for a time, but cannot avert, war. In process of time the same conditions will again prevail, the same nerve strain be again encountered. The causes of world anarchy and distrust are far more fundamental than those which can be appeased by the sacrifice of one country.

And why should Czecho-Slovakia be sacrificed? The very suggestion is sacrilege, and is contradictory to that spirit of justice which is our high boast.

The nation of Czecho-Slovakia came into being twenty years ago. It is republican in constitution and its individuality as a nation has been recognised in three separate Treaties: the Treaty of Versailles, signed 28 June, 1919, Germany being a signatory; one with Austria, on 10 September, 1919; and one with Hungary, on 4 June, 1920. The independence of Czecho-Slovakia, therefore, as a nation is fully established.

In the census of 1930 the population was stated to be just over 14½ millions. This total gives roughly two-thirds population to the Czecho-Slovaks and one-third to nationals of other countries. Germans are said to number about 3¼ millions.

* * *

Now it is the unchallenged right of every independent country to govern itself by the laws instituted by itself. With a new country, when once its borders have been defined by treaty and accepted by the rest of the nations, the same unchallenged right becomes theirs. And just as Britain, France or America would tolerate no external interference with their internal method of government, so the Czechs have the same right to independence of action.

Under democratic laws and principles, the voice of the two-thirds should be paramount, and no other country has the right of interference. If the Sudeten Germans are not satisfied with Czech law, they should remove themselves back to the Fatherland. And for Hitler to demand a plebiscite in another country is the crowning proof of an unbalanced mind. That Mr Chamberlain can agree is unthinkable, or that Britain and France will consent to the sacrifice of Czecho-Slovakia is equally unthinkable. It would be the grossest betrayal of history.

There is one sure thing emerging out of the whole debacle. However much we follow the habit of the ostrich, hiding our heads in the sand and pretending it does not exist, it is there. The system of exclusive nationalism is a menace to world peace. It always has been; it always will be. And, just as exclusive nationalism is a menace, so, too, are exclusive alliances. They are as futile to preserve order and bring about security as though they did not exist. All that follows is that, instead of one nation being armed against another nation, groups of nations are armed against other groups. In either case, millions of pounds have to be spent upon weapons of destruction. The same trouble is there; all that is altered is the volume. Group alliances produce antagonistic group alliances, and so the folly goes on.

* * *

From a purely materialistic point of view, the only royal road to world peace is internationalism. I do not mean an alliance of nations armed to the teeth for aggression, but a Federation of nations determined to preserve peace.

Suppose such a Federation came into existence at this moment – a Federation of nations outside the dictatorship states. From the combined Federation, an International Police Force could be organised and dispatched at once to the Sudeten area. Hitler would then have no excuse to intervene by force of arms on behalf of the Sudeten Germans.

The International Police Force would preserve order, even as the International Military Force did on the Saar. It was only when the Saar became demilitarised that Hitler sprang his dramatic surprise. Without even a "By your leave", he advanced his troops into the forbidden zone. If order was preserved on the Saar without bloodshed by an International Force, surely it can be done again in Sudetenland by an organised International Police Force. Surely this is possible, and surely it is infinitely preferable to the present muddle and constant sense of insecurity.

But there is yet another point of view arising out of the crisis in which we find ourselves. And in this point of view I intend to be very deliberate.

A writer in "The Sunday Pictorial", Mr Charles Wilberforce, has an article entitled "Wake up, Britain". It is an article which must have caused the hearts of munition manufacturers to flutter with excited admiration, and the believers in conscription to dance for joy. It is written in the true "Britain rules the waves" style, and I have little doubt that many read the article with pleasure and with agreement to text and context.

Mr Wilberforce seems to see the salvation of Britain through and by the force of arms. "Whether the country likes it or not," he writes, "it has to be put on a potential war footing." And again: "National registration of every man and woman with a view to conscription for labour and military service in case of war." For "what nation, however bellicose, would dream of attacking Britain organised for instant and efficient defence?" Anti-aircraft defence, ships, arms, etc, all must be increased and strengthened. And so on. In bold type we read, "Britain has got to wake up! We have got to wake up or perish!"

I give Mr Wilberforce credit for his opinions – opinions which will be endorsed by thousands. There are thousands of my fellow countrymen who honestly believe that the power vested in guns and ships is the only solution to preserve Britain's life. A greater error has never been made. Many nations and empires have crumpled into dust because they had no other idea of preservation than this. And other nations will meet a similar fate whose god is mammon and whose defence is lethal force.

* * *

During the past week we have had one of the strangest contrasts ever witnessed – the churches thrown open for prayer to a God in whom the nation has no faith or trust. No nation can have implicit trust in God whose sole defence is armaments. Thousands of prayers have been prayed during the last twenty years which had no more virtue than wind. "Give peace in our time, O Lord", and we do not trust Him to do it.

We rather depend upon a visible gun for peace. A good stout ship, bristling with armaments, and we can rest comfortably in our beds. What fools we be, to be sure!

Someone has said that we are a nation of shopkeepers. It would have been more true to say that we are a nation of hypocrites. And in face of this we expect God to do what we ourselves should have done. Twenty years of sheer waste. Nothing constructive. And, now, all we can contribute to world peace is the fitting of gas-masks to babies. We had our opportunity of discovering the truth that "Blessed is the nation whose God is the Lord", and we have stifled it. We now have to pay the penalty.

* * *

I have written the above because I have believed, and still believe, that Great Britain is the most potent factor for good in the whole world. I believe she has a destiny which, if she will permit herself to be stripped of her gross materialism, will give her such power that all other nations will look to her for guidance. It may be that, even in the darkness of this hour, another chance may be given us to fulfil that destiny. Prayer may be heard and answered. The crisis may pass.

Will there, then, be a great return to the things which matter most – a sincere and unquestioning faith in the God who is supreme? Or will there be a return to materialism and Mammon? One more chance – and the choice is ours.

Gleanings [74, extract]
(First published: October 21, 1938)

I view, with considerable misgivings, the renewed feverish activities in war talk and in war preparations. It seems to me that we are the most illogical and inconsistent of folk. Personally, I try to give to other folk credit for their opinions provided those opinions are consistent. It is the inconsistencies of folk that "gets my goat".

A fortnight since, under the stress of our great need, we crowded the churches that we might implore Divine help against war. At that moment, with sinking dread in our hearts, we were, of all folk, the most sincere. The Press wrote of the power of prayer. The BBC became super-zealous in giving Church dignitaries the opportunity of telling their flock how wonderful God could be in an emergency. And then we were told that God had answered prayer. He had intervened, and war was stayed.

But is this true? If it is true, then surely there is no need for further dismay. If we honestly believe that God did answer prayer, can we now believe that he will yet again answer our prayer?

* * *

But why prate of pious beliefs? And why be such hypocrites? Here is the unpalatable truth: war was stayed because both France and Britain found they were not in a position for a major conflict. And when that position is stiffened, by added recruitment, by a modified conscription, and a fully-organised Air Raid Precautions scheme, with all the ramifications pertaining to "defence", Britain and France will dictate the terms – or go to war.

Gleanings [75]
By George E Hobbs
(First published: October 28, 1938)

In last Friday's issue of "The Evening Advertiser" there appeared an article by Mr JA Spender under the title of "Two roads for Britain to choose from".

Articles from the pen of this gifted writer frequently appear in the columns of "The Evening Advertiser" and of "The Swindon Advertiser". They are always worthwhile, and usually provoke thought which will not be denied. The one quoted above was a worthy companion to its predecessors.

The article in question pivots upon a series of queries. Emerging therefrom, two ways were suggested by which Britain could direct her future contribution towards solving the European muddle.

The writer dealt with Mr Churchill's broadcast to America. With that part I am not at present concerned. I am concerned rather with his suggestion of the two-road choice.

Mr Spender thinks of Britain and France as the principals of the League Powers, and asks: "Why have we not succeeded in these twenty years in establishing collective security – security for all against war and for each against aggression – as intended when the League was drawn up? Why has the League" – still thinking in terms of Britain and France – "failed in promoting disarmament and treaty-revision, the two essentials of pacification, and the only conditions on which it could have applied sanctions without the risk of great and dangerous wars?"

Sanctions against whom is revealed in the reason given to the "whys".

"Britain and France," wrote Mr Spender, "have been pursuing contradictory policies at the same time – the policy of keeping Germany down and the policy of appeasing her – and between the two we have succeeded neither in keeping her down nor in appeasing her."

The choice of roads, then, is alternatively repression of, or appeasement to Germany. The former, of course, means war; the latter (to which Spender is inclined) may be "the sole alternative to accepting a sentence of doom for the next and coming generation".

I think we are all agreed that peace is the most desirable thing in the world. We feel, with a passion never before experienced, that we would like to awaken tomorrow morning and know that all these nightmare problems were settled for all times. What a Doxology would rise from our hearts! But alas, it will not be so, and one fears it will be a long time before that Doxology will be sung.

* * *

At the moment human nature is such (both in the individual and in the community) that selfishness predominates over selflessness. And even in the hour of extreme human need, when the highest and best of our natures should be revealed, the revelation unfortunately is base and low. We do not rise superior to self, but grovel in the dust to it. And just so long as this obtains, so will the spectre of the rule of force remain. It must be so because the expression of brute force (war) is but the outward sign of the inward cancer, the clash of self-interests and desires.

During the last twenty years a subtle and vital change has been occurring in the political thinking of the world. In some nations the term "self-interest" has changed into something dynamic – something which bears the sinister title of "determinism". Self-interest has been translated into self-determination, and this, not as a national ideal, but as a collective political formula for supremacy. So powerful has this formula become that it has challenged the stability of civilisation.

The principles of the struggle for supremacy are now well defined. They lie between the political faiths of democratic states, whose rules are 'government of the people, by the people, for the people', in which freedom is enjoyed within very wide limits, and totalitarian states, whose rules are opposite. Totalitarianism literally means dictatorship, regimentation, cog-precision, a lifeless sub-ordination of the individual to the State. Not, however, to its moral and spiritual good, but to its physical supremacy. Under this system, freedom is not possible, even within narrow limits. All that leads to essential knowledge is censored. The Press and wireless are restricted, and free speech is unknown. Life under conditions such as these become meaningless, for it is robbed of all sweetness and joy.

Knowing now the issue, let us return to the two-road choice. I think it is without question that an attempted repression of totalitarian states would mean the reign of jungle law – the law of tooth and claw. When Hitler said he was prepared to risk a world war, he meant what he said. There was no play upon words. Hitler was ready to meet its demand.

* * *

Then what of appeasement? Or, if it sounds better, what of negotiations as a means of appeasement? Let me review the question on the principle that man must work out his own salvation with fear and trembling. On that principle, I very profoundly suggest that appeasement as a means of avoiding war is futile. It is impossible to satiate the insatiable. Before the visions of Germany, Italy and Japan there is world domination, and nothing short of that will satisfy them.

Germany, with Italy behind her, and Japan, a sly but efficient ally, in the background, form the strongest combination against the rule of civilised law that history has known. Japan will conquer China, and could have done so long before this, had she so wished. But her wish is not to bring about a hasty conclusion to hostilities. In that far-away zone, Japan is concentrating upon perfecting a war technique which will eventually be the pattern upon which Germany and Italy will mould their resources. When that technique is perfected, and every detail scientifically weighed and analysed, then will come the world challenge – and damn the consequences! That is why I feel appeasement to be futile as a means of avoiding war. Colonies may be restored to Germany and half Europe given her as a sop, but sooner or later she will come again and ask for more.

* * *

In a letter to "The Listener", of 6 October, Mr Wickham Steed, quoting a Sudeten German industrialist, wrote: "The German annexation of Sudeten German regions will not be the end, but only the beginning, of German expansion eastwards." And there can be but little doubt that this statement will be realised.

If repression would be fatal to peace, and appeasement, in the long run, no less fatal, surely in a sane world of thinking there must be yet another road which may be explored. Surely it is better to try the unexplored than continue the road which must lead to disaster.

Someone has said that "in a heavily-armed world, moral force counts for little". I am not sure that I can subscribe to that dictum. In our own country I look upon our Civil Administration (Courts of Law and the Police Force) as a moral force. Justice is a moral quality, and has moral virtue in its essence and in its functioning powers. The law-abiding citizen is protected, and the citizen who has a grievance can find redress through the Courts. The fact that a policeman carries a truncheon in no way detracts from the fact that he is a moral factor in our corporate life.

One of our laws prescribes that no person may carry a firearm except under a rigid licence. If everybody were permitted to carry guns it is not difficult to see that the functions of the police to maintain order would be almost impossible. Therefore the law is that the police must know where every firearm can be located. And so smoothly do the wheels of law administration run that a major conflagration is impossible. A little trouble here and there, but it is soon rectified. Imagine what our country would be like without its Courts of Justice and its Police Force: anarchy, disorder, chaos.

Surely the same principle could be applied to international affairs. It serves no useful purpose to say that the difficulties in the way of such a principle are insurmountable. Progress is possible only by surmounting difficulties. And they can be surmounted, given the will to begin.

It seems to me so illogical to prefer old roads which we know must lead to disaster because we fear that a new, unexplored road may not be successful. It is even more illogical when the new road to international peace and security has already proved its worth in preserving peace within a nation's borders.

Never was the time more opportune to explore the validity of this great principle. Procrastination is not only the thief of time. It maybe the cause of universal disaster.

The Root Cause of War
By George E Hobbs
(First published: December 8, 1939)

By the time this appears in print, three months will have passed since that fateful Sunday, when over the air, came the ominous proclamation: "We are now in a state of war with Germany." Personally I did not hear it. At the moment when those shattering words were spoken, I was conducting a religious service. I had previously arranged with a friend to go into the street and ascertain the news – Peace or War? Presently the door opened. For one dread second, I paused. He gave the old Roman sign of "War".

I continued with the service. The die was cast!

Twenty-five years ago, similar conditions prevailed. The world entered into that struggle believing that when peace came, no future war would be possible. "A war to end war" was the slogan, and one which, from the allied peoples in the combat, at least, was a sincere ideal.

But the people of the world were to learn once more a lesson so often taught – and just as often forgotten. There can never be a war to end war. To have faith in such a claim is tantamount to a faith in the historic truth of "Jack and the Beanstalk". Both have the same and equal virtue. It is the virtue of the fairytale. Ever since man became man, his long tangled history has proved, over and over again, that war cannot be eliminated by war.

It is a far cry from the "Battle of the Kings" (roughly 1939BC) to the war of 1939AD. In that period of approximately 4,000 years, thousands of wars have raged. Each succeeding war has been spawned from its predecessor and has become, in turn, the pestilential breeding-ground for its successor. Egypt, Babylonia, Assyria, Persia, Greece, Rome, Turkey, Spain, Holland, France, Germany and Britain – all have tried to attain permanence by force of arms, and each and all have proved its futility.

At the close of 1917, envisioning the New Earth which would follow the then existing chaos and disorder, a writer penned these brave words:

> "At the close of the Great War, a new era will open in the world's history. We can never go back entirely to the old order, and few would wish us to… It will be a time of great opportunity. The task before mankind will be to rebuild civilisation on a surer foundation than that of the past. A great task of reconstruction lies ahead, and we must begin to prepare ourselves to take advantage of the unparalleled opportunity afforded by the war for overhauling our whole national life, and moulding it in accordance with the requirements of the New Age."

The Great War terminated. The new era dawned – the era which was to be "a time of great opportunity", and one in which civilisation was to be built on a surer foundation than that of the past. Before the dawn had lengthened into day, the night shadows had fallen. To change the metaphor: The oasis, so full of promise, had dissolved once more into a mirage.

Long after the guns had ceased to thunder out their message of death and destruction, long enough for some evidence of the "surer foundation" to reveal itself, another writer penned these words:

> "When the great calamity overtook the world there were many young hearts that gladly offered all they had in response to the cry for men to fight and, if necessary, to die that freedom might not perish. The years that have since elapsed have been years of disillusionment!"

Under the present system of thinking it cannot be otherwise.

* * *

But to revert to the slogan, "War to end war".

One can conceive of an interpretation of the slogan which could be literally true – that definitely there is a way in which war would end war. In order to prove the interpretation logical, the fundamental cause of war must be ascertained and understood.

Physical war (war in which lethal weapons are used to kill and maim) is the vicious effect of a vicious cause; it is the outward sign of an inward malady. That malady is deep-seated in human nature; it is no more in one nation than in any other; it is no less in one nation than in any other. Wherever man is, there it is to be found. The malady is summed up in a word which has no frightfulness at all in its oral expression – selfishness. "Murder" is a word ugly in sound and meaning. "Selfishness" is robbed of its ugliness, even as it is uttered, yet in its implications it is as deadly and ugly as murder. Every wrong, every injustice, every act of aggression can be traced back to selfishness.

Dictionaries, by their very nature, must be dignified in defining the meaning of a word. It is because of this limitation that no dictionary can possibly define "selfishness" adequately. Seeing that it is the root from which every branch of evil springs, it is almost puerile to say that "selfishness" means "justification of one's self", or even that "selfish" means "chiefly or wholly regarding one's own self; void of regard to others". The explanations lack the "punch" necessary to reveal the true nature of selfishness.

Selfishness is as cruel as hell, for it can count profits as of more value than human lives. It is hydra-headed in its expression. It can be disguised as "democracy", "defence" and "expediency". So treacherous is it that there is not a single high ideal or lofty aspiration but what it can effectively parody. It expresses itself in commerce, in the factory life, in the national legislature, and in the civic council chamber. It is revealed in social life, and even where it is not expected – in Church life. It is in the heart of the writer of this article and in the hearts of those who will peruse the article. It is of the devil, devilish.

* * *

Here, then, we have the unmistakable root cause of war, and until the root has been grubbed out and destroyed, wars will continue. Physical war can never outlaw physical war, because the root cause remains. Only as the root cause is crushed and broken beyond a possible resurrection can physical war be eliminated from international affairs. A war upon selfishness will terminate all strife and aggression.

Unpalatable as it is, the fact remains that every individual who cannot claim exemption from selfishness has his and her share of responsibility in the present war. Too often we attempt a distinction between human faults and term them greater and lesser. In essence, no such distinction is possible. The gigantic profits of vested interests, the vicious circle of "graft", the use of the purchasing power of higher salaries in order to accumulate commodities to the detriment of the lowest paid – all stand impeached before the bar of equity and justice as crimes of equal merit. And even in the humbler circles of humanity – where, one may argue, self-preservation is sufficient excuse – if the same spirit is revealed, that, too, is a crime equal to that shown by the lords of "graft" and of huge profits. The one merits no more and no less condemnation than the other.

It is this spirit – the spirit of selfishness, operating through the individual and finding mass expression through the nations – which has caused not only the present war, but every war throughout the ages. And as long as we permit this bondage to self, then just so long will the cry against black-outs, rationing, inconveniences, pain, tears and slaughter be futile. The world must groan in its anguish until the individual has dethroned the devil of selfishness and enthroned the God-like characteristic of selflessness.

Chapter 11

Beyond the Veil: Adventures into Spiritualism and the Afterlife

The consciousness that spiritual intercommunication was attainable was the hope to which my soul has ever been anchored...
(George Ewart Hobbs, April 19, 1918)

As Europe descended into war and George was destined for a premature death at the age of just 63 in 1946, it seems rather appropriate to round-off this book with two chapters that look again at his lifelong interest in what was to follow, *beyond the veil* of death. It is a subject that featured heavily in *A Swindon Wordsmith*, and in this chapter we look again at his preoccupation with spiritualism, including an encounter with a giant of literature, before finishing with a more theological examination of immortality.

Can Mortals Hold Communion With The Spirit World? – Yes! (published on April 19, 1918) represents George's first known prose on the subject of spiritualism. In it we hear of George's fourth (and apparently successful) attempt at communing with the spirit world by intensive concentration.

He uses the term 'penetrate the veil' and refers to the spirit being at his side – something which has echoes of a further such encounter that he wrote about in the pages of the *Swindon Advertiser*, nine years later. He emphasises that this was attained by 'concentration of the mind' – and not via a third party, such as a medium.

And by the time of his second successful contact with the hitherto unnamed spirit, George feels emboldened to make the following declaration:

> As a full revelation can only come by passing through the gateway of physical death, I do not hereby claim that I received a full revelation. But I assert most emphatically that my discovery was such as to lead me to understand that the spirit "land" was essentially one of individual conscious perception. I want to remember this great discovery; for not only do I now know that spirit life is ever around me, I also know that when the final change is at hand, I have no "journey" to face, but merely a change of perception.

In **The Revelation of Love** (appearing in four parts between June and August 1918), we get to hear that George goes on to achieve conversational 'spiritual communion' with an old man, a young girl, a mother and son and, finally, with two lovers, in his quest to find the real meaning of love.

This really wasn't a flight of fancy as far as George was concerned. In fact, he was profoundly serious, and later went out of his way to dispel any suggestion this was the either the result of a 'hallucination of the mind' or 'a spectral illusion'.

In the science fiction series *A Visit to Venus* which appeared in the *Swindon Advertiser* in 1927 (and published as a companion to this book), we intriguingly find George relating one of his very own, personal psychic experiences via one of its main characters, namely Jim. Indeed, George adds a footnote to the piece explaining that 'this is a true experience of the narrator'.

The following extract from Chapter 11 of *A Visit to Venus* gives an insight into George's beliefs about spiritualism:

> It occurs to me to tell you of an incident which I can vouch for as truth. It is quite inexplicable to me, yet the facts are just as I relate them.
>
> "There was a time when I was greatly interested in spiritualistic phenomena. I accepted nothing as proved. I was just an investigator.
>
> "During the period of my interest, a meeting was advertised at which a lady was to give the tenets of spiritualistic beliefs, after which she would prove the fact of clairvoyant perception.
>
> "At the meeting I found myself one of an audience of between sixty and seventy, composed of both sexes of adult age. I knew several of the audience, and knew them to be men and women of no mean intelligence.
>
> "I will pass over the first part of the proceedings as being of no interest to us at the moment. Then came the part which proved so inexplicable to me. I may say in passing [that] the lecturer was a complete stranger to the town, this being her first visit. She intimated there were folk present who were

invisible to every other person except herself. She saw them clearly, and would describe them. A generalisation, however, was no concrete proof, therefore she would particularise to a definite individual who was present in the room.

"With dramatic suddenness the lecturer turned to where I was sitting and, pointing to me, asked if I would agree to her describing folk who were standing close to my side. I agreed to her proposition, but laid it down very definitely that the proof would have to be flawless for my consent to her description. I should agree to no vague description or suggestion. I would have no one imagine there was collusion between lecturer and subject.

"The lecturer smilingly accepted my conditions, saying that the descriptions given would be flawless and convincing. And to my utter amazement it was even as she declared. The descriptions were perfect and could admit of not the slightest deception.

"Two years previous to this meeting, two cases of malignant illness and subsequent death occurred with which I was intimately acquainted as visitor and friend. One was a girl, eighteen years of age, who died of a malady unknown to me, apart from her case. The other was that of a man in late middle life who died with cancer in the throat. The features of both were known to me to the minutest detail. One (the girl) stood by my right shoulder, said the lecturer. The other (the man) stood by my left shoulder.

"As she first described the girl and then the man, I should have been false to truth had I said I did not recognise them. As clearly as I knew them in life so mentally I saw them again. Every feature, look and gesture was described, and such was the faithfulness of delineation that I had no hesitation in believing she actually saw them. There can be no other explanation possible."

And, in the next chapter of *A Visit to Venus*, we read:

"And you say that is a true experience, Jim?" queried Sandy, upon the conclusion of my narrative. I could not help but detect a world of longing in his query.

"It is just as I have told you, Sandy," I responded. "I have exaggerated nothing. I have kept nothing back. Every detail I have given you could be vouched for by each member of that audience who followed the demonstration with breathless interest. The descriptions were perfect, and no other explanation can be given, but that what she described she actually saw."

The real significance of this revelation only becomes clear, years later on December 9, 1938, when George recalls this very same incident in his Gleanings series – something which forms part of a larger discourse on death and the conscious survivability of the spirit. All of the related pieces are reproduced below, as part of this chapter.

And to provide some further context for this chapter on spiritualism, the following paragraph – full of poignancy – appears in *A New Year's Message*, dated January 4, 1929:

> And to those who face the New Year with the hand of bereavement heavy upon them: death is inevitable, it is the lot of all, yet its presence is never felt without grief. But could we glimpse behind the veil, how much would our sorrows lessen. We cannot see – or, at least, many of us cannot – and all that we see and feel is loss – just loss.

It's difficult to draw any other conclusion but this is George's own pain, writ large, for all to see. But, of course, we're bound to ask what prompted George's interest in spiritualism in the first place? While it is accepted that he had an insatiable intellectual curiosity, as well as a personal religious imperative to pursue the search for truth, it probably went way beyond that, and might well have had its origins in the deaths in infancy of his two sons (Reginald, aged only 11 months, in 1907 and Ivor, aged nearly three, in 1919).

Of course, the obvious thing would be to try to discover the date of the meeting where George bore witness to the demonstration of clairvoyance and mediumship – an event which apparently persuaded him as to the verities of the movement, in no small part by the surprising accuracy of the information revealed to him by the two spirits via the lecturer. Although this matter is the subject of ongoing research, there's no doubt that it was a watershed moment in George's life and long after accepted by him as confirmation of the survivability of the soul.

George wrote extensively on the subject of Darwinian evolution, and warmly embraced its teachings. He believed that early man was bestowed with an immortal spirit by a supernatural creator, as a separate, divine act. Spiritualism advanced the belief that the afterlife/spirit world allowed the departed to 'evolve' to higher spiritual states 'at a rate more rapid and under conditions more favourable to growth' than man found on Earth. References to this very concept can be found in *A Visit to Venus*, the science fiction story he wrote in 1927 (republished as a companion to this book in 2021).

Whilst Spiritualism had become increasingly popular in the late 19th century (according to Wikipedia, by 1897 there were more than eight million followers in the United States and Europe, mostly drawn from the middle and upper classes), it was during and after the First World War that it was to see its biggest expansion. For example, it is reported that the Spiritualists National Union had

145 affiliated societies in 1914, yet by the end of the conflict in 1918, this number had 'more than doubled to 309'. And, according to Steven J Sutcliffe in his book, *Children of the New Age*, 'in the late 1920s and early 1930s there were around one quarter of a million practicing spiritualists, and two thousand Spiritualist societies in the UK.'

Many adherents at the time would doubtless have cited the ghostly 'goings-on' by Mr Splitfoot at the home of the Fox sisters in Hydesville, New York in 1848, and subsequent revelations as evidence that:

The spirits of the dead really do exist
They desire to communicate with the living
They can and do communicate

And so emerged a plethora of spirit mediums, such as Florence Cook, Emma Hardinge Britten and Estelle Roberts, who, via 'demonstrations' of mediumship, clairvoyance and materialisation, as well as other manifestations, sought to spread a message of hope to those whose faith in life after death was being encouraged (rather than challenged, as one might expect) by the emergence of science and technology.

For example, the invention of photography (1826), the electrical telegraph (1838), the telephone and loudspeaker (1876), the phonograph (1877), moving pictures (1890), cinematographic motion pictures (1895) and radio (1897) permitted disembodied voices to emerge from mysterious devices and for the images of people to be retained on paper or celluloid – even long after they had died. To quote Kirsty Logan from the excellent Radio 4 series, *A History of Ghosts*, 'Everyday was a haunting.'

And side by side, there eventually emerged an industry led by sceptics and would-be believers alike who, when attending seances, simply wanted incontrovertible proof that such phenomena were taking place as suggested. The field of study known as parapsychology (originally coined as psychical research) thereafter spawned its own organisations and newspapers devoted to establishing the truth and exposing those they would regard as fraudsters and charlatans. For example, The Ghost Club was founded in London as early as 1862, and the Society for Psychical Research was also established there, 20 years later.

As for George, it seems he fell into both camps, even though one could argue strongly that he simply needed to believe, both as an affirmation of the Biblical promises of immortality and of the hope that one day he would be reunited with his two boys.

You'll find elsewhere in this context that George quotes from the eminent French chemist and biologist, Louis Pasteur, who shared a similar yearning. Upon further investigation, we can understand why. This is a quote from *Life of Pasteur* by Bene Vallery Kadot, translated from the French by Mrs KL Devonshire, and published by Constable & Co Ltd (1923):

> 'My philosophy is of the heart and not of the mind,' wrote Pasteur from the bedside of his dying daughter, 'and I give myself up, for instance, to those feelings about eternity which come naturally at the bedside of a cherished child drawing its last breath. At those supreme moments there is something in the depths of our souls which tells us that the world may be more than a mere combination of phenomena proper to a mechanical equilibrium brought out of the chaos of the elements simply through the gradual action of the forces of matter.'

For a while at least, his own research and his sateless curiosity provided him with the comfort he sought. But as time progressed, was it the case that his inquiring mind remained convinced?

The following examples have been chosen to demonstrate George's feelings about spiritualism – although we aren't absolutely sure that he wrote the first two, the first published locally and the second in a national spiritualism journal: **Life After Death – Sir A Conan Doyle in Swindon** (*North Wilts Herald*, April 30, 1920) and **Sir A Conan Doyle in the West** (*The Two Worlds*, May 7, 1920).

Given that the lecture took place a full two years after he had first started writing in the *Advertiser* about his own experiences of spiritual intercommunication, could he have resisted such an opportunity, not only to further his own understanding of the belief system, but to make his own assessment of the evidence underpinning it all?

Besides, the visit of the author of the Sherlock Holmes stories was a really big event for Swindon, coming as it did at the end of a short tour of the West Country by the celebrated author and physician, and immediately prior to his departure for Australia and New Zealand on spiritualist missionary work.

A shorter report of the same event appeared in *The Two Worlds*, a weekly newspaper founded in Manchester in 1887, by Emma Hardinge Britten. Declared to be 'a Weekly Journal devoted to the Phenomena, Philosophy and Progress of Spiritualism,' it was regarded as the voice of Spiritualists in the north of England in particular, and a publication of which George admitted to being an avid reader – for a while at the very least.

Nearly two decades later, in **Gleanings [40]** (February 18, 1938), George commences his investigation into spiritualism *per se*, although there are many earlier articles where he has expanded on his thoughts on immortality, the conscious survivability of the soul and his neo-transcendental experiences of intercommunication with the spirit world.

We learn for the first time that he has 'read extensively, both of the activity of the Psychical Research Association and of the Spiritualist Society', and that he was not only a reader of *The Two Worlds*, but also a contributor of articles to its pages 'in the years that are gone'.

In the circumstances, it was imperative that we tried to locate these articles ahead of the publication of this book. Consequently, much time was spent in trawling through the online archive of *The Two Worlds* newspaper in the hope of recovering George's contributions, but sadly to no avail. The only conclusion we can draw is that this all happened sometime between the years 1895 and 1918 (inclusive), where sadly, there is a gap in the record, but it does, at least, strengthen the theory that he was the author of pieces about Conan Doyle's talk in Swindon in 1920.

We get to hear of his conviction that 'some phenomena occur, under control of psychic law' and the fact 'that such exist has been proved to me absolutely without question', although he states that he 'cannot agree that they actually demonstrate a proof of immortality'.

Despite an interlude of many months, George picks up where he left off in **Gleanings [80]** (December 2, 1938) with investigations into the phenomena of death and whether this marks the annihilation of the individual concerned or, alternatively, whether it marks the point at which we all pass into a new state of conscious survival.

Although not specifically named, the reference contained in the penultimate paragraph is to the medium Estelle Roberts and her 'spirit guide,' the native American Indian known as 'Red Cloud'.

Reportedly considered by the British Spiritualist Movement as 'one of its finest exponents of mediumship in the 20th century', she was a superstar of her day. Just as George was writing this piece, she had already embarked on a tour of England, sponsored by the *Sunday Pictorial* newspaper, taking in Manchester Free Trade Hall, two meetings at the Royal Albert Hall, one at Birmingham and one at Sheffield. In all, she is estimated to have demonstrated her professional skills to around 60,000 people.

In **Gleanings [81]** (December 9, 1938) part two of the December 'Spiritualism trilogy' as it were, George tackles the difficult subject of mental capacity and in a style considered clumsy and simplistic by modern standards, seeks to define and quantify the potential for 'personality'.

His line of reasoning appears to be that science accepts as fact that the 'personality' or 'soul' (call it what you will) expires with the physical 'self' at the point of death. And if this is the fate of those blessed with high intelligence, then there is absolutely no chance of 'survival' with those of lower intellectual function.

However, he seeks to contrast this 'inevitability' with the teachings of the spiritualist movement, where 'every human being, irrespective of brain capacity, survives death in a state of living consciousness' and that 'in the new experience, all malformations and defects are corrected'.

It is also in this article that George recounts his experiences of clairvoyance at the (hitherto undated) spiritualist meeting in Swindon – details of which originally appeared in print in 1927.

Our research will continue in an attempt to find out more about this encounter, which, for him anyway, proved to be a transcendent turning point. It's likely to have taken place sometime between 1911 and 1918 (inclusive).

Unfortunately, *Gleanings* [82] (December 16, 1938), is currently missing from the record, but is the subject of ongoing research. The third of the series of three articles devoted to spiritualism, it is known to contain not only his thoughts on 'Revelation' (the disclosure of divine truths through communication with a supernatural entity), but is also intended to be a summary of his beliefs.

Nevertheless, the succeeding articles and reports do allow us to fill in many of the gaps, and get an overall understanding of his critical thinking and conclusions.

We have included two articles from **Psychic News** (December 24, 1938 and January 7, 1939) because they refer to George.

Founded in 1932 as a weekly newspaper by Psychic Press Ltd, *Psychic News* was, however, closely associated with the Spiritualists' National Union, who actually went on to acquire the publication themselves in 1995, and retained ownership until 2010. Proclaiming in 1938 to be 'The Spiritualist Newspaper with the World's Largest Net Sale', this article refers to George by name and features large sections from his own piece on the demonstration of mediumship and clairvoyance that appeared in the *Advertiser* on December 9.

The latter of the two is useful in that it contains a number of quotes from the missing article that appeared in the *Advertiser* on December 16. But, more importantly, it contains the key elements of his evaluation of (and support for) spiritualism, which, for the writer of the news item at least, wasn't quite as unequivocal as he/she would have liked.

In **Gleanings [86]** (January 20, 1939), George responds to the criticism as to why he couldn't yet endorse the verities of spiritualism – despite having been overwhelmingly convinced by the demonstration of clairvoyance that he attended some years previously.

His hesitancy seems to revolve around the fact that the use of a third party in dialogue with the 'spirits of the dead' laid the whole process open to deception – yet he is keen to emphasise that as a student of the spiritualist movement, he had not yet come to any firm conclusions and was eager to continue his investigations 'with caution and care'.

Finally, we include another article from *Psychic News* (February 4, 1939). This is the last known episode in the spat about metaphysics between George and *Psychic News* – only this time it is penned by Chief Reporter AW Austen, one-time secretary to the well-known editor, Maurice Barbanell.

Whether George enjoyed the 'communication' metaphor contained in the short piece or whether he was ever convinced about the truths of spiritualism and its attendant manifestations, we'll probably never know for sure; the discourse on this subject appears to cease at this point.

Life After Death
Sir A Conan Doyle in Swindon

(First published in *North Wilts Herald*, April 30, 1920, writer uncredited)

The ever-engrossing subject of the after-death state was discussed at some length by Sir Arthur Conan Doyle, in a lecture on "Life and the hereafter," which he delivered to a rapt audience at the Swimming Baths, Swindon, on Thursday evening.

The Mayor (Mr SE Walters), who presided, mentioned as a preliminary that there was an increasing desire to know more about the spirit world. They all recognised Sir Arthur Conan Doyle as a real and earnest seeker after truth, and because of that they were anxious to take a lead from him.

Sir Arthur Conan Doyle, who was received with loud applause, observed that his principal reason for coming to Swindon was that there was no centre for the study of spiritualism. He had set himself the mission, not to proselytise, but to preach the message he had received from the spirit world; and it was his intention in a while to tour New Zealand, Australia and America with the same object. Coming as he did amongst the unconverted, he thought he might be pardoned if he traced the early history of the spiritualistic movement; and so he took his audience back to the year, somewhere in the forties of the last century, when communications with the spirit world were first established in the home circle of a family named Fox in America. That, Sir Arthur declared, was an epoch, a turning point in the history of the human race; it was an event far more important than wars, the rise and fall of dynasties, or international treaties.

The speaker then went on to talk of his own association with the movement. Like many others, he had been a sceptic, a materialist, and had been inclined to view rather disparagingly anything that savoured of other-worldliness. But he had given years of careful study to the subject, observed closely the phenomena which had been produced as innumerable scenes, and had now accepted final proof of the broad claims of spiritualism.

But spiritualism, unfortunately, had been laid open to the charges of fraud and trickery through the malpractices of charlatans, who endeavoured to exploit it for their own profit. However, the genuine seekers after truth and enlightenment were increasing in number as a result of the war, and what had previously been a craze, a cult, was now becoming a guiding philosophy.

Just after the war broke out, there was staying at his house a lady who was highly mediumistic and had developed the faculty of automatic writing. She received messages from relatives who had been killed in the war and gave information about things that were about to happen – and that did actually happen afterwards. This and other experiences of a private and intimate character had told him to accept the truths that were half-hidden in the spirit world.

It was to be confessed that many of the phenomena that had been produced were liable to be classified as childish and stupid, but in such cases regard must be had not for the phenomena themselves but for the spirit, the message, behind. The numerous rappings and tappings were but signals from the spirit world to attract the attention of a very material generation.

"All the time the bell has been ringing, and we have refused to take off the receiver," Sir Arthur added very aptly. Communication with the spirit world was becoming clear and clearer, which was a fact that was being more readily appreciated by the many who had lost loved ones in the war.

The New Testament was an open book to the student of spiritualism, declared the speaker. St Paul had preached that there was a natural body as well as a spiritual body. At the moment of death the inner, the etheric or astral body floated out of the physical body, of which it was a duplicate. Immediately after dissolution the disembodied soul came face to face with those it had loved on this earth; and it was a fact worthy of note that frequently a dying person murmured words of endearment to absent relatives and friends. This was called mind-wandering by the people who did not know; but it was really a beginning of the visions which followed on death.

Life and experience on the other side were much the same as we found them on the physical plane. But the dual forces of love and sympathy dominated everywhere, and drew souls into perfect harmony. As the eye grows dimmer on this side, it becomes ever clearer on the other side.

Sir Arthur refuted the theological view that we are "all miserable sinners". "We are not," he declared. "We have not deserved all punishment, but require some compensation. We have been through a great deal in this world, and we shall surely get that measure of justice, of compensation which we have earned." In the after life there would be a period that could be likened to a "rest cure." Bullying husbands and nagging wives would not be present to spoil the innocent enjoyment of their partners. Men's lost strength and women's lost beauty would be renewed, for the physical disabilities would be removed. The testimony obtained from persons who had "passed over" led to the conclusion that they did not desire the return to this "mud bath" of ours.

Spirituality was not attained by religious forms and ceremonies, but by striving after spiritual things: love, sympathy, charity, gentleness, unselfishness. We should have to pass through successive stages before we reached the goal: each death was but a "promotion" to a higher state; and so we should go on climbing the heights until we attained the topmost point and be finally merged in the Divine Spirit.

The Mayor acknowledged his own as well as the audience's indebtedness to Sir Arthur Conan Doyle for his most illuminating address, and the latter briefly replied.

Sir A Conan Doyle in the West
(First published in *The Two Worlds*, May 7, 1920, writer uncredited)

The meeting at Swindon on the 22nd was presided over by Ald Walters (Mayor of Swindon) who stated that his presence there was to give welcome to a distinguished visitor whose worth and fame were known wherever the English language was spoken. As chief magistrate – whilst he could not claim to be a spiritualist – he was the representative of the citizens, and it had been his rule to be the servant of them all. At the same time, he thought that any man unwise who closed his ears and mind to new truths, and he was sure that Sir Arthur would not espouse any cause unless he had sufficient grounds of faith and reason for so doing.

He (the chairman) was there to listen, and perhaps to learn, and he was sure his fellow townsmen would give their honoured visitor a hearty welcome. (Applause.)

Sir Arthur, on rising, took his audience to Hydesville and delineated in detail the momentous happenings which ushered in the New Revelation. Criticisms and misstatements of the original facts were ruthlessly exposed, and the speaker showed how solid was the foundation laid in 1848 and succeeding years.

He traced the spread of the movement through the New World and the Old, and concluded that the spirit world had now such a hold on this, that to sweep back the tide of new truths was an impossibility. It had come in force, and had come to stay.

He then outlined the researches of the early band of scientific experimenters, and contrasted them with the latest researches of Drs Crawford and Geley, showing that all results pointed to the same fact, ie, that the spirit world was behind the Movement. Its real significance, however, was spiritual and not phenomenal, the latter being merely fingerposts to spiritual life.

An audience of nearly one thousand people listened with rapt attention to an address lasting an hour and a half, and there is some likelihood of a society being formed in this important railway centre as a result of the meeting. Several earnest spiritualists reside in the town, and steps are being taken to get them together.

Sir Arthur finished his tour tired, but happy, and success attended every effort.

Gleanings [40]
By George E Hobbs
(First published: February 18, 1938)

This week I want to get down to a question which, by the very nature of our physical constitution, we all have to face. Yet it is one of those questions from which, usually, we shrink. What happens at death? Are we still conscious of existing? Or do we become completely annihilated – matter, mind and spirit?

A friend has passed out. He could talk, think and act. Now the powers which enabled him to do this have forsaken him. The will to compel his being to function no longer expresses itself. The personality which was labelled by his name has vanished. All that belonged to him as an individual being has ceased to have value. It is pulseless and dead. Just what has happened? Is everything gone and lost forever? True, there is memory but that belongs to those who have survived him. What of him?

I had written thus far when news reached me of a second passing. A friend with whom I had worked day by day for 14½ years had died. To what? To where?

Many have faced up to this problem and to many it is still a problem – unsolved and full of mystery. Can no light be given to those who are searching in the darkness? Let us examine the problem frankly, and as fully as our limited powers will permit.

Now it is perfectly true that the instinctive desire of every individual is for life. We literally yearn for life in which we are conscious of existing. We are here existing, conscious and we are satisfied with the knowledge that we exist and are conscious. We shrink from death – well, to put it bluntly, because we fear the unknown, the uncharted seas from which travellers have never returned to tell us of their experience.

Is it fear which has produced the demand for immortality. Is it that human hearts compel a belief in immortality because the opposite is nauseating? Or is this yearning for life the mystic urge of an inward self, conscious of its indestructibility?

* * *

Let us commence our inquiry with the statement that things are believed in for one of two reasons. Either they can be demonstrated to the senses or, failing demonstration, a belief in them is logical. Can therefore, immortality be demonstrated? Or failing demonstration, is it logical of belief? Let us examine the problem.

If we turn to science for some solution we find not merely antagonism but a positive denial of its possibility. Haeckle, who was an eminent German scientist and philosopher, has left it on record that "The idea of the personal immortality of the soul is scientifically untenable. Death puts an end to the physiological functions of the cerebral neuroma – the countless microscopic cells the collective activity of which is known as 'the soul'."

Sir Arthur Keith, our own eminent scientist, has declared without compromise that: "The brain is not a tenement inhabited by a spirit or soul. The 'spirit' or 'soul' is but the name for the manifestations of the living brain.

Beyond a doubt, our thoughts, feelings, aspirations and passions are manifestations of the brain. When they are narcotised, destroyed or dead, consciousness disappears."

And then he adds: "Man has the seeds of immortality within him. But the gift is for the race, and not for the individual." In other words, Sir Arthur Keith sees immortality only in the continuance of the species, and not in the continuance of the individual.

In contradistinction to the declaration of science against, there are the avowed claims of spiritualists FOR immortality. No useful purpose is served in ridiculing these claims. They are either true or untrue, and they must be judged by the logic or illogic of their appeal.

Spiritualists claim that immortality is not only true, but that it can be demonstrated. They further claim that they have established materialisation and intercommunication – that they have seen the "dead" and that they have talked with them.

Now I do not pretend to any exhaustive knowledge of this claim. I have read extensively both of the activity of the Psychical Research Association and of the Spiritualist Society. For many months I was a reader of "The Two Worlds" – the official organ of the Spiritualist organisation – and, in the years that are gone, have contributed articles to its pages.

That some phenomena occur, under control of psychic law, I am convinced. Whether that law is good and permissible, or dangerous and questionable, I do not pronounce upon. That such exist has been proved to me absolutely without question.

During the test of those proofs, no collusion or mere guess-work was possible. The proof was so irrefutable that to deny it would have been just stubborn foolishness. As I say, some phenomena do occur, but personally I cannot agree that they actually demonstrate a proof of immortality. In such matters we tamper with laws which are but little known or understood. And it has long been suspected that the nature of these laws is such that they operate adversely upon the mental stability of the investigator.

It is here that I see the possibility of deception – not deception by the investigator or demonstrator, for in the main they are folk of high integrity and of moral standing, but deception through the laws by which the investigator works. The investigator is deceived into believing something for which his heart yearns while actually and really it is not the truth. Personally, while there is much in the logical doctrine with which I profoundly disagree, there is one aspect with which my intelligence compels agreement. It is that, while a good and beneficent Personality exists to direct humanity towards the highest and best, there also exists an evil and malevolent Personality which seeks to mislead and deceive humanity – one that lures humanity into false conclusions. I leave it there.

There is yet another avenue of investigation left to us. It is that of revelation. We shall conduct our investigation along this avenue with the same impartiality as we did the claims of spiritualism. Is a revelation possible? If so, is it one [upon] which we can depend? Let us see.

* * *

I think it is logical to assume that the yearning for immortality is intellectual in its basis and expression. So far as we know, man is the only creature that yearns for immortality. It is not the result of fear of the unknown, but what I may term the instinctive urge of the wanderer seeking his way home. Man feels the sense of "a temporary resident" as he thinks upon his physical existence. He knows that the physical expressions of life are not permanent. And this instinctive urge therefore, is the awareness that a fuller, a more expressive, a permanent life awaits him at the end of his physical wanderings – that he will eventually find himself at home.

It is in this instinctive urge where I first see a declared revelation. The wanderer, right down in his inner, conscious self, is "told" that physical death does not mean extermination, but rather it is the entrance to a continuity of conscious existence which is more complete.

If we take the Bible as the written revelation of the truths of immortality, we find the strongest truth possible of its certainty. While the Old Testament, in places, is vague – even pessimistic – its general teaching is that man is a creature whose personality is imperishable and immortal.

But what the Old Testament lacks, the New Testament supplies with a clarity which is amazing. Gone are the half-formed wishes, the half-destroyed doubts. In their place radiates the certainty of a positive assurance that "Death is swallowed up in victory. That man dies but can live!

And so we will leave Huxley when he says: "We poor mortals have to be content with hope and belief in all matters, past and present. Our sole certainty is but momentary." And with fuller confidence we will turn to FW Myers, in his "Human Personalty": "Beyond us is still mystery; but it is mystery lit and mellowed with an infinite HOPE. We ride in darkness at the haven's mouth;

but sometimes through rifted clouds, we see the desires and needs of many generations, floating and melting upwards into a distant glow. Up through the light of seas, by the moon's long, silvering ray."

Man's end is not physical death. That is the portal into fuller life.

Gleanings [80]
By George E Hobbs
(First published: December 2, 1938)

At the outset of this article I wish to say that, while I shall write upon a poignant subject, there will be nothing morbid in its presentation. Even those of my readers subject to mental gastritis may read this article without a feeling of nausea. I shall write upon the phenomena of death and of the implications arising therefrom.

Very few traverse far along the path of life without coming up against the presence of death. To young folk it is mysterious and somewhat frightening; to adults it is not mysterious in its process, and should not be frightening in its effects. The mystery – if mystery there be – is not in death itself, but rather in the problem of conscious survival. And we may as well admit at the onset that so far as actual knowledge of survival is concerned – that is, the knowledge one has of having been to and returned from, say, Westminster Abbey, or to and from a lecture or reading, or back from the magnificent buildings or India – we are just where Shakespeare's "Hamlet" was in 1604. It is still:

"The undiscover'd country from whose bourn
No traveller returns –"

That is, no traveller has ever returned to give a personal account of a personal experience.

Death is an experience which every human being must encounter. None is exempt. All who live must, by the very constitution of their being, die. Human beings do not die because of a curse pronounced upon the race. To assert such is to declare a travesty of logic and a contradiction of natural law. The truth of "As in Adam all die" is simply the truth of the inflexible operation of natural law. Human beings are composed of such materials as are subject to the law of all physical things. Birth, development and death are all controlled by this law. There is therefore, no problem involved in death. The problem lies in what follows death.

I imagine that this search for knowledge began with the dawn of human thought. Probably at that crucial moment when, as the race was emerging from its sub-intellectual to its intellectual stage, the first reasoned love began to reveal itself. The newly-conditioned race wished to know what happened to their loved ones at death.

While death should not be frightening, seeing it is a natural process, it is true that the flesh shrinks from the thought of it. And I imagine the reason to be that the primal instinct and desire of every normal individual is for life which is consciously experienced.

> "Whatever crazy sorrow saith,
> No life that breathes with human breath
> Has ever truly longed for death.
> 'Tis life of which our nerves are scant,
> O Life! not death, for which we pant;
> More life, and fuller, that we want—"

The human heart ever yearns for life. More than ever it yearns for life when death approaches.

But is this yearning merely the outgrowth of fear? Do we demand and compel a belief in conscious survival because we fear its opposite? Or is this yearning the mystic urge of a spiritual self, conscious of its indestructibility?

* * *

Are we annihilated at death? Or do we survive its tremendous test?

In all our investigations of truth we must remember that universal belief does not constitute truth. The slogan that a hundred million people cannot be wrong is not always true. We have only to remember the days in which Galileo lived – the late 16th and early 17th centuries. The universally accepted belief was that the earth was stationary and the whole of the visible heavens revolved around it. This, it was declared, had the sanction of Divine literature – the Bible. The time came when the very opposite was found to be the truth. So that we may say that belief in itself does not establish truth.

We will, however, commence with belief, and say things are believed in for one of two reasons. Either they can be demonstrated to the senses, in which belief may become the knowledge of truth. Or, while demonstration is not possible, a logical faith may verify not only its possibility, but also its truth. Can, therefore, survival be demonstrated? Or, failing demonstration, will a logical faith yield belief in the truth of its claim?

If we invoke the aid of science in our investigation we immediately meet with disturbances to the claim of survival – that is, of a conscious or personal survival. Many scientists – certainly not all – seem to take their stand by the side of the writer of Ecclesiastes. Says the "Preacher":

> "For that which befalleth the sons of men befalleth beasts; even one thing befalleth them; as the one dieth, so dieth the other; yea, they have all one breath; so that a man hath no pre-eminence above a beast. All go unto one place; all are of the dust, and all turn to dust again."

It is somewhere here that Sir Arthur Keith, the eminent scientist, would take his place. He would see, more or less, a common status of man and beast, except for the higher development of the brain in the case of man. It is not that he would agree to the fact of the indestructibility of matter and deny the indestructibility of the soul – the extra part of man. Sir Arthur will not agree man has that "extra part". At least, this is how he puts it.

"The brain," says he, "is not a tenement inhabited by a spirit or soul. The 'spirit' or 'soul' is but the name for the manifestations of the living brain." He further asserts that human aspirations, passions, thoughts and feelings are the expressions of the physical brain, from which, if it was destroyed or dead, consciousness disappears. And then he continues, "Man has the seeds of immortality within him: But the gift is for the race and not the individual.

Sir Arthur sees not the continuance of the individual, but only of the race. In continuing the race the individual dies, or rather, he is completely destroyed. In this he but qualifies the dictum of Haeckle, the late eminent German scientist and philosopher: "The idea of the personal immortality of the soul," wrote Haeckle, "is scientifically untenable."

And yet, although many scientists decide upon such a cold, test-tube conclusion to human life, I imagine that quite often their inmost hearts crave for some tangible contradiction. They analyse every portion of the human body and reduce it all to the terms of chemistry. The most vital organ of the body (the brain) is therefore just a mass of nerves – truly exquisitely compounded, I accept – but just a wonderful power station which, at death, will fall in decay and dust. In their worship of the actual and physical they give no room to the possibility that the unseen, that wonderful thing which, for want of a better term, we can only call the "personality", may be more real than visible. And because this personality cannot be revealed in the test-tube, to them it is non-existent. To me it seems such an unreasonable attitude to adopt.

In the Wells-Huxley tome, "The Science of Life," the joint authors ask this question: "Alone, in the silence of the night and on a score of thoughtful occasions we have demanded, can this self, so vividly central to my universe, so greedily possessive of the world, ever cease to be? Without it surely there is no world at all!"

* * *

In my next article I want to continue the investigation. We shall explore along the avenues of Spiritualism and of Revelation.

For a week or so past some of the largest halls in the country have been filled to capacity while a well-known medium has attempted to prove her powers of penetrating the veil of death. Hundreds of folk [who leave the hall] believe she has established contact with the other world. But is this really true? If it is true, then conscious survival is established as truth and also that a link connects the seen with the unseen.

This will be our next investigation.

Gleanings [81]
By George E Hobbs
(First published: December 9, 1938)

In my last article we found that, so far as the reasoning of physical science is concerned, conscious survival of death is not admitted. If we counter that "personality" demands the admission of survival, the physical scientist retorts that personality is but the accumulated expression of the individual unit, and is conditioned by the efficiency of its physical machinery.

To put it in a general way, physical scientists declare that the brain is the vehicle by which and through which thoughts, desires, aspirations and passions express their presence and power. By this argument – which it would be futile to refute – it would seem that the brain is the seat of personality, because these powers (the powers of thought, desire, aspiration and passion) are the "ingredients" which go to form that wonderful something we term "personality". Therefore personality is conditioned by brain capacity. We are not thinking now in terms of academic capacity, but in terms of moral capacity.

If the brain functions with exquisite clarity, and is disciplined so that it can assimilate and express in thought and conduct all that is noble and beautiful, then the personality is of a high order. But if, on the other hand, the brain does not function clearly (that is to say, if there can be no response even under discipline to that which is noble and beautiful) then personality will be of a low order. In both cases, whether of a high or low order, the brain is the conditioning instrument. And, says the physical scientist, as the brain at death disintegrates and falls into dust, that which it has accumulated will also perish and die.

It would seem, then, that there can be no personality without brain capacity. Even if a normal person were granted survival it would rule out altogether the unfortunate imbecile. Made in perfect human form, but with an imperfect brain – no personality. Let me quote an extreme case.

Some years ago I stood looking through the window of a friend's house in the country. A short distance away stood another house, from the front door of which came a little girl of about five years of age along with a splendid specimen of young manhood. He was about 5ft 10ins in height and of excellent physique. His age was about 19 or 20. The little girl had a picture-book and she and the youth sat upon a garden seat to look at the pictures. She was a lovely little thing, happy and free, and she laughed gaily at the pictures in her book.

From where I stood I heard the youth speak. I was puzzled. Then my heart missed a beat! An unaccountable lump came to my throat – I knew! The little girl of five was the youth's superior. She, in her baby way, could appreciate the pictures. He, tall and finely built as he was, could not. The machine was there, for he was sensitive to pain, but the pleasures of appreciation were denied him. Arrested development came upon him almost from birth.

I have quoted this extreme case because I want to give full appreciation to the considered judgement of the physical scientist. Personality is conditioned by the capacity of the brain to function. Hence, with the death and disintegration of the brain, personality is destroyed. If, therefore, survival is denied to "personalities" of outstanding merit, much less can it be permitted to the unfortunate individual whose brain cannot function.

And now, in contradistinction to the sweeping denial of survival by physical scientists, I want to try and show that every human being, irrespective of brain capacity, survives death in a state of living consciousness. Also, that in the new experience, all malformations and defects are corrected.

Let us follow our investigations first, however, before we sum up our findings.

The declarations of Spiritualism for survival are as positively insistent as are the declarations of physical scientists against it. An avowed spiritualist would as soon deny his own existence as deny the fact of survival. He claims that his is the positive knowledge of demonstration. He may agree that he himself is neither clairvoyant nor clairaudient. But, by means of an accredited medium under spirit control, he has proof positive of survival.

While to the uninitiated, this savours of the ridiculous, we get positively nowhere by mere ridicule. Let us give the spiritualist credit for his beliefs, and let our demand for proof have the dignity of a sane investigation.

Spiritualists begin with the assumption that man is more than physical. They contend that he is a spiritual entity, the spiritual "fabric" being housed within the physical organism during the life-cycle of the person. This spiritual "self" is composed of refined, attenuated materials which the physical senses are far too gross to recognise while the person is living upon the physical plane. When death occurs this spiritual "self" is released and goes out into the spirit world.

* * *

It will be noted that this assumption goes beyond our first suggestion – that personality, manifesting itself through the physical brain, was the indestructible part of man. Spiritualists claim that the indestructible part is a complete counterpart of the physical. They claim that when those who have passed over have been materialised to the view of the clairvoyant medium it is the complete form that is seen. To buttress this contention they quote the scene which occurred upon the Mount of Transfiguration. Peter and John saw and conversed with Moses and Elias.

Now I am not going to dispute the claims of spiritualism (I shall deal with my own personal views when we come to discuss "Revelation") – first, that man is a spiritual being; and secondly, that the spiritual part of man is indestructible; and, thirdly, that survival of death is a conscious existence. Nor shall I dispute the further claim of intercommunication with those who have passed over. I cannot dispute something of which I know so little.

That some wonderful powers are given to certain folk the following, I think, will prove. I can vouch for every word of that which I now write for it is my own personal experience.

Some time ago a woman lecturer came down from the North of England to Bristol to lecture upon spiritualism. Spiritualist friends here persuaded her to come to Swindon for one evening, and she came. Knowing that I was interested in this matter, they invited me along. When I arrived I found myself one of an audience of perhaps eighty. So that I could take notes for criticism, I sat as far away from the lecturer as possible, and was convinced I was lost in the crowd.

For the first half the lecturer dealt with the claims of spiritualism. Then she paused. Looking over the audience, she declared quite casually that she was clairvoyant. She was quite square about the matter. She would deal with a positive case and not a figurative one. For this she would need a subject to check her declarations. To my dismay she stood upon her toes, and over the heads of the audience pointed to me. I agreed, but first I gave the audience to understand that as this was the first time the lady had been in Swindon, it naturally was the first time we had met. I informed them that the lecturer could in no circumstances know anything of my life, etc, and also that what she had to declare I would scrupulously check. If true, I would declare it true; if false I would declare it false. With a smile she agreed.

I have no hesitation in saying that she startled me with the accuracy of her descriptive vision. She told me that by my right shoulder a young girl stood. She described her features in the minutest detail. Did I know her? Yes, quite well. She had passed over about a year, and I had visited her for about six months before she died. The lecturer pictured my young friend as clearly as though I held her photograph in my hand. Then by my left shoulder stood a man. Again a description of features, clear and faithful. Did I know him? Yes, I knew him. A mate with whom I had worked for years, and who had passed over 18 months before. I had been with him when he passed out.

Without the slightest hesitation she gave me an accurate description of the cause of death in each case. There was no "guessing" but just plain fact. And I am convinced that what she described she saw.

I give this experience for what it is worth. It is a true experience. But does it prove survival of death? Or is there some other explanation?

In my next article I want to deal with Revelation, and then generally to sum up.

Medium Startles Reporter by Her Accuracy

(First published in *Psychic News*, December 24, 1938, writer uncredited)

"In contradistinction to the sweeping denial of survival by physical scientists, I want to try and show that every human being, irrespective of brain capacity, survives death in a state of living consciousness," wrote George E Hobbs in the

Swindon Advertiser, a few days ago. "Also that in the new experience, all malformations and defects are corrected."

Hobbs fairly outlined the case for spiritualism, but reserved his own judgement, and then told of an experience of his own, which occurred at a spiritualist meeting in Swindon.

"When I arrived I found myself one of an audience of perhaps eighty," he wrote. "So that I could take notes for criticism, I sat as far away from the lecturer as possible."

Describing how the medium after her address, demonstrated clairvoyance, Hobbs went on... But Hobbs did not say whether he thought his experience proved survival. He merely printed the facts, and promised to sum up in a future article.

Reporter Has Spiritualism Proved To Him – Then Talks of "Danger"
(First published in *Psychic News*, January 7, 1939, writer uncredited)

George E Hobbs who has been writing a series of articles on survival in the "Swindon Advertiser," has a curious outlook on life after "death".

He has written three, fairly long articles debating the possibilities of continued existence, he has searched the Bible for texts that support his opinion, but is apparently not in the least interested in what form that life would take.

In a previous article, he told how a medium picked him out, a stranger, and described to him two people whom he had known before they "died". He said he did not dispute that the medium saw the people whom she described.

Now, in his summing up, he writes:

"I have sympathy, too, with my friends the spiritualists. They seem not to be satisfied with Revelation, but must probe the veil between the two worlds. The great trouble is that it lends itself to deception.

"I do not doubt for one moment the probability of contacting with those who have passed over. Strange powers are given to some folk, and if those powers are used wisely I imagine they may be powers for good.

"At the same time I realise that a danger always exists when one is dealing with laws little understood. It is best, I think, to go forward in such investigations with caution and care."

Then Hobbs gave his own view: "So far as I personally am concerned, I am satisfied with revelation. I am convinced [of] survival of death. And I am equally convinced that that survival is one of complete consciousness. We shall know there and then that we are."

But if Hobbs's faith in survival is based on the three texts that he quoted in his articles, then it has a very thin foundation. Before coming to a hasty conclusion and condemning spiritualists for their boldness, he should have read just one further text: "Add to your faith knowledge."

If he had done that, he would not be content with "revelation". He would want to know.

Gleanings [86]

(First published: January 20, 1939)

I note that the Editor of the "Psychic News" has taken me gently to task over my recent articles on "Survival", published in "The Swindon Advertiser." I was rather surprised to see the headlines printed in bold type: – "Reporter has Spiritualism proved to him – Then talks of danger."

Incidentally, I seem to be in good company, for Beverley Baxter, MP, described as "The Voice of Britain", is accused of writing nonsense and of being ignorant. And Ernest Oaten, Editor of "Two Worlds," also comes under criticism.

Coming to the mild criticism of my articles, the Editor of "Psychic News" writes: "He has written three fairly long articles debating the possibilities of continued existence, he had searched the Bible for texts that support his opinion, but is apparently not in the least interested in what form that life will take." And finally: "But if Hobbs' faith in survival is based on the three texts that he quotes in his articles, then it has a very thin foundation. Before coming to a hasty conclusion and condemning spiritualists for their boldness, he should have read one further text – 'Add to your faith knowledge.'

"If he had done that, he would not be content with 'Revelation.' He would want to know."

There is nothing in the criticism about which to raise a storm. It is, however, misleading for the Editor has read into my articles what is not there. I did not come to a "hasty conclusion". And I certainly did not "condemn spiritualists for their boldness". Nor did I search for texts "that supported his opinion". And, again, I am interested in what form "that life will take".

I am not sure, as yet, that I have come to any final conclusions, save that I am convinced of survival. It is not an opinion, but a conviction. It is my conviction that the real personality is an immortal entity, and that, at death, released from the limitations of the earth body, it passes over into a world of which it is conscious. With honest conviction I believe in the continuity of conscious existence. I believe, again with honest conviction, that this continuity of existence is the heritage of all mortal beings, irrespective of their manner of living.

The picture I have in mind at the moment is that given by St Paul. In that picture he suggests that during mortal life we gather to ourselves certain properties. On the one hand these properties may be likened to "gold, silver and precious stones"; on the other hand they may be likened to "wood, hay and stubble". When we pass over we take with us our indestructible part – our spirit being, and the part that may or may not be destroyed – the properties of characteristics we have accumulated during our earthly passage through life. If the characteristics can be likened to gold, silver and precious stones, they will pass over us, and be to us as "mansions". But if they are likened to wood, hay and stubble, they will be destroyed "as by fire," and we shall pass over unclothed and naked. On the one hand a good start will be made towards higher service and activity; on the other hand a fresh start will have to be made.

* * *

In regards to spiritualism, I have come to no hasty conclusions. I am still a student, reading all I can upon the subject and talking it over with spiritualistic friends. The one thing which puzzles me considerably is that all communications which are supposed to come from the other side can come only through a medium. If communication is possible – and I am not foolish enough to assert with positive conviction it is not possible – why cannot I communicate with those who have passed over? It seems to me just here where deception may creep in.

With "revelation" everyone who can read or who can hear the word read stands equal to reception. But it is not so with the Spiritualistic Faith. It is those who claim clairvoyant powers to see "through the veil", and those who claim clairaudient powers who hear the voice from the other world. Those to whom the mediums communicate what they see and hear have to take things on trust. I suppose my friends of the Spiritualistic Church will tell me that it is a matter of atonement. Even so, I should like a little more light upon this extraordinary phase. If communication is possible then it should be within the power of all to do so.

Again I assure that, so far as I personally am concerned, I am satisfied with Revelation. I am convinced that survival of death is a reality. And I am equally convinced that that survival is one of complete consciousness. We shall know there that we are.

But, while saying this, I have not closed the door of my conviction with finality. I am open to add to my knowledge of truth even from my friends the spiritualists.

All Worlds Are One
[Extracts from Comments Column by Chief Reporter, AW Austen]

(First published in *Psychic News*, February 4, 1939)

What Does He Glean?

I cannot understand George E Hobbs of Swindon, who writes "Gleanings" in his local paper. He indignantly rejects the suggestion made in Psychic News a few weeks ago that he is not interested in what form life in the spirit world will take, though he is convinced of its reality. Yet he repeats, "I am satisfied with Revelation."

It would seem to me that if he wants to know more he cannot be satisfied with what is already revealed!

The Essential Medium

Hobbs cannot understand why a medium is necessary to communication. He does not see why spirits cannot talk to him direct.

If he is logical, he will not accept letters from the postman but will insist on his friends, or enemies, bringing their messages direct. He should refuse to listen in, for that means accepting his wireless set as an intermediary instead of the speakers talking to him direct.

The postman and the wireless receiver save him and his friends trouble. So does the medium, for he saves Hobbs the trouble of developing his own psychic gifts. If Hobbs likes to spend a few years developing the powers we all possess, he can talk to his spirits direct. Until then, he must use a medium if he wants to communicate with the "dead".

Chapter 12

Immortality, the Meaning of Death and Other Theological Ideas

> *Man, by the fact that he is made in the image of the undying, is natural heir to immortality. It is not conditional – neither can he be disinherited*
> **George Hobbs, July 20, 1928**

George commences his examination of the theories relating to the 'soul' (the seat of conscious thought and self-awareness – call it what you will) and once again, it's clear that he had already read extensively on the matter.

Prompted to commence this eight-part series following the address given by the Scottish anthropologist Sir Arthur Keith at Manchester University on May 9, 1928, George debates whether the 'spirit' exists separately within the physical structure of the human body, or whether, like all other mammals, it is merely a function of the brain and nervous system – and therefore dies when the body perishes.

He states at the beginning of part 8 of the series, called simply Immortality:

> When I set out to write this present series it was not a sudden whim which prompted me. I have been anxious to write upon this subject for many months past, but the time never seemed opportune. Not only so, but I knew that months of thought and careful reasoning had led me to conclusions which were the antithesis of orthodoxy. But when, as the result

of Sir Arthur Keith's lecture, the public mind seemed awakened to its issue,
I felt the time was then opportune.

It's worth pointing out at this juncture that George uses the word 'psychic' fairly liberally in these discussions and, rather confusingly, it is applied to mean 'matters relating to the soul or mind' as well as in the context of 'faculties or phenomena that are apparently inexplicable by reference to natural laws'. The latter definition (which relates to supernatural abilities such as clairvoyance and mediumship) is the one which is in more common usage today (and something explored at length in the previous chapter).

George was never one to follow the pack, and the following is a further example of his willingness to put his head above the parapet and challenge mainstream scientific thought in situations where it appears to stray into matters of faith (and *his* faith in particular).

So, does the mind exist separately from the body? And is the belief in immortality 'torn asunder' by advances in anatomy, biology and evolution theory? George appears to take comfort from comments attributed to Sir Arthur in which he says that 'I do not think my statement destroys the theory of immortality', although this may simply be an occasion where the scientist draws a distinction between what can be proven, and matters of faith which are beyond his bailiwick.

Then follows an examination of how ancient peoples embraced the notion of immortality and even of secondary egos as a means of comprehending events 'experienced' during dreamtime. Thereafter, we are taken on a journey through some ancient belief systems, including animism and Native American funerary ritual, and then to an analysis of theology and the Scriptures, encompassing both immortality and resurrection.

By part 4, George is expounding his own creed, proudly announcing: 'Do I believe in immortality? Most certainly I do. And as shocking as a positivist's attitude may seem, I believe in it wholly and without reservation.'

His conviction is founded on the belief that man was imbued with immortality at the point at which he was 'made in the image of God' – that image being spiritual, not physical.

The reasoning around immortality becomes even more nuanced in part 5. Here we find George seeking to draw a distinction between man's activities which are of molecular constitution and those 'higher' activities which are psychic or spiritual and therefore 'free activity exclusive of atomic constitution'.

He boldly asserts that: 'No one today will be hardy enough to attempt an intellectual denial of the existence of a Creator. This Creator we call God.'

Some readers may be forgiven for thinking that George had made quite a big assumption at this juncture, but his reasoning is, nevertheless, fascinating. In summary, this amounts to the belief that the universe was designed by an intelligent entity, and it follows that this Being must have 'also existed for millions of years'. And if 'this Being has existed from eternity, then He must be altogether free of atomic constitution'.

According to George, this is a demonstration that conscious life can and does exist independently of physical limitations. And it follows that if God made man in His own image, then it must be the case that God dwells in man – so every human being must therefore be immortal.

In part 6, discussions centre on the subject of brain activity – in particular, aspects of academic achievement and moral conduct – and then take a rather interesting turn. What George refers to as 'soul capacity' (defined by him as 'the highest psychic expression') is something which he states 'does not of necessity rest upon any particular development of the brain' and amounts to '[mental] capacity independent of reason' – that is: regardless of intellect.

This segues into an examination of whether soul capacity is independent of molecular activity. Meanwhile, George asserts (somewhat controversially) that the 'poor imbecile' cannot possess any soul culture or any psychic expression by virtue of a malformed brain, devoid of functional powers – as distinct from the brain of someone with low intellect. However, once free of this mortal coil, the malformed brain finds happiness.

The reader may struggle with much of George's thinking in this respect, particularly with the following, rather bullish, statement:

'We have seen that life, free of atomic renewals, is known to exist. I use the word "known" because it cannot be denied without violating reason. This free, unfettered life is the life of God.'

And we get to hear that in his opinion, it is 'soul life which gives distinctive personality to the individual' and it is this which is 'impervious to death'.

Ahead of the final part, in which the question is raised as to the end state or condition of those who have succumbed to physical death, George declares: 'I understand that many articles have been written recently on this question, none of which have I read or wished to hear discussed, as I am extremely anxious to keep my mind clear to the issues of this present series.'

By the eighth and final part, we get more of an insight into George's absolute commitment to tenets of his faith, even if, by his own admission, he doesn't fully understand them. He then seeks to provide an answer to the age-old question of where the souls of the deceased go at the point of death.

And finally, in tackling another Biblical doctrine head on, George declares that there really is no such thing as eternal punishment and that man's ultimate destiny is… happiness.

Also included are two extracts and some *Advertiser* correspondence from later in the same year, in which George seeks to dispel the Old Testament teaching that physical death is the result of Adam's disobedience in the Garden of Eden.

And we conclude the examination of physical death by including the final two chapters of a series entitled *Origins*, dating from 1935. Here, once again, he expands his thinking with reference to the doctrine of original sin and man's eventual resurrection.

In paragraphs three and four of Part 5, George sets out a personal statement on his approach to tackling controversial parts of the Bible – further evidence if needed that he was prepared to break free from religious dogma, be true to himself and enjoy true liberty of thought.

The fact that he was prepared to put himself at risk of opprobrium (or even eternal damnation, as some would have it) for daring to reject a literal interpretation of Biblical teaching, speaks volumes for his moral and ethical integrity, let alone his well-known dislike of convention.

Immortality [1]
First of a Series of Talks
By George E Hobbs

(First published: May 25, 1928)

The deductions of Sir Arthur Keith, the eminent surgeon and biologist, are by no means new, and should occasion no dismay to those who rest upon a belief in Immortality.

Haeckel, in his "Evolution of Man", published as far back as 1874, says: "Physiology teaches us further, on the ground of observation and experiment, that the relation of the soul to its organ, the brain and spinal cord, is just the same in man as in other mammals. The one cannot act at all without the other; it is just as much bound up with it as muscular movement is with the muscles. It can only develop in connection with it."

Again he says, speaking of the Dualistic (body and soul in one organism) belief: "If then, we must reject these popular and, in some respects, agreeable Dualistic theories as untenable, because inconsistent with the genetic facts, there remains only the opposite or Monistic conception, according to which the soul is, like any other animal soul, a function of the central nervous system, and develops in inseparable connection therewith."

But while Sir Arthur Keith, with true scientific reserve, keeps within the bounds of that which can be demonstrated, Haeckel could not resist speculation. Said he: "From all these facts" – two volumes of them – "sound reason must conclude that the still prevalent belief of the immortality of the soul is an untenable superstition."

What are the Facts?

Just as Haeckel propounded the belief that psychic activity and development was based upon a physical cause – the brain – so Sir Arthur has re-affirmed it. No useful purpose is served by ignoring discovered facts, and these cannot be made any less true by refutation.

What are the facts? How can they be stated so that the ordinary individual may understand them?

The brain is an organ of intense complexity, [but] of much less complexity in the lower species of life, rising higher, until its highest complexity is reached in man. The superlative position of man in the scale of sentient beings led early scientists to declare there were distinctive organs in the human cerebrum – the fore brain – which were absent in all other creatures. Painstaking examination, however, proved this declaration false. It was discovered that the characteristic features of the human cerebrum were found in a rudimentary – or undeveloped – form in the lower apes, and more or less fully developed in the higher apes.

While it was known that the brain was the functional organ of all movement, the great difficulty was the seat of location of that mysterious process known as "thought impressions". [Where lay the mind, the psychic life of man? Was it in some second self, distinct from the physical? Or did it lay in the physical?] That was the intriguing query ever before the mind of the investigating scientist.

It was known that if certain areas of the brain were injured or diseased, the power of movement in definite members of the body would cease. I believe I am correct in saying that paralysis of the right arm or leg would indicate the cause to be centred in a localised area of the brain's left hemisphere. Roughly speaking, the left hemisphere of the brain governs the right side of the body, and the right hemisphere the left side of the body.

It was natural to discover that the physical governed the physical. But did the physical govern the psychical? The movement of an arm, the flicker of an eyelid, sight to the eye, sound to the ear, all revealed that the brain was functioning normally. But what was the cause, and where was the seat of thought, desire, aspirations, hopes, fears, love and hate?

No Act Without Thought

We may now advance a step farther in the quest. A little reflection will prove that movement or action is an effect and not a cause. Action is the culmination of a process. Every action is first preceded by a thought. The duration between the two may be a second or a year, but whether a second or a year, the same process is followed.

I submit I speak truth when I say there is no such possibility as a thoughtless action. There are acts performed by wrong thought and by insufficient thought, but never without thought. To take a simple illustration. An adult climbs the stairs to the bedroom. It seems absurd to suggest that every time the stairs are negotiated there is a mental registration of the action. Yet such is the case if a close investigation be given. When that adult was a small child the parents were exceedingly careful the child should come to no harm when ascending the stairs. Verbal instructions and cautions would be given in the lifting of one foot and then the other, and in process of time not only would the thought impressions of the instructions be registered, but also the number of stairs to be negotiated. And so, when the adult stage is reached, every time the stairs are ascended there is a sub-conscious memory lifting first one foot and then the other, and calculating the number of steps in the ascent.

The truth of this simple illustration is the same of every action. Conscious or sub-conscious thought precedes every action. Conscious thought would precede an act not previously performed, and sub-conscious thought an act that had become habit.

If this be true, that thought must precede action, and action is functioned from or by the brain, then it seems to lead to the fact that thought and action must function from a common source. And this leads to a further deduction. If thought and action function from a common source, then it seems to suggest that if molecular disturbance is the basic cause of action, it must also be the basic cause of thought. This would mean that just as the physical governs the physical, so the physical would govern the *psychical*.

I rather hate to quote the following because of what is involved by its implications. The absolute necessity of these experiments is a debatable point. I leave it there. The following is taken from a scientific treatise:

"We can remove the large hemispheres, piece by piece, from the mammal without killing it, and we then see how the higher functions of consciousness, thought, will, and sensation are gradually destroyed, and in the end completely extinguished. If the animal be fed artificially, it may be kept alive for a long time, as the destruction of the psychic organs by no means involved the extinction of the faculties of digestion, respiration, circulation, urination – in a word, the vegetative functions. It is only conscious sensation, voluntary movement, thought, and the combination of various higher psychic functions that are affected."

Sir A Keith's Deductions

Having these facts in mind it is little wonder that Sir Arthur Keith, himself a Positivist by physical demonstration, should say in his address: "Mind has a material basis. The brain is a piece of living machinery. It consumes fuel and transmutes energy into feeling, thought, and memory.

"Every fact known to medical men compels the inference that mind, spirit, soul are the manifestations of a living brain, just as the flame is the manifest spirit of a burning candle. At the moment of extinction both flame and spirit cease to have a separate existence. However much this mode of explaining man's mentality may run counter to long and deeply cherished beliefs, medical men cannot think otherwise if they are to believe the evidence of their senses."

Suppose these deductions are true, do we dispose of Immortality? Even Sir Arthur will not go that far. In an interview following his address he said: "I do not think my statement destroys the theory of immortality. Religion has no bearing on our teaching. We are out only to discover and understand the human body and to find the exact way of curing diseases." Sir Arthur is evidently too much of a scientist to be positive in theory.

In my next article I want to try and evaluate the many varying beliefs in this great subject.

Immortality [2]
Second of Series of Talks
By George E Hobbs
(First published: June 1, 1928)

Last week I gave what seemed like a refutation of the belief in Immortality, based upon arguments by Haeckel and Sir Arthur Keith. The premise, that the psychic life of man was based upon molecular processes in the cerebrum – or forebrain – being accepted. It was also suggested that the acceptance of this premise in no way precluded the possibility of immortality. Now, perhaps, we may traverse farther along this fascinating pathway.

It will be admitted, I think, that almost from the dawn of human consciousness, a continuance of life beyond physical death held some place in human thought. But just as in all evolutionary growth, the first ideas would be hazy and even grotesque. Imperfect knowledge must always lead to distorted vision. Even in these days, after thousands of years of accumulated data, not only is controversy still rife, but to many thousands the question is still pregnant with grotesque ideas.

Believing that early man postulated a belief in the continuity of life beyond physical death, it is not a little intriguing as to the cause for this belief. Did man argue from himself, or was the process reversed and argued back to himself? There was a phase in religious development known as "animism" or "animatism". This was a belief that every material object – trees, rivers, animals, the heavenly bodies, etc – possessed a soul and a personality. Was "animism" an extension of his own soul consciousness or, having decided that these objects possessed souls, did he then argue back upon himself, that he, too, possessed a soul? The probability is that man argued outwards to animism [and not the other way round], with animism being the cause of his soul consciousness. I have long thought upon this point, and am wondering if the following fanciful sketch supplies a possible solution.

Story of a Hunter

The hunter was caught far from his home when night approached. He sought a secluded cave for his couch. In the morning he was still in the cave, in the very spot he had fallen asleep. He knew he had not traversed one step outside that cave during the hours of dark, yet he had followed the buck tirelessly and had killed it. Not only so, but his brother, who had been killed by a cave bear, had come to him. He had conversed with his brother, though he knew he had seen him interred in the customary crouched position. What did it mean? Did he actually kill the buck? There was no sign about him of a kill. Did he actually see his brother? How could he when that brother had long since been dead? What, then, did it signify?

Was it these very phenomena of sleep, the return of consciousness after slumber, and the strange experiences of life and adventures in dreamland while asleep that led early man to the idea, and then to the belief, that he possessed a double or second self? If so, then from the belief progress would soon be made to the supposition that this secondary personality would continue to exist after death.

Lewis Spence, a high authority upon early religious beliefs, tells us that the early Egyptian belief was that man possessed a soul, the symbol for the soul (the ba) being a man-headed bird. Mr. Spence continues:

> "Now the conception of a soul as a bird is a very common one among savages and barbarians of a low order. To uncultured man the bird is always incomprehensible because of its magical powers of flight, its appearance in the sky where dwell the gods, and its song, approaching speech. From the bird the savage evolves the idea of the winged spirit or god, the messenger from the heavens."

(The idea expressed here seems to suggest the man argued outwards.) Writing again along similar lines, Mr. Spence says:

> "Many American Indians believe that birds are the visible spirits of the dead. The Powhatans of Virginia believed that birds received the souls of their chiefs at death, and the Aztecs that the spirits of departed warriors took the shape of humming-birds and flitted from flower to flower in the sunshine. The Boros of Brazil believed that the soul has the shape of a bird, and passes in that form out of the body in dream."

Myths and Legends

It is rather interesting to continue with Mr Spence for the moment. In another book of his, "Myths and Legends of the North American Indian", he says:

> "The idea of a future life was very widely disseminated among the tribes of North America. The general conception of such an existence was that it was merely a shadowy extension of terrestrial life, in which the same round of hunting and kindred pursuits was engaged in. The Indian idea of eternal bliss seems to have been an existence in the Land of the Sun, to which, however, only those famed in war were usually admitted.
>
> "American funerary ritual and practice throughout the northern sub-continent plainly indicates a strong and vivid belief in the resurrection of the soul after death. Among many tribes the practice prevailed of interring with the deceased such objects as he might be supposed to need in the other world. These included weapons of war and of the chase for men, and household implements and feminine finery in the case of the women.
>
> "Most of the tribes appear to have believed that the soul had to undertake

a long journey before it reached its destination. The belief of the Chinooks in this respect is perhaps a typical one. They imagine that after death the spirit of the deceased drinks at a large hole in the ground, after which it shrinks and passes on to the country of the ghosts, where it is fed with spirit food and drink. After this act of communion with the spirit-world it may not return.

They also believe that every one is possessed of two spirits, a greater and a lesser. During illness the lesser soul is spirited away by the denizens of ghost-land. The Navahos possess a similar belief and say that the soul has none of the vital force which animates the body, nor any of the faculties of the mind, but a kind of third quality, or personality which may leave its owner and become lost, much to his danger and discomfort. The Hurons and Iroquois believe that after death the soul must cross a deep and wide stream, by a bridge formed by a single slender tree, upon which it has to combat the attacks of a fierce dog. The Athapascans imagine that the soul must be ferried over to a great water in a stone canoe, and the Dakotas believe that departed spirits must cross a stream bridged by an enormous snake."

(To be continued)

Immortality [3]
Third of Geo E Hobbs' Talks
(First published: June 15, 1928)

In my last article I gave instances of the beliefs in a future life by the early Egyptians and the North American Indians. The beliefs of the North American Indians were instanced because they were the established possession of this race ages before western adventurers discovered their land. I am persuaded in my mind these two instances will be sufficient to establish the fact that primitive man postulated a belief in immortality. To cite further would be mere repetition, because with very few modifications, the experience of the one is the experience of all. No theological difficulties disturbed their minds. Their beliefs were simple but definite.

But when we come to the modern aspect of the case we approach it knowing that controversy and debate have torn it asunder with sharp incisive claws. It ceases to be the "instinctive possession of the race" and becomes a bone of contention between religionists. That views, ideas, and opinions should vary is consistent with reason. But the astonishing part is that each opposing school of thought claim, as the basis for their particular belief, "divine inspiration". How on earth "divine" inspiration can give two ideas of each opposing the other passes my comprehension. And when it comes to three and even more distinct and contradictory ideas, all divinely inspired, then the whole suggestion reduces itself to a farce. No two men can claim divine inspiration for their beliefs if those two beliefs are antagonistic to each other. Obviously one must be wrong, and, perhaps, both are wrong.

Why not let us be frank and honest? Let us admit that in all questions which engender controversy our deductions are "humanly" inspired by the reasoning faculties with which a benignant Creator has endowed us. Knowing then our limitation, we should cease to be dictatorial, dogmatic and intolerant.

Body and Soul

I must now ask the reader for a little patience. When one begins to quote the theologians, patience is indeed needed.

Hodge, in his "Systematic Theology", says the Scriptures teach that God formed the body of man out of the dust of the earth, and breathed into his nostrils the breath of life, and he became a living soul. According to this account, man consists of two distinct principles: a body and a soul; the one material, the other immaterial; the one corporeal, the other spiritual. It is involved in this statement, first, that the soul of man is a substance; and secondly, that it is a substance distinct from the body. So that in the constitution of man, two distinct substances are included. Texts of Scripture are quoted to support this view:

Eccles XII, 7: "Then shall the dust return to the earth as it was, and the spirit shall return unto God who gave it." Is X, 18: "Shall consume... both body and soul." Dan, VII, 16: "I, Daniel was grieved in my spirit in the midst of my body." Matt, VI, 25: "Is not the life (soul) more than meat, and the body than raiment?" Matt, X, 28: "Fear not them which kill the body, but are not able to kill the soul; but rather fear him which is able to destroy both soul and body in hell."

Here Hodge states, and backs up his statement with Scripture, that man is distinctly dualistic in his constitution; that the soul is as realistic as the body and that it was breathed into man immediately after his bodily creation. So far so good. But is the soul immortal, ever-living? Hodge says:

> "According to the Scriptures the probation of man ends at death. As the tree falls so it lies. He that is unjust let him be unjust still, and he that is righteous let him be righteous still. When the bridegroom comes, they that

are ready enter in, and the door is shut. It is appointed unto all men once to die, and after that, the judgement. The destiny of the soul is decided at death."

From this we infer that the immortality of the soul is taught, the writer using scriptural phraseology in his statements.

Again, writing of the doctrine of future punishment, he says: "It is an almost invincible presumption that the Bible does teach the unending punishment of the finally impenitent, that all Christian churches have so understood it. There is no other way in which this unanimity of judgement can be accounted for. The church believes it because it must believe it, or renounce faith in the Bible and give up all hopes founded upon its promises."

I would like the reader to understand I am giving no opinion of my own. I am simply recording the opinions of a theologian. When the time comes I shall give my own thoughts fearlessly.

According to Professor Hodge, the Scriptures teach, first, that man is a composite creature, consisting of body and soul, and second, that the body perishes at physical death, but the soul continues to live either in bliss or never-ending woe. Now let us see what a more modern religionist than Hodge says upon this matter.

Robert Roberts, in his "Christendom Astray", says:

> "The doctrine of the immortality of the soul is an untrue doctrine, which effectually prevents the believer of it from truly apprehending the truth concerning the work and teaching of Christ."

In order to buttress this contradiction to Hodge, Roberts appeals to Scripture. Says he:

> "Now, in opposition to this view (that man is a creature in whom God breathed immortal life) we shall show that, according to the Scriptures, man is destitute of immortality in every sense, that he is a creature of organised substance subsisting in the life-power of God, which he shares in common with every living thing under the sun; that he only holds this life on the short average tenure of three-score years and ten, at the end of which he gives it up to Him from whom he received it and returns to the ground, whence he originally came, and meanwhile ceases to exist. Such a proposition may well be shocking to ordinary religious susceptibility; but it demands investigation."

So that in contradistinction to Hodge, Roberts says man is destitute of immortality in every sense; that he is a creature of organised substance subsisting in the life-power of God, which he shares in common with every living thing under the sun.

But while Roberts declares that man is destitute of immortality he does not preclude the possibility of his becoming immortal. Quoting extensively from texts of Scripture, he says that at death man ceases to exist; he is nowhere; but should he ever live again "it will be the result of a fresh effort on the part of Almighty power".

The Resurrection

Although man, being nowhere and utterly losing his identity, Roberts says according to the Scriptures there is to be a resurrection. The righteous passing to eternal felicity and bliss, and the wicked to where? Here are his words:

"This resurrection to damnation, however, is not a resurrection to unending life, or to hell fire in the popular acceptation. It is a resurrection to judicially administered shame and corruption… They rise to the shame and confusion of a divine and growing rejection, in which "few stripes" and "many stripes" are inflicted, according to desert… differences in the duration and intensity of suffering as justice may demand, after which the wicked are finally engulfed in the second death, which obliterates their wretched existence from God's creation. Being of no use, they are put out of the way, and disappear for ever."

Thus Hodge says the Scriptures teach that man is immortal; that the good receive eternal joy and the wicked eternal sorrow. While Roberts says that the Scriptures teach man is not immortal; that by a "fresh effort on the part of Almighty power" he will rise on the resurrection morning, the good passing to bliss, the wicked to conscious punishment and then to final obliteration and extinction.

(To be continued)

Immortality [4]
Fourth of a Series of Talks
By George E Hobbs

(First published: June 22, 1928)

In the present series I have tried to be as brief and as concise as possible. Two illustrations only were given showing that primitive man had beliefs in immortality. Two illustrations only were given to show the opposing views of modern religionists upon this matter. Hence we have up to date:

(1) The scientific view which we found, apparently, contradictory to any idea of immortality,

(2) The divergent views of Christian religionists in that on the one hand immortality is claimed from the Scriptures to be an unconditional verity, and on the other from precisely the same sources it is found not to be the possession of the race, but may possibly be "due to a fresh act of Almighty power", the good passing to eternal bliss, the evil resurrected for punishment and finally annihilated.

Now, perhaps, I can traverse a freer road in that I may postulate my own creed. It matters not a jot to me whether I be orthodox or unorthodox, but it does matter considerably whether I be true to the convictions within me. I have been accused of many things, all of which leave me unruffled in the gladness and buoyancy of, to me, incontrovertible certainty.

"Without Reservation"

Do I believe in immortality? Most certainly I do. And, shocking as a positivist's attitude may seem, I believe in it wholly and without reservation. My convictions must be told in my own way.

The story recorded in Genesis, known as the "creation" of man story, is marvellous in the grandeur of its basic truth. The writer probably knew nothing of chemical constituents, but from practical experience had probably seen sufficient evidence to support his theory that man was made from earth elements. Mortified flesh, or bones crushed by the impact of boulders, had soon lost their identity in the surrounding soil. Bone, flesh and soil were soon of like identity. Hence, with no exaggeration, "Man was formed out of the dust of the ground."

Though evolution, as we understand it, was to the writer a sealed book, he distinctly recognises a development, a change. True, his description of that change is contrary to present day advanced thought, nevertheless an epoch-making change is recorded. The dust-constituted man "falls". He is given a test, and in the test he fails. Yet, to me, the record of that failure is the very place where I see the first glimmer of immortality. The possibility is reached where man is made in the image of God. Not that God fails, but that man can achieve. The blind instinct of the beast is now substituted by the powers of reason. Long had this wonderful factor been fighting for expression in the fast-developing man, but the time came when he could say "I will" and "I will not."

I suggest, in passing, that the reason why the writer records a "fall" to early man is that the tremendous power of evil had to be accounted for. Instead of, as we see it, the divine emerging from the beast, he sees the "perfect" besmirched by a sudden evil.

When the Light First Came

I have often thought how close is the analogy between physical light and mental, moral and spiritual light. If we take as an example the creation and development of the former and then by comparison review the latter, it seems to me that many of the difficulties immediately vanish. I am not now concerned so much with man's "knowledge" of immortality as I am in trying to assign a definite period when the first light came.

In words noble and grand, the record states that the Spirit cried: "Light be!" and Light was. But we make a very profound mistake if we think that full refulgent light came instantaneous with the command. Countless ages elapsed before the first faint nebulistic glow made itself manifest. The process was long and the progress slow. Matter in its elemental constituents had to be brought together, and the huge, unwieldy mass set in motion. Slow at first but ever gaining speed, until energy, diffusing through its mass, began to make its presence known in the first faint glow.

But though it was slow it was sure, ever increasing, until, through myriads of years, light came to perfection. The Creator saw the Light and was satisfied with the result. In this brief survey we have Plan, Development, Purpose and Achievement. And I would suggest that the process and progress of mental, moral and spiritual light is identical to that of physical light. And just as light was light when motion vitalised the mass with energy, so man became an immortal being when he was vitalised with the possibility of volitional choice.

Man, emerging from the beast, like material elements, had to pass through the stage of primeval darkness, crudity and chaos. In process of time his moral ignorance is challenged by the dawning light of moral greatness. He sees something beyond mere animal cravings, something which will give him power. In his ignorant eagerness he stretches out his hands to the full light – to the "Knowledge of the gods" – and meets, as one would expect him to meet, with failure.

Unthinkable!

But what is failure? A dead man cannot fail. A live animal cannot fail in the moral sense. It takes a live man to fail, and when man "failed" he had traversed a long way along the road which led to the knowledge of his kinship with the immortal. He is alive with a new outlook, and to a new responsibility. He is aware that a gulf now separates him from his former life. He has the making of something which he finds difficult to define, but towards which he steadfastly sets his face. The distance which separates him from the beasts is of a very narrow margin, but in that narrow margin lies the glory of his new experience. As Padraic Colum expresses it in his poem, "The Plougher":

> The brute-tamer stands by the brutes, by a head's breadth only above them!
> A head's breadth, aye, but therein is Hell's depth, and the height up to Heaven,
> And the thrones of the gods, and their halls and their chariots' purples and
> splendours.
> It may be only a head's breadth, but therein is the "height up to heaven".

I cannot close this week's contribution without quoting these lines of Omar Khayyam, the astronomer-poet of Persia. Says he, in declaring that the making of man was "surely not in vain":

> Surely not in vain
> My substance from the common Earth was ta'en,
> That He who subtly wrought me into Shape
> Should stamp me back to common Earth again.
> Why, ne'er a peevish Boy
> Would break the Bowl from which he drank in joy,
> Shall He that made the vessel in pure Love
> And Fansy, in an after rage destroy?

Is it possible that God, having made the vessel for His purpose and for His glory, should destroy it? It is unthinkable.

(To be continued)

Immortality [5]
George E Hobbs Continues His Talks
(First published: June 28, 1928)

In my last article I recorded my belief that man became heir to immortality at the period of his evolutionary separation from the brute creation. I suggested that then it was when "man was made in the image of God", the image of God in man being spiritual, not physical. We may now proceed further in our quest.

Man having now been made in the image of the undying will possess the undying in his own nature. But the difficulty arises as to what is the nature of that element which is impervious to death, and where is it housed? Apparently, everything known to man may conveniently be tabulated under the heading of substance or matter. Even the invisible can be a substance. The perfume of a flower may be ascending particles of the flower or gases radiating from it. Assuming it to be attenuated gases, it is still matter, in that it consists of elemental properties. And this would lead one to suppose that as all things upon this terrestrial globe are of elemental structure, the ultimate destiny of all life and form is the release back into its several basic constitutions.

The atom of hydrogen in a tree and the atom of hydrogen in man will in process of time be atoms of hydrogen in soil or atmosphere. The atom of hydrogen in man will have no superiority over the atom of hydrogen in a frog or in a cesspool. The tree will lose its identity as a tree, and the human body will lose its identity as a human body, but the atoms of hydrogen in both will remain atoms of hydrogen.

But is everything of atomic constitution? The highest expression of man's activities is his psychic life. He can think and reason; he can love to the extent of selfless sacrifice, all of which indicates his alliance to the undying. Then what of this psychic life?

Man lives his physical life by atomic renewals. Every particle of his being is in continual flux. There is a constant discarding and renewing. But can this apply to the whole realm of his psychic life? This may seem an absurd question for the moment, but I plead for patience in the quest.

That the psychic life grows and develops is a truth too obvious to be discussed. It is a fact of experience. Yet growth and development can, apparently, only be associated with atomic additions and renewal. If, then, man's psychic life is purely of molecular constitution, it would seem that the case for immortality is lost. For our comfort, however, there is an avenue of escape from this negation. We can postulate free activity exclusive of atomic constitution.

The Creator We Call God

No one to-day will be hardy enough to attempt an intellectual denial of the existence of a Creator. This Creator we call God. Now there are certain features about the Creator which, to deny, would be tantamount to denying one's own existence. We are surrounded by facts which indicate design, by effects which demand a cause. Design indicates intelligence, and intelligence indicates an entity – a being.

The Being who creates the universe must of necessity be greater than His creation, and again of necessity, must have life at least of equal duration. Without stressing the point, as we know that the visible universe has existed for many millions of years, we are led to the conclusion that the Being who created it has also existed for millions of years. To make use of a term which human thought can scarcely comprehend, we are led to the conclusion that this Being has existed from eternity. If from eternity, then He must be altogether free of atomic constitution.

Little as we know of God it would violate our reason to believe that God is older to-day than yesterday. If He develops then He is subject to physical laws and must be atomically conditioned. Such a suggestion must be absurd in the extreme. God is not only free from all the limitations of space, but is also exalted above all the limitations of time. With Him there is no distinction between past, present and future, but all things are equally and always present to Him. With Him duration is an eternal now.

We have here demonstrated that free, conscious life can and does exist independent of physical limitations, and that that life is the life of God, the life of the undying. And this leads us to a further consideration. It would violate our reason to imagine that this life is an isolated one. A lonely Creator, isolated from companionship, is unthinkable. With Him, surrounding Him, must be intelligences of like nature to Himself. This is the very extension of reason itself, and need not be due to Christian faith or a divine revelation. The galaxy of like intelligences need not be for assistance in creation or maintenance of created things, but it needs must be for that which even the highest intelligence yearns – fellowship and companionship. Hence we may affirm that not only one life exists which is free of atomic structure, but myriads.

Man Immortal

Now, perhaps, we may see one greater meaning in the suggested fact that man was made in the image of God. Or, to say the same thing in a better way, that God made man in His own image. To put it briefly: God made man the residence of and for His image. Just as a newly-built palace, however ornate, could never be a royal residence until the monarch resided there, so man was but potentially immortal until the residence was complete and ready for the entering in of the undying. God in-dwelling in man – which is not a theological doctrine, but the possession of every human being – makes man immortal.

Man, physically, is made to function in surroundings peculiar to his constitution. And just as reason has shown that every phase of his physical life follows and obeys natural law, so I think it can be shown that the expression of the undying, though infinitely higher than the physical, can only function through the physical.

(To be continued)

Immortality [6]
Sixth of Geo E Hobbs' Interesting Talks
(First published: July 6, 1928)

We have now approached to the most difficult phase of our investigation. The phase is appalling in the profundity of its scope, seeing we have now to try and find the base and the medium of that which is impervious to death. The general question as to whether the psychic life is altogether impossible apart from a physical medium is so fraught with complications that it first must be reduced to its simplest form. Let us ask: does the psychic life find its expression by and through a physical medium? Let us consider that mysterious function known as thought processes.

A person who has capacity for solving recondite problems is said to possess wonderful brain capacity, not wonderful heart or lung capacity, but brain capacity. Both the heart and lungs may be diseased or injured, yet the intellect may be unimpaired. But let the cerebrum, or fore brain, be diseased or injured, then intellectual capacity is impaired to the extent of the injury.

The difference between one who is at ease with the higher reaches of mathematics and one who is unable to grasp the significance of two multiplied by two is the difference of mental capacity. If an investigation of the two brains were possible, it would be found that the brain of the clever one was characterised by a number of convolutions and fissures, while in that of the one of low mentality the convolutions and fissures were far less in number and of inferior development. Here, then, we have two very interesting facts. First, that intelligence is impaired only by some disease or injury to the brain, and, second, that the presence or modification of a certain characteristic indicates a low or advanced mentality. In the face, therefore, of these two facts it will not be overstating the case to say that thought processes are associated with the brain.

But may I suggest – and I use this term for want of a better – that academic attainment is but one aspect of the psychic life. And if I may be pardoned for the thought – not the highest aspect. I have in mind these words – I quote the sense if not the actual words: "Be good, sweet maid, let those who will be clever."

Some Strange Contrasts

There is the aspect of moral conduct. And here we are met by some strange contrasts. Clever folk, geniuses, are not always folk of high moral attainment. The two may and sometimes do coincide. But it is not a fact of necessity that the two should companion together. Academic achievement is something for which one may legitimately strive; its realisation something of which one may be proud. But it is not that which has the greatest effect upon life.

It is a remarkable feature of experience that high moral virtues are often found where academic mentality is low. There may be absolute inability to appreciate the constitution and function of the heavenly bodies, but there is a keen appreciation of the difference between right and wrong. Mathematics may be an impenetrable forest, but the pathway up to God is open and unobserved.

The sneer often levelled at religion is that it is all very well for simple minds. The sneer is not intended to mean those who have singleness of purpose, but minds of average and low mentality. If this article hid a sermon I should unhesitatingly say that therein lay its glory and strength. If it were not "all very well for simple minds" then it would have no value for me. I form one of the great majority of simple minds.

But to retrace. Is this higher manifestation of the psychic life functioned by a physical medium? I very definitely laid down my belief that the element of the undying came to humanity at the dawn of volitional choice. Not when man left the cave to construct for himself his first rude house, or to make his first instruments of agriculture. Not when he was first conscious of the rising and setting of the sun and the constancy of the stars. These were but developments of something which had already been instituted.

I want to stress this point because it seems to me that the powers to achieve academically – of which house building, agriculture, etc, constituted the very rude beginning – does not of itself propound alliance with the undying. But soul capacity – the appreciation of a more noble outlook; the desire to love, sympathise and be of service – does propound the link of oneness with God.

I think we have now seen sufficient to formulate the proposition that soul capacity – the highest psychic expression – does not of necessity rest upon any particular development of the brain. In other words, there is capacity independent of reason. And one would go farther and say there is capacity which sets reason at defiance – a capacity of the unreasonable. This truth is confirmed by the poet in these lines:

> Where Reason fails with all her powers
> There Faith prevails and Love adores.

A Verity of Experience

This is not something we wish to admit in order to buttress the case for immortality. It is something we are bound to accept because it is a verity of experience.

The idea of the undying indwelling in man is of such profundity that the keenness of the highest intellect could not apprehend it without the assistance of that capacity which sets Reason at defiance. Yet, such is its all-pervading penetration, the humblest intellect can delve into its secrets without the semblance of a headache.

Academic learning – that mighty force, which by its application is gradually wresting from nature her secrets – may be likened to the thundering of mighty waves upon a rocky coast. But soul capacity is mirrored in the beautiful words of the Psalmist: "He leadeth me beside the still waters." In the former there is pleasure but no rest. In the latter there is pleasure, refreshment and rest. In the former each strives to achieve for selfish motives. In the latter selfishness is eliminated, and service becomes the soil in which soul expansion is developed.

There are other aspects of the psychic life, but these two will be sufficient for our present purpose. We found that the first – thought processes which led to high mental attainment – functioned in perfect accord with convolutional development of the brain, but that the second – soul capacity – could be developed to a high degree with an indifferent mentality.

Does this mean that soul capacity is altogether independent of molecular activity? In my next article I want to examine this.

(To be continued)

Immortality [7]
Geo E Hobbs Continues His Talks
(First published: July 13, 1928)

Up to this point of our investigation we have been traversing the preliminary stages of a great and wonderful quest, the final stage of which will be the investigation of the "place" or state of those who have passed through the phase of physical death. I understand that many articles have been written recently on this question, none of which have I read or wished to hear discussed, as I am extremely anxious to keep my mind clear to the issues of this present series.

We have found that thought processes which lead to all degrees of academic learning are due to a particular condition of brain formation. We also found that soul capacity of high development was possible with indifferent mentality; that soul expression and culture did not depend upon any particular condition of the brain. Yet, strangely enough, in speaking of soul capacity, we are still in the realm of thought processes. No soul-life can develop without thought. I do not suggest that soul capacity is non-existent without thought. That would be a most foolish mistake to make. I simply say that soul-life cannot develop without thought. For instance, a twelve-month-old child is unconscious of thought processes, yet it has soul capacity. It has soul capacity by sheer right of birth, because it is made in the image of the undying – of God. The seed of soul life is there, but it remains dormant until quickened or awakened by a process which is as tender as the "still dews of eve".

The writer of the allegorical story of Genesis records this awakening in a very beautiful way. He says: "And they heard the voice of the Lord God walking in the garden in the cool of the day." Every child soul is quickened by the voice of God in the morning of their years. And no allegory could be more delightfully clear than to represent the awakening occurring in the garden. Here, amidst the sweetness and fragrance of the flower-bedecked garden of babyhood, the call to soul development is heard.

Hence, according to the response of the individual to soul culture, the degree of development will naturally follow. And it may be that when adult stage is reached, folk will say, as folk have said of thousands, he or she is by no means brilliant, but he or she possesses the character of nobility.

The "character of nobility" – the highest psychic manifestation – is possible only by thought processes. For the moment, therefore, we will agree that the brain is the organ of function. And this conclusion we may amplify – again for the moment – by the examination of a second instance.

There is nothing in life so worthy of pity as an imbecile. To see a human form grow and develop almost to perfect physique, yet with a mind dark and chaotic, is pitiable in the extreme. One wishes one could avoid this aspect, but it is of such paramount importance to the investigation that it must be dealt with.

The outward form is almost perfect. In many cases eyesight and hearing are unimpaired. The lungs function correctly, for they experience no difficulty in respiration. The heart beats normally. Food is assimilated and goes to form all that is needful to physical development, yet is there something abnormal; something which speaks of an underdevelopment. The trouble lies in the brain. The organ which normally is the functional agent of thought processes is malformed. Therefore, there can be no psychic expression, no soul culture.

The thoughtful reader will kindly note the terms used. I have not suggested there is no soul capacity in a hopeless imbecile. Soul capacity is there by the same right as was that of the twelve-month child – by right of its human birth – the difference being that in the imbecile it cannot manifest its presence because the organ by which manifestation is possible is malformed. That malformation must of necessity render void all powers of psychic expression.

I use the term "soul capacity" in its widest sense. If terrestrial life is the limit to capacity then never can there be soul development. But, thank God, capacity is not limited to terrestrial life. When the poor malformed brain, in weary acquiescence, surrenders to physical death, the bonds are broken and the soul commences its expansion and expression unhampered and free. There for the first time it knows itself, and in that state where malformation is unknown it finds happiness.

Without further stressing the point I think sufficient has been shown to prove that the highest life – psychic life – can manifest itself only by the brain, but, providing that functional powers are there, the degree of brain development does not control or govern the degree of soul expression. In contradistinction to the powers of soul expression, academic learning does depend upon the degree of brain development.

Here, then, I think we find the positive scientist's difficulty. By an investigation of two brains the scientist is able to declare that one is the brain of high mentality, the other is the brain of low mentality. But in no wise way can he declare by investigation that one is the brain of high soul-attainment and the other is the brain of low soul-attainment. High mental achievement is stamped upon the brain. High soul-attainment is not evidenced there, therefore it is impossible of analysis. But to say that soul life – that part of man which is impervious to physical death – is non-existent because it is not subject to analysis is manifestly contrary to logic.

We have seen that life, free of atomic renewals, is known to exist. I use the word "known" because it cannot be denied without violating reason. This free, unfettered life is the life of God. When, in the process of development, man became fit for the indwelling of the undying, that great and wonderful possession became his. And it is his by inalienable right.

Having arrived thus far in our investigation it is now but a matter of pure logic to see that the activity of soul life must manifest itself through a physical medium. It could not be otherwise. The receptive seat of soul life, therefore, is the brain.

It is the soul life which gives distinctive personality to the individual. The degree of soul life development is the degree of character development. And it is this distinctive personality which is impervious to death. Just as true as sunrise follows sunset, and sunset follows sunrise, so true is it that this reinforced personality will pass unhampered through the gateway of physical death, or into the limitless realm of possibilities until development reaches perfection.

Next week I hope to examine the question of the "place" or "state" of those who have passed through the first stage of their psychic development.

(To be continued)

Immortality [8]
Mr George E Hobbs Sums Up His Beliefs
(First published: July 20, 1928)

When I set out to write this present series it was not a sudden whim which prompted me. I have been anxious to write upon this subject for many months past, but the time never seemed opportune. Not only so, but I knew that months of thought and careful reasoning had led me to conclusions which were the antithesis of orthodoxy. But when, as the result of Sir Arthur Keith's lecture, the public mind seemed awakened to its issue, I felt the time was then opportune.

The fact of my unorthodoxy still causes me a few qualms. Not, however, with the worry of being different to someone else, but with the worry that inadvertently I may cause some good orthodox friend pain. But as I said in one of my former articles, I cannot give assent to something I do not and cannot believe. An untruth is an untruth whether in business dealings or in matters of nominal religious belief. There are many things I do not understand, and in these matters I assent belief by faith. But where a doctrine shocks my reason and violates the principle of Divine Goodness, then I cannot nor will not say I believe.

One of the doctrines to which I can subscribe a whole-hearted acquiescence is that of immortality. It has long since passed the stage of "doctrine" with me, and has become a principle, a certainty of exquisite definiteness. I know there are many who share in this wonderful certainty, but the parting of that ways comes in the interpretation of its mode. Let us consider this in detail, and although I write boldly, I pray I do not write presumptuously. May God save me from that sin.

Man, by the fact that he is made in the image of the undying, is natural heir to immortality. It is not conditional, neither can he be disinherited. Whatever effect this suggestion may have upon the reader, I feel I must stress this point. Even though the condition of a man be similar to that of Israel in the days of Isaiah ("The whole head is sick, and the whole heart faint. From the sole of the foot even to the head there is no soundness in it; but wounds and bruises and putrefying sores") – even in this deplorable condition, man does not lose or forfeit his hereditary right to immortality. No moral disorder can blot out the image of the undying. Past all the filth of unwholesomeness, Supreme Compassion still "looks and loves His image there".

Where are the Dead?

If then, irrespective of his moral condition, man is heir to immortality, what is meant by the "place" to which man goes after passing through the gateway of physical death? In other words, and to make use of a question which at the present time seems to occupy a deal of the public thought: "Where are the dead?"

First as to its geographical position. I use the misplaced term "geographical position" for simplicity of idea. Someone has said that the whole conception of man living again is absurd from the fact that no "place" could house the millions who have died and the millions who will die. But I would suggest that the absurdity turns back upon the doubter seeing that he has misconceived the whole idea of "place". Is not the universe the home of God? And is not the universe boundless? A little consideration will show the absurdity of "lack of room".

Of two opposites one must be right. Space is either limited or limitless. Human intelligence falls before the idea of a limited space and while it is altogether unable to grasp the significance of a limitless space, yet the latter is the more logical. In that part of this infinity of space with which we are familiar there are thousands of suns visible to the eye every night when the sky is free of cloud. Hundreds of these suns rival our sun both in size and light. We now know the function of our sun, in that he [the sun] controls a retinue of dependants. His work is to govern eight planets, about 700 asteroids – tiny worlds, ranging from ten to a few hundred miles in diameter – and 26 moons.

The whole swings upon an orbit the outer diameter of which is approximately 5,020 millions of miles. Upon one of the planets at least – the earth – there is sentient life. In common fairness to the glorious annals of ascertained knowledge, while it is known that planets circle the sun and that one at least sustains life, no other such system is known to exist. And for a very logical reason.

The only means such a system could reveal itself is by a diminution of the light of the primary (the individual sun) as the planets of that system circled round. This obviously is impossible seeing that the circling planets would be infinitely smaller than the sun concerned. The same principle holds good to the dwellers of earth in the transits of Venus and Mercury. When Venus transits the sun, there is no diminution of the sun's light.

Contrary to Logic

But to say that no such system exists because it is not subject to observation is contrary to logic. The inference is very definite that such systems do exist. Given the logical possibility that hundreds, probably thousands, of such systems existing, the idea of lack of room to house the "millions who have died and who will die" vanishes into thin air. I believe that the whole universe is at the disposal of those who have passed through the gateway of physical death.

Here, then, opens a vista of exquisite promise. The wrongs of earth life, its inequalities, the sorrows and poignant anguish, all pass through a compensatory process – the process of physical death. Man finds his destiny and that destiny is perfected happiness.

Before concluding this series, may I just touch upon an old topic. There are some who still believe in that most horrible of all doctrines – eternal punishment. I imagine their position to be that they feel under an obligation to believe it repulsive as it must be to them because they feel it is the teaching of "God's Word". Without introducing levity, is not this position similar to that of the old lady who said, relative to the story of Jonah and the whale: "If the Bible said that Jonah swallowed the whale instead of the whale swallowing Jonah, I should believe it."

To say the least, is not such a position unwise? I remember my own position. There was a time when I felt I ought to teach it, but all the time I had to stifle my own sense of justice. Every time I tried to teach it I felt I was giving a picture of God altogether antagonistic to His nature. Mercy became meaningless and love was transformed into vindictiveness. For months in an agony of soul I wrestled with this problem, and the day came when I not only discarded it as unthinkable, but actively preached against it. It was only then that I felt happy. The God that I know is far too big to be vindictive. Eternal punishment is a fallacy. It is more. It is treachery to the Loving Father to teach it. Man is destined to happiness, and that will be his ultimate life.

(The End)

Bible Narratives for Young Students [7, extract]
By George E Hobbs
(First published: October 12, 1928)

But I find I must guard against sermonising. It is a natural pit into which a preacher is apt to fall when writing.

I said a moment since the writer of Genesis has discovered a great, physical fact. In his allegory he depicts the newly-formed man about to take up his duties as custodian of the garden. But, before he assumes those duties he is cautioned. "In the day that thou eatest (of the forbidden fruit) thou shalt surely die."

The newly-formed man is scarcely conscious of living when he is faced with the possibility of death.

What a profound student of nature this scribe must have been. He has discovered that life from the moment of birth is a constant battle against death, that every human being entering into life enters it with a caution. His vision is even wider. He sees that mystic something, which can only be described as death, standing before the newly-awakened and challenging it with the certainty of its fate.

He has probably seen death so many times that he agrees it is common to all. At last he reasons that if death be common to all then there must be a common cause. What can be that common cause?

He probably knows nothing of ailments, but in his brooding for a solution, he presently sees something that will fit the case. He is already acquainted with a moral code of action, and he sees that the violation of that moral code is common to all men.

He therefore implies in his allegory that if death ensues then it is directly the result of disobedience. He did not know as we know today that physical death is the natural termination to physical life. It does not come as a punishment or as a result of disobedience, but as a natural and logical sequence to life.

Yet, though this is known to all men, the doctrine is still taught that death is the result of disobedience. It was quite a natural solution to the writer in the faraway age, but the modern age should view it in a very different light. Physical death is the compensation to physical life, not its punishment.

Bible Narratives [8, extract]
By George E Hobbs
(First published: October 19, 1928)

Answer to Critics

In concluding my article for this week, I wish to refer to last week's article. I am glad to say I have been taken to task somewhat strenuously for "suggesting death not to be due to disobedience". As this anticipates the third chapter of Genesis, I shall only deal here with the criticism offered me, due to what I wrote last week.

It was understood, of course, that I meant physical death and the "sin" of Adam. In this connection I want to say, I more than suggested it. I very definitely declared that death was not the result of disobedience. I say again: physical death is not due to the "sin" of Adam.

Physical death is the natural sequence to physical life, and I challenge a logical contradiction to this truth. If I could so blind my eyes — to use a twisted metaphor — and believe that physical death came to the earth because of the "first man's sin" and came as a punishment, then I must also believe it to be the most unjust punishment ever inflicted by a wise Creator.

Animals die. Birds die. Fish die. These have never been guilty of disobedience, so why pass the punishment on to them? Where is the logic?

Bible Narratives
(First published: October 26, 1928)

Sir – I am obliged to Mr Chas Lee for his letter published in last Friday's Advertiser. I have had many verbal criticisms, kindly and otherwise, in connection with my "Bible Narratives". But Mr Lee's letter is the first published comment, for which I am truly grateful.

Mr Lee would like to know how I can reconcile my theory – that physical death is the natural sequence to physical life, and has not come upon humanity as a punishment – with certain passages quoted from the Bible.

I trust Mr Lee will not object to my method, but instead of answering him direct and attempting a reconciliation, let me put the case thus: if it can be proved that physical death existed before man came to the earth, then I claim to have proved my case. For physical death to be the direct result of disobedience, then physical death was unknown until a conscious, responsible being made it possible. This would naturally coincide with the advent of man.

Shall we mutually agree that millions of creatures existed before man came to the earth that did not exist when he did make his appearance? What became of these creatures? The "days" of the creation period were of great length, and countless ages must have elapsed between the time when life first dawned, to the time when man first walked the earth as a man.

During all that long period creatures were growing, developing and – what? The law of physical life tells me they were dying. Millions of creatures lived, developed, declined and died long ago, before man came. Then, if physical death was the natural sequence to physical life previous to the advent of man, how can the physical death of man be the result of disobedience?

I am sorry to put it this way, but before I attempt an answer to his query, will Mr Lee tell me his agreement or disagreement with this statement?

George E Hobbs

Origins: Part IV
By George E Hobbs
(First published: January 25, 1935)

We shall now deal with a very difficult problem in our study of "origins". We have tried to interpret – fearlessly and honestly – the origins of man's physical, mental, moral and spiritual development. We hope, as fearlessly and as honestly, to face the problem with which we are now about to deal. We face it with the knowledge that we may be called before the bar of man's judgement for the convictions herein expressed. No fear of an adverse criticism, however, should ever deter us from an investigation into the claims of Truth. At the same time, no claim should be approached iconoclastically. Our best method of approach is to determine upon an analysis of the facts, or aspects, presented.

The most certain of all human experiences, as at present constituted, is that of physical death. From the moment we become separate entities at birth, physical death has waged incessant war against us.

The phenomenon of physical death is not an intellectual problem. It becomes a problem only when shrouded in theological mists. When we are informed that physical death originated in "man's first disobedience" we have a problem created for us where none should exist.

We readily grant that individual opinions and convictions will be moulded entirely upon the conception the individual holds as to the "creation" of man. If the conception is that of a literal interpretation of the Genesis narrative – that man was created physically perfect, mentally acute, with moral and spiritual affinities to the Creator Himself, and that under the sinister influence of he serpent, through the woman, he fell from his lofty estate – then the origin of physical death is plain.

A Problem for Early Thinkers

But – to change the person – I claim, and in the past few weeks I have tried to prove its truth, that we cannot accept such a narrative except as allegory. Truth is foreshadowed, but the vehicle of conveyance is allegory.

I have said that the phenomenon of physical death is not an intellectual problem. It must have been a real problem, however, to the early thinkers of the race. And I suggest that there is little difficulty in reconstructing the process of thinking which led to the "death penalty for sin" idea.

It is very probable that primitive man was unacquainted with "natural" death among animals. Animals were killed for food or, if not for food, because they were a menace to human life. Primitive man had probably seen animals dead apart from those he slew. But they bore the marks of a titanic struggle upon them, as animals would when fighting to the death through sex instinct or for survival. Placid, unmarked death was probably unknown. Death from "natural" causes, as distinct from acts of violence, was a phenomenon which happened only to human beings. Why was this? And so primitive man began his quest for an explanation.

I have explained in previous articles that to the primitive mind, nothing could or did happen unless "someone" made it to happen. Behind every "happening" there was a distinct personality. Hence the galaxy of gods, or super-men, which the primitive minds evolved. This process of reasoning was applied to the "happening" of physical death. It could be explained only by the fact that an invisible spirit preyed upon men and captured them sooner or later. None could really escape the clutches of this invisible power. Sometimes the spirit could be propitiated and rendered less malevolent, as in the case of one who recovered form a serious illness. But, in the end, this power was victorious.

The transition from the fact of this presence to the purpose of its existence was but a matter of time and deduction. Death was universal. It came upon all men. Then death came because men had incurred the displeasure of the gods. Men were mortal because they were evil in their thoughts and deeds. It was just the simple reasoning of simple minds.

Unfortunately this explanation does not end our problem. The fact must be faced that men of wise thinking and of astute mind have, throughout the ages, given their consent to the belief that physical death originated as a penalty or punishment. This belief is taught even to-day.

Now I claim very positively that if physical death be tabulated as a penalty or punishment – in the sense, of course, under discussion – then physical life must also be tabulated in the same category. Death is the perfectly natural sequence to life. And, inversely, life is the cause of death. Death cannot come to that which does not exist. When it does exist, whether it be with solar systems, worlds, trees, flowers, insects or man, physical death must of necessity, by the very law of their constitution, be their ultimate fate – at least, so far as men are concerned, their transitional fate. That, however is another and different problem.

Physical death was in the world long, long ages before man came to be. The trilobite, the ammonite, the huge ungainly saurians and sabre-toothed tiger, the mammoth and the mastodon all died in the long struggle for survival. And each, in turn, gave place to new forms of life which again died.

I think no one would be hardy enough to suggest that physical death was a punishment upon the millions of creatures that preceded the coming of man. Such a suggestion would be too utterly absurd. And yet, while we know that life and death alternated through all the stages of man's physical development, the suggestion is applied to him. Is not this equally untenable and absurd?

Illustrating the Point

Let me construct a simple allegory. I agree at the outset that there will be something missing but it will serve to illustrate the point at issue.

John was a man 60 years of age. His life has been a very strange one. At birth it was seen he was sadly afflicted: he was born blind. In a few months it was seen he was deeply afflicted: he was an imbecile. So he grew up unconscious of sight and of reason.

When he was 30 years of age a brain specialist examined him, and found that an operation upon a particular nerve centre of the brain would give to him a glimmer of reason. He also thought that in process of time his patient would possess a brain equal to that of a normal man.

The operation was performed, and in ten years John had the powers to distinguish between right and wrong. His blindness, however, could not be cured.

When he was 40 years of age he committed a very grave wrong. For this offence he was taken before a Judge, who took a serious view of the case.

John's defence was that having lived between 30 and 40 years without the powers of knowing right from wrong, his newly-acquired powers had somewhat disconcerted him. He was very sorry and would try to do better in the future.

The Judge, however, would not accept his plea, and sentenced him to be blind for the rest of his life, as a punishment for his sin.

Physical death came to "man" before man had moral perceptions, even as blindness was John's before he did wrong. Then how can physical death have its origin in "man's disobedience"?

The real significance of the allegory will be explained next week.

Origins: Part V
By George E Hobbs
(First published: February 1, 1935)

I intimated last week that this week's article would be an attempt to interpret the real significance of the Genesis narrative of "origins". I want to concentrate on one aspect only, because it seems that this constitutes the greatest difficulty of all. It is the doctrine, or belief, that death originated in man's first disobedience.

I want to make it clear that this is not an impetuous and hastily-considered interpretation. I shall interpret as I see it through a long and patient study of the details presented. I have studied it with an ever-growing appreciation of the profundity of its teaching and truth of the law it propounds.

No one is more conscious than myself how difficult it is to escape the thraldom of preconceived ideas – ideas which have been fastened upon one by teaching; teaching which has been forced home by the application of penalties and fear. I remember, all too vividly, how I struggled with a mighty fear in my heart that the monstrous threat was true of hell fire awaiting those who did not take the Bible literally. That fear has long since passed. It passed because I discovered that God was not the frowning, petulant, policeman-judge fostered by medieval theological thought. I discovered that He could not be so petty as to give man a capacity for intelligence and then prohibit him its use under penalties of punishment – punishment too terrible even to contemplate.

There came a day when I determined that in no circumstances would I tolerate a ban upon my thinking. The Bible was open for my study, and I claimed the right to say that I should accept as truth and what I should reject. I came to the conclusion that if, for the sake of convention, or because of a fear of "being lost", I subscribed my consent to something which was logically unsound and ethically wrong, I was untrue to myself. On more than one occasion I found myself guilty of a falsehood in my "beliefs". Only as I freed myself from this intolerable mental prison could I find true liberty of thought. Now to get down to the narrative.

An Illogical Method

The idea that death came upon man as a punishment for sin springs from the allegory itself. God's charge to Adam was clear and concise: "But of the tree of the knowledge of good and evil, thou shalt not eat of it: for in the day that thou eatest thereof thou shalt surely die." Adam did eat of the tree, but he did not die!

This difficulty, however, is surmounted by the literalists. Unfortunately they do not seem to appreciate that their explanation but makes the problem more difficult. They affirm that Adam did die, or, at least, that from the moment he disobeyed God he began to die, the idea being that, previous to his sin, Adam was immortal. He was incorruptible. His disobedience brought the seeds of corruption to his body. Hence he began to die.

This however, seems to me a very illogical method of dealing with the problem. Such an explanation makes the Creator capricious. He creates an immortal being who cannot die, and then changes him into a mortal being for doing something He knew he would do. Such argument cannot stand the light of serious investigation.

But we cannot dismiss the problem with such ease. It would seem that the Apostle Paul gave his sanction to the idea of the death penalty for sin. Writing to the Corinthians, he makes use of the phrase: "For since by man came death".

Taken from its context, the phrase has but one meaning (a danger is ever present when separating text from context). The meaning is that Paul believed it to be disputably true that death came because of man, by man and through man.

If, however text and context are placed in true perspective the phrase takes on a much different meaning. The attitude of mind of the writer is defined, and his aim is clearly seen.

Release From Bondage

The Apostle is concerned with the dynamics of a new and vital conception of life – a conception he had assimilated with much difficulty. It had been too stupendous, too illogical, too much against the laws of natural science. Against the logic of his previous profound reasoning. Paul is now convinced that He who had died upon the cross had definitely risen from the dead. His Lord had actually grappled with, and overcome, the "power" which had held men in bondage with chains. The Apostle, therefore, takes man as he finds him, mortal – as he knows all human beings to be – and with the fear of death ever before him. To this state of depression and mental fear Paul brings the joyful knowledge of release from bondage. Hence I suggest that the great thought behind the Apostle's phrasing is not "For since by man came death, by man came also the resurrection of the dead" but rather, "For since in man is death, in man also is the resurrection of the dead."

The latter, which I suggest is the truer interpretation, first recognises the fact that man is, and always has been, mortal, and in the fulness of time must meet the dissolution of his physical frame. It further recognises that death no longer is to be feared. Its hold upon men has been broken. The fount of power to break that fear has been discovered in man, just as death was in man. It is the indisputable recognition of the fact that man has the seed of immortality within himself.

This thought is amplified in the next utterance Paul writes: "For as in Adam all die, even so in Christ shall all be made alive." The idea herein expressed is clear. It is this: "For as the physical body must yield itself to physical death, so the psychic body, through that power which was in Christ, shall manifest itself in spiritual existence."

Such an interpretation enhances the truth contained in the allegory of Genesis. Man was "fashioned" in the image of God. How close was the "fashioning" was but dimly sensed until the Christ made it plain to his Apostles through His own victorious and revealing transition. The Psalmist had caught a fleeting vision of the truth when he wrote: "Thou wilt guide me with Thy counsel and afterwards receive me to glory."

Physical death did not come upon man as a penalty for sin. Physical death came upon man through the constitution of his being. Of the dust of the earth, he must return to the dust. But his ego, his personality, himself is not of the dust. He is fashioned for eternity.

This will end the series.

Chapter 13

The Final Acts

Give me one hundred men who fear nothing but sin and desire nothing but God, and I care not whether they be clergyman or laymen, they alone will shake the gates of Hell and set up the kingdom of Heaven upon the earth.
(John Wesley)

George's last known contribution to the *Swindon Advertiser* was a letter that appeared on Friday, May 10, 1940, extolling the virtues of the dandelion. Far from being considered a noxious, perennial weed, he recommends that they are used as a salad leaf substitute or alternatively, boiled as you would garden greens.

George's great-grandson, Peter Field, recalled that George's daughter, Dorothy (Peter's grandmother), would often suggest to him and his brother, Tim, that they went looking for dandelions for sandwiches. "I would have been about seven," said Peter. "We were told to try to avoid places where cats had been, which I think might have dampened our enthusiasm over time!"

We thought it fitting that, in addition to a transcription of George's letter, we should include page 151 of the *Observer's Book of British Wild Flowers*, which provides a concise write-up, all about the dandelion.

That would normally be reason enough, but this first edition from 1937 once belonged to his former Even Swindon School headmaster and mentor, Henry Day, one of the first members of the North Wiltshire Field and Camera Club (founded in Swindon in 1898), and a former Vice-President.

He is also someone to whom George once wrote the following, in a letter dated February 21, 1916:

> I will certainly say this, whatever success I have attained since my schooling days terminated, that success has been directly attributable to the tuition I received from yourself. I often look back to the last two years of my school days, when I was in the sixth and seventh standards, with great pleasure.
>
> One of the things, among others, that I like to remember is the memory of morning prayers. I was certainly thoughtless in those days, thoughtless to the nobler and grander things of life, yet as you conducted prayers morning by morning, there were times when I saw in you a something that I could not define then, but now I know it was the fact that you had indeed grasped the nobler and grander life, and you revealed it to me (unconsciously, perhaps, on your part) in the way you conducted morning prayers.

And in a piece written for the *Swindon Advertiser* in 1919, marking Henry's forthcoming retirement, he added: 'But to you, sir, I owe more than words can express.'

It was hard to know how best to conclude this book. Should we end it on a fanfare or with something more measured? For a man who gave so much of his life to Swindon and its people, you could be forgiven for thinking that his obituary in the *Swindon Advertiser* – though fulsome – was deserving of more column inches. And this for a man who had made regular contributions to newspapers and publications for over 25 years, had ministered to his fellow Methodists (and other denominations) as a local preacher for over 35 years, and had served the Great Western Railway for more than half a century, 20 years of which were spent as Foreman-in-Charge of X-Shop.

Of course, his premature loss in December 1946, at the age of only 63, would have been most acutely felt by his wife, Agnes; his daughter, Dorothy; son-in-law, Joe Shailes and his grandchildren, Peter and Margaret.

He lived his life modestly and was said to have given freely of his own money. He was highly critical of those in the Church who took a penny more in their stipend than they actually needed to meet their day-to-day needs, and jealously guarded his own probity as a preacher. He remained a tenant for the whole of his married life, and left an estate barely worth the same amount as he received as an annual salary.

A cutting of the actual obituary that appeared in the *Swindon Advertiser* on January 10, 1947 is reproduced in the following chapter. An almost identical piece appeared in the pages of the *North Wilts Herald and Advertiser* with the headline 'A Noted Lay Preacher and Writer of Swindon'.

He lived and died within the bosom of working class Swindon, and was finally laid to rest in an unmarked grave at Radnor Street Cemetery. Only relatively recently has the exact location of his grave been rediscovered and a small marker added – all this as we continue to publish his body of work and argue for his rightful place among the town's celebrated 20th century citizen journalist/writers.

Dandelions as food
(Letter to the *Swindon Advertiser*)
(First published: May 10, 1940)

Sir, – Saturday's "Swindon Diary" in "The Evening Advertiser" contained an item entitled "Noxious Weeds," stating that "along Cricklade-road, Swindon, is a picture of the 'yellow peril,'" the "peril being the dandelion. The item ends with the somewhat pathetic plea, "Why is action not taken under the Noxious Weeds Act?"

Noxious weeds? Tut-tut. Dandelion leaves are edible, and far surpass mustard and cress or lettuce for making green sandwiches. And if a second vegetable is needed for dinner, none better than dandelion leaves can be obtained. It beats garden-gown greenstuff into a cocked hat. I had a boiling of dandelion leaves quite recently and they were delicious. A supper can be made a delightful repast with bread and cheese and freshly picked dandelion leaves.

To prepare them is quite an easy matter. As the stalk is rather too bitter for my palate, I first remove it from the leaf. Then soak the leaves in water for a few minutes, adding a small piece of salt. Then, according to the quantity gathered, the leaves can be used for sandwiches, salads, or cooking. For cooking they are boiled in exactly the same way one would boil garden greens.

So, friends of Gorse Hill district, take your baskets and bags, gather the "peril" for food. They can be had for the picking, apparently, and can be enjoyed without having "digging for victory" lumbago.

Yes, I know it is the flower which constitutes the difficulty. Lack of sugar will prevent the making of wine this year. Still, as one picks the leaves, the flower can be removed at the same time and destroyed.

Yours, etc,
George E Hobbs

Above: a book that belonged to George's headmaster at Even Swindon School, Henry Day, and the page featuring dandelions (opposite) (author's collection).

DANDELION
Taraxacum officinale

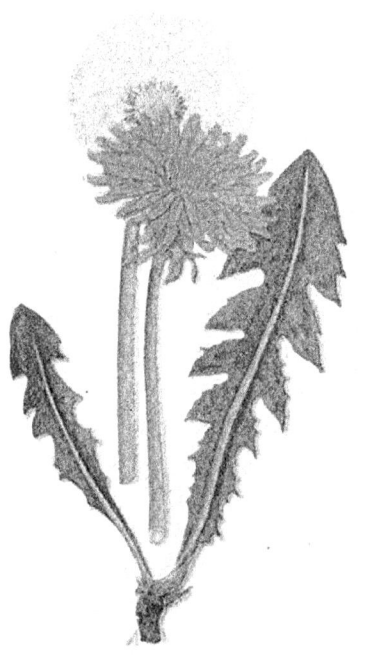

In meadows, pastures, cultivated and waste places everywhere the Dandelion is to be found.

It is a perennial. It has no proper stem, the leaves springing directly from the long, thick root, which is black on the outside and very bitter.

From their midst arise the golden-yellow flower-heads on their hollow stalks. Both stems and leaf-stalks exude a milky juice when broken. The involucre consists of a double row of bracts, the inner long and erect, the outer short, but turned back and clasping the stem.

The florets are all strap-shaped, and each is a perfect flower, containing both anther and stigma. The ovary is crowned by the corolla, which is invested by a pappus of soft, white, silky hairs, representing the calyx. After fertilization the corollas wither, the bracts open, and each pappus spreads into a parachute, the whole constituting a fluffy ball. A light wind detaches them and they float off to disperse the seeds far and wide.

Flowering from March to October.

Illustrations

A detail of a photograph taken at a Band of Hope meeting or outing, c1898, with George Hobbs (possibly holding a framed copy of his temperance pledge certificate) behind his father.

George Hobbs and his future wife, Agnes, c1901 (courtesy of Peter Field).

Two views of the chapel in Percy Street that George attended from a young age and where he later became a lay preacher. Top: the chapel under construction; it opened in 1898. Above: the interior of the chapel at an unknown date (both photos courtesy of the Swindon Society).

Hillside Chapel, Wootton Bassett, where George Hobbs sometimes preached, pictured c1910 (top, courtesy of Wootton Bassett Town Hall Museum) and in 2021 (author's collection).

Grove Methodist Church, Wantage, another place where George Hobbs was a lay preacher, pictured c1970 (top, courtesy of The Vale & Downland Museum, Wantage) and in 2021 (author's collection).

More places where George Hobbs preached; top: the Methodist chapel, Purton, in 2021 (courtesy of Sylvia Freemantle); above: the former Little London Mission in Old Town, Swindon, during work to convert it into private dwellings; opposite, top: the Methodist chapel, Wroughton (courtesy of Duncan & Mandy Ball); opposite, bottom: Wootton Bassett Wesleyan Chapel (date unknown, courtesy of Wootton Bassett Town Hall Museum).

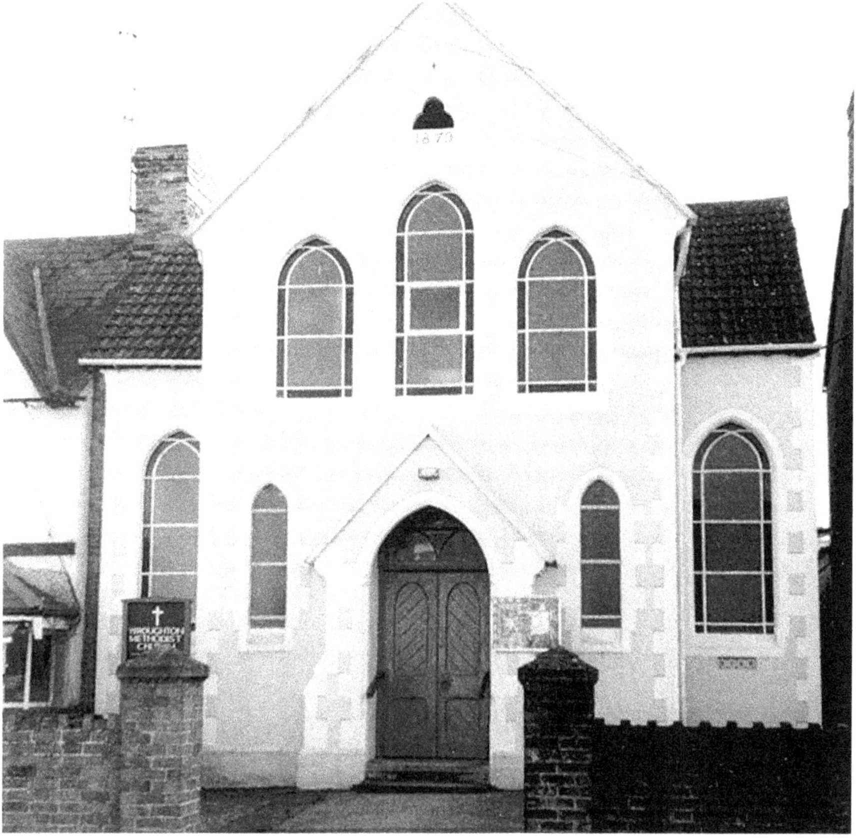
1879
METHODIST

Wootton Bassett
Wesleyan Chapel.
T.A. Teagle.

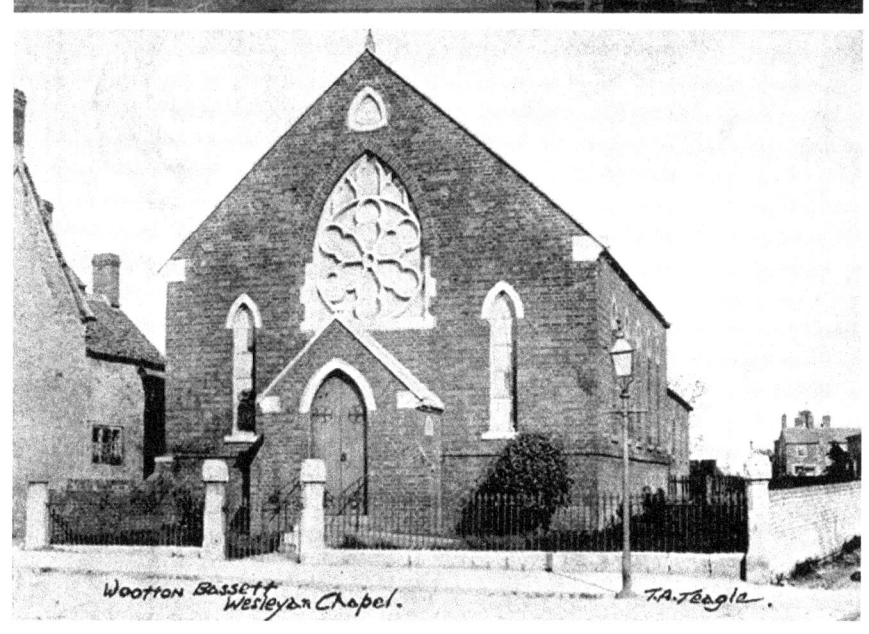

The official programme printed to mark the total solar eclipse of 1927, which George Hobbs visited Southport to witness (see page 137).

A souvenir from speedway racing at Wroughton in 1937/8 (courtesy of Local Studies, Swindon Libraries/Kevin Leakey) (see page 194).

THE TWO WORLDS

A WEEKLY JOURNAL devoted to the PHENOMENA, PHILOSOPHY, and PROGRESS of
SPIRITUALISM,
Founded]   also to RELIGION IN GENERAL and to REFORM.   [1887

No. 1628—Vol. XXXII.   FRIDAY, JAN. 24, 1919.   [REGISTERED AT THE G.P.O. AS A NEWSPAPER.]   PRICE TWOPENCE.

Marylebone Spiritualist Association, Ltd.,
will, until further notice,
HOLD SUNDAY EVENING MEETINGS at 6-30 p.m. at STEINWAY HALL, Lower Seymour Street, LONDON, W.
(Just off Oxford Street, close to Portman Square)

SUNDAY, JAN. 26TH, Mr. THOS. PUGH, of Manchester.
SUNDAY, FEB. 2ND, Mr. P. E. BEARD.
Admission Free. Collection. Inquirers Cordially Invited.
Doors open at 6 p.m. No admission after 6·45 p.m.

LONDON SPIRITUAL MISSION.
13, PEMBRIDGE PLACE, BAYSWATER, LONDON, W.

SUNDAY, JAN. 26TH, at 11, Mrs. MARY DAVIES.
At 6-30, Mr. P. E. BEARD.
WEDNESDAY, JAN. 29TH, at 7-30, Mr. G. PRIOR.

WIMBLEDON SPIRITUALIST MISSION.
THEO' PASSAGE BETWEEN 4 & 5, BROADWAY, WIMBLEDON.

NEXT SUNDAY, at 6-30, Mr. HARRY FIELDER.
WEDNESDAY, PUBLIC CIRCLE, at 7-30, Mrs. Cannock.
WEDNESDAYS.—Psychic Healing, 3 to 5. From 5 to 6, Mr. RICHARD A. BUSH attends to give information about the subject of Spiritualism. Enquirers welcomed.

N. L. S. A.
GROVEDALE HALL, GROVEDALE RD., HIGHGATE TUBE STN.

SUNDAY NEXT, at 11-15, Sergt. CAMPAIGNE. At 3, LYCEUM. At 7, Mr. and Mrs. W. F. SMITH.
WEDNESDAY, JAN. 29TH, at 8, Mrs. A. JAMRACH.
SUNDAY, FEB. 2ND, at 11-15, Mr. T. DAVIS.
At 7, Mr. G. TAYLER GWINN.
WEDNESDAY, FEB. 5TH, at 8, Mr. & Mrs. PULHAM.
SUNDAY, FEB. 9TH, at 11-15, Mr. T. O. TODD.
At 7, Mrs. A. BODDINGTON.
WEDNESDAY, FEB. 12TH, Mrs. PODMORE.

SOUTH LONDON SPIRITUALIST MISSION.
LAUSANNE HALL, LAUSANNE RD., QUEEN'S RD., PECKHAM, LONDON, S.E.

SUNDAY, JAN. 26TH, at 11-30, **PUBLIC CIRCLE.** At 7, **Mrs. CANNOCK,** Address and Clairvoyance.

THURSDAY, JAN. 30TH, at 8-15, Miss ELLEN CONROY, M.A., will give a Lecture on "The Symbolism of Colours."

SUNDAY, FEB. 2ND, at 3 and 7, Mr. J. DUNN will give an Address at both meetings.

SUNDAY, FEB. 9TH, at 7, Mrs. MARY GORDON.

Members' Circle, WEDNESDAYS at 8. Door closed at 8-15

Metaphysical & New Thought Lending Library
Comprising works on Metaphysics, New Thought, Astrology, Palmistry, Occultism, etc., by the best Authors at low prices. Full particulars and catalogue of books will be sent on receipt of request (for 4d.).
C. Maurice Dobson, Publisher and Bookseller, 146, KENSINGTON HIGH STREET, LONDON, W. (8.)

MAN'S PLACE IN THE UNIVERSE.
By ALFRED RUSSEL WALLACE,
O.M., LL.D., D.C.L., F.R.S., ETC.

Cloth. Pocket size. 283 pages. 1/11½ post free.

SALE SPIRITUALIST CHURCH SERVICES

SUNDAY : LYCEUM, 10-30. OPEN CIRCLE, 3. EVENING SERVICE, 7, at the FREE LIBRARY.
WEDNESDAY : MEMBERS' CIRCLE, Temperance Hall, at 7
THURSDAY : PUBLIC CIRCLE at Free Library at 7.

TO STAND STILL IS TO GO BACK.
Organ Fund : Donations respectfully solicited.
Piano Fund : Lyceum urgently require a Piano.
Propaganda Fund : We want £500 for this Fund.
New Members : 200 New Members wanted at once.
The Lyceum : Another 100 children members required.
Speakers : Paid and unpaid Platform Speakers wanted.
Clairvoyants : Gifted exponents should send open dates.
Library : Gifts of Spiritualistic books urgently needed.
Financial Sec. : Mr. J. LONGBOTTOM, 19, Old Hall-rd., Sale.
Hon. Sec. : Mr. T. PUGH, 16, Poplar Grove, Sale.

NATIONAL HOME CIRCLE UNION.

HOW TO BECOME YOUR OWN MEDIUM.

On account of the great public interest in this epoch-making movement, a **CONFERENCE** will be held in London as well as Manchester, due notice of which will appear in this column.

It will be spiritually conducted, and controlled by a council of twelve representative Spiritualists, including delegates from any Church or Society, irrespective of creed.

Every Spiritualist Society will have an opportunity of becoming affiliated.

All wishing to attend the Conference should make application at once.

The writer will be glad to have the views of Spiritualists and mediums as to how, in their opinion, Home Circles should be conducted.

The large number of sincere investigators who have responded already makes it imperative that the public demand for intelligent information shall be met, and the writer takes this opportunity of thanking everyone who has written. Write to THOMAS PUGH, 10, Broad Street Avenue, London, E.C.

HOME CIRCLE COMPETITION.

£5 CASH PRIZES TO BE GIVEN AWAY

On behalf of the HOME CIRCLE UNION, I am prepared to give

PRIZES TO THE VALUE OF £5

to the competitors who, in a 1,000 or 1,500 word article, send in the best and most practical essay by Jan. 31st, 1919, on

"HOW TO CONDUCT HOME CIRCLES WITH OR WITHOUT A MEDIUM."

The articles will be adjudicated by a Committee, full particulars of which will appear on this page.

Competitors should send in their articles to **THOMAS PUGH, 10, Broad Street Avenue, London, E.C.**

Opposite: the front page of The Two Worlds, *the publication for spiritualists read by George Hobbs, in 1919. Top: the advertisement from* The Two Worlds *in January 1920, featuring Sir Arthur Conan Doyle's impending visit to Swindon (courtesy of IAPSOP). Above: a front page from another spiritualist publication,* Psychic News, *in 1939 (courtesy of UM Digital Collections) (see Chapter 11).*

Reuben George (courtesy of Local Studies, Swindon Libraries) (see Chapter 7).

Swindon Town's official team picture for the 1926-7 season, during which George Hobbs witnessed their local derby match with Bristol City, through the eyes of Mrs Crabthorn (see page 90). The team included one of the club's greatest players, centre forward Harry Morris (middle row, sixth from the left). After joining Town from Swansea during the close season for a princely transfer fee of £110, Morris scored hat-tricks in each of his first two games, and a further three goals in the next two games. And as he had found the net in each of the four previous games before playing Bristol City, as well as in each of the following 11, the match is remarkable for the fact that Morris didn't *score! Later in the season he scored five in the 6-2 hammering of Queen's Park Rangers, a feat he would repeat in 1930, against Norwich City. Harry Morris ended his career with 229 goals in 279 appearances; no wonder even Mrs Crabthorn was anxious to watch him play!*

The Evening Advertiser's front page on September 3, 1939 (courtesy of Local Studies, Swindon Libraries).

Methodist Lay Preacher of Many Interests

Swindon Loss by Death at 63 of Mr. George E. Hobbs

A METHODIST lay preacher since his young days, and a contributor to the Evening Advertiser of many years' standing, Mr. George E. Hobbs, whose death is reported, was widely known throughout the Swindon area.

Sixty-three years of age, Mr. Hobbs was not only a native of Swindon, but had lived in Jennings-street practically the whole of his life. He also carried on the tradition of his father as a regular attender at the Percy-street Methodist Church.

MISSION GIFT

An enthusiastic preacher, he was also very tolerant in his attitude, and had frequently addressed congregations of different denominations. Some of his

MR. HOBBS

most outstanding work was at the Little London Mission and one of his most treasured souvenirs was a fountain pen presented to him on behalf of that Mission.

In days gone by, he often travelled to the outlying areas in a horse-drawn trap, in order to keep his engagements.

A story writer of no mean ability, he was a valued contributor to both the North Wilts Herald and the Evening Advertiser for many years.

As foreman of the Points and Crossings Dept. in X Shop, G.W.R. Works, a position he had held for 23 years, he was extremely conscientious, and during the war years had to reduce his outside activities in order to keep pace with the extra work that arose.

He started with the G.W.R. after leaving school, and originally was in the "G" Shop, being a fitter and turner by trade. One of his most interesting experiences was joining the reporters from London when Queen Mary and the late King George V. visited the G.W.R. works, so that he might write an account of the visit.

KEEN ASTRONOMER

On another occasion, being a keen astronomer, he went up to Stockport in order to gain the best point of vantage for studying a total eclipse of the sun.

He will be remembered also for his association with the Rowing Club at Coate.

He leaves a widow, and a married daughter, Mrs. J. Shailes, who lives at Farm cottages, Rodbourne.

The Rev. F. Clark officiated at the funeral service, which took place at the Wesleyan Chapel, Percy-street, Swindon, and also at the interment which followed at Radnor-street cemetery.

Mourners were: Mrs. A. Hobbs (widow), Mr. and Mrs. J. Shailes (son-in-law and daughter); Peter and Margaret Shailes (grandchildren), Miss Joan Stone and Mr Bob Field, Mrs. E. Ponting, Devizes (sister); Mr. E. Dummer (nephew), Mr. and Mrs. Neate, M. and Mrs. G. Rich, Mr. N. Little (Cricklade), Mr. B. Harbour, Mr. L. Harris, Mr. S. Silkman (London), and representatives from X Shop, G.W.R. as well as many friends from different churches.

The Swindon Advertiser's report of the death of George Ewart Hobbs in December 1946 (courtesy of Peter Field).

George Ewart Hobbs's grave in Radnor Street Cemetery, Swindon. It was unmarked until this handmade marker was installed by Noel Ponting in 2019 (author's collection).

Mrs Crabthorn – an artist's impression by Lydia Ponting (see Chapter 4).

Appendix A:

The Known Works of George E Hobbs (1924-1940)

*Republished in full or extract in this book
**Republished in full or extract in *A Swindon Wordsmith*
†Republished in full in *A Visit to Venus*

Note: numbering or apparent sequencing errors are due to mistakes made during the original newspaper publication

Answers to Correspondents [1] (April 17, 1924)
Answers to Correspondents [2] (April 25, 1924)
Answers to Correspondents [3] (May 23, 1924)
A Pen Picture of the Royal Visit to Swindon (Great Western Railway Magazine, June 1924)**
The Conversion of Z – A Little Story for Hospital Week (June 13, 1924)
A Mystery (June 27, 1924, letter)
Trip (July 3, 1924)**
Beauties of Wye Valley – A GWR Shop Outing (September 5, 1924)*

[Nothing found for 1925]

A Bird-Cage Mystery – Mr GE Hobbs Propounds a Problem (August 13, 1926 (letter))
Mrs Crabthorne at a Football Match – Her "Impressions" of the Leadership Fight (October 29, 1926)*
Listening-In to Mars – A Comedy of the Crabthorne Household (November 5, 1926)*
Good, Bad and Indifferent (December 17, 1926, letter)

Rev W Clifford – A Pen Picture of the Pulpit [10] (January 14, 1927)
A Visit to Venus Chapter I – Recorded by George E Hobbs (January 7, 1927)†
A Visit to Venus Chapter II – Recorded by George E Hobbs (January 14, 1927)†

A Visit to Venus Chapter II [continued] – Mr GE Hobbs Continues His Narrative (January 21, 1927)†
A Visit to Venus Chapter III – Mr GE Hobbs Continues his Narrative (January 28, 1927)†
A Visit to Venus Chapter IV – Mr GE Hobbs Continues his Narrative (February 4, 1927)†
A Visit to Venus Chapter V – Mr GE Hobbs Continues his Narrative (February 18, 1927)†
A Visit to Venus Chapter VI – Recorded by George E Hobbs (February 25, 1927)†
A Visit to Venus Chapter VII – Recorded by George E Hobbs (March 4, 1927)†
A Visit to Venus Chapter VIII – Recorded by George E Hobbs (March 11, 1927)†
A Visit to Venus Chapter IX – Recorded by George E Hobbs (March 18, 1927)†
A Visit to Venus Chapter X – Recorded by George E Hobbs (March 25 1927)†
Butler's Hudibras (March 25, 1927, letter)
A Visit to Venus Chapter XI – Recorded by George E Hobbs (April 1, 1927)†
Victoria Hospital – Impressions of a Visit (April 1, 1927)
A Visit to Venus Chapter XII – Recorded by George E Hobbs (April 8, 1927)†
A Visit to Venus Chapter XIII – Recorded by George E Hobbs (April 15, 1927)†
A Visit to Venus Chapter XIII [continued] – Recorded by George E Hobbs (April 22, 1927)†
A Visit to Venus Chapter XIV – Recorded by George E Hobbs (April 29, 1927)†
A Visit to Venus Chapter XIV [continued] – Recorded by George E Hobbs (May 6, 1927)†
A Visit to Venus Chapter XV – Recorded by George E Hobbs (May 13, 1927)†
A Visit to Venus Chapter XVI – Recorded by George E Hobbs (May 20, 1927)†
A Visit to Venus Chapter XVII – Recorded by George E Hobbs (May 27, 1927)†
A Visit to Venus Chapter XVIII – Recorded by George E Hobbs (June 3, 1927)†
A Visit to Venus Chapter XIX – Recorded by George E Hobbs (June 10, 1927)†
A Visit to Venus Chapter XX – Recorded by George E Hobbs (June 17, 1927)†
A Visit to Venus Chapter XXI – Recorded by George E Hobbs (June 24, 1927)†
Pen Picture of the Solar Eclipse (June 30, 1927)**
A Visit to Venus Chapter XXI [continued] – Recorded by George E Hobbs (June 30, 1927)†
A Visit to Venus Chapter XXII – Recorded by George E Hobbs (July 8, 1927)†
A Visit to Venus Chapter XXIII – Recorded by George E Hobbs (July 15, 1927)†
A Visit to Venus Chapter XXIII [continued] – Recorded by George E Hobbs (July 22, 1927)†
A Visit to Venus Chapter XXIV – Recorded by George E Hobbs (July 29, 1927)†
A Visit to Venus Chapter XXIV [continued] – Recorded by George E Hobbs (August 5, 1927)†
A Visit to Venus Chapter XXV – Recorded by George E Hobbs (August 12, 1927)†
A Visit to Venus Chapter XXVI The End – Recorded by George E Hobbs (August 19, 1927)†
The "Fall" – Historic or Symbolic? (October 7, 1927)*
"Vigilans Non Cadet" – Story of Human Weakness Told in Allegory [1] (October 28, 1927)
The Solar Eclipse – Impressions of a Swindon Lecture (November 2, 1927)*
"Vigilans Non Cadet" – Story of Human Weakness Told in Allegory Chapter III [Chapter II] (November 4, 1927)
The Significance of 11 November (November 9, 1927)
"Vigilans Non Cadet" – Story of Human Weakness Told in Allegory [3] (November 11, 1927)
"Vigilans Non Cadet" – Story of Human Weakness Told in Allegory [4] (November 18, 1927)
"Vigilans Non Cadet" – Story of Human Weakness Told in Allegory [5] (November 25, 1927)
"Vigilans Non Cadet" – Story of Human Weakness Told in Allegory [6] (December 2, 1927)
"Vigilans Non Cadet" – Story of Human Weakness Told in Allegory: The End (December 9, 1927)
The Reconciliation – A Christmas Story (December 23, 1927)

The Coward – Chapter 1 [fiction] (January 6, 1928)
The Coward – Second Instalment [fiction] (January 13 1928)
The Coward – Chapter 3 [fiction] (January 20, 1928)

The Coward – Chapter IV [fiction] (January 27, 1928)
The Coward – Fifth Instalment [fiction] (February 3, 1928)
The Coward – Sixth Instalment [fiction] (February 10, 1928)
The Coward – Seventh Instalment [fiction] (February 17, 1928)
The Coward – Last Instalment [fiction] (February 24, 1928)
A Day With The Relaying Gang (May 18, 1928)
Immortality [1] (May 25, 1928)*
Immortality [2] (June 1, 1928)*
Immortality [3] (June 15, 1928)*
Immortality [4] (June 22, 1928)*
Immortality [5] (June 28, 1928)*
Immortality [6] (July 6, 1928)*
Immortality [7] (July 13, 1928)*
Immortality [8] – The End (July 20, 1928)*
The Creation of the World [1] – First of Series of Articles (August 17, 1928)
The Creation of the World [2] – Bible Narratives for Young Students (August 24, 1928)
The Creation of the World [3] – Bible Narratives for Young Students (August 31, 1928)
Bible Narratives for the Young Student [4] (September 7, 1928)
Bible Narratives for Young Students [5] (September 14, 1928)
Bible Narratives for Students – The Second Chapter of Genesis [6] (October 5, 1928)
Bible Narratives for Young Students [7] (October 12, 1928)*
Bible Narratives [8] – George E Hobbs Continues His Talks (October 19, 1928)*
Bible Narratives [9] – George E Hobbs Continues His Talks (October 26, 1928)
Bible Narratives (26 October 1928, letter)*
Bible Narratives [10] – George E Hobbs Continues His Talks (November 2, 1928)
Bible Narratives [11] – George E Hobbs Continues His Talks (November 9, 1928)
Bible Narratives [12] – George E Hobbs Continues His Talks (November 16, 1928)
Bible Narratives (November 16, 1928, letter)
Bible Narratives [13] – George E Hobbs Continues His Talks (November 23, 1928)
Bible Narratives (November 23, 1928, letter)
Bible Narratives [14] – George E Hobbs Tells the Story of the Deluge (November 30, 1928)
A Relaying Gang at Work (Great Western Railway Magazine, December 1928)**
Bible Narratives [15] – George E Hobbs on the Story of the Flood (December 7, 1928)
Bible Narratives [16] – George E Hobbs Continues His Talks (December 14, 1928)
Bible Narratives [17] – George E Hobbs Continues His Talks (December 21, 1928)

A New Year's Message (January 4, 1929)
Permanent Way Fittings and their Manufacture (GWR Mechanics' Institute/Swindon Engineering Society, February 5, 1929)**
Bible Stories [1] – Geo E Hobbs Resumes His Narratives (April 12, 1929)
Bible Stories [2] – Geo E Hobbs Resumes His Narratives (April 19, 1929)
Bible Stories [3] – Mr Hobbs' Interesting Narratives (April 26, 1929)
Bible Stories [4] – Mr Hobbs' Interesting Narratives (May 3, 1929)
Bible Stories [5] – Geo E Hobbs Continues His Narratives (May 10, 1929)
Bible Stories [6] – Geo E Hobbs Continues His Narratives (May 17, 1929)
Bible Stories [7] – Geo E Hobbs Continues His Narratives (May 24, 1929)
Bible Stories [8] – Geo E Hobbs Continues His Narratives (May 30, 1929)
Bible Stories [9] – Geo E Hobbs Continues His Narratives (June 7, 1929)
Bible Stories [10] – Geo E Hobbs Continues His Narratives (June 14, 1929)

Bible Stories [11] – Geo E Hobbs Continues His Narratives (June 21, 1929)
Bible Stories [12] – Geo E Hobbs Continues His Narratives (June 27, 1929)
A Story with a Moral (July 5, 1929)
Bible Stories [13] – Geo E Hobbs Continues His Narratives (July 12, 1929)
Bible Stories [14] – Geo E Hobbs Continues His Narratives (July 26, 1929)
Bible Narratives [19] – Romance of Joseph, the Son of Jacob (2 August 1929)
Bible Narratives [20] – Joseph Becomes the Slave of Potiphar (9 August 1929)
Bible Stories [15] – Geo E Hobbs Continues His Narratives (August 16, 1929)
Bible Stories [16] – Geo E Hobbs Continues His Narratives (August 23, 1929)
Bible Stories [17] – Geo E Hobbs Continues His Narratives (August 30, 1929)
Percy Street Wesley Guild (August 30, 1929, letter)
Bible Stories [18] – Geo E Hobbs Continues His Narratives (September 6, 1929)
Bible Stories [19] – Geo E Hobbs Continues His Narratives (September 13, 1929)
Bible Stories [20] – Geo E Hobbs Continues His Narratives (September 20, 1929)
Bible Stories [21] – Geo E Hobbs Continues His Narratives (September 27, 1929)
Bible Stories [22] – Geo E Hobbs Continues His Narratives (October 4, 1929)
Bible Stories [23] – Geo E Hobbs Continues His Narratives (October 11, 1929)
Bible Stories [24] – Geo E Hobbs Continues His Narratives (October 18, 1929)
Bible Stories [25] – Geo E Hobbs Continues His Narratives (October 25, 1929)
Bible Stories [26] – Geo E Hobbs Continues His Narratives (November 1, 1929)
Bible Stories [27] – Geo E Hobbs Continues His Narratives (November 8, 1929)
"All Quiet on the Western Front" (November 8, 1929, letter)
Bible Stories [28] – Geo E Hobbs Continues His Narratives (November 15, 1929)
Bible Stories [29] – Geo E Hobbs Continues His Narratives (November 22, 1929)
"All Quiet on the Western Front" (November 22, 1929, letter)
Bible Stories [30] – Geo E Hobbs Continues His Narratives (November 29, 1929)
Bible Stories [31] – Geo E Hobbs Continues His Narratives (December 6, 1929)
Bible Stories [32] – Geo E Hobbs Continues His Narratives (December 13, 1929)
A Christmas Story (December 20, 1929)

The Return of Mrs Crabthorn – George E Hobbs Revives an old Character (January 24, 1930)*
Mrs Crabthorn Has A Day Out [1] – The First Stage of a Visit to Clifton Zoo (January 31, 1930)*
Mrs Crabthorn's Visit to Clifton Zoo [2] – Her Experiences on the Journey from Swindon to Bristol (February 14, 1930)*
Mrs Crabthorn's Visit to Clifton Zoo [3] – George E Hobbs Continues the Story of Her Adventures (February 21, 1930)*
Mrs Crabthorn at the Zoo [4] – The Final Episode (February 28, 1930)*
Mrs Crabthorn Demands An Explanation (March 7, 1930)*
The Crabthorns and The Dunmow Flitch – The First Rehearsal (March 14, 1930)*
The Crabthorns and The Dunmow Flitch – The Second Rehearsal (March 21, 1930)*
Spring Cleaning [1] – *Mrs Crabthorn Makes a Start* (March 28, 1930)*
Spring Cleaning at the Crabthorns [2] – *George E Hobbs Continues the Story of His Adventures* (April 4, 1930)*
Spring Cleaning at Crabthorns [3] – *Final Episode* (April 11, 1930)*
The Crucifixion (April 17, 1930)
Capital Punishment (April 25, 1930)
Mrs Crabthorn's "Gost" (May 2, 1930)*
"The Acorn": A Fable (May 9, 1930)
The Evil Genius – Chapter I [fiction] (May 16,1930)

The Evil Genius – Chapter II [fiction] (May 23, 1930)
The Evil Genius – Chapter II (continued) [fiction] (May 30, 1930)
The Evil Genius – Chapter 3 [fiction] (June 6, 1930)
The Evil Genius – Chapter 8 [sic] *[Chapter 3 continued]* [fiction] (June 13, 1930)
The Evil Genius – Chapter 4 [fiction] (June 20, 1930)
The Evil Genius – Chapter 5 [fiction] (June 27, 1930)
The Evil Genius – Chapter 6 [fiction] (July 4, 1930)
The Evil Genius – Chapter 6 (continued) [fiction] (July 11, 1930)
The Evil Genius – Chapter 7 [fiction] (July 18, 1930]
The Evil Genius – Chapter 8 [fiction] (July 25, 1930]
The Evil Genius – Chapter 9 [fiction] (August 1, 1930)
The Evil Genius – Chapter 9 (continued) [fiction] (August 8, 1930)
The Evil Genius – Chapter 10 [fiction] (August 15, 1930)
The Evil Genius – Chapter 11 [fiction] (August 22, 1930)
The Evil Genius – Chapter 12 [fiction] (August 29, 1930)
The Evil Genius – Chapter 12 (continued) [fiction] (September 5, 1930)
The Evil Genius – Chapter 13 [fiction] (September 12, 1930)
The Evil Genius – Chapter 14 [fiction] (September 19, 1930)
The Evil Genius – Chapter 14 (continued) [fiction] (September 26, 1930)
The Evil Genius – Chapter 15 [fiction] (October 3, 1930)
The Evil Genius – Chapter 15 (continued) [fiction] (October 10, 1930)
The Evil Genius – Chapter 16 [fiction] (October 17, 1930)
The Evil Genius – Chapter 17 [fiction] (October 24, 1930)
The Evil Genius – Chapter 18 [fiction] (October 31, 1930)
The Evil Genius – Chapter 19 [fiction] (November 7, 1930)
The Evil Genius – Chapter 19 (continued) [fiction] (November 14, 1930)
The Evil Genius – Chapter 20 [fiction] (November 21, 1930)
The Evil Genius – Chapter 21 [fiction] (November 28, 1930)
The Evil Genius – Chapter 22 [fiction] (December 5, 1930)
The Evil Genius – Chapter 22 (continued) [fiction] (December 12, 1930)
The Evil Genius – Chapter 23 [fiction] (December 19, 1930)
The Evil Genius – Chapter 24 [fiction] (December 24, 1930)

The Evil Genius – Chapter 25 [fiction] (January 2, 1931)
The Evil Genius – Chapter 26 The End [fiction] (January 9, 1931)
Controversy [1] [fiction] (January 23, 1931)
Controversy [2] [fiction] (January 30, 1931)
Controversy [3] [fiction] (February 6, 1931)
Controversy [4] [fiction] (February 13, 1931)
Love's Message (February 20, 1931)
Controversy [Final Part] [fiction] (February 27, 1931)
The Fear of Heights (March 6, 1931)
Power (March 13, 1931)*
Power [continued] (March 20, 1931)*
Heroism – The Scott Expedition (March 27, 1931)
Heroism No 2 – The Titanic Disaster (April 2, 1931)
Heroism No 3 – Grace Darling (April 10, 1931)
Heroism No 4 – Florence Nightingale (April 17, 1931)
Heroism No 5 – Mary Slessor (April 24, 1931)

Heroism No 6 – Boadicea (May 1, 1931)
Heroism No 7 – Charles Bradlaugh (May 8,1931)
Heroism [No 8] – David versus Goliath (June 5, 1931)
Heroism No 9 – Daniel The Hebrew Prophet (June 12, 1931)
Heroism No 10 – Elijah (June 19, 1931)
Heroism [No 11] – Moses (June 26, 1931)
Heroism No 12 – Peter (July 2, 1931
Heroism No 3 – Peter continued (July 10, 1931)
Heroism No 14 – Saul of Tarsus (Paul the Apostle) (July 31, 1931)
Heroism No 15 – Jesus Christ (July 24 1931)
The Book of Job No I (July 31, 1931)
The Book of Job No II (August 7, 1931)
The Book of Job No III (August 14, 1931)
The Book of Job No V (August 21, 1931)
The Book of Job No VI (August 28, 1931)
The Book of Job No VII (September 4, 1931)
The Book of Job No VIII (September 11, 1931)
The Book of Job No IX (September 18, 1931)
The Book of Job No X (September 25, 1931)
The Book of Job No XI (October 2, 1931)
The Book of Job No XII (October 9, 1931)
The Book of Job No XIII (October 16, 1931)
The Book of Job No XIV (23 October 1931)
The Book of Job No XV (October 30, 1931)
The Book of Job No XVI (November 13, 1931)
The Book of Job No XVII (November 20, 1931)
The Book of Job No XVIII (November 27, 1931)
The Book of Job No XIX (December 4, 1931)
The Book of Job No XX (December 11, 1931)
The Book of Job No XXI (December 18, 1931)
The First Christmas (December 24, 1931)*

A Message And A Forecast! (January 1, 1932)
The Book of Job No XXI (January 8, 1932)
The Book of Job No XXII (January 15, 1932)
The Book of Job No XXIII (January 22, 1932)
Adventures [1] – Introducing "Bill" (January 29, 1932)
Adventures [2] – "Bill" Goes to Sea (February 5, 1932)
Adventures [3] – Bill's Education Begins (February 12, 1932)
Adventures [4] – Bill Is a Hero (February 19, 1932)
Adventures [5] – Bill Is a Hero Part II (February 26, 1932)
Adventures [6] – The Skipper Gets Bitten (March 4, 1932)
Adventures [7] – Bill Gets a Fright (March 11, 1932)
Adventures [8] – A Chapter of Accidents (March 18, 1932)
Adventures [9] – The Burglary (March 24, 1932)
Adventures [10] (April 1, 1932)
Adventures [11] – 'Men are Monkeys' – Vide Bill (April 8, 1932)
Adventures [12] – "Black Dan" (April 15, 1932)
Adventures [13] – Bill's First Love Affair (April 22, 1932)

Adventures [14] – The Storm Part 1 (April 29, 1932)
Adventures [15] – The End of the Storm (May 6, 1932)
Adventures [16] – How "Simple" Rode to Victory (May 13, 1932)
Adventures [17] – Bill's Striking Yarn (May 20, 1932)
Adventures [18] – The "Devil-Fish" (May 27, 1932)
Adventures [19] – Hep's Romance (June 3, 1932)
Adventures [20] – Hep's Romance Concluded (June 10, 1932)
Adventures [21] – "Ginger" (June 17, 1932)
Adventures [22] – "Black Dan" Again (June 24, 1932)
Adventures [23] – The Battle (July 1, 1932)
Mrs Crabthorne Prepares For Trip (July 7, 1932)*
Adventures [24] – Pirates: The Attack (July 15, 1932)
Adventures [25] – "Pirates" – Concluded (July 22, 1932)
Adventures [26] – "Simple" Passes Out (July 29, 1932)
Adventures [27] – Death to the Despoiler (August 5, 1932)
Adventures [28] – Death to the Despoiler Concluded (August 12, 1932)
Adventures [29] – "Wreck of The Hermione" (August 26, 1932)
Adventures [30] – "Wreck of The Hermione" (September 2, 1932)
Adventures [31] – Bill is Defiant (September 9, 1932)
Adventures [32] – Bill's Romance (September 16, 1932)
Adventures [33] [The End] – The Last Voyage (September 23, 1932)
The Crime (September 30, 1932)
And The Prize Vanished (October 7, 1932)
The Carstairs Mystery (October 14, 1932)
The Carstairs Mystery – Concluded (October 21, 1932)

An Open Letter To Mr Reuben George (January 20, 1933)*
Freedom (February 24, 1933)*
World Peace In Peril (March 3, 1933, letter)*
The Chain Letter Pest (March 31, 1933, letter)

Tin Foil For The Hospital (September 14, 1934, letter)
Wireless Talks [1] [War, pacifism & the sky at night] (October 26, 1934)*
Wireless Talks [2] [Sir James Jeans: A Tour Through Time and Space] (November 9, 1934)
Wireless Talks [3] [Sir James Jeans: A Tour Through Time and Space] (November 16, 1934)
Wireless Talks [4] [Sir James Jeans: A Tour Through Time and Space] (November 23, 1934)
Wireless Talks [5] [Sir James Jeans: A Tour Through Time and Space] (November 30, 1934)
Wireless Talks [6] [Sir James Jeans: A Tour Through Time and Space] (December 7, 1934)
Wireless Talks [7] [The Very Rev WR Matthews] (December 14, 1934)
One Aspect of The Incarnation (December 21, 1934)*
Resolutions (December 28, 1934)

Origins [1] [A new interpretation of Genesis and the meaning of death] (January 4, 1935)
Origins Part II [A new interpretation of Genesis and the meaning of death] (January 11, 1935)
Origins Part III [A new interpretation of Genesis and the meaning of death] (January 18, 1935)
Origins Part IV [A new interpretation of Genesis and the meaning of death] (January 25, 1935)*
Origins Part V [A new interpretation of Genesis and the meaning of death] (February 1, 1935)*
Origins (letter by 'XY') (February 8, 1935)

Personal Freedom (February 8, 1935)*
Personal Freedom: Part II (February 15, 1935)*
Personal Freedom: Concluded (February 22, 1935)*
Personal Freedom (letter by Believer) (March 1, 1935)
Personal Freedom (letter by GEH) (March 8, 1935)*
Personal Freedom (letter by A Believer) (March 15, 1935)
The Call To Prayer (September 6, 1935)*
The Choice (September 13, 1935)
What Is Prayer? (October 4, 1935)
A Fantasy (December 20, 1935)

"Rules" of War (January 17, 1936)*
Reflections (February 21, 1936)
The "Bombshell" (March 13, 1936)*
An Open Letter to Mr WW Wakefield MP (April 8, 1936, letter)*
The Futility of Capital Punishment (April 24, 1936)
Byron: The Man & The Poet (May 1, 1936)
The "Children's Charter" (May 8, 1936)
"Victory" And Annexation (May 15, 1936)*
Life Sketch of Major-General Sir Henry Havelock KCB (May 22, 1936)
"Love Triumphant" (June 5, 1936)
In Remembrance [of Reuben George] (June 12, 1936, letter)*
Life's Success (June 19, 1936)*
The Late Mrs Reuben George (26 June 1936, letter)*
The Humour of Life (June 26, 1936)*
Life's Problems (July 3, 1936)
Holidays (July 9, 1936)*
Perusing An Old Journal (July 17, 1936)
The New Methodist Hymnal (July 24, 1936)*
The New Methodist Hymnal (continued) (July 31, 1936)*
"The Swindon Advertiser" – 1870 (August 7, 1936)
A Delve Into The Past (August 14, 1936)
"The Man Himself" (August 21, 1936)
Is Nature Crazy? (August 28, 1936)
Is Nature Crazy? Part II (September 4, 1936)
Peace (September 11, 1936)*
Toy Soldiers (September 17, 1936, letter)
Mythology (September 18, 1936)
Mythology (continued) (September 25, 1936)
Letter by GE Hobbs (September 25, 1936 (missing from the record))
The Hidden Years (October 2, 1936)
Lessons of Harvest (October 9, 1936)*
The Joy of Life (October 16, 1936)
Internationalism (October 23, 1936)*
Internationalism (continued) (October 30, 1936)*
Remembrance Day (November 6, 1936)
The Wonders of Ant Life (November 13, 1936)
The Wonders of Ant Life (continued) (November 20, 1936)
"World Peace" (November 27, 1936)*

Whither? (December 4, 1936)
New Aspect of The Incarnation (December 18, 1936)
The Inn At Bethlehem (December 24, 1936)

"Quo Vadis" (January 1, 1937)
Letter-Writing (January 8, 1937)
The Bible (January 15, 1937)
South With Captain Scott (January 22, 1937)
Light (January 29, 1937)
Light Part II (February 5, 1937)
Light Part III (February 12, 1937)
Light Part IV (February 19, 1937)
The Present Menace (February 26, 1937)*
Light No V (March 5, 1937)
Light No VI (March 12, 1937)
Light No VII (March 19, 1937)
Kingship: A Good Study (March 25, 1937)
The Return From The South Pole (April 2, 1937)
A Saga of The Seas (April 23 1937)
The Problems of "Defence" (April 30, 1937)*
Gleanings [1, marriage] (May 7, 1937)
As Others See Us (May 14, 1937, letter)
Gleanings [2, marriage and children] (May 14, 1937)
Gleanings [3, coronation of King George VI] (May 21, 1937)
Gleanings [4, democracy and the Church of England] (May 28, 1937)*
Tribute To Vicar (June 4, 1937, letter)
Gleanings [5, the National Anthem, conventions and Sir John Betjeman] (June 4, 1937)
Tribute To Vicar (June 11, 1937, letter)
Gleanings [6, Lord Kitchener] (June 11, 1937)
Gleanings [7, conventions and censorship] (June 18, 1937)
Gleanings [8, peace, multilateralism and internationalism] (June 25, 1937)
Gleanings [9, the Wesley brothers] (July 2, 1937)
Gleanings [10, holidays] (July 8, 1937)*
Gleanings [11, "McGlusky's Great Adventure" by AG Hales] (July 16, 1937)
Gleanings [12, cyclists and road safety] (July 23, 1937)*
Gleanings [13, Wroughton Sunday speedway, the Church and modern youth] (July 30, 1937)*
Gleanings [14, talent and ability] (August 6, 1937)
Hands off Cyclists (August 6, 1937, letter)
Gleanings [15, secret weapons and internationalism] (August 13, 1937)
Gleanings [16, meteorology and climate change] (August 20, 1937)
Gleanings [17, knowledge, reasoning and examinations] (August 27, 1937)
Gleanings [18, the battle of the sexes] (September 3, 1937)
Gleanings [19, Alderman Reuben George] (September 10, 1937)*
Gleanings [20, Seamark's 'The Mystery Maker', drugs and hopelessness] (September 24, 1937)
Gleanings [21, the bombing of Nanking and Canton; internationalism] (October 1, 1937)*
Gleanings [22, hope in the Bible and dreams of a better world] (October 8, 1937)
Gleanings [23, the limitations of pacifism] (October 15, 1937)
Gleanings [24, the meaning of harvest] (October 22, 1937)
Gleanings [25, wildlife conservation and national parks] (October 29, 1937)

Gleanings [26, microscopic life] (November 5, 1937)
Gleanings [27, Armistice Day and HG Wells] (November 12, 1937)*
Biology (November 19, 1937, letter)
Gleanings [28, NSPCC, bad parenting and child neglect] (November 19, 1937)*
Gleanings [29, George responds to letter by Mr GV Smith] (November 26, 1937)
Gleanings [30, Jack London's 'Iron Heel.' Power, inequality & oppression] (December 3, 1937)
Gleanings [31, Dr David Livingstone] (December 10, 1937)
Gleanings [32, New Internationalism as advocated by Sir Fabian Ware] (December 17, 1937)*
The Story of Love (December 23, 1937)
Gleanings [33, acts of love and service, duty and obligation] (December 31, 1937)

Gleanings [34, world peace and the creation of a better society] (January 7, 1938)
Why Planet Swerved (January 13, 1938, letter)
Gleanings [35, Grace Darling] (January 14, 1938)
Gleanings [36, the new Church of England doctrine] (January 21, 1938)
Gleanings [37, church unity, Little London Mission and Object Reinmuth 1937] (January 28, 1938)
Gleanings [38, the Swindon Stadium controversy, gambling – skill or chance?] (February 4, 1938)
Gleanings [39, Astrology and astronomy] (February 11, 1938)*
Gleanings [40, Spiritualism, psychic phenomena and immortality] (February 18, 1938)*
Gleanings [41, A call for a code of international law] (February 25, 1938)
Gleanings [42, Are churches teaching really what Christ said?] (March 4, 1938)
Gleanings [43, the Battle of Majuba Hill] (March 11, 1938)
Gleanings [44, live boxing from USA; Anschluß and the League of Nations] (March 18,1938)*
Gleanings [45, photojournalism & war; the aerial bombing of civilians] (March 25, 1938)*
Gleanings [46, a bumper book of facts] (April 1, 1938)
Gleanings [47, a story in allegory] (April 8, 1938)
Gleanings [48, a story in allegory] (April 14, 1938)
Gleanings [49, a story in allegory] (April 22, 1938)
Gleanings [50, a story in allegory] (April 29, 1938)
Gleanings [51, a story in allegory] (May 6, 1938)
Gleanings [52, a story in allegory] (May 13, 1938)
Gleanings [53, a story in allegory] (May 20, 1938)
Gleanings [54, a story in allegory] (May 27, 1938)
Gleanings [55, a story in allegory] (June 3, 1938)
Gleanings [56, a story in allegory] (June 10, 1938)
Gleanings [57, a story in allegory] (June 17, 1938)
Gleanings [58, a story in allegory] (June 24, 1938)
Gleanings [59, a story in allegory] (July 1, 1938)
Gleanings [60, Christianity, church and state] (July 7, 1938)
Gleanings [61, life cycles; the rise and fall of maritime nations] (July 15 1938)
Gleanings [62, Dr Spencer Jones and speculation about extraterrestrial life] (July 22, 1938)*
Gleanings [63, Dr Spencer Jones and speculation about extraterrestrial life] (July 29,1938)
Gleanings [64, Dr Spencer Jones and speculation about extraterrestrial life] (August 5, 1938)
Gleanings [65, Dr Spencer Jones and speculation about extraterrestrial life] (August 12, 1938)*
Gleanings [66, fear of the unexplained, events in nature and child protection] (August 19, 1938)
Gleanings [67, the Old Testament story of Jacob and Esau] (August 26 1938)
Gleanings [68, freedom of thought, expression and conscience] (September 2, 1938)*
Gleanings [69, the pursuit of rest, peace and contentment] (September 9, 1938)*
Gleanings [70, Hitler, Chamberlain and the Sudetenland] (September 23, 1938)*

Gleanings [71, the threat to Czechoslovakia and a plea for peace] (September 30, 1938)
Gleanings [72, 'as war been averted?'/hoarders and profiteers in Swindon] (October 7, 1938)
Gleanings [73, solutions to the threat of war and the importance of little things] (October 14, 1938)*
Gleanings [74, a few days on holiday in Walton-on-Thames] (October 21, 1938)*
Gleanings [75, procrastination and appeasement are the enemies of peace] (October 28, 1938)*
Gleanings [76, astronomy, preaching and child neglect] (November 4, 1938)
Gleanings [77, Ezekiel's vision of resurrection & the failure of peace-making] (November 11, 1938)
Gleanings [78, encouragement to young scholars, especially plodders] (November 18, 1938)
Gleanings [79, the persecution of Jesus and the fall of nations] (November 25, 1938)
Gleanings [80, the phenomena of death] (December 2, 1938)*
Gleanings [81, spiritualism, death and survival] (December 9, 1938)*
Gleanings [82] (December 16, 1938 (missing from the record))
Gleanings [83, Christmas 40 years ago, iceskating and climate change] (December 23, 1938)
Gleanings [84, a look back at the state of the world] (December 30, 1938)*

Gleanings [85, proposed penal reform for juveniles] (January 6, 1939)*
The Late Mr JG Wise – An Appreciation (*North Wilts Herald*, January 13, 1939)
Gleanings [86, new social conscience; spiritualism] (January 20, 1939)*
Gleanings [87, an appeal to all those suffering from worry and depression] (January 27, 1939)*
Gleanings [88, George sent to interview a baby girl!] (February 3, 1939)
Gleanings [89, childhood anxiety and mental health; child neglect] (February 10, 1939)
Gleanings [90, the origin of religion] (February 17, 1939)
Gleanings [91, the growth of religion – series stops abruptly] (February 24, 1939)
Cinema Grievance (August 11, 1939, letter)
British Nazis? (September 22, 1939, letter)
The Root Cause of War (December 8, 1939)*

Dandelions As Food (May 10, 1940, letter)*

Appendix B

Glossary of Words and Phrases

Admonition: a firm warning or rebuke
Blamed: polite form of 'bloody'
Brake: a colloquialism for an early type of motorised vehicle
Chimerical: illusory
Decalogue: the Ten Commandments
Dial: face
Doxology: a hymn, verse or form of words in Christian liturgy, glorifying God
Dry Bob: a teetotaler
E Dunno Where 'E Are: song recorded by Gus Elen (1931)
Fiat: proposition
Gage: (archaic) a valued object deposited as a guarantee of good faith
Gin: gin trap
Gone on the club: taking sick leave
Hardihood: daring
Hors de combat: unable to fight in a time of war
Intensitive: increasing the force of
Leaven: a pervasive influence that modifies something or transforms it for the better
Lim: something on the edge or marginal
MSS: manuscript(s)
Ninny: a foolish and weak person
Parlour: the front room of a working class home, often containing a (seldom used) piano
Propitiate: to win or regain the favour of God
Public weal: the public good
Quilted: covered, ie concealed
Raiment: formal clothing
Repast: meal
Thraldom: the state of being in slavery to another person
Vapourings: bluster
Wee drappie: a small drop of spirits
Whit: a small amount

Appendix C

Bibliography

Akers, Peter & Reid, Alastair (eds), *Alternatives to State Socialism in Britain: Other Worlds of Labour in the 20th Century* (London, Palgrave, 2016)
Child, Mark, *The Swindon Book* (Warminster: Hobnob Press, 2013)
Child, Mark, *The Swindon Book Companion* (Warminster: Hobnob Press, 2015)
Mattick, Dick, *The Robins* (Buckingham: Sporting and Leisure Press, 1989)
Ponting, Noel & Carter, Graham, *A Swindon Wordsmith* (Gloucester: Hobnob Press, 2019)
Sutcliffe, Steven J, *Children of the New Age* (Abingdon: Routledge, 2002)
Swindon Advertiser/Swindon Evening Advertiser/Evening Advertiser/North Wilts Herald (Swindon: multiple issues 1924-1940)

www.ancestry.co.uk
www.ancestry.com.au
www.archive.spectator.co.uk
www.arthurconandoyle.co.uk
www.bible-history.com
www.biblehub.com
www.biblestudytools.com
www.breweryhistory.com
www.brin.ac.uk
www.britannica.com
www.british-history.ac.uk
www.britishnewspaperarchive.co.uk
www.cambridge.org
www.digitalcollections.lib.umanitoba.ca
www.digitalcommons.law.yale.edu
www.digitalstroud.co.uk
www.dmbi.online
www.dunmowflitchtrials.co.uk
www.encyclopedia.com
www.en.wikipedia.org
www.eprints.lse.ac.uk
www.goodreads.com
www.google.com
www.hansard.parliament.uk
www.history.wiltshire.gov.uk
www.hymnary.org
www.hymnlyrics.org
www.iapsop.com
www.jstor.org
www.labology.org.uk
www.library.um.edu.mo
www.lyricsplayground.com
www.military.wikia.org
www.mymethodisthistory.org.uk
www.myprimitivemethodists.org.uk
www.mywesleyanmethodists.org.uk
www.onlinelibrary.wiley.com
www.onthisday.com
www.religionmediacentre.org.uk
www.rodbournehistory.org
www.royalalberthall.com
www.rhs.org.uk
www.sf-encyclopedia.com
www.swindonadvertiser.co.uk
www.swindonfc1879.com
www.swindonphotosoc.org.uk
www.swindonweb.com
www.tandfonline.com
www.teslauniverse.com
www.theatlantic.com
www.theotherpages.org
www.traditionalmusic.co.uk
www.virtualshanghai.net
www.wiltshire-opc.org.uk
www.ww2db.com
www.1900s.org.uk

So-called 'ordinary' working towns sometimes hide their lights under bushels, *A Swindon Wordsmith* aimed to put the record straight to some extent – by paying tribute to one of the town's forgotten writers.

George Ewart Hobbs deserves to be remembered alongside fellow Swindon writers Alfred Williams and Richard Jefferies, particularly as his works tell us so much about the times through which he lived (1883-1946).

Despite working full-time, for more than half a century, as a Great Western Railway engineer, George was a prolific writer, most of his works commissioned as weekly columns in the *Swindon Advertiser*.

For the first time, this book republishes a sample of his works, including articles about many of the subjects that fascinated him – religion, philosophy, astronomy, spiritualism, engineering and more. But it also includes poetry, eyewitness reports on remarkable events of the day, pioneering comic sketches and even science fiction stories.

As well as this literary legacy, Hobbs's vivid writing provides us with a unique and brilliantly observed insight into everyday and so-called 'ordinary' life in Swindon, a century ago.

A Visit to Venus is a result of the remarkable vision and creativity of Swindon writer George Ewart Hobbs (1883-1946).

Hobbs, whose life and works are also explored in *A Swindon Wordsmith* (published in 2019) and *A Swindon Radical* (2021), worked full-time as an engineer with the GWR, for more than half a century, but was still a prolific writer, across a dazzling range of (fiction and non-fiction) subjects.

A companion book to *A Swindon Radical*, *A Visit to Venus* was originally serialised in the *Swindon Advertiser*, and although it is not Hobbs's only work of science fiction, it is the longest and most ambitious, made all the more remarkable by the fact that it was written in 1927, when the genre was in its infancy.

With its believeable characters and the philosophical and theological questions it raises, *A Visit to Venus* sits alongside other quality (but much later) examples of the genre in its purest form, most notably Star Trek, boldly dealing with what science fiction is always about in the end: man's ultimate solitude.

Because this is a story seeking not just what's *out there*, but rather what's *inside us*.

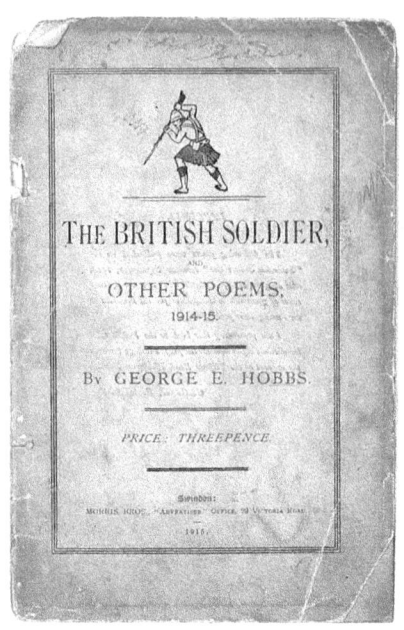

The first (and until *A Swindon Wordsmith* and *A Swindon Radical* the only) anthology of George Hobbs's work to be published was *The British Soldier and Other Poems 1914-15*.

Morris Bros, publishers of the *Swindon Advertiser*, produced the booklet, which contained 24 poems, 23 of which had appeared in the paper during the period October 1914 to July 1915.

It is now extremely rare, but readers may obtain a PDF of it by emailing shresearch2@gmail.com.

About the Authors

Noel Ponting

Noel was raised in Cirencester, and had a career in the real estate sector. He started writing for *Swindon Heritage* in 2014 and became a regular contributor through to its final edition in late 2017. He co-authored *A Swindon Wordsmith* in 2019. His great-great-grandfather, William 'Billy' Thomas founded the London Stout House (now known as the Glue Pot) public house in Swindon's Railway Village.

Graham Carter

A co-founder and vice-chair of the Alfred Williams Heritage Society, in 2014 Graham co-wrote (with Caroline Ockwell) *The Shadow of the Workhouse*, a part-history of the workhouse at Stratton. He was a co-founder and the editor of *Swindon Heritage*, and wrote, designed and edited *A Swindon Timecapsule*, which won the Chartered Institute of Library and Information Professionals' Alan Ball Award in 2018 for Outstanding Local History Publication. Like George Hobbs, Graham is a former journalist, and continues to write a weekly column for the *Swindon Advertiser*.

www.ingramcontent.com/pod-product-compliance
Lightning Source LLC
Chambersburg PA
CBHW070935180426
43192CB00039B/2187